MW01487349

Ancient Wisdom for Polarized Times

THE WORLD OF HERODOTUS
5TH CENTURY BCE

SCYTHIA

Black Sea

Ister

ITALY

Adriatic Sea

PAIONIA

Strymon

MACEDON

Lake
Prasias

Propontus

PAPHLAGONIA

•Taras

*Tyrrhenian
Sea*

•Dodona

GREECE

Sestos•
Troy
Hellespont

Lemnos
Methymna•
Lesbos
Chios

•Mytilene
LYDIA

PHRYGIA

•Sardis
IONIA
Priene•

Samos
Mycale•
Delos Lade
Naxos

CARIA
•Miletus
•Halicarnassus

LYCIA

Sicily

Crete

Rhodes

Cyprus

MEDITERRANEAN SEA

LIBYA

EGYPT

Heliopolis•
Memphis•

*Lake
Moeris*

Nile

•Artemisium

ACARNANIA

Thermopylae•

PHOCIS •Abae

Delphi•
Lebadaea•
BOEOTIA

Euboea

•Eretria

Thespiae•
•Thebes
Plataea•
Asopos
Hysiae•

Amphiareion•
•Aphidna
•Marathon

•Pallene
Nisaea• Eleusis•
•Athens

Gulf of Corinth

Corinth•
Salamis

•Phaleron
ATTICA

PELOPONNESE

•Olympia

Mt.
Parthenion ▲
•Tegea

•Argos

Troizen•

Aegina

Cape
Sounion

Sparta•

Aegean Sea

Cape Tainaron

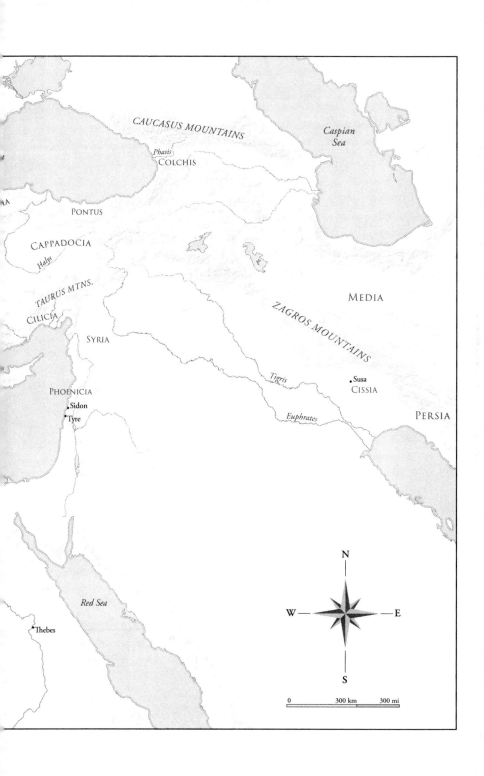

CAUCASUS MOUNTAINS

Caspian
Sea

Phasis
COLCHIS

PONTUS

CAPPADOCIA

Halys

MEDIA

TAURUS MTNS.

CILICIA

ZAGROS MOUNTAINS

SYRIA

Tigris

Susa
CISSIA

PHOENICIA

Sidon
Tyre

Euphrates

PERSIA

Red Sea

Thebes

N

W — E

S

0   300 km   300 mi

Ancient Wisdom for Polarized Times

*Why Humanity Needs Herodotus,
the Man Who Invented History*

EMILY KATZ ANHALT

Yale UNIVERSITY PRESS

New Haven and London

Published with assistance from the foundation established in memory of Philip Hamilton McMillan of the Class of 1894, Yale College.

Yale University Press books may be purchased in quantity for educational, business, or promotional use. For information, please e-mail sales.press@yale.edu (U.S. office) or sales@yaleup.co.uk (U.K. office).

Frontispiece: Beehive Mapping.

Set in Minion type by Westchester Publishing Services.
Printed in the United States of America.

Library of Congress Control Number: 2025931247
ISBN 978-0-300-27287-1 (hardcover)

A catalogue record for this book is available from the British Library.

Authorized Representative in the EU: Easy Access System Europe, Mustamäe tee 50, 10621 Tallinn, Estonia, gpsr.requests@easproject.com.

10 9 8 7 6 5 4 3 2 1

MIX
Paper | Supporting responsible forestry
FSC
www.fsc.org
FSC® C008955

For my daughters, Erica Lesley Anhalt and Ariela Claudia Anhalt

πρὸς δὲ τόδε μέγα θαῦμα, ὅου κλέος οὔποτ᾽ ὀλεῖται,
κοῦραι Δηλιάδες, ἑκατηβελέταο θεράπναι·

(And, in addition, this great marvel, whose glory will
never perish,
young women of Delos, attendants of the far-archer
Apollo)

—*Homeric Hymn to Apollo* 155–156

Contents

Author's Note

All translations of ancient Greek passages included in this book are my own. I intend this book for readers who may be unaware of Herodotus's value for us today. To help readers engage directly with Herodotus's *Histories*, chapters include my translations of selected passages of Herodotus's Greek text. In the accompanying expository discussions, I hope to introduce readers to Herodotus's illuminating and multifaceted wisdom as it emerges from the *Histories*. Notes identify sources and offer merely a representative sample of the vast scholarship on Herodotus in English.

I have translated all of the tales and quoted passages of the *Histories* included in this book from the Oxford edition of Herodotus's Greek text: *Herodoti Historiae*, 2 vols., edited by C. Hude, 3rd ed. (Oxford: Oxford University Press, 1927) (1st edition 1908). Passages selected for translation reveal a pattern of emphasis and a set of insights drawn from Herodotus's diverse, wide-ranging compendium of stories, culminating in his detailed account of the Persian Wars (490s–479 BCE) occurring a half century before his own time.

In translating, I have attempted to transmit content, themes, and emphases manifest in the Greek text, but the *Histories* challenges any effort to provide a readable English translation. Herodotus writes in a discursive, paratactic style, adding thoughts and clauses as they occur to him, and sometimes changing grammatical structure mid-sentence. Greek words often do not have precise single English equivalents, and no English translation can directly capture Herodotus's word order, grammar, and idioms. I have often had to divide Herodotus's longer sentences into shorter ones. Nevertheless, in translating, I have tried to transmit something of the experience of reading Herodotus in Greek, preserving as closely as possible the literal meaning of his words and phrasing while still yielding sense in English. I fervently hope that a glimmer of Herodotus's storytelling artistry survives the arduous, transformative journey from Greek to English.

Many highly readable recent English translations of Herodotus exist, including *Herodotus: The History*, translated by David Grene (Chicago: University of Chicago Press, 1987), and *Herodotus: The Histories*, translated by Tom Holland (London: Penguin Classics, 2014). Many also include excellent introductory essays, explanatory notes, and appendixes, e.g., *Herodotus: The Histories*, translated by Robin Waterfield, with introduction and notes by Carolyn Dewald (Oxford: Oxford University Press, 1998), and *The Landmark Herodotus: The Histories*, edited by Robert Strassler and translated by Andrea Purvis (New York: Pantheon Books, 2007).

Acknowledgments

Family, friends, colleagues, and students have been enormously helpful and encouraging. All have been most tolerant of my obsession with Herodotus and my efforts to enlist his aid for today's turbulent times. I am grateful to my brilliant, dedicated agent Jennifer Lyons for believing in this project from its embryonic form and for making the book a reality. Thank you to editor Heather Gold and her expert team at Yale University Press, including Elizabeth Sylvia, Susan Laity, and Beth Lindop, and to copyeditor Eliza Childs. They have improved this project tremendously, as did two extremely astute anonymous reviewers for Yale University Press, who generously offered meticulous, constructive advice. I owe a great debt to colleagues and friends too numerous to list but including especially my agent and friend Jennifer Lyons and my allies and friends in the academic trenches April Mosolino, Fred Smoler, and Tristana Rorandelli. A course-release grant from Sarah Lawrence College in the spring of 2023 and a sabbatical the year following (2023–2024) enabled me to complete this book.

My greatest debt is to my family. My husband Eduardo enlightens, elevates, and encourages me daily, even as I test his patience regularly by reacting to current events with versions of "How do people not realize this already?! Herodotus exposed it long ago?!" I dedicate this book to my wonderful daughters Erica and Ariela, two extraordinary, brilliant, kind readers, writers, and thinkers. Both have helped me to develop, organize, and articulate my ideas. Both have been loyal, encouraging supporters of this and other projects. I thank Erica and Ariela especially for constituting—in their ingenuity, wisdom, humor, kindness, and hard work—my greatest hopes for the future. My brother and sister-in-law, Jimmy and Dena Katz, have also been a cheering source of intellectual and emotional support.

I drew inspiration for this book from Hannah Arendt's incisive observation in *The Origins of Totalitarianism* that "the ideal subject of totalitarian rule is not the convinced Nazi or the convinced Communist, but people for whom the distinction between fact and fiction (i.e., the reality of experience) and the distinction between true and false (i.e., the standards of thought) no longer exist." Herodotus's *Histories* reminds us that humane critical discernment remains humanity's best defense against poisonous ideologies and toxic misuses of powerful technologies.

Ancient Wisdom for Polarized Times

Introduction
Inventing History

According to Herodotus, as the Persian empire, ruled by King Cyrus, expanded rapidly westward around 546 BCE, Greeks on the western coast of Asia and nearby coastal islands asked the Spartans of mainland Greece for help repelling the Persian advance. The Spartans refused to help, but they sent messengers to the Persian king. Sparta's messengers informed the king that the Spartans would absolutely not tolerate the Persians harming any Greek cities.

King Cyrus had no idea who these Spartans were. He had to ask. Told about Sparta and its inhabitants, Cyrus responded disdainfully, insulting the Greeks for having in their cities central meeting places where they held assemblies and bought and sold goods. Cyrus threatened darkly that the Spartans would soon be discussing their own troubles rather than those of the Greeks on the Asian coast.[1]

Is this story true? Maybe. Thanks to Herodotus, the question can and must be asked.

In our current brave new world of digital engagement, virtual reality, and artificial intelligence, the ancient Greek prose writer Herodotus (ca. 484–post 430 BCE) recalls us to our capabilities and responsibilities as sentient human beings. Scant biographical information about Herodotus survives, but he was probably researching and writing throughout the 450s–420s, with 430 the date of the latest event he mentions.[2] Throughout his *Histories*, a lengthy, eclectic collection of tales culminating in an account of the Greco-Persian Wars of the early fifth century, Herodotus cultivates the skills and the motivation required to defend ourselves against a massive, targeted, multipronged assault on the real, the actual, the verifiable. Artist of inquiry, weaver of tales, Herodotus literally made history.[3] In the second half of the fifth century, as the Athenians experimented with the world's first-ever direct democracy, Herodotus introduced the concept of a factual, verifiable narrative. Though Herodotus was not born in Athens, his work indicates a close, yet nonpartisan, connection with the city.[4] Agnostic about the authenticity of ancient tales long accepted on faith, Herodotus presents instead the results of his own investigations and assessments. In place of the unverified and unverifiable traditional stories of long ago, Herodotus narrates more recent events. His *Histories* (ca. 430s BCE) exemplifies a fresh new method of evidence-based inquiry and rational evaluation.

In today's volatile political environment, reality is under siege. Influential voices at all extremes of the political kaleidoscope—some cynical opportunists, some blinded by ideological certainties—craft narratives and interpretations drawn not from fact but from fantasy. Purveyors of falsehoods prey on human gullibility. Exploiting others' reluctance to do the hard work of evidence-based analysis, authoritative voices entice the undiscerning to accept fictions and fabrications on faith. In consequence, millions of people believe—to their core—things that are demonstrably not true. Not an exclusively left-wing or right-wing problem, the denial of evidence and logic characterizes political extremists of every variety. Extremists gain powerful support from anyone uninterested in learning facts or unwilling to moderate an opinion based on evidence and logic. Some argue that we are each entitled to our own reality, or that objective facts are inherently prejudicial, or that factual evidence is fake news. Captivated by misleading and demonstrably false narratives, we forfeit our capacity for compassionate, humane interactions and we imperil human survival itself.

Authoritarian falsehoods endanger civil society, threatening to obliterate democratic ideals and institutions and the rule of law. Propaganda, intimidation, violence—hallmarks of abuses of power, whether left-wing totalitarianism or right-wing fascism—are not new or transient phenomena, but modern technology vastly potentiates their toxicity. Disinformation for profit has become an increasingly powerful economic force. Amplifying extremist falsehoods, social media exacerbate the gap between people who value objective evidence and rational argument and those who do not. So-called mainstream media, in their pretense of equitable reporting, like to insist that they present "both sides" of every issue. Since most issues are multifaceted, this posture reduces complex problems to simplistic binaries and often validates objectively nonsensical opinions, equating fanciful, unsubstantiated, or patently false claims with evidence-based, rational arguments.

Conflating fact with fiction, this poisonous brew imperils our survival as individuals and as members of communities. To survive and thrive, we must have some measure of basic agreement on the nature of reality as perceived by our senses and as governed by the laws of physics. Without exception we all view the world through the lens of our own nature, personality, talents, environment, and experience. We can interpret factual evidence in different ways. We can select facts to emphasize and facts to ignore. Since rational deductions drawn from empirical evidence must be provable or disprovable, an objective explanation remains provisional, necessarily alterable if new evidence emerges. If we abandon the requirement that claims of fact be verifiable and verified by objective evidence, then we have no shared tools for measurement and assessment and no shared language in which to communicate. If "your reality" conflicts with "my reality," as it inevitably will, verbal persuasion becomes useless for conflict resolution. Foregoing verbal debate, we succumb to primitive violence—but now armed with cutting-edge twenty-first-century weaponry.

Investigating and writing just as a violent, deeply polarized Greek world was launching a catastrophic civil war (the Peloponnesian War, 431–404 BCE), Herodotus commended rational thought and self-control as survival skills. Now as then, Herodotus cultivates his readers' ability to distinguish fact from fiction. His stories reveal natural and predictable causes and consequences of human decisions and events. Herodotus's *Histories* encourages readers to value discussion over autocratic pronouncement, real substance over deceptive appearances, and humanity over barbarity. Containing multifaceted wisdom on a range of subjects, including faith, sexual violence, deception, tyranny, empiricism, political equality, and self-control, Herodotus's narrative reads as an effort to recall his contemporaries to their better, smarter, more constructive selves. Thucydides later criticized Herodotus as unreliable for writing about the past rather than his own present.[5] Implicitly dismissing Herodotus as a mere entertainer addressing his work to his contemporaries, Thucydides claimed to have produced his own work as a "possession for always."[6] But Herodotus was a political thinker addressing his contemporaries.[7] Concerning Herodotus's conception of the usefulness of narratives of the past, scholarly opinions vary.[8] But Herodotus addresses future readers as well as his contemporaries.[9] Insights in the *Histories* remain as vital for human survival and success now as they did in Herodotus's own times.

In developing the idea of history as distinct from myth, Herodotus simultaneously made himself a source of truth and a liar. He termed his approach *historiē*, a noun derived from a verb meaning "to have seen and (therefore) to know." (The title of the work, *Histories*, is not Herodotus's, though it is ancient.[10] And *historiē* did not come to mean "history" until a century after Herodotus.)[11] Herodotus's concept of *historiē* has parallels in ancient Greek judicial arbitration processes.[12] In the ancient epic the *Iliad* (ca. 750 BCE), a *histor* appears depicted on the shield of Achilles as a mediator or arbitrator, empowered to hear both sides and determine restitution in a case of wrongful death.[13] Herodotus develops the evaluative role of the *histor* into his process of *historiē*, an inquiry into the facts so as to make an informed, rational assessment. Centuries later, the Roman statesman, legal advocate, and philosopher Cicero (106–43 BCE) famously called Herodotus the "father of history."[14] Subsequently, however, the Greek writer Plutarch (46–post 119 CE) denounced Herodotus as mendacious, accusing him of innumerable "falsehoods and fabrications."[15]

"Father of history" and purveyor of falsehoods seem antithetical designations, but they are two sides of the same coin. Only once you have a concept of historical fact can you recognize ahistorical, counterfactual, or magical narratives as false, fictional, fantastical. If some narratives are "true" by virtue of being verifiable and verified, then antithetical, unverified, and unverifiable narratives, by definition, are not. In devising *historiē*, Herodotus himself introduces the very criteria by which today we distinguish his more evidence-based tales from his less credible ones. Herodotus's trove of empirical evidence includes the stories that people tell. Many of these seem implausible, if not downright impossible, and Herodotus often dramatizes even plausible scenes as if drawn from eyewitness reports that he cannot possibly have accessed. Even some of Herodotus's claims of firsthand observation may not all be literally true.[16] Many of the *Histories*' most memorable and powerful tales—by Herodotus's own criterion of verifiability—remain instructive parables rather than records of factual historical events.[17]

The *Histories* equips us to learn, however, not only from Herodotus's well-substantiated, most factual stories but also from his less validated, less plausible, even impossible tales. Stories make sense of our lives. They organize disparate events into meaningful narratives. But any selection, collection, and arrangement of even empirically verifiable and verified elements is by definition a fabrication. The identification and sequencing of significant components necessitates choices. Distinguishing causation from correlation requires judgment. Herodotus models and trains readers in the process of assembling facts and assessing them on their merits. He reminds us that stories can entertain, enlighten, even elevate us, but they can also enthrall, ensnare, captivate, deceive. Herodotus helps us to tell the difference.

The inventor of history offers an essential antidote to counterfactual narratives plaguing modern political discourse and generating fear, hatred, and violence, our most destructive and self-destructive passions. As both a factual narrator and a fanciful storyteller, Herodotus insists on the survival value of critical discernment. His stories encourage skepticism in interpreting empirical evidence and invite readers to learn from the characters' decisions and experiences. Herodotus models and fosters an open-minded eagerness to encounter foreign peoples, cultures, and stories. He makes moral evaluations, but he also permits readers to draw their own conclusions.[18] Many tales offer direct guidance and cautionary warnings for Herodotus's Greek contemporaries.[19] Having less at stake than they in the outcomes of these stories, we can assess more objectively the words and actions of the people within them. Stories of long-ago people and conflicts do not enflame our passions and partisan affiliations as stories about our own times might. We can learn from these characters' mistakes and their successes. Throughout the *Histories*, Herodotus recalls us to the necessity of evidence-based moral reasoning, and he coaches us in how to do it.

Herodotus's distinction between myth and history provides a path to authenticity in our increasingly virtual modern world. In the fifth century BCE, the first generations of Athenians, themselves raised on fanciful narratives of their past, were creating and learning to use the world's first-ever democratic political institutions.[20] Herodotus introduced the concept of objective truth, derived not from personal preference or authoritative pronouncement (whether by a political or divine authority) but from factual investigation and empirical deduction and analysis. Deploying the then still quite new artistic medium of prose writing, Herodotus recorded his own and others' eyewitness reports, and he tried to identify his sources.[21] When possible, he provided material evidence as corroboration. His claims regarding his investigative methods may not be entirely reliable.[22] But Herodotus cautioned against the seductiveness of narratives.[23] While incorporating mythic material into his work, Herodotus invited his contemporaries to engage their critical faculties in the arduous process of acquiring and assessing authoritative narratives and reconciling conflicting accounts. He invites us to do the same. Though Herodotus not infrequently violates his own proclaimed methodology and also succumbs, at times, to the fantastic, the fanciful, the unverifiable, he aims at the facts. His *Histories* exposes the toxicity of authoritarianism and cultivates judicious, independent thought.

In identifying myth as unverifiable and developing the concept of history, Herodotus forged tools essential for refining and sustaining a radical departure from traditional, authoritarian, and hierarchical power structures—now as then. From the eighth through the fifth centuries BCE, the Greeks experienced the world's first-ever movement away from autocracy and toward broader forms of political participation, exemplified most famously by the Athenian democracy of the fifth century BCE. Scholars continue to debate the precise nature of the ancient Athenian attitude toward the rule of law.[24] But throughout the history of the world, democracy is not the norm but the bizarre exception. Normal is leaders and followers, warlords and tribesmen, monarchs and subjects, landlords and serfs, bullies and victims. The ancient Greeks were crafting something entirely new. In the twenty-first century, however, we appear to be regressing, abandoning democratic norms and degrading democratic institutions and the rule of law. All varieties of radical voices today—"progressives" and "conservatives" alike—eagerly promote authoritarianism or authoritarian populism even as they masquerade as defenders of democracy, equality, and justice. Undermining regressive, dogmatic absolutism, Herodotus encourages readers to engage thoughtfully with every narrative, however authoritative. He encourages us to think about how *and why* the ancient Greeks managed to conceive of and attempt democratic government in the first place. His insights undergird the ideals of equality, justice, and humanity necessary to create and sustain democratic freedoms and obligations anywhere and everywhere.

Promoting an empowering and liberating alternative to authoritarianism or authoritarian populism, Herodotus's *His-*

tories cultivates in readers that most democratic of all skills: the capacity for complex, nuanced independent thought. Autocrats and demagogues of every variety reduce human experience to a rigid opposition between good and evil, friend and foe. The simplification offers the seduction of certainty in uncertain times and the comfort of feeling part of a righteous—if undiscerning—like-minded group. But it cannot capture the reality of human experience or help us to navigate it. Reinforcing prejudice and exacerbating anger, hatred, and violence, absolutist divisions of human existence into friend versus foe impel us to deny the fundamental humanity of people with whom we disagree. An us-versus-them mentality deprives us of compassion for other human beings and prevents us from acknowledging either suffering or achievement that does not conform to our ideological framework. While moral complexity can seem scary and stressful, the *Histories* encourages us to face reality with courage and ingenuity.

Did Herodotus intend any of this? We cannot know. Apart from the *Histories* itself, hardly any evidence about his life and purposes survives. No essays, journal entries, interviews, or podcasts exist that might corroborate any assertions about Herodotus's intentions. Arguments concerning the author's intention drawn from within the text of the *Histories* inevitably appear circular, for one can only claim, "The *Histories* conveys these ideas because Herodotus intended to convey them. We know that Herodotus intended to convey these ideas because the *Histories* conveys them." Lack of evidence external to ancient Greek epics and tragedies similarly undermines arguments drawn from within the texts concerning the intentions of Homer, Aeschylus, Sophocles, and Euripides. (Perhaps Sophocles intended to write comedy but was not very good at it?!) Instead of ascribing intentionality to Herodotus in order to account for any interpretation of the *Histories,* it is better to think of Herodotus as an unreliable narrator revealing more than he himself knows or intends.

As an unreliable narrator, Herodotus engages readers in the process of moral evaluation. The *Histories* exemplifies the prejudice, sexism, and misogyny of its own times—and so many others. But it also subtly undermines these traditional attitudes and norms. Herodotus is prejudiced; he identifies a set of characteristics for each ethnic group, and he attributes these characteristics to every individual member of that particular group. But Herodotus's prejudice does not align with modern racism because it derives not from skin color, physical traits, or even perceived mental abilities but from language, geography, and culture. Herodotus also differs from modern racists in his eagerness to learn from the ways and experiences of peoples very different from him. Inviting readers' moral discernment, Herodotus fails to reject the sexism and misogyny of his own text and times. And yet, he exposes the costs of these views and behaviors—to men. An openness to "otherness" and the realization that sexism and misogyny also harm men help to undermine poisonous racist, sexist, and misogynistic attitudes and policies of today.

One premise of my work is that stories have a profound influence on who we are and who we become. When Herodotus was writing, prose was a brand new art form but storytelling in poetic verse was not. For centuries, ancient Greek myths, told in epic poetry and later retold in tragic plays, had been shaping and shifting Greek attitudes and values, gradually moving the Greeks away from their traditional enthusiasm for hierarchical power structures and toward a preference for more egalitarian, group decision-making. Three thousand years ago—maybe even earlier—stories later comprising two vast epic poems, Homer's *Iliad* and *Odyssey* (ca. eighth century

BCE), introduced the radical idea that the powerful have a responsibility toward those subject to their authority, that the powerful are accountable for the quality of life of everyone in their community.[25] This was and remains a thoroughly revolutionary idea. Throughout history and still today, rulers and powerful individuals frequently pursue power not to help those subject to their authority but to promote their own interests at others' expense. Over centuries, ancient Greek epic poetry (and later tragic poetry) gradually helped the Greeks to understand, as by now we must, that not only autocrats, oligarchs, or unelected revolutionary leaders or councils but also popular majorities and even democratically elected politicians may misuse their power, indulging their worst impulses and appetites in prioritizing their personal interests over those of everyone else.

The ancient Greeks coined the term *dēmokratia*, "democracy," and they were the first to attempt the experiment—with mixed results. A combination of *dēmos* and *kratos,* meaning "people power," the word does not in itself define the identity of "the people" ("everyone," "the many," with "the few" excluded?) or how they wield their power (with what methods, goals, and results). By the time Herodotus was writing his *Histories,* the Athenians had experienced some form of democratic government for more than two generations (since 508/7 BCE). By 461 BCE Athens had a radical, direct democracy with most significant political decisions made by direct vote (what we would call a referendum) by all male citizens. Every male citizen—rich, poor, well-born, low-born—had one vote.[26] Decision-making may have been more by consensus than by direct majority voting.[27] But in either case, the Athenian democracy was never remotely egalitarian by twenty-first-century standards: women remained second-class citizens, subject to male authority and unable to participate in politics.[28] The Athenians kept many people enslaved.[29] They subjugated other citizen-communities, often with appalling brutality. Athenian democracy and Athenian imperialism had a complicated relationship.[30] But, arguably, modern, anachronistic assumptions about the Athenians' conception of their own democratic identity render the contradiction paradoxical; the problem would not have troubled Herodotus's contemporary Athenians.[31] Supremely confident in their own ethnic and cultural superiority, ancient Athenians of Herodotus's day were patriarchal, imperialist, misogynistic, and xenophobic.

The Athenian model of direct democracy should remind us that democratic procedures and institutions are only as good, humane, and beneficial as the people who participate in them. A majoritarian voting process merely reflects the understanding and the values of a majority of those voting. Majorities can get things right, but they can also get things horribly wrong. There can be a vast gulf, even a fundamental antithesis, between the understanding and beliefs of popular majorities and the factual knowledge of experts. Cynical, unscrupulous opportunists exploit the irrational credulity of majorities for their own personal political and financial gain. Would-be dictators, authoritarian populists, and their enablers prey on the ignorance, fears, prejudices, animosities, and gullibility of popular majorities.

The ancient Greeks were certainly not paragons of equity and inclusion, but their history and literature provide instructive models of admirable as well as reprehensible behavior, conduct to emulate or to avoid. In two previous books, I have examined the role of ancient Greek myths in fostering humane, egalitarian political ideals and institutions: *Enraged: Why Violent Times Need Ancient Greek Myths* and *Embattled: How Ancient Greek Myths Empower Us to Resist Tyranny*. Both books examine stories told in Homer's *Iliad* and *Odyssey* and in a few Athenian tragic plays.

We cannot know, however, whether tales told in ancient Greek epics and tragedies (eighth to fifth centuries BCE) are factually true, and we owe that realization to Herodotus. Like archaic epics, most fifth-century Athenian tragedies dramatized stories that we would call "mythical" today. Aeschylus's *Persians* (472 BCE), depicting the battle of Salamis of just eight years earlier, remains the sole extant tragedy with a contemporary event for its plot.[32] Not sharply dividing ancient myth from recent or contemporary history, ancient Greeks had long accepted stories of the Trojan War and its aftermath as accounts of their own ancient history. Dismissing long-ago tales as unverifiable, concentrating instead primarily on contemporary or closer-to-contemporary events, and relying on eyewitnesses and material evidence whenever possible, Herodotus brought narrative storytelling to a democratic age.

To develop this new approach to storytelling, Herodotus drew on the ancient Greek narrative tradition of stories focused on conflict. The *Iliad* introduced the idea of a great war as a major force of disruption, a significant driver of historical change. Herodotus follows suit, choosing a much more recent war for which eyewitnesses in his own time could still be found. He may have intended his war narrative to revisit, even rival Homer's.[33] The first four books of the *Histories,* ranging far and wide in space and time, reveal Herodotus's varied interests as an ethnographer and geographer.[34] But books 5 to 9 narrate the Persian Wars of the generation before his own, the massively bloody conflicts between Greece and Persia in the first two decades of the fifth century.[35]

Focused on conflict, Herodotus also follows epic tradition in eliciting the audience's ethical judgment. The Homeric epics introduced the concept of the audience as critical moral thinker. By providing a broader view than the perspective available to mortal characters within the stories, Homer's epics place the audience in a position to evaluate the characters' priorities and conduct. Herodotus similarly offers readers more information than his characters possess, and he invites readers to participate in the process of analysis and assessment. His selection and arrangement of material and frequent authorial intrusions influence readers' responses.[36] In shaping his material for a Greek audience, Herodotus also prompts critical self-reflection.[37] He equips readers—now as then—to measure characters' claims and choices against the consequences that result. Some goals, priorities, and decisions appear useful and commendable—but others not so much. Engaging with Herodotus cultivates our own ability to think critically and to learn from stories about other people, some of them very much like ourselves, some of them disturbingly alien. The *Histories* helps us to overcome any inclination to view "difference" with automatic hostility.

Unlike the epic and tragic tales of Herodotus's predecessors and contemporaries, however, the tales in the *Histories* do not demand or permit us to accept them on faith. Herodotus's stories derive from no supernatural source or political authority, and they include no supernatural protagonists.[38] They emerge instead on Herodotus's own authority and from his own process of rational inquiry and investigation. Although Herodotus frequently violates his own claim to provide firsthand, eyewitness accounts and even includes many implausible and impossible tales, he focuses on the role of human choices and actions in precipitating events.[39] Herodotus accepts divinities and portents as real and influential.[40] He sometimes includes divine forces and oracular pronouncements as explanations after the fact. But human beings emerge as the primary agents or causes of events.[41] Thanks to Herodotus's own insistence on the value of empirical inquiry, we can reject many of his tales as fabrications rather than fact, but his clear delineation of human agency makes ex post facto supernatural or magical explanations of causality appear redundant.

Describing the wars between Persia and Greece in the early fifth century BCE as well as peoples, places, and events preceding the conflicts, Herodotus offers numerous cautionary tales. He identifies lack of self-restraint and lack of intellectual insight as drivers of self-destruction. He warns against lust, ambition, overconfidence, and vengeance, forces that overwhelm our capacity for evidence-based, rational, creative, and farsighted decision-making. Like many ancient Greek authors, Herodotus emphasizes the disastrous consequences of unrestrained, unreflective passions—for everyone, not merely the preyed-upon but also and especially the predators themselves. The *Histories* warns explicitly against sexual predation, against unfettered and unaccountable autocratic power, and against mistaking power and military success for moral virtue.

In conjunction with these cautionary warnings, Herodotus's tales commend evidence-based analysis, merit-based leadership, and a free exchange of opinions as vital to individual and communal flourishing. The *Histories* emphasize the survival value of accurately interpreting and evaluating the reality perceived by the senses. In numerous tales, self-restraint and intellectual discernment promote resistance to tyrannical deception and oppression. Depictions of characters' discussions—some constructive, some not—develop readers' capacity for rational, productive debate. Herodotus exposes the fallacy of equating material wealth with happiness or virtue. He invites readers—now as then—to envision moral excellence to include nonmaterial goods of ingenuity, courage, empathy, self-control, discernment, and rational decision-making.

Even as it commends evidence-based, rational inquiry, the *Histories* suggests that objectivity is a goal, not a fully achievable final destination. Herodotus himself does not achieve objectivity; he remains firmly convinced of Greek cultural superiority. But his Greek cultural bias includes a distinctive preference for evaluating facts and narratives—Greek as well as foreign ones—on their merits. His eagerness to learn from the cultures and experiences of others offers a constructive model and guide. Herodotus recognizes that no one can be absolutely right (or absolutely wrong) all of the time. He reminds us that contact with others—even and especially people very unlike ourselves—can be illuminating. In his openness to "otherness," Herodotus cultivates attitudes and skills essential to combatting false racist, misogynistic, and xenophobic narratives of today.

The ancient Greeks always recognized that democracy is very fragile. Democracy is an attempt to protect individuals and the community as a whole against tyrannical abuses of power, but it is itself vulnerable to abuses of power. Institutions alone cannot protect us from denials of the very existence of objective, verifiable, and verified truths. Democratic institutions offer only part of the solution to the problem of good government. Our stories must do the rest. Stories profoundly influence our goals and aspirations and the ways that we treat one another.

The widespread circulation and acceptance of nonfactual or counterfactual stories today suggest that many of us are energetically collaborating in undermining our own best interests, but Herodotus reminds us that we have an alternative. By promoting empiricism and a logical understanding of causality, the *Histories* empowers us to resist the increasing use of falsehoods, violence, and intimidation in the political process. Herodotus recalls us to the necessity of distinguishing fact from fiction. Encouraging us to draw logical deductions from factual evidence, the *Histories* equips us to learn from experiences, our own and those of other people. Herodotus's compendium of ancient tales offers life-saving strategies for making constructive choices in our own lives, for evaluating leaders and policies, and for ensuring the beneficial, humane use of political power and human ingenuity. A closed, incurious, unreflective mind characterizes both the tyrant and the citizen in a tyrannical society, whether a right-wing, fascist dictatorship or a left-wing, totalitarian regime. And a well-intentioned but unwary citizen unguardedly facilitates both extremes. By contrast, Herodotus suggests that an open, inquiring, critical mind characterizes both the political leader and the citizen of a thriving democratic society.

Long ago, the inventor of history introduced vital truths to a myth-loving age. He can do it again.

1

On Faith

With his very first words, Herodotus implicitly rejects the unquestioned authority of faith. In place of traditional tales of men and gods, handed down for centuries, validated by a supernatural source, the Muse, and accepted on faith, Herodotus substitutes himself and his own process of inquiry and analysis.[1] His *Histories* brings storytelling down to earth. Denying supernatural origins for his work and omitting supernatural characters, Herodotus finds the source of narrative truth not in faith but in critical inquiry. Much of human experience remains beyond human control, but Herodotus begins by encouraging readers to focus on human agency and the more predictable aspects of human experience: the consequences of human beliefs, decisions, and actions. His *Histories* begins:

[*Proem*] This is the display [*apodexis*] of the results of the inquiry [*historiēs*] of Herodotus of Halicarnassus, in order that the experiences of human beings not be forgotten with the passage of time and in order that great and marvelous deeds [*erga megala te kai thōmasta*]—some displayed [*apodechthenta*] by Greeks, some by foreigners [*barbaroisi*]—not be without verbal commemoration [*aklea*], both with respect to other things and in regard to the cause of their making war against each other.

Every writer struggles with beginnings. Herodotus begins with himself. His own name is the first word of his work. The Greek text begins, literally, "(Of) Herodotus [*Hērodotou*] of Halicarnassus of the results of the inquiry [*historiēs*] the display is this" or, as English idiom requires, "This is the display of the results of the inquiry of Herodotus of Halicarnassus."

Identifying himself and the content of his work, Herodotus introduces the concept of the author as investigator, mediator, and evaluator. The noun *historiē*, source of the English word "history,"—though pronounced as four syllables, with the emphasis on the third, as "hist-or-REE-ay"—incorporates research, inquiry, and evaluation.[2] The word defines a process of identifying the facts so as to make a valid assessment. Early medical and scientific writers also employed empirical investigation, but Herodotus uniquely focuses not on natural or biological phenomena but on human conduct.[3] Although many of Herodotus's stories lack evidentiary corroboration—some even defying the laws of physics—Herodotus from the start invites readers to join in his essentially historical process of recording, analyzing, and evaluating human events and the tales people tell.[4] The idea of *historiē* derives from a concept long predating Herodotus. The *Iliad*, originating hundreds of years before Herodotus, includes a brief mention of a *histor*, a sort of mediator, a person before whom both sides lay out the facts in a grievous dispute. The *histor* presides over presentations of competing claims and determines proper restitution. The *Iliad*'s narrator describes the process as depicted in a peacetime scene decorating the immortal shield crafted by the god Hephaestus for the great Greek warrior Achilles.[5] In this ancient scene of nonviolent conflict resolution, the *histor* "mediator" appears as an accepted authority figure positioned to determine and evaluate the facts in a dispute over financial restitution for a wrongful death. Introducing his own work as *historiē*, Herodotus broadens the mediator/evaluator role to define the act of examining and assessing human experience, achievements, and conflicts more generally.

It may be difficult for us in the twenty-first century to appreciate the radical departure from tradition of Herodotus's opening words. Beginning his project, Herodotus echoes the opening lines of his epic predecessors.[6] But in the archaic epic poems of Homer and Hesiod, predating Herodotus by centuries, the narrator begins by identifying not himself as narrator or author but the Muse or Muses, supernatural characters, as the source and authority for the tales that he will tell.

Both Homeric epics open with a request to the Muse of epic poetry to provide the substance of the stories about to be told. Homer's *Iliad* (ca. 750 BCE) begins, "Goddess, sing of the rage of Achilles, son of Peleus, / The grievous rage, which made countless sufferings for the Achaians."[7] The epic proceeds to examine the causes and consequences of human passions and violent conflicts. Homer's *Odyssey* (ca. 700 BCE) begins: "Muse, tell me the story of a very versatile man, who was forced / To wander far and wide after he sacked the hallowed city of Troy."[8] This epic proceeds to narrate one man's arduous experiences and extraordinary exploits. We do not know who "Homer" was, and since the epics were most likely transmitted orally for centuries before they coalesced into something like the works we have today and were written down (sixth century BCE), it is best to think of Homer as the name of a poetic tradition.[9] The narrator of the *Iliad* and *Odyssey* is not the source of the stories but a conduit for a supernatural authority, as each epic narrator begins by asking a goddess for the substance of his tales.

Hesiod, an epic poet of the seventh century BCE, similarly gives the Muses the originating authority for his poems and their contents. Hesiod's *Theogony* or "Origin of the Gods" begins by invoking the Muses: "Of [or, from] the Muses inhabiting Mt. Helicon let us begin to sing . . ."[10] Hesiod's *Works and Days* also starts with an invocation to the Muses as the source of its subject, the memorialization of great human achievements, beginning, "Muses of Pieria, who grant glory [*kleiousai*] by means of songs, come hither . . ."[11]

Drawing on ancient storytelling traditions, Herodotus breaks radical new ground.[12] Like his archaic predecessors Homer and Hesiod, Herodotus starts by defining his source and his subject.[13] But unlike Homer and Hesiod, Herodotus identifies not unverified, unverifiable poetic tradition as his source and subject but himself.[14] Herodotus does not address the Muse of epic poetry, and the Muse appears nowhere in his narrative. Moreover, in both Homeric epics, the first word signals the epic's subject. The *Iliad,* a tale of violent passion and its consequences, begins with the noun "rage." The *Odyssey,* a tale of one man's long journey to recover his identity, family, home, and political authority, similarly identifies the subject of the epic with its first word, "man." Hesiod's epics both have "Muses" as their very first word. In striking contrast, Herodotus puts his own name first, presenting himself as the origin and subject of his narrative. In place of traditional, generations-old, oft-told, unverifiable stories, Herodotus substitutes his own evidence-based investigation into human experiences and marvelous achievements and his analysis of the results.[15]

You may be meeting Herodotus for the very first time, but his opening words signaled to his contemporaries that they were stepping into a new branch of a vast river that had been flowing for centuries. Although Herodotus substitutes himself and his own investigations for the Muses as the source and subject of his narrative, he follows his archaic epic predecessors in seeking to commemorate human events and accomplishments.[16] Employing a new medium of prose writing, Herodotus pursues the traditional goals of epic poetry familiar to his contemporary audience: memorialize extraordinary events and deeds and identify causal factors.[17] In the ancient tradition of epic poetry, the Muses preserve mortal exploits for all time by eternally supplying the content of epic tales. Drawing on the Muses as his source, the epic poet aims to preserve and transmit the characters' *kleos,* the immortal glory conferred by eternal remembrance in epic song. The narrator memorializes in his tales the *klea andrōn,* "glorious deeds of men," while mortal characters explicitly pursue *kleos.*[18] Hesiod, using the participle *kleiousai,* "granting glory [*kleos*]," identifies the Muses—supernatural beings, I must emphasize—as the source of the record of human events and accomplishments.[19] Like an epic poet, Herodotus, too, aims to preserve wondrous (*thōmasta*) actions and events, promising to ensure that the great deeds (*erga megala*) of both Greeks and foreigners (*barbaroi*) not be effaced/forgotten (*eksitēla*) by time nor without glory (*aklea*).

Herodotus follows Homer in promising not only to memorialize great deeds but also to identify the causes and consequences of human conflict and struggle.[20] The *Iliad's* narrator begins by seeking the cause of the quarrel between Achilles and Agamemnon, and the *Iliad* as a whole identifies the causes and consequences of that quarrel and other disputes. Herodotus seeks the causes of the great conflict between Greeks and non-Greeks, promising to identify and memorialize exploits of both Greeks and foreigners, "both with respect to other things and in regard to the cause of their making war against each other" (*Hist.* 1, first sentence).[21]

In defining the subject and goals of his inquiry, Herodotus's opening words also reveal that the ancient Greeks divided the world into two categories, Greeks and *barbaroi,* "foreigners." Unlike its English derivative, "barbarians," the Greek word conveys not "savage" or "uncivilized" but "other, foreign, different." *Barbaroi,* the plural, signifies "non-Greek speakers," since the languages of other peoples sounded to the Greek ear like *"bar bar bar bar."* Despite this essentially linguistic distinction, Herodotus does not exclude the achievements of *barbaroi* from his inquiry, record, and evaluation. Foreigners may not speak Greek, but Herodotus's introduction to his project implies that even so their deeds are worth remembering and we can learn from them.

Ancient Greeks had long valued the capacity to learn from experience. In focusing on the causes and consequences of human decisions and actions, both Homeric epics depict empiricism as a source of knowledge. The *Iliad* and *Odyssey* distinguish the perspective of the epics' external audience from that of the characters within the tales. Both epics enable their audience to evaluate the characters' statements and actions by exposing their consequences. The broader perspective encourages the audience to learn from the characters' experience. The *Odyssey*'s protagonist epitomizes the ability to learn from experience. The epic's narrator introduces Odysseus as one who knows by seeing. ("He saw and came to know the citadels and the thoughts of many men.")[22] Throughout the epic, the capacity for empirical learning promotes Odysseus's survival and success. A generation before Herodotus, Aeschylus's tragedy *Agamemnon* (458 BCE) explicitly articulated the idea that wisdom comes from experience and especially from suffering, as the play's Chorus attributes to Zeus the principle for mortals of *pathei mathos,* "learning by experience/suffering."[23]

But Herodotus goes further, for he finds the great value of empiricism not only in physical action but also in the mental process of assembling factual evidence and assessing human experience. Suggesting that he himself as investigator, recorder, and evaluator is as noble and necessary as any warrior or statesmen, Herodotus innovatively places *historiē* itself among the great accomplishments of human beings. He focuses (like archaic Greek epics and fifth-century Athenian tragedies) on human agency and the human ability to learn from experience. But as researcher, chronicler, and authority, Herodotus transcends the traditional epic narrator's role of conduit for a supernatural storytelling source. In identifying his own work as an *apodexis,* "display" or "showing forth," Herodotus uses the same concept for his product as a prose writer as he uses for the "great and marvelous deeds—some displayed [*apodekhthenta*] by Greeks, some by foreigners." Both *apodexis* and *apodekhthenta* derive from the same verb.[24] Herodotus thereby *equates* his production of a written, evaluative record with the great and memorable actions and experiences of his own and preceding generations.[25]

Situating the chronicler's new investigative, evaluative role among the greatest of human achievements, Herodotus departs from the traditional stories' mixture of human and divine protagonists. Throughout the *Iliad* and *Odyssey,* gods participate energetically, while words and actions of human characters drive the plot. Both epics contrast divine power and invulnerability with mortal limitations and vulnerabilities, exposing the consequences of human choices. The *Odyssey* overtly draws on divinity to emphasize human responsibility for human fortunes, as the great Olympian god Zeus complains at the outset that mortals are responsible for exacerbating their own suffering but blame the gods for it.[26] Athenian tragedies similarly include divine characters while emphasizing human responsibility for human experience. Like the archaic epics, Athenian tragedies contrast mortal ignorance and vulnerability with divine imperviousness to suffering.[27] Herodotus, however, excludes divine protagonists.[28] He includes no scenes of gods on Olympus or scenes among the dead in the underworld. He recognizes an interaction between fate or destiny and human motives and actions.[29] He records human beliefs in supernatural forces and human claims of divinities and other supernatural forces intervening in human life. But he narrates no such tales on his own authority. Herodotus sometimes attributes causality to divine agents as an explanation after the fact. And his characters often act relying on faith. But the *Histories* concentrates on human conduct, beliefs, and choices and their consequences. Not divine but human behavior emerges as a potent force for change in human events.

The exclusion of a supernatural source and supernatural protagonists enables Herodotus, as inquirer and chronicler of events, to assume subjective, fully human authority for the content of his stories. Long before Herodotus, the *Odyssey* had already begun to distinguish between truth and falsehood in narrative storytelling.[30] But the many lies of the protagonist Odysseus appear to the epic's external audience as fictions only because they contradict facts established by the third-person narrator. The Muse herself guarantees the truth of the narrative.[31] Lacking any external, objective corroboration, Homer's audience must accept the narrator's claims, validated by the Muse, on faith. Homer's narrator, a mere conduit for the divine Muse, can be proven neither false nor true. In place of this traditional supernatural narrative authority and unquestioning faith, Herodotus substitutes his own knowledge and reasoning. By asserting entirely human responsibility for his stories, Herodotus invites his readers to engage their critical faculties in evaluating his tales. Tales derived from supernatural authority admit no rational challenge to their veracity. Tales proffered on human authority do. As a fully human narrative authority, Herodotus precludes acceptance of the veracity of his tales on faith.

As a human narrator describing human beings rather than divinities and depicting events exclusively in the mortal realm, Herodotus invites readers to learn from his investigations and from the experiences of the human beings in his tales. Given that so little is in our control, the effort to understand and control the elements that do lie within our purview can maximize our chances of survival and success. Accidents, natural disasters, illness, death—we can attribute these to divine forces, to luck, chance, fortune, or fate, or to our genetic inheritance. We may have comparatively little real control over the circumstances and direction of our lives. But we do have some. Many illnesses may be pre-baked into our DNA and therefore inevitable, but others become increasingly likely if we smoke, consume alcohol excessively, or eat exclusively junk food. Automobile accidents may be beyond our control, but texting while driving improves our chances of causing one. Herodotus begins his work by drawing our attention to real-life human causes and their consequences. He reminds us of our own power, limited as it may be, to influence our own fortunes.

Faith in narratives concerning supernatural forces constitutes a large part of human experience, however, and a great source of human conflict. Human beings—individuals and groups—disagree about the nature of divinity and the role of supernatural forces in human life. Not infrequently, such disagreements turn nasty. Religious intolerance and faith-fueled violence have wrought havoc throughout history, as they continue to do today. Claims about the supernatural admit no proof or disproof. Faith invites, and often permits, no discussion. In the absence of indisputable material evidence, faith admits no possibility of verification. Verbal persuasion becomes, if not impossible, then very difficult. Lacking convincing evidentiary proof, devout believers may resort to intimidation or even violence.

Herodotus's *Histories* offers a path away from faith-based violent conflict and toward self-understanding and mutual understanding. Archaic Greek epics emerged in a world of rigid social and political hierarchies long before democracy was even a concept. Writing at the dawn of democratic ideals and institutions, Herodotus turns his attention, and ours, away from supernatural forces and toward human achievements and conflicts. Stories give meaning and structure to human life. They are a potent social, political, and economic force. Uncritical acceptance of unquestioned or unquestionable (e.g., supernatural or imaginary) narratives yields and sustains authoritarianism and often promotes political violence. The ability to question authoritative narratives remains fundamental to the functioning of democratic politics and peaceful conflict resolution. Much as we might wish to, we do not in fact inhabit a nonmaterial realm constrained only by our own imagination. We exist amid real-world forces and events. Herodotus begins his innovative project of *historiē* by evoking not faith but reality-based rational judgment.

2

On Myth

Moving beyond faith, Herodotus proceeds to move beyond myth. He begins by making the familiar unfamiliar, narrating not the distant past as his Greek contemporaries understood it but an "alternate history," tales of ancient times as told to him by Persian storytellers (*logioi*)— or so he claims (1.1–5).[1] We need not, and probably should not, accept this account as genuinely Persian. Whether authentically Persian, Greek-inflected, or significantly shaped by Herodotus himself, however, this version of events, as Herodotus recounts it, does not align with well-known Greek stories.

Whereas *historiē* makes verification necessary and possible, myth, like faith, admits neither contradiction nor confirmation. Herodotus incorporates mythic material and patterns into his narrative.[2] But his record of the Persians' alternate version of the past undermines confidence in any authoritative, unverifiable narratives of events long distant in time. Recognizing that the passage of time prevents the possibility of certainty, Herodotus invites rational comparison of conflicting accounts, but he declines to validate any version. Evoking his readers' skepticism and capacity for comparative analysis,

Herodotus commences his *historiē* by challenging the authority of ancient myth:

[1.1.] Persian storytellers say that the Phoenicians were the
cause of the disagreement. For they say that the Phoenicians,
having come from the sea that is called the Erythraean Sea
[modern Indian Ocean and its gulfs] to this sea and inhabiting this land which they now inhabit, immediately occupied
themselves in making long voyages, carrying off Egyptian
and Assyrian merchandise. They went into other places and
especially to Argos. [2] (Argos during this time was preemi-
nent among all of the places in the land that is now called
Hellas [Greece].) Arriving in Argos, the Persians say, the
Phoenicians set out their cargo for sale. [3] On the fifth or
sixth day following the day of their arrival, with nearly all
their merchandise already sold, many women came to the
sea—according to the Persians—and among them, in particular, the daughter of the king of Argos. Her name, the
Persians say (and the Greeks agree), was Io, daughter of
Inachus. [4] The Persians maintain that while these women
were standing around the stern of the ship buying whatever
goods they most desired, the Phoenicians, having encouraged
one another, rushed against them. Most of the women fled,
but Io and some other women were seized. The Persians say
that the Phoenicians put the women on board the ship and
went sailing away to Egypt.
    [1.2] This is how the Persians say that Io came to Egypt.
But it is not how the Greeks say it happened. And this, say
the Persians, first began the injustices. The Persians claim that
after these events some of the Greeks (they are not able to
identify which ones), having put in to Phoenician Tyre,
kidnapped Europa, the daughter of the king. These would

have been Cretans. To the Persians, this second rape made
things equal. But afterward, in their opinion, the Greeks were
responsible for a second injustice: [2] For, according to the
Persians, the Greeks sailed in their long ship to Colchian Aia
[in modern Georgia] and to the river Phasis. From there,
having accomplished the other matters for the sake of which
they had come, these Greeks kidnapped the king's daughter
Medea. [3] The king of Colchis sent a herald to Greece to
demand restitution for the rape and to demand the return of
his daughter. But, say the Persians, the Greeks replied that
just as the Phoenicians did not make any restitution to them
for the rape of Argive Io, neither, therefore, were they themselves going to give anything to the Colchians.

[1.3] The Persians say that in the second generation after
these events, Alexandros, the son of Priam, hearing these
tales, wanted to get a woman from Greece for himself by
means of rape, completely understanding that he would not
pay a penalty because those prior abductors had paid no
penalty. [2] So, when Alexandros kidnapped Helen, it seemed
best to the Greeks to send heralds first to demand both the
return of Helen and restitution for the rape. According to the
Persians, when the Greeks put forward these claims, the
Trojans brought up the rape of Medea, maintaining that
having paid no penalty nor returned Medea when this was
demanded, the Greeks now wanted there to be restitution to
themselves from others.

[1.4] Up to this point, therefore, according to the
Persians, it was just rapes and thefts alone between each
other. But after this, they claim, the Greeks, surely, were
greatly responsible. For the Greeks began to launch an attack
against Asia before they themselves attacked Europe. [2]
Now, the Persians consider the raping of women to be the
work of unjust men, but they believe that making a fuss about

pursuing vengeance for raped women is characteristic of
fools—whereas paying no heed regarding raped women is
characteristic of wise and prudent men. For it is clear, the
Persians believe, that if the women themselves did not want
to be raped, they would not keep on getting raped. [3] The
Persians claim that men from Asia take no account of women
being raped but that Greeks, because of a Spartan woman,
gathered a great expedition and then, going to Asia, destroyed the power of Priam [king of Troy]. [4] From this, the
Persians say, they always considered the Greeks their enemies. For the Persians claim as their own Asia and the
barbarian races living there. They consider Europe and
Greekness entirely separate, different, and at variance.

[1.5] This is how the Persians say that it happened, and
they identify the sack of Troy as the origin of their hatred for
the Greeks. [2] But the Phoenicians do not agree with the
Persians about the story of Io. They admit that they brought
Io to Egypt but they claim that they did not rape her and take
her against her will. They say that Io had sex with the ship's
captain and that, when she discovered she was pregnant, she
was ashamed to tell her parents and therefore sailed willingly
to Egypt so that her condition would not become manifest.
[3] These are the things that the Persians and the Phoenicians
now say. But I am not here for the purpose of saying that
these events occurred in one way or another. Instead, I will
identify the man whom I know [oida] first began the unjust
acts against the Greeks. Having indicated him, I will proceed
with my account, detailing small and large communities of
human beings equally. [4] For many communities that were
great long ago have now become small, and many that were
great in my time were small before. Understanding well that
human happiness [eudaimoniē] never remains in the same
place, I will mention both equally.

The *Histories* begins by enlisting myth in pursuit of narrative truth. The Persians' alternative retelling of long-ago events elicits the critical discernment of Herodotus's contemporary Greek audience. Many scholars find humor or parody in *Hist*. 1.1–5.[3] And yet, contrasts between this Persian account and traditional Greek stories locate the origin of the East-West conflict in a serious clash of moral values. Modern scholars identify concepts of the "West" and "Western civilization" as recent constructs.[4] But Herodotus here introduces a moral opposition between Greek and Persian storytelling. Numerous, extensive Greek tales of the well-known distant "past" offered moral instruction. But in retelling the abbreviated version that he attributes to Persians, Herodotus portrays Persians as supremely uninterested in learning from past events. These "Persian" storytellers merely identify a series of reciprocal rapes, culminating in the theft of Helen by the Trojan prince Alexandros (also called Paris) and followed by the Greeks' gratuitous desire (gratuitous in the Persians' opinion) for violent revenge, this last deemed by the Persians "the work of fools" (1.4.2). Using a grammatical construction signifying indirect discourse (i.e., reported speech) throughout the Greek text of the passage, Herodotus emphasizes repeatedly that not he himself but Persian storytellers provide this version of events. The Persians insist, essentially, that "the Greeks started it." As Herodotus reports it, their reductive account offers no moral wisdom.[5]

As recounted by Herodotus, the Persians' alternate version of well-known long-ago events directly contradicts the ancient *Greek* tradition of remembering the past *so as to learn from it*. The Greek noun *aletheia*, "truth," literally means "not forgetting." (In the ancient Greek conception of the underworld, mortals drink the water of Lethe to forget their past lives. The alpha at the beginning of *alētheia* equates to the English prefix "non," meaning "not," so that the word signifies

the act of not forgetting.) Herodotus has promised to identify
the cause of the conflict between Greeks and *barbaroi*, "foreigners," but his Persian storytellers offer a simplistic, unenlight-
ening explanation. Herodotus does not delineate the contrasts
between the Persian and Greek accounts because he does not
need to. His contemporaries knew the Greek tales intimately.
For centuries, tales of the Trojan War, told in epic and then
tragic poetry, constituted the Greeks' understanding of their
own distant past and its moral lessons.[6] Attributing an unreflective, reductive account to Persian storytellers, Herodotus
makes the Persians indirectly and inadvertently condemn
themselves for their inability to learn from experience.

Unlike these purportedly unreflective Persian storytellers,
Herodotus's Greek contemporaries knew well the warnings
against mortals' sexual predation transmitted by the *Greek* accounts of these events. Told and retold in epic and tragic poetry for centuries, Greek tales depict a cascade of needless
catastrophes begun by sexual assault. Traditionally acknowledged as a record of long-ago events, Greek stories expose the
suffering not only of an initial, opportunistic predator but of
everyone touched by events initiated by rape. In the *Iliad*, Hel-
en's abduction catalyzes massive carnage for both Trojan perpetrators and Greek avengers in a ten-year war. Though the
Trojan War provides the context and opportunity for men to
display both admirable and not so admirable words and actions, the *Iliad* emphasizes above all the dire consequences of
Alexandros's theft of Helen: innumerable, heart-rending deaths
of young warriors in their prime, the terrible grief of bereaved
parents and wives, the imminent destruction of a beautiful city
and the enslavement of its survivors.

In Greek stories, Alexandros's rape of Helen catalyzes not
only a catastrophic war but also that war's terrible aftermath.
The *Odyssey* and many Athenian tragedies further emphasize

the grief and suffering of victors and vanquished alike. The victorious Greek king Agamemnon gets murdered on returning home, a direct consequence of his long absence besieging Troy. Even Odysseus, celebrated architect of the Greek victory, experiences ten long years of hardship and misery following the fall of Troy, while he strives to recover his home, family, and political authority. The *Odyssey*'s narrator even likens the wandering Odysseus to a grieving, about-to-be-enslaved widow of a Trojan warrior.[7] Athenian tragedies depict the suffering of the erstwhile victorious Greeks as well as the brutal enslavement of Trojan women and children. Lack of restraint in victory redounds on the Greeks, for they anger the gods by desecrating their temples, and many Greek warriors perish on the homeward voyage, their ships wrecked by divinely sent storms.[8]

In contrast to Greek stories exposing extensive suffering consequent on one act of rape, Herodotus has the Persians offer a simplistic narrative lacking any instructive value. Herodotus's Persian storytellers seem unwilling—or perhaps unable—to perceive either the cascading or the self-inflicted costs of sexual assault. They merely recount a laundry list of reciprocal rapes, beginning with the rape of Io and culminating in the rape of Helen and an unprovoked, unwarranted Greek attack on Troy. (Assuming no responsibility for the Persians' view, Herodotus consistently employs a grammatical construction signifying that he merely reports what the Persians say.) Herodotus need not specify that the Persian tale of the rape and theft of Io from Argos—by Phoenician traders who subsequently sail merrily off to Egypt (1.1)—completely contradicts the Greek account. As Herodotus's Greek audience well knew, in Greek stories the powerful Olympian god Zeus rapes Io and transforms her into a cow in order to avoid detection. Zeus's wife Hera finds out, sends a gadfly to torment Io, and forces her to wander miserably—until Io arrives in Egypt, regains her human form, and becomes the ancestor of the great Heracles (= Hercules).[9] The rape has no adverse consequences for Zeus, obviously. He is a god. What could he suffer? In Greek tales, Zeus's sexual assaults, *because* they present no problem for Zeus, offer a pointed contrast with the self-destructive consequences of mortals' sexual assaults, such as Alexandros's rape of Helen. Omitting Zeus entirely, the Persians' version of Io's story offers no constructive counter-model. Just a casual, callous, terrible tale of rape.

Uninterested in moral instruction, Herodotus's Persian storytellers merely keep score. In response to the theft of Io, they continue, "some Greeks" went to Tyre in Phoenicia and stole the king's daughter Europa. Though these Persian storytellers seem uninterested in precision, Herodotus supplements Persian ignorance, clarifying, "These would have been Cretans" (1.2.1). But Greeks knew very well that in this instance, too, Zeus was the culprit. Assuming the form of a bull, Zeus carried Europa off to Crete, with Zeus's divine status giving him complete impunity.[10] Omitting Zeus once again, the Persians now call the score even—until Greeks gratuitously steal Medea, the king's daughter, from Colchis (on the eastern edge of the Black Sea). Explaining that Greeks commit this second crime after "having accomplished the other matters for the sake of which they had come" (1.2.2), the Persian storytellers allude dismissively to a much-celebrated Greek tale, the glorious quest for the Golden Fleece by Jason and the Argonauts.[11] Indifferent to (or ignorant of) the famous Greek story, the Persians identify this third rape as merely yet another unprovoked, opportunistic theft.

Herodotus's apparently partisan account of the Persians' version of these long-ago events begins to expose a vast gulf between Greek and Persian culture. Whereas the Greeks craft meaningful narratives and learn from them, the focus of the

Persian storytellers, as Herodotus presents it, remains not moral but transactional. The Persians maintain that the Greeks refused to return Medea and pay a penalty on the grounds that the Phoenicians gave no recompense for their theft of Io. These tales of uncompensated, unpenalized rape motivated Alexandros to steal Helen, since he expected to suffer no adverse consequences. But when the Trojans ignored Greek requests for compensation and the return of Helen, the Greeks started the war against Asia. To the Persians, this decision appears senseless and completely unprovoked for, as Herodotus explains, "The Persians consider the raping of women to be the work of unjust men, but they believe that making a fuss about pursuing vengeance for raped women is characteristic of fools—whereas paying no heed regarding raped women is characteristic of wise and prudent men. For it is clear that if the women themselves did not want to be raped, they would not keep on getting raped" (1.4.2). (That disgusting and self-absolving male misconception has proven sadly durable.) In contrast to this revolting assertion, *Greek* tales reveal that Greeks care very much when women are raped. Not at all out of concern for the experience of the women themselves, it must be admitted, but for the resulting harm to *men*—and the cautionary lessons manifest to later generations.

Obscuring any moral instruction, the Persian account implies that there is nothing to see here, nothing to learn. Just the basic premise that one rape begets another and also that women acquiesce in their own rape. (Although male characters in the *Iliad* do not deem Helen complicit in her own abduction, both Homeric epics evoke her subjective experience and agency, and archaic and classical Greek sources consider the question of her willing participation.)[12] Herodotus's Persian storytellers fail to learn from investigating the past.[13] And they explicitly prefer injustice to foolishness.[14] Their version of events

also includes the somewhat illogical claim, given the reciprocal series of rapes begun not by Greeks but by Phoenicians, that
the Greeks initiated the conflict between East and West. The
Persian storytellers maintain that "the Greeks began to launch
an attack against Asia before they themselves attacked
Europe" (1.4.1) and the destruction of Troy caused the Persians' hatred of Greece (1.5.1). But even the Persians' reductive
retelling reveals that the Greek expedition against Troy was
not unprovoked.

While Herodotus presents the Persians as deriving no educational value from their own narrative of past events, ancient Greek tales show human sexual predation causing not
success but suffering. In Greek stories, predatory *divinities* may
proceed unscathed but not mortal men. Long before Herodotus, the Homeric epics emphasized that gods can commit sexual assault with impunity because gods are immortal and
impervious to harm. The great Olympian god Zeus, for example, appears in ancient Greek tales as a world-class sexual ath-
lete, raping not only Io and Europa but as many young victims
as he pleases and fathering numerous divine and semi-divine
children. Other male gods do the same. By contrast, in these
same tales, *mortal* sexual predators harm themselves. Alexandros's theft of Helen directly causes the destruction of Troy, its
royal family, and Alexandros himself. In the *Iliad*, a second act
of sexual appropriation, the theft by the Greek king Agamemnon of a captive girl previously awarded as a sex slave to another warrior, alienates the Greeks' greatest fighter and ensures
countless deaths among Agamemnon's own warriors and allies.
As reported by Herodotus, Persian tales conspicuously reduce
such cautionary warnings to a trivial retributive series of theft
and counter-theft. Herodotus's Persian storytellers insist that
men rape other men's women with impunity—with Alexandros
the sole exception. Omitting gods from their account, the Per-

sians describe purely human—though inhumane—interactions. Even the Phoenicians' alternative explanation for Io's abduction, that she was pregnant with the child of the ship's captain and left with him voluntarily out of shame, attributes responsibility to Io herself and lacks any supernatural element or moralizing lesson.

Although Greek tales portray sexual assault as self-destructive for male sexual predators and harmful to all mortals, the focus remains male experience. With women as collateral damage, ancient Greek epics and tragedies emphasize men's choices and the consequences of these choices—for *men*. In the *Iliad*, the decision to treat women like objects to be captured, given, or stolen proves to be a disastrous mistake. The epic depicts not women but their male "owners" as the victims of other men's appetites. Mortal women in the *Iliad* have scant opportunity to speak for themselves, and mortal men's sexual predation appears as a supreme act of *self*-harming. Outspoken female characters in Athenian tragedies, uttering speeches written by men and spoken by male actors, illustrate the harmful effects of male immorality and abuses of power not especially on women but on men.[15]

The depiction of sexual assault in ancient Greek stories as self-destructive for mortal men fails to dent misogyny much, but it nevertheless contains small seeds of progress toward sexual equality. A surprising number of epic and tragic tales do illustrate women's experiences. Homer's portraits of Andromache and Hecuba in the *Iliad* and of Penelope in the *Odyssey*, for example, and numerous female characters in fifth-century tragedies, heartrendingly evoke female suffering.[16] Without recognizing women as equal to men and deserving of the same rights and responsibilities, the ancient Greeks did seem to perceive that only gods can commit sexual assault with impunity. This farsighted realization—that sexual predation can and will backfire and harm the *mortal* predator—is a place to start. Even the modern fight for legal equality for women in the United States in the 1970s began, it seems, by showing the harm that sexual inequality causes not for women but for men.[17] The realization that mortal sexual predators *harm themselves* constitutes a groundbreaking idea for any society, particularly one as male-dominated and insensitive to women's humanity and experience as ancient Greece. By contrast, the Persians' "alternate history" lacks any cautionary warning against sexual predation.

Herodotus's invitation to reconsider what we might term "myth" focuses, however, not on misogyny but on narrative truth. Offering the Persians' version of ancient events, Herodotus shows the value of comparing divergent accounts. Comparison exposes both the difficulty of authenticating tales of long ago and the benefits of encountering foreign views. Herodotus's Greek contemporaries cannot fail to notice contrasts between the Persians' narrative and the traditional Greek stories of these well-known and consequential events. Unlike Greeks, Persians learn nothing from even their own tales, but comparison proves illuminating. The trivializing Persian account highlights the Greek capacity to deduce powerful, cautionary moral lessons from ancient stories.

Refusing to authenticate any narrative of long-ago events, Herodotus draws a sharp distinction between unverifiable tales of the distant past and tales derived from human empirical knowledge. In offering an obtuse Persian narrative, Herodotus indirectly emphasizes the instructive value of the Greek version of past events, and yet he concludes by insisting, "I am not here for the purpose of saying that these events occurred in one way or another." Instead, Herodotus will proceed from his own knowledge, explaining, "I will identify the man whom I know [*oida*] first began the unjust acts against the Greeks" (1.5.3). The perfect indicative *oida*, "I know," literally means "I have seen," that is, "I have seen and therefore I know." The verb identifies a directly empirical conception of knowledge.[18] By substituting empirical knowledge for uncritical acceptance of traditional stories, Herodotus undercuts the authority of myth and evokes his readers' logical reasoning abilities.

Just as Greeks can learn from comparing alternative stories to their own, they—and we—can learn from perceiving repetitive patterns within narratives. Unlike the tales that Herodotus attributes to Persians, ancient Greek epics and tragedies consistently show a repeating pattern of mortal sexual predators causing harm to themselves. Assembling and evaluating evidence of more recent human events, Herodotus identifies an overarching pattern of historical change: cities rise and fall; human fortunes vary.[19] He concludes this opening section of the *Histories* by promising to be an equal opportunity reporter, describing cities both great and small, since, as he explains, "Many communities that were great long ago have now become small, and many that were great in my time were small before. Understanding well that human happiness never remains in the same place, I will mention both equally" (1.5.4).

In recognizing the variability of human fortunes, Herodotus draws on an ancient theme. The *Iliad* emphasizes the vicissitudes of fate, foreshadowing the fall of Troy and the destruction of its royal family, once rulers of a great city but now soon to be dead or enslaved. The *Odyssey* similarly exposes the fluctuation of human fortunes in its vivid account of the much-traveled Odysseus, a king and conquering warrior turned reluctant wanderer, shipwreck survivor, destitute beggar, and then king once again. In both Homeric epics, the human enthusiasm for violent revenge exemplifies the rise-and-fall pattern in human fortunes and the complicity of human choices in perpetuating it. Both epics depict vengeance

as reciprocal and ever escalating. Vengeance killings perpetuate cycles of success and failure, one furious avenger soon falling victim to the next. In the *Iliad*, vengeance killing follows
vengeance killing as each aggrieved warrior seeks revenge for
a previously slain comrade. In the *Odyssey*, Odysseus's successful return and reestablishment as king of Ithaca requires him
to destroy the predatory suitors occupying his household in his
absence. But the suitors' death enrages their kin, who seek vengeance in their turn. Only the supernatural intervention of a
goddess prevents this particular vengeance cycle from devas-
tating an entire community.[20]

In alignment with Athenian tragic playwrights, Herodotus exposes still further the role of human beings in precipitating or delaying the rise-and-fall pattern of human fortunes.
Aeschylus identifies the responsibility of a ruler for hastening,
exacerbating, ameliorating, or delaying disaster for himself and
his people.[21] While the *Iliad* presents Troy's Queen Hecuba, for
example, as a victim of a malign fate, Euripides portrays Hecuba
as the victim of human greed and cruelty.[22] Similarly focused
on human agency, Herodotus depicts patterns of historical
change as explicable but not predetermined.[23] Human fortunes
may inevitably fluctuate, but Herodotus's *Histories* will reveal
that human passions and decisions directly determine the timing, duration, and extent of the cycles.

Emphasizing human agency, Herodotus draws a line between myth and history by refusing to authenticate any version
of events long distant in time. His account of the Persians' alternative version of the past vividly illustrates the problem of
verification. Lacking corroborating evidence, neither Persian
nor Greek accounts can be proven true or false. Myth can only
demand acceptance. *Historiē* invites critical reasoning. Herodotus does not always adhere to his own promise of stating only
what he himself knows (cf. *oida* at 1.5.3), as we will see. Many

stories in the *Histories* defy verification. But Herodotus accomplishes a stunning break with tradition nevertheless. Unlike ancient myths, authenticated by a supernatural source, no human narrative can command unquestioning acceptance, even if uttered by a powerful political ruler or religious authority. Truth must be objectively verifiable. "True" and "false" cannot merely mean my preferences or yours.

From the outset, *historiē* confronts myth as Herodotus introduces a new source of knowledge: empirical observation and rational deduction. In Homeric epic and Aeschylus's tragedies, *muthos* means a spoken word or story precipitating action, but Herodotus uses the term infrequently, identifying written tales (his own and those of others) not as *muthoi* but *logoi*.[24] Exposing contrasts between tales of long-ago events, Herodotus encourages skepticism regarding the source and content of any narrative. Refusing to validate one account of unverifiable events or another, Herodotus introduces the radical, crucial understanding that only something verifiable and verified can be true. Anything else is supposition, superstition, counterfactual.

Long ago, Herodotus distinguished myth from history, but myth remains a perennial tool of political extremists, endangering democratic institutions and democratic ideals of humanity, equality, and justice. Disinformation and evidence-free conspiratorial narratives are not a new menace, but modern digital technology greatly augments their power. Designed to maximize profits by creating addiction and modifying human behavior, digital algorithms—*by design*—specifically target human vulnerabilities and amplify lies, disinformation, and discord. Users unconsciously mistake the resulting "alternate reality" for the real thing. Spreading modern myths, internet platforms have been meticulously designed to deprive users of personal agency, empathy, and the capacity for rational, analytical thought.[25] Artificial intelligence promises to take this process to new levels, and governmental regulations thus far offer inadequate protections.

Providing a vital defense against this powerful assault on reality-based rational thought. Herodotus's distinction between myth and history sustains democratic politics. Democracy requires resolute resistance to counterfactual statements and narratives. Democratic political participation requires a sincere desire to ascertain facts, understand relationships between facts, and identify patterns of causality. Democratic political participation requires individuals to evaluate a variety of reality-based options. The free exchange of opinions and ideas enables the best ideas, political leaders, and policies to prevail. In a democracy critical thought is not merely a right, it is an obligation. Nonviolent democratic change relies and thrives on verbal conflict. We can and will (and should) disagree on priorities and policies. If we cannot agree on questions of basic fact, however, if we abandon the requirement that anything deemed a fact be verifiable and verified—if we cannot distinguish myth from history, in other words—then democratic discussion and debate cannot even begin, let alone succeed.

As the first extant Greek text to differentiate what we might term "myth," an unverified, unverifiable story, from *historiē*, a process of evidence-based critical inquiry, Herodotus's *Histories* fostered the ancient Greeks' unprecedented rejection of tyranny and the development of democratic political ideals and institutions in the fifth century BCE. Modern historians identify numerous benefits derived from historiography and the study of history.[26] But the concept of verifiability remains today the cornerstone of democratic political discourse and our best protection against tyrannical forces of propaganda and disinformation. Our own capacity for intellectual discernment remains our most vital tool for self-preservation. Beginning his project by reporting an alternative version of well-known ancient stories, Herodotus cultivates readers' capacity for logical comparison and analysis. By introducing the criterion of verifiability, Herodotus equips his readers to identify impossible and implausible tales. His *Histories* can help us preserve the distinction between "myth" and "history" today.

3

On Sexual Violence

Today's news often includes shocking stories of the predatory sexual behavior of powerful people, and the opening tales in the *Histories* attest that such narratives have a long, appalling history. Having refused to confirm either the Persian or the ancient Greek accounts of the long-ago rapes of Io, Europa, Medea, and Helen, Herodotus proceeds to a more recent story, a sordid tale of sexual violation that results in regime change. These initial stories emphasize the connection between sexual desire and material greed.[1] And the *Histories* as a whole connects sexual lust to imperial expansion.[2] The Persians' trivializing account of rapes and counter-rapes, as Herodotus reports it (1.1–5), highlights by implicit contrast the instructive value of ancient Greek tales warning against mortal sexual predation. The next tale, a colorful story about a king of Lydia named Candaules, continues to foreground sexual violence as a potent and durable force for generating narratives, conflict, and catastrophe:

[1.6] Croesus was Lydian by race and the son of Alyattes, tyrant over the peoples dwelling within the boundary of the river Halys, which flows from the country toward the south, between the Syrians and the Paphlagonians, and goes out toward the North Wind into the sea that is called Euxine. [2] This Croesus is the first of the foreigners [*barbaroi*] of whom we know [*idmen*, 1st person plural of *oida*] to subjugate some of the Greeks to payment of tribute to himself, while he added others as friends. . . . [3] Before the rule of Croesus, all Greeks were free . . .

[1.7] The sovereignty of Lydia, formerly belonging to the Heraclidae [the descendants of Heracles/Hercules] came around to the race of Croesus, who were called the Mermnadae, in this way: [2] Candaules—whom the Greeks call Myrsilos—was tyrant over the people of Sardis. Candaules was descended from Alcaeus, the son of Heracles. . . . [3] [Previously,] . . . the land's rulers were descended from Lydus, son of Atys, from whom this whole people has been called Lydian. . . . [4] [But now] the Heraclidae [descendants of Heracles] held sovereignty . . . and they ruled for twenty-two generations of men, that is, five hundred and five years, with son accepting the rule from father—until Candaules, the son of Myrsus.

[1.8] This Candaules, then, fell in love with his own wife. And being in love, he believed that his wife was the most beautiful by far of all women. And so, believing this—for he had a favorite bodyguard, Gyges, son of Dascylus, to whom he used to disclose the most serious of matters of business—to this Gyges Candaules particularly kept on praising the beauty of his wife. [2] Before long—for it was necessary that things turn out badly for Candaules—Candaules said the following to Gyges: "Gyges, I do not think that you are persuaded by me when I speak about the beauty of my wife (for men's ears happen to be more distrusting than their eyes). See to it, therefore, that you manage to view her naked." And Gyges, shouting out loudly, said, [3] "Master,

what unhealthy word are you speaking, commanding me to
behold my mistress naked? Together with the stripping off of
her undergarment, a woman is stripped of her modesty and
dignity. [4] Long ago, noble things were discovered by men,
and it is necessary to learn from these. And among them is
this one precept: that a man should look upon his own
property. I am persuaded that she is the most beautiful of all
women. And I ask you not to ask me for what is contrary to
law, custom, and tradition [anomōn]!"

[1.9] Saying such things, Gyges fought back, fearing lest
something bad happen to him from these matters. But the
king answered with the following: "Be bold, Gyges, and fear
neither me—lest I speak this word for the purpose of testing
you—nor my wife, lest some harm happen to you from her.
For from the outset I will contrive it in such a way that she
will not learn that she has been viewed by you. [2] I myself
will station you behind the opened door in the chamber in
which we go to bed. And after I come in, my wife also will be
present for bed. A chair lies near the entry. Upon this, she
will place each of her clothes, taking them off one by one, and
she will provide you with much leisure for viewing. [3] And
whenever she walks away from the chair and toward the bed,
and you are behind her back, from this point, take care that
she not see you as you leave through the doors."

[1.10] Since, indeed, Gyges was not able to escape, he
was ready. When it seemed to Candaules to be time for bed,
he led Gyges into the chamber. Immediately after this, his
wife also was present. Gyges observed her as she entered and
placed her clothes. [2] And when he was behind the back of
the woman as she headed toward the bed, he departed,
slipping out secretly. *And the woman sees him going out!* But
understanding the thing that her husband had done, she did
not shout out, although she had been shamed, nor did she

appear to understand—having it in mind to take vengeance on Candaules. [3] For among the Lydians, and among nearly all other foreigners [*barbaroisi*], even for a man to be seen naked brings great shame.

[1.11] At the time, surely, in this way revealing nothing, she kept quiet. But as soon as it was day, having readied her most faithful servants, she summoned Gyges. And he, expecting that she knew nothing of what had been done, came when called. For he was accustomed, previously, to go to the queen whenever she called. [2] And when Gyges arrived, the woman said the following: "Now, Gyges, of two paths that you are facing, I give to you the choice as to which you want to take. Either kill Candaules and have me and the kingship over the Lydians or it is necessary for you yourself to die immediately, so that you will not in future, obeying Candaules as to everything, view things that you ought not to see. [3] But it is necessary either for that man—the one who planned these things—to be destroyed or for you to be destroyed, you who saw me naked and did things that violated custom." Gyges for a time wondered at the words that were spoken, but then he begged her not to constrain him to need to make such a choice. [4] But he did not persuade her. Instead, he saw the necessity truly lying before him: either to kill his master or be killed himself by others. He chose to survive. But of course he had questions: "Since you force me against my will to kill my master," he said, "come, let me hear how we are going to set upon him." [5] In reply, she said, "The attack will be from the same place where that man displayed me naked. You will assault him while he is sleeping."

[1.12] Thus, they readied their plan. And when it was night—for Gyges was not released nor was there any escape for him; it was necessary that either he or Candaules die—he

followed the woman into the bedroom. Giving him a small
dagger, she hid him behind the very same door. [2] Afterward, Gyges slipped out and killed Candaules while he slept.
And Gyges held Candaules' wife and his kingship. This is the
Gyges whom the poet Archilochus of Paros, who lived at the
same time, mentioned in an iambic trimeter poem.

[1.13] Gyges held the kingship, and he was confirmed by
an oracle in Delphi. For when the Lydians took up arms,
considering what had happened to Candaules to be a terrible
thing, both the partisans of Gyges and the other Lydians
came to an agreement: if the oracle declared that Gyges was
king of the Lydians, then he would rule, but if not, then he
would give back the sovereignty to the descendants of
Heracles. [2] The oracle gave its response, and thus Gyges was
king. The Pythia, however, said something further: there
would be vengeance by the Heraclids on Gyges' descendant
in the fifth generation after him. The Lydians and their kings
took no account of this prophesy, until it was accomplished.

[1.14] In this way, the Mermnadae held the tyranny,
having done away with the descendants of Heracles, and
Gyges, having acquired the tyranny, sent not a few offerings
to Delphi. In fact, most of the offerings of silver that there are
in Delphi are his. Besides the silver, he dedicated both an
extraordinary amount of gold and also—most worthy of
mention—six golden bowls. [2] These stand in the treasury of
the Corinthians, and they weigh thirty talents. To speak truly,
the treasury does not belong to the Corinthian public but to
Cypselus, son of Eëtion. This Gyges was the first of the
foreigners [barbarōn] whom we know [idmen)] to dedicate
offerings at Delphi—after Midas, son of Gordias, king of
Phrygia. [3] For surely Midas dedicated the royal throne
upon which he sat when he made judgments, and it is worth
seeing. The throne sits there in the very same place where

Gyges' bowls stand. This gold and silver that Gyges dedicated
is called Gygian by the Delphians, named after the man who
dedicated it.

In moving beyond faith and myth, Herodotus presents a
challenge, because he is not the most reliable of narrators. He
introduces direct empirical knowledge as the source of the
distinction between myth and his own project of *historiē*, but
he immediately proceeds to violate his own principle. Herodotus is the first extant Greek author to suggest, "You know
what? Those stories that we have been telling ourselves for
centuries, that is, the tales in the epic poems of Homer and
Hesiod and later revised and retold by Athenian tragic playwrights, those stories all happened way too long ago to be
verifiable." Herodotus claims that he will narrate instead what
"I know" (*oida* at 1.5.3, meaning literally "I have seen and
[therefore] I know"). He will later clarify that his narrative
includes his own direct observation as well as tales told him
by others (e.g., 2.99).[3] Dismissing ancient stories as empirically unverifiable, Herodotus focuses instead—though not
exclusively—on more contemporary, or closer to contemporary,
events. He claims to draw on firsthand information, his own
or that of other eyewitnesses, but the first tale that Herodotus
tells on his own authority, the first tale that he claims to know,
concerns people who lived many generations before his own
time: this very first tale he tells as his own, not as a retelling of
someone else's narrative, powerfully dramatizes the self-
destructiveness of sexual violence.

Undeniably not factually certain, this story establishes a
pattern of cause and effect manifest throughout the *Histories*
as a whole: excessive passion and lack of self-restraint bring
disaster. The Persian storytellers' claims notwithstanding,
Herodotus's Greek contemporaries knew that ancient Greek

tales show human sexual predators causing suffering not only for their victims but also and especially for themselves. Herodotus's tale of King Candaules—though not verifiable by inquiry and empirical assessment—reaffirms traditional ancient Greek warnings against sexual assault.

Like the Persians' "alternate history," the story of Candaules invites readers to engage constructively with the past. Although Herodotus claims now to draw on his own knowledge instead of other people's tales, again he reports a story of long ago, not an event with available firsthand evidence. Herodotus promises to "identify the man whom I know [*oida*] first began the unjust acts against the Greeks" (1.5.3). That man is Croesus, king of Lydia. But Herodotus does not begin with Croesus. The first story that Herodotus tells on his own authority (not as a retelling of the narrative of others) involves not Croesus but Croesus's great-great-grandfather Gyges, bodyguard of an impressively short-sighted king. Historical or not, this story encourages readers to begin to think historically, that is, to identify patterns of cause and effect and to learn from the experiences of others.

Herodotus's tale of King Candaules has all the moral grandeur of a salacious soap opera, but this story of a villainous husband and a ruthless wife—or a hapless husband and a victimized wife—has a crucial moral message. You do not need to sympathize with either the king or the queen or even with the "helpless" bodyguard Gyges to get the point: a powerful, libidinous king lacked impulse control. He had no qualms about violating traditional customs or gratuitously hurting others. He lacked the ability to foresee predictable consequences of his transgressive actions. He overvalued his own ability to control events. He lost his political authority and his life for no good reason, just through his inability to control his passion or to care about its costs to others.

Candaules' family had ruled Lydia for twenty-two generations, sovereignty passing peacefully from father to son (1.7.4).
Candaules, however, "fell in love with his own wife" (1.8.1).
Maybe it was love. Maybe it was lust. Candaules could not have
told the difference. (In an era of arranged marriages for political
and/or economic purposes, either might seem strange.) Not
content to experience this love (or lust) privately, Candaules insists on boasting about his wife's beauty to his bodyguard Gyges, deciding eventually that Gyges must view the queen naked.
Only then will Gyges be convinced that she really is the most
beautiful woman in the world. Dismayed, Gyges protests, "I am
persuaded that she is the most beautiful of all women. And I
ask you not to ask me for what is contrary to law, custom, and
tradition [*anomōn*]!" (1.8.4). Gyges knows that the king's demand is a very bad idea. But the king ignores these objections,
and he never once considers his wife's feelings. He is confident
that he can set up the situation so that Gyges will be able to view
the queen as she undresses for bed without her realizing that
she is being viewed. Since Gyges has no choice, he reluctantly
agrees to the scheme.

Of course it does not work. After undressing, the queen
sees Gyges and instantly knows what he and her husband have
done. Despite her horror and shame, she restrains herself from
crying out. She lets Gyges depart unaware that she has seen him
commit this terrible violation. Herodotus explains that "among
the Lydians, and among nearly all other foreigners [*barbaroisi*],
even for a man to be seen naked brings great shame" (1.10.3).
Calling Gyges to her the following morning, the queen gives
the bodyguard a stark choice: either kill the king and take the
kingdom and gain herself as his wife, or be killed immediately
(by the queen's attendants, presumably). As before, Gyges acts
reluctantly, but he really has no choice. Herodotus observes
simply, "He chose to survive" (1.11.4). And the queen has a plan

worked out. Just as her husband choreographed the visual assault on her, she choreographs the murder of her husband. Again, Gyges follows instructions. He murders the king in his sleep and takes over the kingship and the king's wife. The story emphasizes not the queen's experience but the king's irrational and cruel sexual violation and its predictable and symmetrical consequences. We may acknowledge the queen's impressive self-control and her ability to turn a terrible event to her advantage. She manages to retake control of her body—but only sort of—by giving it to another man. And she achieves her revenge. But Herodotus's contemporary audience in the fifth century BCE, accustomed to male dominance, is unlikely to have admired or approved of the queen's actions. Herodotus never even tells us her name. He calls her "the queen" or "Candaules' wife." The tale offers some acknowledgment of the woman's experience and agency.[4] But Herodotus focuses not on the queen but on the bizarre and unnecessary form of King Candaules' sexual lust, his irrational desire to show his wife naked to his bodyguard. The method of the king's assassination mirrors his own violation of the queen, with Gyges hidden behind the same door. Self-restraint and a little forethought or imagination might have saved this king, but he never dreams of such a thing.

This story does not qualify as historical, in the modern sense, but Herodotus begins to exhibit and engage instincts that we today can recognize as historical. Though dismissive of reductive ancient Persian tales and agnostic regarding the veracity of ancient Greek ones, Herodotus nevertheless spins a tale as ancient and unverifiable as any. He fails to fulfill his promise to "identify the man whom I know [oida] first began the unjust acts against the Greeks" (1.5.3), beginning not with Croesus but with Croesus's great-great-grandfather Gyges. And how could Herodotus possibly know what the king, queen, and

Gyges said and did? But fictional amplification does not seem to have contravened the ancient conception of historical truth.[5] Moreover, like a modern historian, Herodotus identifies the causes and consequences of human behavior. For Herodotus, this tale exemplifies the causal forces in history.[6] He contextualizes the story as the catalyst for regime change. He also makes an effort to supply objective corroboration, drawing on literary and material evidence. He cites a poem of the archaic poet Archilochus, explaining, "This is the Gyges whom the poet Archilochus of Paros, who lived at the same time, mentioned in an iambic trimeter poem" (1.12). He cites, too, material artifacts, the so-called Treasure of Gyges, a thank offering still apparently extant at Delphi in Herodotus's own day (1.14).

Herodotus may or may not have been familiar with an alternative ancient story about a man named Gyges, but his version reads as a realistic counterpoint to a most fanciful tale.[7] In Plato's *Republic* (fourth century BCE), one of Socrates's interlocutors tells a story about a man called Gyges, a tale similarly involving acts of adultery, murder, and regime change. Plato's Glaucon narrates a story that he claims men tell of a Lydian shepherd named Gyges who finds a ring with the power to make its wearer invisible. Empowered by this magical ring, Gyges proceeds to seduce the Lydian queen, murder the king, and take over the kingship.[8] In direct contrast to the Gyges of Glaucon's narrative, Herodotus's Gyges is not an eager adulterer, assassin, and usurper but a reluctant voyeur turned unenthusiastic murderer, new husband, and king. Herodotus may not have known the version of the tale as it appears in Plato's (much later) text, but his story of Gyges exposes the magical power of invisibility for the impossibility that it is. In the *Histories*, Candaules apparently fancies that he himself has the power to make Gyges invisible and able to view the naked queen without being seen by her. Reality intervenes. In Plato's *Republic*,

Glaucon's version provides a thought experiment to corroborate the claim that no one would refrain from committing injustice if he could do so with impunity. Herodotus offers instead
a reality-based, cautionary parable: *never* expect that you can
commit injustice with impunity. Just imagine that you have the
power to ensure someone's invisibility. See how well that works
out for you.

Herodotus is not yet writing history, but like a historian,
he identifies patterns of behavior that produce predictable
results. Like both the Persian and the Greek accounts of ancient stories, the tale of Candaules emphasizes the reciprocal
nature of gratuitous violence and establishes a pattern visible
throughout the *Histories*.[9] Recognizing the variability of
human fortunes, Herodotus encourages readers to focus on
the role of human agency in precipitating and perpetuating
human success or failure. Not all things are in our control, of
course, but Herodotus suggests that we would be wise to pay
attention to the ones that are.

The tale of Candaules exemplifies a direct causal link between human actions and their consequences. In this story, an
autocrat's misogyny, insecurity, lack of concern for others, and
lack of imagination cost him his political power and his life. Far
from validating or celebrating sexual violence, Herodotus exposes its toxicity, not merely to victims but especially to perpetrators. The freedom to do whatever he wishes permits a
powerful ruler to destroy himself and deprive his descendants
of their patrimony. Some might choose to attribute Candaules'
destruction to fate or ill luck.[10] But Herodotus does not present
fate as the causal factor. Translations may obscure this, however. I translate *chrēn gar Kandaulēi genesthai kakōs* as "for it
was necessary that things turn out badly for Candaules" (1.8.2).
(Cf. Grene: "For it was fated that Candaules should end ill," and
Purvis: "It was fated that things would turn out badly for

Kandaules.")[11] The verb *chrēn* can mean "it was fated" and/or "it was necessary." The ambiguity here seems essential. Perhaps Candaules' destiny (or his DNA, as a modern alternative) determines his actions, but Herodotus emphasizes in detail the counterproductive nature of this autocrat's *choices*. Not fate but his own decisions doom Candaules.

Interested in causality and in the predictable consequences of human behavior, Herodotus encourages a critical, historical stance toward even unverifiable tales of long ago. He begins his inquiry into great achievements and the causes and consequences of human disputes with a series of tales of grievous sexual predation. Offering as "Persian" an uninstructive account that his contemporaries would perceive as an alternate version of historical events, Herodotus implicitly validates as distinctively Greek the tradition of learning from past events. The subsequent tale of Candaules reiterates the warning against mortals' sexual predation implicit in the Greek versions of the tales of Io, Europa, Medea, and Helen: sexual assault harms the perpetrator. The implications of Candaules' story will resonate throughout the entirety of the *Histories*.[12] This first tale, narrated not as a recap of other people's tales but on Herodotus's own authority, directly warns against predatory sexual behavior: a ruler or powerful person who fails to restrain his lustful impulses and indulges his ability to harm others brings ruin on himself and his descendants.

The example of Gyges also suggests that acquiescing in doing harm, even under authoritative pressure, ensures the suffering of future generations. Gyges gains comparatively temporary success. Herodotus introduces the story to explain how a long-running tradition of peaceful hereditary sovereignty imploded (1.7.1.). An oracle at the time promises that Gyges' descendant in the fifth generation will pay for his ancestor's wrongdoing (1.13.2). A fifth-century Athenian might expect his descendants, by their achievements, to cast retroactive glory on himself.[13] We may not share the ancient Greeks' abiding interest in the success of descendants as a source of honor to preceding generations. We may be less troubled than ancient Greeks by thoughts of adverse consequences for our descendants. But unlike Gyges, we require no divine oracle connecting unbridled human appetites to current and future economic, ecological, social, and political perils. We can see the causal connections already operating. Attribution of supernatural agency seems beside the point.

Even under democratic government, the ancient Athenians never achieved an egalitarian society, but ancient Greek *stories* gradually influenced attitudes and aspirations. The ancient Greeks deserve our condemnation for their embrace of slavery, misogyny, and abuses of power, just as we must condemn prejudice, misogyny, oppression, and abuses of power in every time and place, including and especially our own. Democratic political institutions alone do not solve the problems of injustice and inequality. Ancient Greek epics and tragedies, however, introduced the very ideals of humanity, equality, and justice by which today we measure the ancient Greeks' inadequacy and our own. Like epic and tragic tales, Herodotus's tale of Candaules shows the foolishness of failing to restrain destructive passions—particularly sexual lust (but also, by extension, anger, greed, cruelty, etc.).

By focusing on human behavior and its consequences, Herodotus cultivates our ability to learn from our own experiences and the experiences of others. The desire to objectify and demean others and treat them with callous cruelty endures today, driven not only by proud, self-avowed, even politically successful sexual predators and their enablers and admirers but also by anyone who mistakes self-objectification for self-empowerment. Herodotus offers nothing to admire, however, in King Candaules' ability to harm others, his inability to control his lust, his violation of social norms, and his disregard for his wife's (and his bodyguard's) experiences and feelings. Even the queen's story cautions against participating in one's own dehumanization by embracing the status of sexual object. Candauless wife betrays her husband in reestablishing the custom that only a husband can see his wife naked, and her lack of desire undermines the traditional association between female beauty and female passion, as she coolly takes control and gets her revenge.[14] But Candaules' wife fails to gain bodily autonomy. Unnamed, she also gains no posthumous glory. The consequences for both king and queen suggest that objectifying a human being—even if that human being is oneself— brings only temporary or illusory power.

Initiating the process of historical inquiry, Herodotus invites readers—now as then—to take responsibility for our own role in achieving success or failure. He urges us to think deeply about our own best interests. He encourages us to consider how we do and should treat one another and use our power. Like ancient Greek epic and tragic tales, Herodotus's story of Candaules demonstrates that indulging the impulse to commit sexual violence ensures suffering, for perpetrators and victims, now and in the future. Herodotus could draw on no eyewitness to the story of Candaules and Gyges, but by emphasizing the dire consequences of sexual violence, Herodotus insists on the value of facing the facts.

4
On Fact

Acknowledging the importance of facts, Herodotus helps us to confront toxic forces of propaganda and disinformation in the twenty-first century. Another lively tale in the *Histories* affirms, by allegory, the vital role of historical inquiry for deploying objective fact in pursuit of truth and justice. Claiming to report what "I know," Herodotus incorporates not only purportedly eyewitness accounts but also the remarkable stories that people tell.[1] This includes the tale of Arion and the dolphin, an anecdote of dubious credibility inserted early in book 1. Herodotus's account of Arion's lengthy dolphin ride seems both vaguely historical and charmingly fanciful. The story interrupts Herodotus's account of a reliably historical figure, Periander, tyrant of Corinth from approximately 627 to 587 BCE.[2] The tale of Arion initially appears as a brief, perhaps inconsequential, digression.[3] But this memorable story emphatically illustrates the power of fact to refute nefarious falsehood:

[1.23] Periander [Herodotus narrates] was the son of Cypselus . . . and tyrant of Corinth. The Corinthians say that the greatest marvel [*thōma*] in life happened to him. And the

people of Lesbos agree with them. They say that Arion of
Methymna [on Lesbos], who was second to none of the
citharodes [singers] of that time, was carried to Tainaron
upon a dolphin. Arion was the first of those we know [*idmen*] to make and name the dithyramb [a choral song in
honor of Dionysus] and teach it in Corinth.

[1.24] They say that Arion, having spent a great deal of
time with Periander, desired to sail to Italy and Sicily. Having
made a lot of money there, they say, Arion wished to return
to Corinth. [2] He set out now from Taras and hired a ship
of Corinthian men, since he trusted no others more than
Corinthians. But when they were on the open sea, the
Corinthian sailors plotted to cast Arion overboard and have
his money. Understanding this, Arion offered them his
money but begged them to spare his life. [3] Of course, he did
not persuade them. Instead, the sailors ordered Arion either
to kill himself, so that he might have a burial on land, or to
leap into the sea as quickly as possible. [4] In dire straits due
to their threats, Arion entreated them, since their decision
seemed best to them, to permit him to sing while standing on
the rowers' benches and wearing his full singer's costume.
Arion promised that after singing he would kill himself. [5]
And the sailors, anticipating the pleasure of hearing the best
singer of all men, went up from the stern to the middle of the
ship. Arion, donning his full singer's costume and taking up
his lyre, went through the High-pitched Clear Song [song in
honor of Apollo]. Having completed this, they say, Arion
threw himself into the sea, just as he was, wearing his full
singer's costume. [6] The sailors sailed off to Corinth, but—
according to the story—a dolphin took Arion up from
underneath and carried him to Tainaron [on the southern
coast of the Peloponnese]. Stepping off the dolphin, Arion
went to Corinth with his singer's costume. Arriving there, he

reported the whole event. [7] But they say that Periander did not believe Arion and held him under guard, not releasing him. Periander looked out well for the arrival of the sailors. When they arrived Periander summoned them and inquired if they had anything to report about Arion. The sailors replied that Arion was safe in Italy when they left and doing well in Taras. Right then, Arion appeared to them exactly as he was when he leapt off the ship. And the shocked sailors, when interrogated, could deny nothing. [8] These things now the Corinthians and the Lesbians say. And there is an offering of Arion at Tainaron, a bronze statue—not large—of a man upon a dolphin.

Herodotus's tale of Arion and the dolphin amalgamates plausible historicity with naturalistic whimsy. Arion seems to have been a historical figure of the late seventh century BCE who visited the tyrant Periander in Corinth. Arion is credited with introducing to Greece the dithyramb, a sacred choral song in honor of the god Dionysus and precursor of the genre of ancient Greek tragedy.[4] From the beginning of his work, Herodotus promises to narrate deeds great and marvelous (*erga megala te kai thōmasta, Hist.* 1, first sentence), and he introduces this tale as the greatest marvel (*thōma megiston,* 1.23). Herodotus shows recognizably historical instincts in citing material corroboration for the story, but he can have drawn on no firsthand, eyewitness account of events occurring nearly two hundred years before his own time, so this story can be hearsay or legend at best. Using a grammatical construction signifying indirect speech—as in his record of the Persian storytellers' tales (see chapter 2)—Herodotus emphasizes throughout his narration of this tale that he does not assume authorial responsibility for the story.[5] He employs direct statement—that is, assumes authorial responsibility—for only the last sentence reiterating his sources and adducing the statue as material corroboration (1.24.8). While such a statue did exist in the fifth century, it is unlikely to have been made much before 600 BCE.[6] And although dolphins have been known to buoy distressed swimmers and sometimes to permit human riders, Arion's lengthy dolphin ride strains credulity.[7]

Despite its questionable historicity, Herodotus's tale of Arion's bold leap and marvelous rescue nevertheless seems recognizably historical in its focus on human conduct rather than divine causality. Here, as throughout the *Histories,* Herodotus anticipates modern historiography in featuring not supernatural agency but human behavior and human causality. Unlike ancient epics and tragedies, the *Histories* contains no supernatural characters—only tales people tell and descriptions of mortal characters' beliefs in divine agency, including Herodotus's own. Detailed descriptions of human decisions and actions provide sufficient causal explanation, making assertions of divine causality appear superfluous. Magical and supernatural forces provide not causal but ex post facto explanations. The oracle predicting divine retribution inflicted on Gyges' descendant (1.13.2), for example, offers a retroactive explanation for subsequent events. As recounted by Herodotus, the suffering of Gyges' descendant Croesus—though "predicted" by the oracle—will emerge as the consequence not of divine vengeance but of poor human choices, as we will see (1.86–92).

Focused on human conduct, Herodotus's tale of Arion does not emphasize the power of divinity. Arion may have been connected to ancient rites honoring the god Poseidon, but Herodotus does not mention this.[8] The story undoubtedly also had ancient associations with worship of the gods Dionysus and Apollo as well as Poseidon.[9] But Herodotus omits these connections too. Unlike Gyges, choosing survival over immediate death (1.11.4), Arion bravely confronts a choice that is no choice and opts for death with honor.[10] The theatricality of the singer's leap may exemplify his trust in Apollo.[11] Arion's rescue via the dolphin may also prefigure Apollo's rescue of the Lydian tyrant Croesus later in book 1.[12] (Arion's extraordinary rescue may even prefigure the Greeks' astonishing escape from Persian domination.)[13] But if Arion's choice to sing and then leap affirms symbolically the saving power of Apollo, Herodotus does not explicitly say so. Herodotus focuses instead on the drama of Arion's predicament, not his miraculous rescue.[14] Even the statue cited as evidence depicts an ordinary man, not a man in the singer's regalia associated with service to Apollo.[15]

In Herodotus's telling, the tale fails to affirm not only divine power but also autocratic human authority. Devoid of explicit assertions of religious connections and lacking divine actors, this story highlights human conduct, but it does not validate an autocrat's power to punish at his own discretion. Herodotus concludes his account without saying what, if anything, the tyrant Periander does to compensate Arion or avenge the injustice that he suffered.[16] Herodotus does not emphasize the vengeance theme.[17] He ends the story with the sailors' shocked dismay at the exposure of their lie, reiteration of the source of the tale ("These things now the Corinthians and the Lesbians say"), and assertion of the corroborating material evidence of the small statue of the man on a dolphin (1.24.8). By failing to make any mention of Periander's response, Herodotus's story does not attribute justice to autocratic political power. Focused not on religious belief or political authority but on human beings and their choices, the tale celebrates Arion's bravery and condemns the sailors' rapacious brutality and mendacity. Elsewhere, Herodotus describes tyrannical atrocities of Periander (3.48–53, 5.92η). But here Herodotus distinguishes Periander not for his autocratic power to punish but for his skepticism, his refusal to believe Arion in the absence of evidence.[18]

Herodotus offers the story not as a religious or political parable but as a moral allegory. As such, the tale has elicited diverse interpretations, some less persuasive than others. Arion's decision may validate Herodotus's conviction that death is better than life.[19] The story may foreshadow "proto-Stoic lessons" manifest in the tale of Croesus and useful for Herodotus's Athenian contemporaries.[20] Some scholars maintain that Arion's experience corroborates Herodotus's confidence that destiny inevitably exposes and punishes criminality.[21] But the tale as Herodotus tells it does not in fact directly connect wrongdoing to inevitable punishment; Herodotus fails to mention either divine retribution or the punishment (if any) inflicted on the sailors. In this particular moral allegory, Herodotus emphasizes not the inevitable retributive force of divinities or fate but the ethical or unethical behavior of human beings.

As moral allegory, Herodotus's tale of Arion aligns narrative falsehood with deliberate, unprovoked cruelty, and it enlists objective fact in the service of truth and (potentially) justice. Herodotus depicts Arion as an innocent victim of wicked opportunists. The Corinthian sailors, though paid to convey Arion to Corinth (and, ironically, deemed by Arion the most reliable of men) value material gain over a man's life. Succumbing to greed, they commit a cruel, inhumane deed. In their unscrupulous aggression and mistaken confidence in their own impunity, the sailors epitomize unrestrained, self-destructive abusers of power throughout the *Histories,* beginning with Candaules and including numerous subsequent examples. The sailors appreciate the pleasure of hearing a great singer, but they have no qualms about slaughtering the greatest of all singers for his money. The sailors' refusal to spare Arion's life while taking his money shows that even they appreciate the power of fact. They understand that alive, Arion could, on arrival in Corinth, credibly attest to their crime. And, of course, confronted afterward by Arion, alive and present, the sailors cannot persist in their lie. The story culminates not in Arion's miraculous survival but in the exposure of the sailors' falsehood.[22] Arion's unexpected arrival in Corinth attests that facts persist despite cynical, vehement denial. Arion's survival in and of itself refutes the sailors' lie. And the indisputable fact of Arion's survival makes justice not inevitable but possible.

Perhaps fabricated and certainly embellished, Herodotus's tale of Arion and the dolphin epitomizes both the power and the limits of art—a singer's, a historian's—to educate and elevate. Though not exactly qualifying as history in the modern sense, this story, prominent early in book 1, reveals the constructive potential of historical inquiry to identify and preserve facts and expose wrongdoing. Arguably, this tale encompasses the themes of the *Histories* as a whole.[23] The story may even implicitly align Arion the singer-poet with Herodotus himself, the inquirer and narrator of events.[24] Arion's story does seem to form part of a pattern validating material evidence and autopsy.[25] But the sailors' witless relegation of great art to nothing more than pleasing entertainment tacitly condemns them for their inability to learn from it. Hearing Arion's song in honor of Apollo—great god of poetry, art, prophecy, healing, truth—makes the sailors rethink their ruthless rapacity not at all. Like the song of a great singer, *historiē* may fail to exert a constructive influence on everyone.

In the *Histories*, Herodotus adopts the goals of an epic poet: memorialize great deeds and identify causes and consequences of human events (*Hist.* 1, first sentence). Thucydides, calling his own work a *ktēma eis aiei*, "possession for always," implicitly disparages Herodotus for aiming to entertain and please—rather than to educate—his contemporaries.[26] No less than Thucydides, however, Herodotus refutes Aristotle's claim that history is fundamentally less philosophical and serious than poetry.[27] As allegory, history offers not "particulars" as Aristotle claims but the very "universals" that Aristotle attributes to poetry. In providing a record and assessment of past events, *historiē* offers a path to narrative truth. Since the Greek word for truth, *aletheia,* means literally "not forgetting," then the opposite of falsehood is enduring memory. Herodotus introduces the improbable tale of Arion as a marvel (*thōma*), but he does not dwell on Arion's dolphin ride. Literal or legendary, that is not the marvel. The marvel is the sailors' inability to maintain their lie in the presence of Arion. The marvel of this tale, as Herodotus tells it, is the power of fact to dispel falsehood.

Though probably itself not factual, the story of Arion's wondrous dolphin ride illustrates the enduring power of evidentiary proof. Addressing his own deeply polarized, violent political moment (440s and 430s BCE), Herodotus deployed his novel invention—a written record of his own inquiries—to save his contemporaries from their rapacious and deluded inhumanity. In our own precarious present of virtual reality, artificial intelligence, and digital disinformation, Herodotus's story of Arion's miraculous survival offers an allegorical remedy for despair. Today's extremists of all varieties—some cynical grifters, others made monstrous by absolute ideological certainty—bombard us with falsehoods, even contradictory falsehoods, so as to eradicate the very concept of objective fact. Arion's unexpected and extraordinary reappearance in Corinth epitomizes the ability of observable facts to refute nefarious fictions. Theft, rage, and violence thrive on falsehoods. Facts make narrative truth and justice not inevitable but possible.

In Herodotus's tale of Arion, art thwarts evil and facts defeat fiction. But Herodotus does not say whether justice triumphs in the end. He fails to mention Periander's ultimate decision about punishment for the sailors or recompense for Arion. By omitting the ultimate outcome, Herodotus suggests that the responsibility for using facts in the service of justice lies not with autocrats—or even authoritative narrators—but with his readers. With us.

5

On Happiness

Although the—admittedly improbable—story of Arion and the dolphin connects truth and justice to factual evidence, Herodotus continues to include many counterfactual and ahistorical tales. He claims to record a conversation between two important historical figures—Solon, the celebrated Athenian poet, statesman, and lawgiver, and Croesus, king of Lydia, purportedly the great-great-grandson of Gyges, Candaules' bodyguard and reluctant voyeur of the naked queen.[1] In this alleged conversation, Solon extols the nonmaterial goods of health, family, and publicly acknowledged virtue. Seeking Solon's affirmation and yet derisively rejecting his claims, the wealthy, powerful Croesus indirectly reveals another crucial component of happiness: the wisdom to appreciate present good fortune. Subsequently, Croesus will reveal by counterexample still another component of happiness: the capacity for the forethought and restraint necessary to *preserve* present goods, as his career trajectory will perfectly exemplify the rise-and-fall pattern of history.

Potent not as history but as allegory, Herodotus's tale of this meeting between Solon and Croesus (and Croesus's subsequent career trajectory) portrays happiness as the product of human attitudes and conduct. Herodotus introduces Croesus as the originator of the conflict between East and West, calling him "the first of the foreigners [*barbarōn*] of whom we know [*idmen*] to subject the Greeks to paying tribute to himself" (1.6.2). Becoming king of Lydia after his father's death, Croesus launches numerous successful attacks on neighboring Greek communities (1.26). After subjugating the Greeks of Asia Minor and forcing them to pay tribute, Croesus starts building ships in preparation for attacking Greek islands in the Aegean:

[1.27] When, therefore, Croesus had forced the Greeks in Asia to pay tribute, he next determined to build ships so as to attack the people living on the islands. [2] But just as everything was ready for the shipbuilding, some people say that Bias of Priene came to Sardis—other people say it was Pittacus of Mytilene who came—and on his arrival Croesus asked him if he had any news about Greece. By his answer, this man put a stop to the shipbuilding. He said, [3] "King, the islanders are buying ten thousand horses. They intend to attack Sardis and you." Croesus hoped that the man was speaking the truth. He said, "I wish that the gods would do this to the mind of the islanders, make them come against the sons of the Lydians with cavalry!" [4] The other man replied, "King, it seems to me that you pray eagerly to catch the island dwellers riding horses on the mainland. In this, you are right to hope. But what else do you think that the islanders were praying as soon as they learned that you were about to build ships to attack them? They were praying to catch the Lydians on the sea, in order to take vengeance against you on behalf of the Greeks inhabiting the mainland, the ones that you have enslaved." [5] Croesus was very pleased by this conclusion, and since the man seemed to him

to speak suitably, he was persuaded to stop his shipbuilding.
And so he established a guest-friendship relationship with
the Ionians living on the islands.

[1.28] With time passing, nearly all of the people
inhabiting the area bounded by the river Halys were subjugated, except for the Cilicians and Lycians. Croesus had
subjugated all the others under his own sway. . . .

[1.29] When Croesus had subdued all of these other
peoples and had acquired them for the Lydians, Sardis was at
the height of its power. And all the wise men who were in
Greece at the time came individually to Sardis. Among these
was the Athenian Solon. Having set laws for the Athenians at
their request, Solon had left Athens for ten years on the
pretext of a sightseeing expedition—but surely it was in order
that he not be compelled to change any of the laws that he
had made. [2] The Athenians themselves were not able to do
this, for they had constrained themselves by great oaths to
use for ten years the laws Solon had set for them.

[1.30] For these same reasons, therefore, and traveling
for sightseeing, Solon arrived in Egypt at the court of Amasis,
and he came especially to Sardis at the court of Croesus. On
his arrival there, Solon was hosted in the royal halls by
Croesus. On the third or fourth day afterward, at the command of Croesus, servants led Solon through Croesus's
treasuries and showed him all of Croesus's great riches. [2]
When Solon had seen and examined everything and Croesus
felt it was the opportune moment, Croesus said, "My Athenian friend, we have heard a lot about you and your great
wisdom and your travels. Pursuing knowledge, you have
covered much territory for the purpose of sightseeing. Now,
therefore, the desire [*himeros*] has come upon me to ask you
if, at present, you have seen anyone who is the most fortunate
[*olbiōtatos*] of all men." [3] Croesus asked this expecting that

he himself was the most fortunate of men. But Solon, flatter-
ing Croesus not at all, instead said what was really true,
replying, "King, that man is Tellus the Athenian." Croesus,
amazed at Solon's answer, asked earnestly, [4] "In what way
do you judge Tellus to be most fortunate?" And Solon
replied, "In this respect: while his community was flourishing, Tellus had noble and good sons, and he saw children
born to them all and all of them surviving. Then, too, when
he had arrived at a time in his life when he was reasonably
well off—by our standards—Tellus had a most glorious end
to his life. [5] For he died most nobly, going to the aid of the
Athenians who were battling their neighbors in Eleusis.
Tellus made the enemy turn and flee. The Athenians buried
him at public expense on the very spot where he fell, and they
honored him greatly."

[1.31] Speaking of Tellus's many riches [*olbia*], Solon
prompted Croesus to ask whom Solon had seen who held
second place after Tellus. Croesus expected very much that
he himself would carry off second prize at least. But Solon
said, "Cleobis and Biton, [2] two men of the Argive race.
They had sufficient financial resources. In addition, they had
such great bodily strength. Both were equally prizewinners in
athletic contests, and in particular the following story is told:
the people of Argos were holding a festival in honor of the
goddess Hera, and the mother of these two men needed to be
carried to the temple by wagon. But oxen were not available
from the fields in time. Constrained by time, the young men
put themselves under the yoke and pulled the wagon with
their mother on it. After traversing forty-five stades [about
five miles], they reached the temple. [3] Having accomplished
this, and having been seen to do it by the full assembly, they
met with the best end of life. And in these men the god
demonstrates that it is better for a human being to be dead

than to live. For while the Argive men were standing around and commending the young men's strength, and the Argive women were commending their mother for having such sons, [4] she, rejoicing both in the deed and in the praise, stood opposite the statue and prayed to the goddess. She prayed that the goddess give to her sons, who had honored her greatly, the thing that is best for a human being to encounter. [5] After this prayer, when they had sacrificed and feasted, the young men lay down to sleep in the temple. They never got up again. Instead, they were held in this end. Making statues of them, the Argives set them up in Delphi on the grounds that they had been the best of men.

[1.32] Solon indeed awarded second prize for good fortune [*eudaimoniē*] to these men. But Croesus, hastening on, said, "Athenian friend, have you dismissed my good fortune [*eudaimoniē*] as nothing, so that you do not consider me worth as much as even private men?" And Solon replied, "You asked me about human matters—I who understand that divine power is entirely jealous and disruptive. [2] For in the long passage of time there are many things to see and to know that one does not wish for—and many things to suffer. For I set seventy years as the boundary for a human life. . . . [4] Of all these 26,250 days in the seventy years, not one day brings anything exactly like another. Therefore, Croesus, a human being is entirely the product of chance [*sumphorē*]. [5] You appear to me to possess great wealth and to be king over many people. But that thing that you asked me I do not yet say of you, until I learn that your life has ended well. For the one who is greatly wealthy is not in any way more fortunate [*olbiōteros*] than the one who has only a sufficiency for his needs of the day, unless good luck [*tuchē*] accompanies him so that he ends his life well, still having all his good things. Many of the men who are very wealthy are unfortu-

nate [*anolboi*], while many who have [only] a moderate
amount for their livelihood are lucky [*eutuchees*]. [6] The one
who is greatly wealthy [*mega plousios*] but unfortunate
[*anolbos*] exceeds the lucky man in only two ways. But the
lucky man exceeds the wealthy and unfortunate man in
many. The wealthy man is able to indulge his passions and to
endure ruinous, divinely sent folly. In these respects, he
surpasses the moderately well-off but lucky man, who is not
as capable as he of enduring ruinous folly and passion. But
good luck [*eutuchiē*] shields the latter against these things. He
lives without injury, without illness, without suffering troubles. He has good children and good looks. [7] If, in addition
to these things, he will still end his life well, this is that man
whom you seek, the one who deserves to be called fortunate
[*olbios*]. Until he dies, refrain from calling him fortunate
[*olbion*] and call him lucky [*eutuchea*]. [8] It is not possible
for one human being to gather together all the good things
that there are, just as no one place is sufficient, providing all
things for itself, but it has one thing and lacks another. The
best land is the one that has the most things. Thus, no one
body of a human being is self-sufficient. It has one thing but
lacks another. [9] Whoever continues in possession of most
of them and then ends his life pleasantly—this man, O King,
seems rightly to carry the name [of 'most fortunate'], in my
opinion. For it is necessary to look to the end of everything,
(considering) in what way it will turn out, for having given a
glimpse of fortune [*olbon*] to many, the god subsequently
overwhelms them utterly."

[1.33] Saying these things, Solon did not in any way
please Croesus. And Croesus sent him away, deeming him of
no account. Croesus believed Solon an ignorant man who
disregarded present goods and ordered him look to the end
of everything.

Despite its granular detail, this conversation between Solon and Croesus lacks historicity. Like allegory, history teaches
by analogy, but not every allegory is historical. Herodotus recognizes that verifiability distinguishes history from myth, but
his tale of Candaules lacks verification. Herodotus identifies the
power of fact to defeat falsehood, but his tale of Arion and the
dolphin seems more legendary than true (though Arion and
Periander are real historical figures). Solon and Croesus, too,
really existed, but such a conversation as this must be ahistorical.[2] Historians have traditionally maintained that Croesus
ruled Lydia ca. 560–546 (or 561–547) BCE, becoming king aged
about thirty-five. Solon established laws for Athens in 595/4 BCE.
If he did really visit Sardis in Lydia soon afterward, as Herodotus maintains (1.29), he would have met with an infant or
toddler Croesus. Recent scholarship has challenged these
traditional dates.[3] But even if Croesus was already on the throne
in the 580s, Herodotus is writing more than a century later. He
can have found no eyewitnesses to a meeting between Solon
and Croesus, and the encounter seems highly unlikely.[4] Though
probably not a factual, historical event, Herodotus's story of this
meeting once again invites readers to think historically, to identify causal factors—and patterns of causality—responsible for
human experience and, especially, human happiness.

Herodotus's account of this conversation between Solon
and Croesus focuses, like the tale of Candaules, on the role of
human attitudes and choices in determining human failure or
success. Herodotus likely shapes Solon's claims to suit his own
goals.[5] And his tale of Croesus has been viewed as program-
matic for the *Histories* as a whole.[6] Candaules appears both insecure (in his assessment of his wife's supreme beauty) and
overconfident (in his ability to control the outcome of his little
staged theatrical drama). Candaules achieves disaster by his
own lack of imagination and unprovoked violation of his wife's

privacy and dignity. A similar blend of insecurity and overconfidence, theatrical display, and lack of imagination characterize the Lydian king Croesus. (And Croesus will proceed to unprovoked aggression. See chapter 6.) Candaules considers his wife most beautiful, puts her on display, and expects to control events. Croesus considers his exorbitant wealth the definition of good fortune, flaunts his riches, and expects to elicit Solon's corroboration. In both tales, not the gods, fate, or chance, but human passions and insecurities drive the plot and determine the outcome.

At first, Croesus seems capable of heeding good advice.[7] When he begins building ships and preparing to attack Greek islanders in the Aegean, a visiting Greek wise man informs him that the Greek islanders are buying horses and planning a cavalry attack against *him* at his landlocked home city of Sardis, far from the coast. The claim is of course false. The islanders are planning no such attack. But Croesus welcomes the idea. *If only the islanders were planning a cavalry attack against me!* he thinks. *I sure wish the gods would make that happen!* He knows that he would easily defeat islanders so inexperienced in land warfare. Well, says the Greek wise man, that is exactly what the islanders started praying when they heard that you were building a fleet. They would love to catch you on the open sea and avenge your enslavement of the Greeks on the mainland. Croesus gets the point. He and his warriors have no expertise in naval warfare. Better stick to land battles. Instead of attacking, Croesus makes an alliance with the Greek islanders (1.27).

Able, initially, at least, to recognize good advice, even if it comes in the form of an analogy, and willing to acknowledge his own limitations, Croesus survives and prospers. He subjugates the Greeks on the mainland so successfully that he and his empire become very wealthy and powerful. Sardis becomes a popular attraction for all the wise men of Greece, the Athenian poet and statesman Solon among them. Herodotus does not explain their motives for visiting Sardis, but the city's great wealth and power must have made it a center of not only economic but also intellectual activity. According to Herodotus, Solon had established laws for the Athenians and then left Athens and traveled for ten years. (The concept of democracy did not exist in 595/4 BCE when Solon enacted his laws, but his innovative legislation put Athens on a path toward democratic government. Solon appears to have attempted to balance the interests of elites and non-elites. He banned loans secured on the person of the borrower, and he opened up political offices to citizens based on wealth rather than birth. Solon is generally credited with instituting a council and general assembly and with establishing public law courts comprising large juries rather than single magistrates.)[8] Arriving in Sardis, Herodotus maintains, Solon visits the phenomenally wealthy Croesus in his palace (1.29).

Croesus's prosperity accompanies a paradoxical combination of overconfidence and uncertainty. Meeting the famous sage Solon, he flaunts his wealth but also exhibits, like King Candaules, an irrational insecurity. Candaules believes his own wife the most beautiful woman of all, but he cannot be content until Gyges views her and agrees. Croesus, too, needs external validation of his own assessment—in this case his assessment of himself. Hosting Solon royally in his palace in Sardis and having ordered his servants to show Solon his extensive treasure, Croesus seeks Solon's affirmation, saying, "The desire [*himeros*] has come upon me to ask you if, at present, you have seen anyone who is the most fortunate [*olbiōtaton*] of all men" (1.30.2). The noun *himeros* denotes not a thought but a feeling, a longing or craving. In posing his question Croesus, just like Candaules, succumbs to an insecure need for another person's affirmation. Certain of his own immense wealth, Croesus thinks that he knows what Solon will answer, but his insecurity requires that he hear the answer from Solon himself.

Like Candaules, Croesus orchestrates empirical, visual confirmation of his own conviction, but Croesus has a very limited, exclusively material definition of "most fortunate." Apparently convinced of his own status as *olbiōtatos*, "most fortunate," because he is "most wealthy," Croesus first ensures that Solon has seen all his material wealth before asking for Solon's affirmation. In formulating his question, Croesus fails to appreciate the various dimensions of *olbiōtatos*. With no direct English equivalent, this multifaceted superlative adjective can mean "most wealthy," but it also comprises "most happy, most blessed, most prosperous." The English "most fortunate" has some of this multiplicity, with "having great wealth" and "lucky" built into the dual sense of "fortune." Croesus does not appear to understand the word's broader sense of "most possessed of happiness, luck, and prosperity."

Confident that he is most wealthy, Croesus seems to expect Solon to identify *him* as most fortunate.[9] But Solon's first pick is an obscure Athenian named Tellus, who lived in a famous city, had noble sons, and lived to see his grandchildren survive to adulthood. Tellus was well enough off, says Solon, by Greek standards. (That could be a subtle dig at Croesus's apparent confidence that everyone, Greeks included, must of course envy his lavish Eastern lifestyle.)[10] Tellus died the most glorious of all possible deaths, fighting in defense of his homeland and forcing his enemies to flee (1.30). This is the best that it gets, Solon suggests.

Irritated and uncomprehending, Croesus asks the follow-up question: All right, who is second most happy-blessed-wealthy-prosperous? Croesus expects that he himself must surely hold at least second place. He still fails to perceive the multiple ways in which a person could be described as "most fortunate," but Herodotus's readers are now beginning to realize the narrowness of Croesus's conception. Second best, says Solon, are these two brothers from Argos (1.31). They had sufficient means to live on. Their bodies were strong, and they were both prizewinners in athletic contests. One day they hauled their mother by wagon a great distance to a religious festival, because oxen were unavailable to pull the wagon. While everyone marveled and praised them for their strength and devotion to their mother, she prayed to the sanctuary's goddess, asking for the best thing that a human being can encounter. After the festival and the feast, the two young men fell asleep and never woke up. This, says Solon, constitutes the second-best thing that a human being can hope for: to die at the peak of one's strength and virtue.

Annoyed that Solon is disparaging his wealth, Croesus persists in missing Solon's point. Solon has to spell it out for him: wealth is impermanent. Lots of bad things can happen to a person, even a wealthy one. You cannot make an overall assessment about any individual's well-being, Solon explains, until after the person has died because you never know what misfortune might yet befall someone (1.32). Obviously, a person who has had great luck so far in life has only one direction in which change *could* occur. Things cannot really get better for that person, but they can surely get worse.

This basic principle applies to communities as well as individuals. At the beginning of his work, Herodotus promises that he will be "detailing small and large communities of human beings equally, for many communities that were great long ago have now become small, and many that were great in my time were small before. Understanding well that human happiness never remains in the same place, I will mention both equally" (1.5.3–4). Herodotus's conception of history rests on the principle that communities and individuals rise and fall.[11] When you are at the top, you can, like Candaules, do things to bring about your own destruction—or you can do everything in your power to remain at the top for as long as possible. Whichever option you choose, your children and grandchildren will inherit the results. And they in turn will face similar options.

Impervious to Solon's insistence on the impermanence of fortune, Croesus also fails to comprehend the idea that fortune could have nonmaterial, intangible dimensions.[12] Solon explains, "Many of the men who are very wealthy are unfortunate [*anolboi*], while many who have [only] a moderate amount for their livelihood are lucky [*eutuxees*]" (1.32.5). The Greek adjective *anolbos*, "unfortunate," has the same root as the superlative Croesus used in his initial question: who have you seen who is *olbiōtatos*, most wealthy, fortunate, happy, prosperous? Solon is trying to point out that you can *have a fortune* but not *be fortunate*. Conversely, you can have considerably less than a fortune and yet be, in fact, fortunate. Finding other criteria more consequential for human well-being than exorbitant wealth, Solon deems good fortune far more desirable than wealth. The wealthy person can indulge his passions and cope more easily with difficulties, but the fortunate person's good fortune excludes difficulties. He lives without pain, illness, or troubles. He has great children and great good looks. Him, you can call fortunate (*olbios*), but only after he is dead. Until then, you can only call him lucky (*eutuxēs*). Solon spells out the point explicitly, telling Croesus, "It is necessary to look at the end of everything, [considering] in what way it will turn out, for having given a glimpse of wealth and happiness to many, the god subsequently overwhelms them utterly" (1.32.9). Despite Solon's directness and clarity, Croesus still fails to understand. His unfounded confidence in material wealth as the definition of success remains unshaken. Croesus considers Solon's advice ignorant nonsense, and he angrily sends Solon away.

Like the tales of Candaules and Arion, this story does not qualify as history in the modern sense, but it affirms Herodotus's conception of the pattern of historical change. If Solon's travels coincided with Croesus's infancy, he is unlikely to have met Croesus at the peak of his wealth and power. But Solon wisely cautions against assuming the permanence of success. Solon's message reiterates Herodotus's previous claim that "human happiness never remains in the same place" (1.5.4). Solon explains that because human fortunes rise and fall, only after someone has completed his life can you accurately call him happy and fortunate (*olbios*) (1.32.7). Croesus completely misses Solon's point, but the remainder of his life will corroborate the claim that human fortunes vary, as Herodotus will soon show.

The tale of Croesus and Solon not only affirms Herodotus's view of historical change but also engages our interpretive abilities. Herodotus does not encourage readers to accept Solon's pronouncements unquestioningly. Croesus's subsequent career will exemplify the impermanence of fortune, but Croesus errs in the present. He trusts only his own limited conception of fortune. He cannot accept new information or conceive of valuable goods that are nonmaterial. His own material success brings him no real comfort or peace of mind. He remains acquisitive and insecure. Solon maintains that only the end counts in making a final determination of another's life, but the example of Croesus reminds us to focus on present circumstances. If fortunes can change in an instant, surely the wise person seeks to enjoy and preserve current good fortune and in bad times takes comfort in hope of a change for the better and tries to achieve it.

Historical inquiry prevents unthinking acceptance of any dogmatic assertions, even those of a famous wise man. Herodotus's tale of Croesus and Solon challenges the narrow definition of happiness as the acquisition of wealth and power, commending instead the nonmaterial goods of a thriving family, health, and virtue. But this story also encourages critical evaluation of Solon's authoritative pronouncements. Just as we need not accept Solon's claim that only the end counts in evaluating someone's life, we also need not unthinkingly accept Solon's assertion that supernatural forces produce the changes in human life. The rest of the *Histories* will *not* corroborate Solon's claim that "a human being is entirely a product of chance [*sumphorē*]" (1.32.4). Using our own capacity for inquiry and assessment and measuring the remainder of the *Histories* against this claim, we will see that human fortunes are indeed precarious, but human decisions and actions play a significant role in determining success or failure. Human happiness proves both effortful and elusive, more dependent on human choices than we might like to acknowledge. Just as Candaules' lust, overconfidence, and lack of imagination ensure his destruction, so too material greed, overconfidence, and lack of imagination will cost Croesus his empire—and nearly his life. Like Candaules, Croesus demonstrates that not chance but human aspirations and conduct permit happiness or preclude it.

Herodotus is not quite writing history, but he is developing his readers' capacity for historical inquiry. To the extent that human beings determine the patterns of historical change— change affecting themselves and others—an awareness of patterns of cause and effect affords some measure of control. Solon distinguishes exorbitant wealth from true happiness. Croesus fails to appreciate present goods. Together they encourage us to reject the fiction that happiness exists only in material acquisition and in some idealized future. They thereby fortify us against influential voices promising utopian futures while creating chaos and misery in the present. Undermining deceptive seductions to material wealth and happiness promised not now

but in some imagined later, Herodotus's tale of Croesus and Solon encourages readers to think critically about the components of happiness. This story reminds us to take responsibility
for choices likely to promote or prevent happiness, not only in
the future but also—and especially—here and now.

6

On Self-Deception

I n his encounter with Solon, Croesus exhibits an impressive lack of imagination and a stubborn imperviousness to wise advice. Unable to recognize that appearances can be deceiving, Croesus mistakes wealth for happiness. He assumes, incorrectly, that Solon will concur. Despite Solon's insistence on the value of nonmaterial goods, Croesus persists in overvaluing material acquisition while remaining unable to enjoy present goods.

Not long afterward, Croesus manifests the same absolute confidence in his interpretation of invisible, supernatural signs as he did in his assessment of the value of material goods. He continues to fail to appreciate the role of his own choices in promoting happiness or disaster. Following his meeting with Solon, Croesus seeks divine affirmation for an intended military conquest by consulting divine oracles. Herodotus may well be misinterpreting or distorting epigraphical evidence.[1] But just as he depicts Croesus trusting his own assessment of the material world, so too he portrays Croesus unquestioningly—and erroneously—trusting his ability to interpret supernatural signs. In his uncritical faith in his assessment of unseen forces operative in human life, Croesus epitomizes the vulnerability of human beings to self-deception. He misinterprets the oracles to suit his own ambitions. Still acquisitive and aggressive despite Solon's efforts, and eager to thwart the rapid expansion of the Persian empire, Croesus decides to attack Persia:

[1.46.2] Therefore, after he formed this intention, Croesus immediately made trial of the oracular sites, both the ones in Greece and the ones in Libya. . . . He sent men to the various oracles in order to test what they knew, so that if it was discovered that one of the oracles knew the truth [*tēn alētheiēn*], he could ask a second question, namely whether he should try to attack the Persians.

[1.47] Sending the Lydians to make trial of the oracles, Croesus instructed them to count the days from when they set out from Sardis and to consult the oracle on the one hundredth day. They were to ask what Croesus, the Lydian king, happened to be doing on that day. They were to write down what each of the oracles answered and bring the response back to Croesus himself. [2] What the rest of the oracles answered has not been reported by anyone, but as soon as the Lydians arrived in the great hall in Delphi for the purposes of consulting the god and asked the designated question, the Pythia said the following in hexameter verse:

[3] I know the numbers of the grains of sand and also the measures
     of the sea.
I understand the speechless, and I hear the one who does not speak.
The smell of a hard-shell tortoise has entered my thoughts.
It is being boiled in bronze together with the meat of lambs.
Underneath, bronze has been laid, and bronze has been set above.

[1.48] The Lydians wrote down the Pythia's answer and headed back to Sardis. And as the other messengers who had been sent to the various places arrived, carrying the oracular responses, Croesus unfolded each message and examined the writing on it. Not a single one was pleasing to him. But when he heard the one from Delphi, he immediately offered a prayer and accepted the message favorably, believing the oracle in Delphi to be the only one that had discovered what he himself had done. [2] For when he sent his messengers to inquire of the oracles in different places, he watched for the designated day and contrived the following: believing that his plan was impossible to discover or conjecture, he himself cut up a tortoise and a lamb, and he boiled them together in a bronze caldron, having placed a bronze lid on top.

[1.49] This, surely, the oracle from Delphi proclaimed in this way to Croesus. I am unable to say what answer the oracle of Amphiareion gave to the Lydians after they performed the customary rites around the temple, for this is not reported— except that Croesus believed that this oracle which he had acquired was also accurate.

[1.50] After this, Croesus kept on propitiating the god in Delphi with great sacrifices. For he sacrificed three thousand animals suitable for sacrifice, and gold-plated and silver-plated couches, and golden bowls for libations. Heaping up purple cloaks and tunics, he burned them up on a great fire. He did this hoping to gain the god's favor even more. And he ordered all the Lydians to sacrifice all their things—in accordance with what each possessed. [2] After the sacrifice, he melted an immense amount of gold and hammered bricks out of it, making the longer sides six palms in length [about 18 inches], the shorter sides three palms in length, and the height one palm. He made one hundred and seventeen of these. Four of them were of refined gold, weighing two and a half talents each [roughly 142 pounds]. The others were of white gold, each weighing two talents [about 114 pounds].

[3] He also had an image of a lion made of the refined gold. This weighed ten talents. When the temple in Delphi burned down [548 BCE], this lion fell from the bricks on which it had been set. It now stands in the treasury of the Corinthians, weighing six and a half talents, for three and a half talents of it had burned.

[1.51] On completing these things, Croesus sent them to Delphi along with other things as well, including two very large measuring bowls, one golden, one silver. The golden one stood on the right-hand side for anyone entering the temple, the silver one on the left. [2] But these were also moved when the temple burned, and the golden one lies in the treasury of the Clazomenaeans. It weighs eight and a half talents and an additional twelve minas [one-fifth of a talent]. The silver one stands upon a corner of the temple's front hall. It holds 600 amphoras [more than 6,000 gallons]. The Delphians use it for mixing at the Theophania festival. [3] They say that it is the work of Theodorus of Samos, and I think so. For it does not appear to me to be an ordinary work. Croesus also sent off four silver jars, which stand in the treasury of the Corinthians, and he dedicated two bowls for sprinkling sacrificial water, one golden, one silver. The golden one has been inscribed. In the inscription, the Spartans claim that the bowl is a dedication of theirs. But they are not speaking correctly. [4] For this also is a dedication from Croesus. One of the people of Delphi wrote the inscription wishing to gratify the Spartans. Although I know his name, I will not mention it. But the statue of a boy with water running through his hand is in fact from the Spartans. Neither of the bowls for sprinkling sacrificial water is from the Spartans, however. [5] Along with these things, Croesus also sent many other unremarkable dedicatory objects, including some round silver bowls and, in particular, the

golden image of a woman, three cubits tall [about four and a
half feet], which the Delphians say is the likeness of Croesus's
baker. In addition, Croesus also dedicated necklaces from his
own wife's neck and also belts of hers.

[1.52] He sent these things away to Delphi. And having
learned of the virtue and suffering of Amphiareius, he
dedicated to him a shield that was entirely gold and also a
spear that was equally solid gold, both its shaft and its
spearpoint. These things were both still in Thebes in my time,
in the Thebans' temple of Ismenian Apollo.

[1.53] To the men of the Lydians who were about to take
these gifts [dōra] to the temples, Croesus commanded that
they ask the oracles if he should make war upon the Persians
and if he should add some army of men as his friend [philon].
[2] And when these Lydians arrived in the temples where
they had been sent, they dedicated the offerings and questioned the oracles, saying "Croesus, king of the Lydians and
other peoples, believing this oracle alone to be prophetic
among human beings, gave you gifts [dōra] worthy of your
prophetic discoveries. And now he asks you if he should
make war upon the Persians and if he should add some army
of men as his ally [summachon]." [3] They asked these things.
And the opinions of both oracles coincided. Both prophesied
to Croesus that if he made war upon the Persians he would
destroy a great empire [archēn]. And they advised him to
seek out the most powerful of the Greeks and add them as
friends [philous] to himself.

[1.54] When Croesus learned the prophecies that were
brought back to him, he rejoiced beyond measure at the
oracular responses. He entirely expected that he was going
to destroy the kingdom [basilēiēn] of Cyrus [king of Persia,
559–530 BCE]. Sending again to Delphi, he learned the
number of people there and he gave them gifts [dōreetai],

two staters of gold for each man [perhaps eight to ten grams]. In exchange for these, the Delphians gave Croesus and the Lydians the right of consulting the oracle first, exemption from all fees, and front seats at festivals. They also offered citizenship in Delphi to any Lydian who wanted it, for all time.

[1.55] Having given these gifts [dorēsamenos] to the Delphians, Croesus consulted the oracle a third time. For, surely, since he accepted the truth of the oracle, he was going to rely on it regularly. Consulting it, he asked whether his monarchy [mounarchiē] would exist for a long time. [2] And the Pythian oracle proclaimed the following:

> But whenever a mule becomes king of the Medes
> At that time, tender-footed Lydian, flee beside the pebbly river Hermus
> And do not remain, nor be ashamed to be a coward.

[1.56] With the arrival of these words, Croesus was delighted most of all, expecting that a mule instead of a man would never be king of the Medes, and therefore assuming that neither he himself nor his descendants would ever be deposed from their sovereignty [archēs].

In this account of Croesus's use of oracles, Herodotus cautions against unquestioning trust in one's own unilateral judgment. Like Candaules, Croesus exemplifies the danger of overconfidence in unfounded assumptions and certainties. Croesus's mistaken belief in his supreme status as "most fortunate" derives from overvaluing visible, material goods. His encounter with Solon cautions against reliance on surface appearances. The reality may be less than meets the eye. But Herodotus's tale of Croesus's subsequent career also cautions against uncritical confidence in a one-sided assessment of the unseen, the invisible forces operative in human life. The reality may be more than meets the eye. Absolute certainty often leads the undiscerning to misinterpret empirical evidence, at great cost to themselves and others. Unfounded certainty similarly causes overconfident individuals like Croesus to misinterpret supernatural signs, again with catastrophic results. Herodotus accepts that portents (and divinities) are real and influential.[2] But his portrait of Croesus (and two other autocrats, Astyages and Cyrus) exposes the problem of interpretation and the vulnerability of human beings to self-deception.

At the very least, the recognition that good fortune is impermanent should promote caution and self-restraint. Croesus fails to understand Solon's insight that "fortune" comprises intangible elements more valuable than material wealth, but the conversation may have taught him to be a little careful. When he decides to challenge the growing power of Persia, he first opts to consult divine oracles to see whether a preemptive attack would be a good idea. Employing a clever test to determine the most accurate of the many Greek oracular sites, Croesus settles on two, the oracle of Apollo at Delphi and one other (1.46–49). Both subsequently predict that "if Croesus made war upon the Persians he would destroy a great *archē*, "empire" (1.53.3). The added advice to acquire allies surely obscures the oracles' ambiguity.[3] But Croesus delightedly—and mistakenly— assumes that by "great empire" the oracle could *only* mean the Persian empire. He never stops to consider that the oracle could be referring to his own.

Croesus interprets this oracle to suit his own desires, but Herodotus, manifesting a proto-historical interest in verifiability, evokes readers' skepticism. Following receipt of the first oracle and unquestioningly trusting the Delphic oracle's veracity, Croesus dedicates lavish gifts to ensure continued favor. Herodotus once again demonstrates recognizably "historical" instincts in scrupulously enumerating as corroboration the material evidence still visible in his own time (1.51–52). Detailing at great length Croesus's many gifts to the oracle, Herodotus emphasizes Croesus's enduring confidence in the supreme value of material goods. Croesus misunderstands the nature of divinity, erroneously expecting the gods to reciprocate his generosity.[4] But since the Greek word for "gift," *dōron*, also means "bribe" (cf. *dōra* at 53.1 and 53.2, *dōreetai* at 1.54.1, and *dorēsamenos* at 55.1), Herodotus's readers may begin to doubt the integrity, independence, or reliability of any oracular pronouncement.

Herodotus also shows that the many gifts/bribes do not benefit Croesus at all, since the problem lies in interpretation. As in his unidimensional understanding of "most fortunate" in his conversation with Solon and "great empire" in the second oracular response, Croesus persists in his inability to imagine that words can have more than one possible meaning. When Croesus consults the oracle a third time, he learns that his own reign will last "until a mule becomes king of the Medes" (1.55.2). The present king of Persia, Cyrus, had subjected the Medes to the Persians—or so Herodotus will maintain (1.123–130)— and the Medes and the Persians currently constitute one realm. By birth, Cyrus is half Persian and half Mede. Croesus can only understand "mule" as an animal born from the mating of a horse and a donkey, and he is certain that a human being will always rule the Persians. It never occurs to him that a man who, like Cyrus, is half Persian and half Mede could be described (offensively and metaphorically) as a "mule."

Even Croesus's effort to determine oracular reliability, his original test of the oracles (1.47–9), cannot solve the problem of interpretation. This piece of the story must be pure fiction. Oracular sites were not accessible every day, and Croesus could not be certain that his messengers could consult the oracle on the specified day.[5] Although Croesus interprets the second oracle unilaterally (assuming the doomed empire could only be the Persians') and the third literally (believing a man could never be, metaphorically, a "mule"), his initial test of the oracles' accuracy has hallmarks of a scientific experiment. But Croesus foolishly accepts the results without skepticism. His question "What will I be doing one hundred days from now?" seems cleverly formulated, and it is remarkable that any of the oracles gets this right. But perhaps the accurate prediction was just a lucky guess. More likely, one of Croesus's attendants might have leaked the information, or bribed the oracle, or doctored the oracular message. Croesus never considers these possibilities. Croesus's response to this first oracle, as to the second and third, exposes his credulousness and his eagerness to believe what he wants to believe.

Despite revealing Croesus's self-deceptive lack of skepticism and failures of interpretation, Herodotus never disputes the connection between oracles and reality. Subsequent events will confirm the accuracy of the second and third oracles: Croesus does destroy a great empire, and it does occur when a "mule" rules the Medes. Herodotus explains that misinterpreting the oracle and expecting to defeat the powerful Persians and their king, Croesus attacks and destroys his own empire. He is utterly defeated and captured by Cyrus, the mixed-race Persian king (1.71–85; 1.91.5–6) [550 BCE]. The effort to gain knowledge of the future proves less than useless. Croesus self-destructively misinterprets the oracles to validate his own aggressive, acquisitive appetite. But oracles do in fact coincide with reality.

Instead of encouraging readers to doubt the accuracy of oracles, Herodotus elsewhere similarly highlights the role of self-deception in skewing interpretation. Like Croesus, the Spartans, for example, accept an oracular prediction as accurate and fail to consider the possibility of alternate meanings. Acquisitive, and motivated by the Delphic oracle's pronouncement that Apollo will grant them land to work in Tegea, the Spartans attack Tegea. Defeated, they do find themselves working the land—as slaves (1.66).[6] The Spartans never succeed in battle against the Tegeans until they successfully interpret a subsequent oracle and fulfill its command. After that, they defeat the Tegeans in battle every time and succeed in conquering most of southern Greece (the Peloponnese) (1.65–70).

Oblivious to the problem of interpretation, Croesus persists in deceiving himself. Although his catastrophic military defeat by the Persians ultimately teaches him the wisdom of Solon's claim that fortune is impermanent, Croesus fails to take responsibility for his own errors.[7] He blames a god for encouraging him to attack Persia (1.87.3), insisting that "doubtless it was dear to a divinity that this all happen in this way" (1.87.4). He accuses the gods of being *acharistoi,* "ungrateful," for all the many offerings he had previously dedicated to them (1.90.4). The Delphic oracle defends Apollo by responding that Croesus has paid for the *hamartas,* "failure" or "error," of his ancestor Gyges" (1.91.1), and that Apollo in fact delayed the disaster for some three years and even rescued Croesus when Cyrus was about to burn him alive. The oracle points out that Croesus himself misinterpreted the oracles. Only then does Croesus accept that the *hamartas,* "error," was his and not the god's (1.91.5).

Croesus belatedly acknowledges his "error," but his self-deception continues. He remains unable to reflect directly on his experience or to reassess his own motives and methods. The Greek noun *hamartas,* used first by Apollo's oracle (1.91.1) and then Croesus (1.91.5), derives from the context of archery; the verb *hamartanō* means "to miss the mark," that is, to miss the target. It suggests not a problem of intentions but a problem of

accuracy. Croesus accepts only that he failed, not that his goals
or methods were mistaken or misguided. Herodotus claims
that when Gyges took control of Lydia from the descendants
of Heracles, the Delphic oracle prophesied that Heracles' descendants would get their revenge on one of Gyges' descendants
in the fifth generation (1.13.2). The archaic conception that an
individual might suffer for an ancestor's misdeed helped ancient Greeks to account for the suffering of apparently innocent
people. But even if we were to agree—as Herodotus's contemporaries might—that *someone* must pay for an ancestor's
error, we would have to ask: Why Croesus? Why not a sibling
or cousin of Croesus? And why at this point in his life and not
later? Unlike Croesus, we can recognize that Croesus brings disaster on himself. Greed and ambition motivate his invasion
of Persia. His unfounded confidence in his ability to interpret
oracles, his failure to consider ambiguities of language, his inability to recognize the possibility of alternate interpretations—
these factors cause him to "destroy a great empire." Not the
Persian empire, as he expects, but his own.

While accepting the veracity of supernatural signs, Herodotus repeatedly exposes the role of self-deception in describing people's reactions not just to oracles but also to dreams
thought to be divinely sent. The capacity for self-deception
makes Croesus confident that a dream, like an oracle, offers
useful foreknowledge: before launching his disastrous expedition against Persia, Croesus dreams that his son will die from
a spear wound. He determines to protect his son by preventing him from participating in warfare, but he allows him to go
on a boar-hunting expedition where he is accidentally and fatally wounded by—yes, of course—a spear (1.34–45). Although
the death of his son convinces Croesus of the accuracy of his
dream, he previously deceives himself in thinking the dream
useful.

Human beings may naturally want advance knowledge of
the future, but Herodotus suggests that accurate interpretation
of any supernatural indication of future events becomes manifest only after the fact. Following the tragic loss of his son,
Croesus identifies the source of his calamity as "one of the gods,
who long ago foretold to me what was going to occur" (1.45.2).
The story validates Solon's claim that "divine power is entirely
jealous and disruptive" (1.32.1). Croesus belatedly accepts that
the gods punished him for his misplaced self-confidence. And
Herodotus introduces the tale of Croesus's defeat as evidence
of divine vengeance, claiming, "After Solon went away, great
retribution from the god seized Croesus, as is likely, because
he believed himself to be most fortunate [olbiōtatos] of all men"
(1.34.1).

For Herodotus's readers, however, such certainty regarding supernatural agency comes to seem beside the point. Maybe
a god or gods did want to punish Croesus. But independent of
divine intentions or actions, belief in accurate foreknowledge
of the future deduced from a dream, as from an oracle, proves
both self-deceptive and irrational. Reacting to his dream, Croesus fails to consider other possible sources of spear wounds
than battle. He deceives himself into thinking that he has taken
precautions by forbidding his son to engage in warfare but allowing him to join a hunting expedition. Croesus does not realize that he cannot have it both ways. Either the dream's prediction
is true or it is not. If Croesus believes that the dream predicts the
future, then his attempt to avert it appears supremely illogical.[8] If
Croesus *could* avert the dream's prediction, would he not thereby
expose the fallacy of accepting dreams as accurate predictors of
the future?

Other powerful autocrats in the *Histories* manifest the
same self-deceptive irrationality. Astyages, for example, grandfather of the Persian tyrant Cyrus, mirrors Croesus in attempt-

ing to prevent an outcome foretold in dreams.[9] For Astyages, a more explicit second dream follows a less clear first.[10] And this king's irrational belief that dreams afford power over the future provokes not merely futile but monstrous action: a failed attempt to murder his own grandson to prevent him from acquiring the Persian throne—followed by horrific vengeance on the subordinate (a blood relative of Astyages) for not destroying the infant grandson (1.107–130). This tale seems ahistorical and full of folktale elements, with details in the second dream suggesting Eastern source material.[11] But in recounting the story, Herodotus emphasizes Astyages's self-deception and irrationality.

Incorporating an account of Astyages's fortuitously surviving grandson, the Persian ruler Cyrus, Herodotus continues to emphasize that oracles and dreams do accurately foretell the future, just not in the way that recipients anticipate. Like his own grandfather and the Lydian king Croesus, Cyrus deceives himself in thinking that a dream affords control over future events. Like Croesus, Cyrus exemplifies the variability of human fortunes.[12] Emulating both his grandfather and Croesus, Cyrus misinterprets a dream to suit his own ambition and makes the dream's prediction accurate by seeking to avert it. Motivated by irrational passion—like Candaules, the Lydian king—Cyrus attacks the territory of others. He "lusted after [*epethumēse*] subjugating the Massegetai" (1. 201.1), and against these people he "had the desire/lust [*prothumiēn*] to make war" (1.204.1). Ignoring good advice (1.206) and preparing to launch his attack, Cyrus unquestioningly interprets a dream to mean that Darius, a young Persian nobleman, is plotting to overthrow him and rule Persia (1.209–210). With the benefit of hindsight and the narrator's omniscience, Herodotus explains the dream's "real" meaning: Cyrus was "thinking that Darius was plotting against him," but in fact "the divinity was showing him before-

hand that he himself was going to die right there in that place
and that his hereditary monarchy was going to be transferred
to Darius" (1.210.1). Cyrus initially prevails in battle over the
Massegetai, but he opts to reject the defeated queen's request
for the return of her captured son. The son kills himself (1. 211–
13), and the queen retaliates, attacking with her full army. In
the ensuing battle—deemed by Herodotus "the most violent"
[ischurotatēn] of all of the battles that "barbarians" ever fought
(1.214.1)—the enemies prevail, killing many Persians, including
Cyrus himself. Although Herodotus invokes a divine explanation, readers of Herodotus's account see that Cyrus's choices directly end his twenty-nine-year reign (1.214.3).

For Herodotus, the human capacity for self-deception
constitutes an unseen but determinative force in human life.
Three powerful autocrats—Croesus, Astyages, Cyrus—deceive
themselves into thinking that supernatural signs validate their
desires and confer control over future events. Just as Croesus
interprets oracles to suit his acquisitive appetite, Astyages interprets a dream to justify killing his own grandson in an effort to retain power, and Cyrus interprets a dream to validate
his irrational passion for conquest. Nothing compels Croesus
to attack Persia, Astyages to try to kill his grandson, or Cyrus
to attack the Massegetai. They just want to. Lust for greater territory and power, like a king's lust for his own wife or sailors'
greed for a passenger's money, needs no further explanation.
But self-deception feeds human appetites and makes supernatural signs worse than useless.

Consistently depicting human agency as a major driver
of historical change, Herodotus emphasizes that human convictions, misconceptions, and decisions shape the contours of
the rise and fall pattern in individual and communal fortunes.
The careers of the ancient kings Croesus, Astyages, and Cyrus
affirm Solon's advice to "look to the end of everything." The pre-

cept should prompt not only an effort to appreciate present goods but also caution, self-questioning, and forethought. Instead, overconfident in their interpretive abilities and lacking restraint, these autocrats rely exclusively on their own uncritical and consequently undiscerning judgment. They yield to their passions without question or counsel. Herodotus repeatedly exposes the folly of entrusting one's fortunes to supernatural signs. Even if oracles, dreams, and portents accurately foretell future events, they offer no benefit in the present. Warning against self-deception, Herodotus implicitly commends self-reflection and self-restraint, timeless survival skills.

Like these ancient autocrats, we deceive ourselves, if we fail to appreciate current good fortune or to question our own certainties, ambitions, and methods. The dangers of decision-making based on uncritical acceptance of supernatural portents extend also to unthinking acceptance of any unfounded predictions or unproven assertions. Today's politicians, pundits, tech inventors, wealthy financiers, and celebrities inundate us with authoritative pronouncements as unsubstantiated and immaterial as any ancient omen, oracle, or dream. We deceive ourselves in succumbing to enticing but fraudulent political promises, digital deceptions, unverified social media posts, or salacious news stories. In his pseudo-scientific effort to evaluate the accuracy of oracles, Croesus offers a lesson in humility to even the most scrupulous modern reader, critic, or scientist. Even the most accurate-seeming explanatory hypothesis may leave various other possible explanations as yet unconceived. Croesus equally constitutes a cautionary example to any exuberant, forethought-free tech inventor or policy maker for whom potentially adverse consequences rarely factor into the planning and calculation of new devices or policies.

Democratic elections give every citizen great power and responsibility, but self-deception thwarts our ability to resist our own irrational passions and preferences. Self-deception prevents us from determining the best future for ourselves and our communities. We all tend to see and believe what we want to see and believe. But actual past experience—our own and other people's—offers a surer guide. (Eugene O'Neill famously suggested that "there is no present or future—only the past happening over and over again—now.")[13] We can choose to ignore the past or to learn from it. Herodotus's examples of overconfident, unreflective autocrats remind us to examine the past and the present from multiple perspectives and to seek verification. Herodotus suggests that foolish certainties and narrow-minded, unsubstantiated assumptions cannot aid us in understanding the past, guiding the present, or improving the future. In encouraging healthy skepticism, Herodotus empowers us against the natural human propensity for self-deception.

7

On Deception

Herodotus interrupts his tale of Croesus to describe the rise to power in Athens of the tyrant Peisistratus (1.59–65.1). Preparing to invade Persia, Croesus accepts the oracles' advice to acquire Greek allies (1.53.3). He proceeds to seek information about the powerful citizen-communities of Athens and Sparta. In Athens, Peisistratus has gained autocratic power by exploiting Athenian factional divisions and religious faith. In his account of this Athenian autocrat's successful power grabs, Herodotus ridicules irrational faith and lack of discernment:

[1.59] Therefore, of these two peoples [Athenian and Spartan], Croesus learned by inquiry that the Attic [Athenian] race was currently held down and torn apart by Peisistratus, son of Hippocrates and tyrant of Athens at the time. . . . [3] . . . When there was civil strife at Athens between men of the coast, led by Megacles, son of Alcmaeon, and men of the plain, led by Lycurgus, son of Aristoleides, Peisistratus, aiming at tyranny, gathered together a third faction. Having collected partisans and calling himself leader of the people of the hill region, he contrived the following plans: [4] he

wounded himself and drove his mule-drawn chariot into the
marketplace on the pretext that he was fleeing enemies—as if
they wished to kill him as he was driving to the countryside.
And Peisistratus asked the people to obtain a protective
guard for himself. (He was famous previously, having held
the generalship against Megara and capturing Nisaea and
displaying other great deeds.) [5] Deceived by Peisistratus,
the Athenian people gave him men chosen from the citizens.
These men became not spear bearers but club bearers of
Peisistratus, for they followed after him carrying wooden
clubs. Joining Peisistratus in rebellion, these men together
with him [i.e., providing a military force for him] took hold
of the acropolis. [6] There, surely, Peisistratus ruled the
Athenians, neither disrupting the current political offices nor
changing the laws. He managed the city according to these
previously established conditions, ordering it nobly and well.

[1.60] After not much time had passed, the partisans of
Megacles and the partisans of Lycurgus [two competing
political factions in Athens], being like-minded, drove
Peisistratus out. Thus, Peisistratus for the first time held
Athens, and not yet having his tyranny very firmly rooted, he
lost it. But the ones who drove Peisistratus out devolved again
into factions and quarreled with each other anew. [2] Troubled by the factional dispute, Megacles sent a message to
Peisistratus asking whether he would be willing to take
Megacles' daughter as his wife in exchange for the tyranny
[autocratic rule over Athens]. [3] Peisistratus accepted the
deal and agreed on these conditions. For the return of
Peisistratus, they contrived the silliest thing of all time, as I
discover (since indeed the Greek race has been judged from
ancient times to be both more shrewd and more free from
simple-minded silliness than the race of barbarians). And
also, at that time, the men in Athens were said to be first

among the Greeks in regard to their prudence and wisdom. Megacles and Peisistratus contrived the following: [4] In the deme [village] of Paiania [in the region of Attica, the area surrounding Athens], there was a woman whose name was Phya. In size, Phya was just three fingers short of four cubits [i.e., about five feet, ten inches] and otherwise well-formed. Costuming this woman in full hoplite [infantryman] armor and setting her on a chariot positioned so that she would appear most glorious, they drove her into the citadel. They sent heralds running ahead. Arriving in the citadel, the heralds announced the things they had been commanded, saying the following: [5] "Athenians! Accept Peisistratus with good will. The goddess Athena herself, honoring Peisistratus most of all men, is leading him back into her own acropolis." Ranging about, the heralds said these things. And immediately the report arrived in the villages that Athena was bringing Peisistratus back from exile. And the people in the citadel, believing that the woman was the goddess herself, worshipped this human woman and accepted Peisistratus.

[1.61] Taking the tyranny in the way just described, Peisistratus married the daughter of Megacles according to the agreement he had formed with Megacles. But since the existing sons of Peisistratus were young men and the descendants of Alcmaeon [father of Megacles] were said to be under a curse, Peisistratus did not want children to be born from this newly married wife. He therefore had sex with her in a way that was not in accordance with custom [ou kata nomon]. [2] At first, the woman concealed these things. But afterward—either on being questioned or not—she tells her mother, and her mother tells her husband. Megacles considered it terrible to be dishonored by Peisistratus. Enraged as he was, Megacles reconciled his enmity with the other political factions. Peisistratus, learning of the actions being

taken against him, escaped from the land altogether. Arriving
in Eretria [a coastal town north of Athens], he took counsel
together with his sons. [3] The opinion of Peisistratus's son
Hippias prevailed: they should recover the tyranny [i.e.,
recover autocratic rule over Athens] for themselves. Thereupon, they gathered together funds from whatever cities
were under obligations to them in any way. Many cities
provided a great amount of money, but the Thebans sur-
passed all in the portion of money that they contributed.
[4] Afterward to speak in brief, time passed, and they readied
everything for their return. Argive mercenaries came from
the Peloponnese, and a man from Naxos arrived, a volunteer
named Lygdamis, who displayed the greatest willingness,
bringing money and men.

[1.62] Setting forth from Eretria, they came back during
the eleventh year. And the first part of Attica that they held
was Marathon [a town on the northern edge of the region
comprising, with Athens, Attica]. They made camp for
themselves in this place. And partisans joined them from the
city and others gathered from the villages, people to whom
tyranny was more welcome than freedom. These men surely
were assembling. [2] But the Athenians from the citadel
considered this of no account, as long as Peisistratus was
gathering money and afterward when he held Marathon. But
when they learned that Peisistratus was making his way from
Marathon toward the citadel, thus indeed they came to the
rescue against him. And these men went with their whole
army against the returning exiles, and the supporters of
Peisistratus, having set forth from Marathon, approached the
citadel. [3] Coming together at the same spot, both sides
arrived at the Temple of Pallenian Athena. There they set
their weapons in place. [4] Thereupon, Amphilytos the
Acarnanian, a soothsayer possessed of divine guidance, stood

beside Peisistratus, and drawing near, he proclaimed an
oracle, saying the following in hexameter verse:

> The cast has been made, and the hunting net has been spread out.
> The tunny-fish will dart through the moonlit night.

[1.63] Divinely inspired, surely, the man spoke these
words, and Peisistratus, grasping the oracle and saying that
he accepted the divine response [i.e., interpreting it as
favorable], led his army on. The Athenians from the citadel
had just then turned toward their midday meal. And after the
meal, some of them had applied themselves to playing dice
and others to sleeping. Falling upon the Athenians [the
factions opposing Peisistratus], the supporters of Peisistratus
routed them. [2] While the Athenians were fleeing, Peisistratus thereupon contrived against them a most clever plan so
that the Athenians would not gather together again and
would be scattered. Mounting his sons on horses, Peisistratus
sent them forth. Overtaking the fugitives, they said what
Peisistratus had commanded them to say, bidding the fugitives to take courage and each go to his own home.

[1.64] The Athenians obeyed. And thus Peisistratus,
holding Athens for the third time, rooted his tyranny firmly
by means of many mercenaries and revenues, some coming
in on the spot, some from the region of the river Strymon.
Peisistratus took as hostages children of Athenians who had
remained and had not fled immediately. He installed them on
Naxos [largest island in the Cyclades] [2] (for Peisistratus had
subdued Naxos in war and handed it over to Lygdamis). In
addition to these things, in accordance with some oracles,
Peisistratus purified the island of Delos [Cycladic island,
birthplace of the gods Apollo and Artemis] in the following
way: As far as the view extended from the temple, Peisistratus

dug up the corpses from every part of this district and moved them to another district of Delos. [3] And Peisistratus was tyrant over the Athenians. Some Athenians had fallen in the battle. Others, together with the descendants of Alcmaeon, had fled from their homeland.

[1.65.1] Croesus learned that such circumstances were now restraining the Athenians during this time. But he learned that the Lacedaemonians [Spartans], having escaped from great troubles, were already having the upper hand in battle against the Tegeans.

In this story of the rise to power of the tyrant Peisistratus, Herodotus directly connects deception with domination and credulousness with subjugation. Deception proves a powerful source of tyranny. Inserted into an account of Croesus seeking Greek allies in preparation for an attack on Persia, the tale depicts autocratic rule as the antithesis of freedom. Inquiring about Athens (one of two currently most powerful Greek citizen-communities, Sparta being the other), Croesus discovers that the Athenians have succumbed to deceptions and have become subject to an autocrat. Croesus learns that the Athenians are "currently held down and torn apart by Peisistratus" (1.59.1). The Athenians first fall for Peisistratus's trick of wounding himself and claiming to have been attacked by enemies. "Deceived" (or "cheated" or "seduced," *eksapatētheis*) by Peisistratus's unsubstantiated claims, the Athenians acquiesce to his demand for a personal bodyguard. This bodyguard provides the force necessary to install the tyrant, for "joining Peisistratus in rebellion, these men together with him took hold of the acropolis" (1.59.4–5).

The autocrat gains power initially by deception, and he resorts again to deception when his rule proves unstable. Peisistratus governs moderately at first, preserving the legal and political institutions established by Solon three decades earlier (1.59.5). But when driven out by the two opposing factions (1.60.1), he regains power by another trick. Conspiring with the leader of one of the opposing factions, Peisistratus dresses up a tall woman (she is about five feet, ten inches) as the goddess Athena, and he parades her through Athens, standing beside her in a chariot. Peisistratus sends heralds ahead proclaiming that Athena herself is escorting him back into power (1.60.5). The Athenians fall for this deception, as they fell for Peisistratus's previous falsehood affirming his need for a personal bodyguard. The Athenians once again mistake the fake for the true and willingly accept the tyrant's authority. But Herodotus exposes the truth behind the charade. He emphasizes the patent absurdity of human beings welcoming Peisistratus back on the basis of the tyrant's dramatic ruse. Herodotus disparages the Athenians for worshipping a human woman as if she were a goddess (1.60.5).[1]

Ancient epic tales had long celebrated cleverness as a valuable survival skill, but Herodotus exposes deception as the tool of a tyrant. Generations before Herodotus, Greeks of the eighth and seventh centuries BCE knew nothing of democracy. The word and concept did not yet exist. Homer's *Odyssey* appears to have gained fixed (written) form sometime during Peisistratus's reign, and the epic as we have it seems both to question and to validate autocratic authority.[2] With democracy not yet imagined, the *Odyssey*'s Odysseus deploys clever deceptions to recover his legitimate and benevolent kingship, the preferable—and sole available—alternative to rapacious aristocratic rule or chaos. But Herodotus and his contemporaries have known (or known of) democratic ideals and institutions for about two generations (since 508 BCE). Unlike Homer's crafty Odysseus deploying calculated cunning in an effort to restore political order and communal well-being, Herodotus's wily

Peisistratus enlists cleverness in the service of tyranny. The tyranny of Peisistratus and then his sons lasted, with interruptions, for half a century (560–510 BCE).[3] Peisistratid rule stabilized—but also forestalled—movement toward democracy initiated by Solon's reforms in 595/4 BCE.

Herodotus commends Peisistratus for preserving the city's current institutions and ruling well (1.59.6).[4] But he forcefully disparages the Athenians for their gullibility. Once again emphasizing the dire costs of unfounded certainty, Herodotus demonstrates that human vision, in the absence of analysis, can mislead. In violating his wife's privacy and dignity, King Candaules relies on the principle that seeing is believing (1.8.2), claiming that "men's ears happen to be more distrusting than their eyes" (1.8.2). But human vision frequently proves inaccurate, as we tend to evaluate visible or invisible phenomena from just one narrow viewpoint. We often see only what we want to see. Herodotus presents autocracy as the opposite of liberty, identifying Peisistratus's supporters as "people to whom tyranny was more welcome than freedom" (1.62.1). The would-be autocrat exploits factional divisions within Athens. He preys on human credulity. Credulousness costs the Athenians their freedom.

In highlighting the Athenians' foolish susceptibility to deception, Herodotus undercuts Greek claims to intellectual superiority. He describes Peisistratus's pretense of being escorted back by Athena as "the silliest thing" ever, particularly given the Greeks' longstanding reputation for exceptional shrewdness and sense and the Athenians' reputation as most prudent and wise of all Greeks (1.60.3). Not even the cleverest of the Greeks, Herodotus seems to be saying, prove immune to tyrannical manipulation of visual images and to their own unfounded trust in the visible manifestation of supernatural forces.

Herodotus's story of Peisistratus's rise to power suggests that susceptibility to deception is not an exclusively Greek but a more universal phenomenon. Though the *Histories* frequently asserts contrasts between East and West, this tale offers instead evidence of interactions and commonalities between them. Despite repeated emphasis throughout the *Histories* on Greek innate superiority to "barbarians" in cleverness and intelligence, this tale in fact aligns Greek and "barbarian" storytelling because it contains numerous folktale elements also present in many ancient Near Eastern tales: for example, the repetition of three attempts, the trickster theme, the gullibility of the trickster's audience (1.59–65).[5] Many Near Eastern folktale elements also appear in the tale of Cyrus's origins at 1.107–130.[6]

And although Herodotus mocks Athenians as uniquely gullible, Peisistratus's contemporary Athenians might well hope that their patron goddess Athena would take a special interest in their city's survival and success, and they would certainly be wary of offending her. Even a century after Peisistratus, in Herodotus's own times, ancient Greeks were only just beginning—and only some of them—to think about natural phenomena in a way that we might term "scientific." Ancient Greeks relied instead on an elaborate system of anthropomorphic gods and goddesses to account for the unseen but powerful forces in human life. Far from all-seeing, all-knowing, and all-just, ancient Greek gods were highly partisan and easily angered. Homeric epics and fifth-century Athenian tragedies present gods and goddesses as narrow-minded, emotional, petty, jealous, lustful, and vindictive. Preoccupied by their own passions and whims, these divinities remain largely indifferent to the welfare of human beings except for a very few individuals or citizen-communities for whom they may have a special affection.

Hoping for divine favor, ancient Athenians also understood that efforts to appease the gods by honoring them with
prayers and sacrifices might bring divine aid—or might not.
Ancient stories reflect that the Greeks understood, as we do,
that even devoutly religious people sometimes suffer terrible
misfortunes and innocent people experience ill-deserved catastrophes. In the *Iliad,* for example, Athena refuses to accomplish a prayer for life-saving assistance for Troy, although
devout Trojan women scrupulously make the stipulated offerings and meticulously conduct the prayer.[7] In Euripides'
Hippolytus, the goddess Artemis fails to protect her devotee
Hippolytus, despite his unerring dedication to her service.
Other examples include Euripides' *Bacchae,* in which the god
Dionysus punishes his devoted worshippers along with the
play's irreverent protagonist.

Ancient Greek epics and tragedies establish no direct correlation between pious worship of the gods and personal success or even survival. But they do depict a much more direct
correlation between offending the gods and suffering disaster.
In the *Iliad,* an affront committed against the goddesses Athena and Hera by the Trojan prince Alexandros/Paris precipitates the Trojan War and the fall of Troy.[8] In Aeschylus's
Agamemnon (458 BCE), gods punish the Greeks for violating
their temples in Troy. In Sophocles' *Ajax* (ca. 448 BCE), Athena
punishes the Greek warrior Ajax for insulting her. In Euripides' *Bacchae* (ca. 406 BCE), Dionysus punishes Pentheus for
disrespecting and attacking him. Tragedies include numerous
other such examples of human beings punished for offending divinities.

Trusting in Athena's patronage and not eager to risk offending her, Peisistratus's contemporary Athenians would not
have doubted Athena's power. Ancient Greeks did not ponder
whether or why to worship the gods. They sought instead to

navigate within the constraints that the gods provide. Their concern was the problem of how to maximize the chances of success in a world governed by unseen and often unpredictable and malignant forces. Like the physical laws of the universe, the ancient Greek gods do not care whether you believe in them or not. Not believing in Athena would be like not believing in gravity. If you fall from a twelve-story window, it does not matter whether you believe in gravity or you do not. You hit the ground just as hard either way. The same goes for Athena and other divinities. Disbelief in Athena (or Zeus or Apollo) does not diminish their power to affect your life. For the ancient Greeks, the gods exist. They do their thing. And the great challenge of human life is to cope.

Never questioning the existence of divinity, Herodotus criticizes the Athenians not for their religious convictions but for their lack of discernment. Peisistratus's ploy might actually have been part of—or a replication of—a traditional religious ritual.[9] But Herodotus ridicules the Athenians for their naïve credulity. The tyrant's pretense of Athena physically escorting him back into power contrasts with the absence of divine characters elsewhere in the *Histories*. Herodotus sometimes belatedly offers supernatural explanations for human experiences, as we have seen. And he includes other people's tales of divine-human interactions. But he does not validate such stories on his own authority (e.g., 6.105 and 6.117.3). Familiar with archaic epic poetry and fifth-century Athenian drama, Herodotus's contemporaries would be especially alert to the glaring absence of divine characters in Herodotus's narrative. Unlike epics and tragedies, the *Histories* does *not* show divinities participating in or directly orchestrating events. In describing the tyrant Peisistratus successfully deploying deception against his credulous Athenian contemporaries, Herodotus emphasizes his own capacity, as narrator, to reveal the truth. Readers of the *Histo-*

ries benefit from Herodotus's ability to distinguish fabrication from fact. As author, Herodotus uses his narrative authority to "pull back the curtain," so to speak, and reveal the reality behind the dramatic illusion. The figure beside Peisistratus in the chariot is not the goddess Athena, just a tall, beautiful woman costumed as Athena.

Herodotus's tale of Peisistratus reminds us that success requires resistance not only to self-deception but also to deception by others. Powerful but undiscerning autocrats in the *Histories* demonstrate the dangers of unilateral decision-making and unchecked power. Mistaken confidence in their own interpretation of dreams, oracles, and even empirical evidence makes autocrats victims of their own worst appetites and impulses. Neither they nor their subjects fare well. In his power grabs, Peisistratus exemplifies successful autocratic deployment of deception. (*My enemies are trying to kill me so I need a personal paramilitary force! A supernatural being wants me back in power!*) If seeing is believing, as these tales indicate, then survival requires not unthinking reliance on surface appearances or supernatural signs but careful reflection and accurate assessment both of what is seen and of what is not seen.

Exposing gullibility as a potential consequence of uncritical faith, Herodotus not only challenges ancient Greek claims to intellectual superiority but also calls into question our own modern ability to resist deception. The Athenians' religious convictions make them vulnerable to a tyrant's unscrupulous ambition, and it is easy to mock—as Herodotus does—Athenian credulity at Peisistratus's "silly" trick. But religion, faith, and belief remain powerful forces still today. We may not share the ancient Greeks' faith in a polytheistic universe, but we accept—whether we are religious or not—that reality includes invisible, intangible elements along with the visible, tangible ones. We recognize emotions and psychological motivations as real, dynamic forces, even though we cannot see or touch them. We now have scientific explanations for forces like gravity, electromagnetism, and DNA, but many things remain unexplained by modern science, and we may still credit as causal agents divine will or purpose—or destiny, luck, or chance. Unlike religious or spiritual beliefs, scientific explanations continue to evolve to account for new facts and empirical evidence, but most of us have to accept the workings of a smartphone or an airplane on faith. Modern technology can seem to the layperson as magical or "supernatural" as divine intervention.

Given recent technological developments and the enduring allure of authoritarianism in our own times, we should not feel too superior to Herodotus's "foolish" ancient Athenians. Modern technology has made us not less but more vulnerable to authoritative trickery. Mainstream news sources and social media have trained many of us to seek—like Candaules and Croesus—not factual information but corroboration of our biases and assumptions. Resistance to deception has become both more vital and more difficult. Inundated by an apparently uncheckable tsunami of deceptive untruths, we may, like Croesus, fail to appreciate ambiguities of language and the distorting influence of desire. We may fail to recognize that evidence, visible or invisible, can yield more than one interpretation. Unthinking trust in the unseen and unverifiable makes us dupes of despotic fraudsters of all varieties and political persuasions. Herodotus's tale of the advent of tyranny in Athens suggests that the absence of critical discernment makes communities dangerously vulnerable to unverified or unverifiable authoritative claims. Once again encouraging prudent skepticism, Herodotus offers a timeless reminder that susceptibility to deception invites subjugation.

8

On Foreign Ways

Broadening readers' field of vision and experience to include foreign places, peoples, and cultural attitudes and practices, Herodotus next takes his readers to Egypt.[1] Book 2 constitutes the earliest surviving and longest classical account of ancient Egypt.[2] Herodotus's open-minded, wide-ranging investigation of Egypt provides a healthful contrast to any narrow-minded rejection of or hostility toward the different or unfamiliar. Herodotus became known as the historian of the Persian Wars (490s–479 BCE), but he likely began as a geographer and ethnographer,[3] and as such he defies description. He does not offer a reliable account of Egyptian history, geography, or culture, as he includes numerous historical errors and logical impossibilities. He draws on Egyptian oral tradition and propaganda, inflected with a mélange of Greek narrative and ethical traditions.[4] Book 2 proceeds unsystematically: history, geographical features, distinctive flora and fauna, religious practices, social customs, divination, botany, medicine, burial practices, fanciful creatures, and improbable or impossible tales all form part of an eclectic mix.

Amid the dazzling eclecticism of this account of Egypt, Herodotus's curiosity and dedicated efforts to find evidence and to verify and evaluate information consistently drive the narrative. Herodotus identifies his analytical methods and sources, drawing on eyewitnesses and material evidence whenever possible. He intrudes frequently into his narrative, offering his own observations and judgments.[5] He encourages readers to learn from the observable experiences of other people. Cultivating readers' capacity for evidence-based cross-cultural comparison, the *Histories* sharpens mental skills necessary for nonviolent civic engagement in our own pluralistic and turbulent times. Throughout his account of Egypt, Herodotus models and encourages a profound openness to the possibility and value of learning from foreign ways:

[2.3] . . . and I also heard other things when I spoke with the priests of Hephaestus. And for these same reasons especially, I took myself to [Egyptian] Thebes and to Heliopolis, wishing to know whether the stories there would coincide with the ones told in Memphis. For the people of Heliopolis are said to be the most learned chroniclers of the Egyptians. [2] I am not eager to describe at length the divine elements of their narratives that I heard—except only the names of the gods, since I believe that all human beings have equal understanding concerning these things. But if I do mention some of them, I will do it because my account requires me to do so.

[2.4] But as for the things that they said regarding human matters, they agreed with one another on the following: they claimed that the Egyptians were the first of all human beings to discover the year, having designated twelve portions of the seasons for it. They said that they had discovered these divisions from the stars. And it seems to me that they do this so much more wisely than the Greeks, in that the Greeks throw in an intercalary month every other year because of the seasons. But the Egyptians give each of the

twelve months thirty days, and beyond that they add another
five days every year. For them, the cycles of the seasons align
with the calendar. [2] They said that the Egyptians were the
first to recognize the names of the twelve gods and that the
Greeks took them up from them. They also said that the
Egyptians were the first to apportion altars, statues, and
temples to the gods and to carve living creatures in stones.
Most of these assertions now they demonstrated in fact as
having occurred in this way, but they said that Min was the
first human Egyptian to be king. [3] They said that during his
time, all Egypt was marshland except for the Theban district,
and that none of the parts of Egypt that are now above Lake
Moeris were above the marsh. To Lake Moeris it is a distance
of seven days' sailing up the river from the sea.

[2.5] They also seemed to me to speak well concerning
the land. For it is clear, surely, even to someone who had not
heard beforehand but having seen with his own eyes—anyone
with intelligence, at any rate—that the Egypt to which the
Greeks sail has been acquired in addition by the Egyptians,
and the land is the gift of the river [i.e., sediments deposited
by the river increased the territory of Egypt, and the river
waters the crops]. So, moreover, are the parts above the lake
up to a distance of three days' sailing. About this, those
[priests] said no such thing, but it is in fact another thing of
this kind. [2] For the nature of the land of Egypt is the
following: first of all, if you are sailing toward Egypt and you
are still at a distance from the land of one day's running, by
dropping down a sounding line, you will bring up clay, even
though you will be where the water is eleven fathoms deep.
This shows that the alluvial deposit extends so far.

These three chapters early in book 2 illustrate Herodotus's
method of inquiry: assemble and assess factual information de-

rived from both verbal accounts and direct personal observation. Herodotus double-checks his sources, investigating whether stories told by priests in Heliopolis and Thebes align with accounts given by priests of Memphis (2.3.1). Interested in reality, Herodotus leaves aside the supernatural; beyond mentioning the names of gods, he is not eager to detail (literally, "lead forth [regarding]") the "divine elements" in the various narratives, recognizing "that all human beings have equal understanding concerning these things" (2.3.2). Herodotus focuses instead on "human deeds/matters" and on trying to find mutually corroborating accounts, reporting, for example, that "they said the following in agreement with one another" (2.4.1).[6] Open to the benefits of encountering foreign ways, Herodotus deems the Egyptian twelve-month calendar much cleverer/ wiser than the Greek calendar in that it aligns with the seasons without needing the insertion of an intercalary month in alternate years (2.4.1). Herodotus uses direct observation and experimentation to determine the nature of the land of Egypt (2.5.1–2).

Although Herodotus spends much time in book 2 describing Egyptian religious beliefs and practices, he is fundamentally an empiricist. He is most interested in information acquired through sense perception—things that he can see for himself or hear from others. He appears to have traveled extensively and questioned as many people as possible, especially priests and priestesses. But he insists that he will focus not on Egyptian "tales" about divine matters but on human "actions" or "affairs" (*apēgēmatōn*, 2.3.2, vs. *prēgmata*, 2.4.1). Less interested in beliefs or stories about supernatural forces, Herodotus is most interested in what human beings actually *do*.

Herodotus's broad and judicious fascination with non-Greek peoples and places also manifests earlier in the *Histories*. Describing Persian religious beliefs, cultural practices, laws, and attitudes (1.131–140), Herodotus mentions most without comment, a few with approval (e.g., 1.136–137). Herodotus says that he will ignore most of the peoples conquered and subjugated by Cyrus and the Persians, but he will focus on the ones who "made the most work for Cyrus" and are "most worth telling" about (1.177). He considers some claims by Babylonian priests *ou pista,* "not credible," but he reports them anyway (1.182). Herodotus even praises a foreign woman, admiring the quick understanding of Nitokris, the Babylonian queen, her defensive precautions in anticipation of Persian invasion (1.185–186), and her clever strategy for preventing the plundering of her tomb (1.187).

Herodotus even appears open to adopting foreign ways—if they improve upon Greek ones. Disturbingly, he considers the Babylonians' "wisest" (*sophōtatos*) custom their practice of distributing wives by auctioning young women. Herodotus deems this practical because the wealthiest men, paying the most for the prettiest women, supply the money to pay other men to take the ugliest women. That way, even poor and ugly women get husbands. By contrast, Herodotus explains, once the Persians conquered the Babylonians, the poorest men had to prostitute their daughters (1.196). Greeks never auctioned young citizen women, and perhaps Herodotus is suggesting that this method could prevent poor Greek men from having to prostitute their daughters. We may fail to see a huge distinction between auctioning young women to the highest bidder and prostituting them, but we can note (with disquiet, I hope) that Herodotus clearly does.

Though manifestly not a proto-feminist, Herodotus values learning about and assessing the ways of foreigners. In the first sentence of the *Histories,* he promises to commemorate "great and marvelous deeds—some displayed by Greeks, some by foreigners [*barbaroisi*]." Though cognate with the

English "barbarian," *barbaros* in Herodotus lacks negative connotations and means simply "non-Greek" or, often, "Persian." Herodotus recognizes reciprocity in the distinction between "us" and "them," even suggesting that *barbaroi* deemed Greeks *barbaroi.*[7] Despite involving a conception of "us" and "them," Herodotus's distinction between Greeks and *barbaroi,* "foreigners," does not align with modern racial or ethnic categorization. For Herodotus and his Greek contemporaries, *barbaroi* differed from Greeks not by physical appearance or intellectual abilities but by language, geography, and culture. Drawing a linguistic distinction between Greeks and non-Greeks, Herodotus and his Greek contemporaries did not define ethnic identity by skin color or physical characteristics. And they had no race-based caste system.[8] Given our modern fixation with skin color as a determinant of identity, we may be surprised that as an ethnographer Herodotus does not use skin color as a distinctive marker of race.[9] No ancient Greek word corresponds to the English "ethnicity," and Herodotus does not seem to have had the concept.[10]

Even ancient Greek slavery had no connection to race, ethnicity, skin color, physical features, or any perceived association between physical features and intellectual abilities. You were enslaved if you were born to enslaved parents. You could become enslaved if your community was defeated in battle. In the *Odyssey,* a king's son, kidnapped as a child and sold into a lifetime of slavery, claims that Zeus takes away half of a man's excellence (*aretē*) when he becomes enslaved.[11] But this same man's intelligence, integrity, and honorable actions in the epic falsify his own claim. Ancient Greek slavery was an economic and political institution.[12] Horrible and deplorable as the system was, slavery was, in fact, an ironically egalitarian feature of ancient Greece, since anyone could potentially come to be enslaved, even members of a royal family, if they were kidnapped or their community was conquered in war. Not visual appearance or perceived racial characteristics determined one's status as enslaved or free but circumstances.[13]

Unconstrained by racialist categorization and eager to learn from foreign peoples, Herodotus repeatedly—even relentlessly—calls attention to his own distinctive method of inquiry, observation, logical analysis, and rational judgment. In book 2, he notes constantly that he is reporting and assessing information that he has heard, insisting, for example, "They said as many things as these, and I also heard other things" (2.3.1). He regularly inserts his own opinions, explaining, "according to what the priests said, and as it seemed best to me " (2.10.1), "I believe the ones saying these things about Egypt, and I consider that they are really and truly so, having seen" (2.12.1), "the priests also told this great piece of evidence to me" (2.13.1), and "these things have been said correctly about the Greeks by the Egyptians" (2.14.1). His process includes assessment, for he explains, "But if it is necessary for me myself to show forth my own opinion/judgment [gnōmēn], having found the opinions [gnōmas] set forth blameworthy, I will declare why it seems to me that the Nile swells in summer" (2.24). He peppers his narrative with such phrases as "according to my opinion/judgment [gnōmēn]" (2.26) and "I hold this opinion/judgment [gnōmēn]" (2.27). He evaluates verbal reports, as in his observation that "this man seemed—to me, at least—to be joking [paizein], in claiming to know truly" the sources of the Nile (2.28.2). If Herodotus sometimes adds the corroboration of an oracle, he does so only after detailing his own calculation. Thus, he reports that "an oracle occurring at Ammon bears witness in my opinion [marturei moi tēi gnōmēi] that Egypt is something as great as I am showing in my account, [an oracle] which I learned later than [forming] my own opinion [*gnōmēs*] about Egypt" (2.18.1). Open to learning about foreign ways, Herodotus uses his own knowledge and experience in evaluating them.

Detailing his methods, Herodotus emphasizes his own extensive travels in Egypt as vital to his research while also acknowledging the limits of his source material. He explains, for example, "I was able to learn nothing else from anyone, but (only) so much else upon furthest inquiry, having gone as an eyewitness as far as the city of Elephantine, and after this inquiring by means of hearsay" (2.29.1) From his own travels, he identifies as known [*ginōsketai*] the course of the Nile in Egypt for a journey of four months, but beyond this, "no one is able to declare clearly" (2.31). "But," he continues, "I heard these things from the Cyrenaean men" (2.32.1). He insists, moreover, "And wishing to see/know [*eidenai*] something clear/certain [*saphes*], from anything that I was able to, I sailed also to Phoenician Tyre" (2.44.1). Herodotus cannot always obtain firsthand reports, explaining, "Concerning none of these things was I able to learn anything from the Egyptians, (while) inquiring [*historeōn*]" (2.19.3). Reliable informants are lacking because "concerning the sources/origins of the Nile, no one is able to say, for Libya through which it flows is uninhabited and a desert" (2.34.2).

Despite the challenges of finding reliable information, Herodotus insists that he is drawing rational conclusions from objective, perceivable facts. He explicitly identifies his method of rational deduction from material evidence, claiming, literally, that he is "putting together/comparing [*sumballomai*] unknown things [*ta mē ginōskomena*], perceiving/ inferring/judging/concluding [*tekmairomenos*] by means of visible/manifest ones [*toisi emphanesi*]" (2.33.2). The words and phrasing are difficult to transfer into idiomatic English, but

the point is that Herodotus does not ask readers to accept his
subjective judgments merely on faith; he is modeling his novel
method of inquiry, observation, and evaluation.

Focusing on observable features, not their ideological
underpinnings, Herodotus attempts to evaluate *on their merits* Egyptian customs and beliefs by means of empirical evidence and logical deduction. He judges the Egyptian calendar
"cleverer/wiser by so much" than the Greek one because it
aligns better with the seasons (2.4). In the same way, he corroborates the Egyptians' conception of the geography of Egypt.
He uses logical reasoning to dismiss Ionian (Greek) claims as
mistaken, deeming the Egyptian account of the origins of the
Delta more accurate (2.5–17). Although mistaken about why the
Nile overflows, Herodotus applies logical reasoning to float—
forgive the pun—his own claims (2.19–27).[14] He admires Egyptian recordkeeping, claiming that "the Egyptians who inhabit
the cultivated part of Egypt, cultivating/practicing the memory of all human beings, are most skilled/learned by far of those
of whom I have encountered and tested" (2.77.1).

Critical but comprehensive, Herodotus includes and evaluates even Greek claims that he rejects. He includes two Greek
assertions about the source of the Nile, which "I deem not
worth mentioning, except for wishing to indicate their content
alone" (2.20.1). Dismissing the first as illogical, he introduces
the second as still more "unknowing, unskillful, unscientific"
[*anepistēmonesterē*] but "more wondrous/marvelous" [*thōma-
siōterē*] to relate (2.21.1). He considers the third Greek explanation for the source of the Nile "most plausible" [*epieikestatē*]
but most untrue [*malista epseustai*] (2.22.1). Recognizing that
claims about the origin of Ocean (understood as a divinity by
Herodotus's contemporaries) go too far back in time to be refuted, Herodotus draws a deduction from Homeric epic poetry,

explaining, "I do not know that any River Ocean exists, but I believe that Homer or someone of the earlier existing poets, finding the name, introduced it into his poems" (2.23). By assembling and examining available evidence, Herodotus judges the Greek account of Hercules less accurate than the Egyptians' account, claiming that "the Greeks say many other things without consideration [*anepiskeptōs*]" and dismissing the Greek version as "simple-minded" or "silly" [*euēthēs*] (2.43–45). Herodotus's description of Egyptian genealogical recordkeeping implicitly undermines Greek notions of genealogy, which include claims of mortal men descended from gods (2.142–3).

Although Herodotus seems ready and willing to appreciate any foreign ideas that are better than Greek ones, his perspective remains relentlessly Greek, constrained by Greek preconceptions.[15] Herodotus's fascination with "self" and "other" provides a mirror for self-reflection.[16] And his focus on "otherness" seems an effort to define "Greekness."[17] Throughout the *Histories*, Herodotus challenges any simplistic binary conception of Greekness versus otherness.[18] But as a Greek writer writing for a Greek audience, Herodotus shares his culture's biases and prejudices. His open-minded and logical approach is itself *evidence* of Greekness. Herodotus exhibits and validates a default Greek assumption that Greek ideas and practices— such as evidence-based, rational investigation and assessment— are essentially normal and best. His "Greek bias" includes a bias toward examining objective evidence and drawing logical deductions. It also includes a distinctive willingness to judge the practices, beliefs, and ideas of others on their merits. Herodotus's openness to encountering and assessing foreign ways contrasts with his depiction of Egyptian closed-mindedness; of the Egyptians, Herodotus observes that "using their ancestral laws/customs/traditions [*nomoisi*], they acquire nothing else" (2.79.1), and "they shun using Greek customs [*nomaioisi*] and, to speak generally, they shun using any customs [*nomaioisi*] of any other human beings" (2.91.1).

In contrast to Egyptian resistance to foreign ways, Herodotus highlights his own broadmindedness and rationality, but as always we need not unquestioningly accept his judgments. His scrupulous identification of his methods and reasoning gives readers tools to critique both. Information gathering and data analysis leave room for interpretation, as Herodotus's account of the origins of the gods reveals:

[2.53] But from where each of the gods originated or whether they existed always, and what forms they had—none of this was known until the day before yesterday, so to speak. [2] For I believe that the age of Hesiod and Homer was older than mine by four hundred years and not more. These are the poets who made the theogony [story of the origins of the generations of the gods] for the Greeks and gave the gods their names, distributed their honors and arts, and indicated the gods' forms. [3] The poets said to have been earlier than these men were later, as it seems to me. I have been reporting what the priestesses of Dodona [in Epirus in northwestern Greece] say, but I myself am stating these things regarding Hesiod and Homer.

[2.54] Concerning the oracles—the one among the Greeks and the one in Libya—the Egyptians tell the following story: the priests of Theban Zeus declared that two women, who were priestesses, were carried off from Thebes [Egyptian Thebes, on the Nile] by Phoenicians. They say that they learned that one woman had been sold into Libya and the other to the Greeks. They claimed that these women were the first to establish oracular sites among the peoples that I have mentioned. [2] When I asked from where they knew this so accurately, they declared regarding these matters that they had made a great search for these women. They were not able to find them, they said, but they later learned these very things that they were saying about them. [2.55] Now, these things I heard from the priests in Thebes, but the priestesses of Dodona say the following: they say that there were two black doves who flew from Egyptian Thebes, one to Libya, and the other came to them (at Dodona). [2] The latter, sitting on an oak tree, announced with a human voice that there needed to be an oracular site of Zeus right there. And the people themselves assumed that the announcement made to them was divine. Because of this, they did it. [3] They say that the dove that went to Libya ordered the Libyans to make an oracle of Ammon there. And this is also an oracle of Zeus. The priestesses of Dodona— whose names were Promeneia, the oldest, Timaretē, the next oldest, and Nikandrē, the youngest—said these things. And the other people of Dodona who were around the temple agreed with them.

[2.56] I myself hold the following opinion [*gnomēn*] concerning these matters: If the Phoenicians truly carried off these holy women and delivered one of them to Libya and the other to Greece, it seems to me that this woman was sold into Thesprotia [region in northwestern Greece], since the same land that is now called Greece was previously called Pelasgia. [2] Then, being a slave there, she established a temple of Zeus under an oak that had grown there. It seems likely—just as she was an attendant at the temple of Zeus in Thebes, she arrived there (at Dodona) and therefore had the memory of her temple service. [3] When she understood the Greek language, she established an oracular site there. She said that her sister had been sold into Libya by the same Phoenicians who had also sold her.

[2.57] The women seem to me to have been called
"doves" by the people of Dodona for this reason: because they
were foreigners (*barbaroi*), and they seemed to them to utter
sounds like birds.[2] But after a time, they say, the dove spoke
with a human voice—when the woman spoke things that
were intelligible to them. As long as she spoke a foreign
tongue, she seemed to them to utter sounds in the manner of
a bird—since in what way could a dove speak with a human
voice? In saying that the dove was black, they indicate that
the woman was Egyptian. [3] The manner of divination in
Egyptian Thebes and at Dodona happen to resemble one
another. And the art of divination from sacrificial offerings
has also come from Egypt.

[2.58] The Egyptians, therefore, are also the first people
who made solemn assemblies, religious processions, and
offerings to divinities, and the Greeks have learned these
from them. To me, the evidence for this is the following: the
Egyptian rituals appear to have been done for a long time,
but the Greek ones were established just recently.

In the passage above, Herodotus features his methods,
meticulously identifying and comparing sources while acknowledging where his informants leave off and his own
opinions begin. He consults multiple sources, noting that "the
Egyptians tell the following story" and "the priests of Theban
Zeus declared" and insisting, "When I asked from where they
knew this so accurately, they declared . . ." (2.54.2). He seeks
corroboration, explaining, for example, "These things I heard
from the priests in Thebes, but the priestesses of Dodona say
the following" (2.55.1) and claiming, "The priestesses of
Dodona . . . said these things. And the other people of Dodona
who were around the temple agreed with them" (2.55.3). He asserts his own opinions, stating, "I have been reporting what

the priestesses of Dodona say, but I myself am stating these things regarding Hesiod and Homer" (2.53.3). He repeatedly inserts his own views, insisting, "I myself hold the following opinion [*gnomēn*] concerning these matters" and "it seems to me . . ." (2.56.1) and "The women seem to me . . ." (2.57.1). Assembling the various accounts and applying his own judgments, Herodotus seeks a chronological timeline, applies logic, and resists supernatural explanations. He recognizes the relative recentness of Hesiod and Homer, deeming their era not more than four hundred years earlier than his own time (2.53.2), and he rejects claims that other poets preceded them (2.53.3). He calls attention to his evidence-based reasoning process, insisting, for example, "To me, the evidence for this is the following" (2.58). He uses logic to assert a probable causal relationship, suggesting that a woman who had been a temple servant in one place might well seek the same role in another (2.56). He rationalizes the priests' magical tale of talking doves, saying of the woman in question, "as long as she spoke a foreign tongue, she seemed to them to utter sounds in the manner of a bird—since in what way could a dove speak with a human voice?" (2.57.2).

Herodotus determines to discover and analyze facts, but preconceptions also shape his judgments. Book 2 is the longest book of the *Histories,* and Herodotus explains that he focuses so much attention on Egypt because Egypt has "the most wondrous things [*thōmasia*]" and "indescribable works" and because most of its customs and ways are contrary to the peoples and customs of other places (*empalin toisi alloisi anthrōpoisi,* 2.35). This conviction frequently distorts and oversimplifies Herodotus's account. Not an objective record, book 2 offers instead evidence of one ancient Greek writer's view of Egypt. It is also a reminder of the great challenge that Herodotus faced encountering Egypt and that everyone faces when seeing or reading anything new or unfamiliar: the challenge to see what is actually there rather than what we expect or want to see.

In his eagerness to examine and assess foreign ways, Herodotus remains certain of Greek cultural superiority. He complicates any simplistic assessment of Greek versus other.[19] But he repeatedly emphasizes contrasts between "barbarian" and Greek sexual practices, for example, likely drawing on ancient Greek cultural stereotypes in suggesting that foreigners (*barbaroi*) are more promiscuous than Greeks and therefore less masculine.[20] Ancient Greek men kept their wives, daughters, and sisters under tight supervision and control, whereas—according to Herodotus—barbarian men cannot or choose not to regulate their women's sexuality properly: women of Lydia, for example, all prostitute themselves in order to finance their own dowries (1.93); Babylonian women have to serve at least once as prostitutes in the sanctuary of Aphrodite, unable to refuse any man or any amount of money (1.99); the Scythian Massegetae have monogamous relationships but freely permit other men to have sex with their wives (1.216.1). Herodotus portrays Egyptian men as effeminate, claiming that they do "women's work" (2.35.2–3). According to Herodotus, other foreign tribes "use" their women in common (e.g., 4.104; 4.172.2; 4.176), have sex like animals (4.180.5), or permit their daughters to be promiscuous (5.6.1).[21] Many of the sexual freedoms that Herodotus attributes to non-Greek cultures contradict patterns normally found in agricultural economies, and his access to sources seems questionable.[22] Unlikely to be factual, Herodotus's depiction of non-Greek sexual behaviors validates the male Greek certainty that women's voracious sexual appetites must be kept under tight control.[23]

Not only cultural prejudice but also flawed logic sometimes undermines Herodotus's reliability. He focuses on observable evidence, but facts are one thing, interpretation another. Discussing Egyptian gods and religious festivals, Herodotus succumbs to the *post hoc ergo propter hoc* fallacy, the Latin phrase meaning, literally, "*after* this thing, therefore *because of* this thing," that is, the fallacy of thinking that because something follows something else it must have been *caused* by that preceding thing. Because Egyptian practices predate Greek ones, Herodotus makes the illogical (and inaccurate) inference that Greeks learned their religious practices from the Egyptians (2.48–58).[24]

Herodotus's inaccuracies exceed errors of logic when he describes Egyptian creatures. Apparently letting his imagination run, he offers bizarre claims about the cat, an animal not found in Greece. Male cats, he claims, kill (but do not eat) their babies to provoke female cats into desiring more sexual intercourse to produce more babies (2.66). He gives a detailed account of crocodiles and the worship of crocodiles by some Egyptians (2.68–70). Hippopotamus, in Greek, means literally "river horse," and Herodotus describes an animal with the mane, tail, and hooves of a horse, though larger and more massive (2.71). He describes as real the phoenix—though scrupulously admitting "I myself did not see it, except in a painting" (2.73)—and winged snakes (2.75–76).

Cultural prejudices, logical errors, and flights of fancy aside, Herodotus's eagerness to encounter and assess foreign ways on their merits stands in stark contrast to two sadly ever-present ideological extremes, both lethal to democratic governance and political equality. One extreme, sometimes called "moral absolutism," deems our own ways the right ways and everyone else's ways inferior or morally wrong. Betraying deep insecurity, moral absolutists denounce criticism or dissent as heresy or treason. Instead of welcoming the opportunity to re-examine their convictions, moral absolutists fear and suppress

intellectual challenges. Their rigid certainty sustains radical intolerance and precludes criticism of their own biases or abuses
of power. Devaluing discussion, debate, and creative compromise, moral absolutism drives both left-wing and right-wing
extremism. With no mechanism for reconciling competing values, moral absolutism often promotes violence if, for example,
ideals of personal freedom conflict with public safety, definitions of political correctness conflict with freedom of speech,
or religious principles conflict with individual autonomy.

An alternative extreme, sometimes called "moral relativism," rejects value judgments, deeming everyone's ways of doing
and being just as good as everyone else's. To the moral absolutist's claim that right is right and wrong is wrong, the moral
relativist illogically replies, "There are no moral absolutes. Um,
except for this one, that there are none." A vast variety of cultural beliefs and practices may be morally equivalent, and tolerance is an essential civic virtue, but moral relativists
self-righteously tolerate even attitudes and conduct that cause
terrible harm. To others' religious and cultural practices of misogyny or child abuse, for example, the moral relativist responds, "Who are we to judge?" Like the certainty of the moral
absolutist, the cultural relativist's certainty that "our ways are
good for us and their ways are fine for them" can legitimize injustice and abuse. In its refusal to make moral distinctions,
moral relativism paradoxically condones and sustains moral
absolutism.

Between the two alternatives of moral absolutism and
moral relativism, Herodotus charts a third way.[25] While both
extreme viewpoints tolerate injustice and preclude the possibility of improvement, the *Histories* offers a far more constructive model of multicultural engagement vital for Herodotus's
own times and ours. Herodotus's account of Egypt suggests that
we need not cling mindlessly to our own cultural certainties or

mindlessly accept those of others as equally good and constructive. Not all ways are equal. Some ways really are better than others. But to discover better ways, we have to be open to new ones. You do not have to accept Herodotus's judgments. Make your own. But notice Herodotus's eagerness to encounter foreign ways. Marvel at his readiness to accept some foreign ideas and practices as better than Greek ones. Critically examine his decisions to accept some behaviors and attitudes as beneficial and to reject others as harmful and/or irrational.

Assessing foreign ways on their merits, Herodotus models a healthy approach to all narratives: proceed with caution and skepticism, and seek corroboration. We are all inclined to believe the stories that we want to believe. This is all the more reason to remain skeptical toward every story—especially ones that align most neatly with our own preconceptions—until verified by factual evidence and/or reliable corroboration. Herodotus exemplifies a Greek cultural bias toward measuring and assessing foreign ways on their merits. We identify his preconceptions and distortions only by employing his methods of assembling factual evidence and subjecting it to rational scrutiny.

Herodotus had to struggle and journey far to find information, reliable or otherwise, but we are flooded with it. The more bizarre, hateful, inflammatory, and counterfactual the story, the more likely we are to see it, and the more it satisfies and benefits its fabricators. Mainstream media outlets and social media platforms vastly broaden our access to foreign and unfamiliar ideas and ways. But they have also made disinformation more addicting, poisonous, and lucrative than ever before. On social media, falsehoods circulate much faster and more widely than truths, with Artificial Intelligence drastically expanding their reach and profitability. The deluge of disinformation diminishes the appetite and aptitude for extended civil conversations about cultural controversies. Open-minded pursuit of evidence, corroboration, and analysis takes goodwill and effort. Abandoning that effort, we remain hermetically sealed in our own dogmatic certainties, locked in by fear, anger, and prejudice—all the while enriching the predatory purveyors of disinformation.

Illustrating the great benefits of diversity, Herodotus reinforces vital attitudes, institutions, and norms imperiled by both "progressive" and "conservative" anti-democratic extremists today. Ancient Greeks originated and developed democratic ideals and institutions, but democracy is fragile. It requires continuous reassessment, reaffirmation, and improvement. Disinformation drives xenophobia, ethnic nationalism, and social and political polarization. Hostile to foreign or unfamiliar ways and toxic to individuals and communities, these powerful forces foment violence. To alter and improve, by nonviolent means, existing laws and ways of doing things—as democratic governance enables and requires—we must each be willing and able to assess all attitudes and practices on their merits. In his account of Egypt, Herodotus validates open-minded and discerning exploration of foreign ways. He demonstrates that broadminded critique of the ways of others can facilitate honest, constructive critique of our own.

9

On Foreign Tales

Herodotus further demonstrates his fascination with foreign ways in his open-minded critique of foreign tales. Retelling two lengthy tales that he heard from Egyptian priests, Herodotus illustrates the educational benefits of cross-cultural comparison, modeling a process of objective comparative evaluation. He understands that stories transmit cultural priorities, and he recognizes that both similarities and differences between stories can be instructive. Using logic and knowledge of human nature, Herodotus reconciles contradictions between the Egyptian and the Greek versions of the story of Helen of Troy, finding the Egyptian account more plausible (2.112–120).[1] Subsequently, a gruesome tale of King Rhampsinitus and the Clever Thief invites reexamination of the long-held Greek cultural value of cleverness (2.121). Drawn from sources of questionable reliability, Herodotus's account of Egypt exposes his own attitudes and those of his Greek contemporaries.[2] But as in his examination of foreign ways, Herodotus shows that evaluation of foreign tales enables open-minded investigators to reassess their own cultural convictions.

Herodotus begins with the Egyptian priests' surprising variation on a most well-known story. According to archaic

Greek epic tales, the Trojan prince Alexandros (= Paris) stole
Helen, queen of Sparta, from his host, Helen's husband Menelaus, and carried her off to Troy. Amassing a huge army, the
Greeks besieged Troy for ten years, demanding Helen's return,
before finally sacking the city and recovering Helen. The Egyptian version similarly condemns Alexandros's theft, but Egyptian priests tell Herodotus quite a different story; they claim that
Helen never actually made it to Troy:

[2.112] The Egyptian priests said that a man from Memphis
[capital of ancient Egypt]—whose name, according to the
Greek language, was Proteus—accepted the kingship from
Pheros. . . . In the precinct of Proteus [in Memphis], there is a
temple named after "Foreign Aphrodite." I gather that this is
the temple of Helen, daughter of Tyndareus—both because
I have heard the story that Helen spent time with Proteus and
also because the temple is named after "Foreign Aphrodite."
For as many other temples as there are of Aphrodite, none is
called with the added designation "Foreign."
     [2.113] As I was inquiring, the priests told me that the
events concerning Helen occurred in the following way: they
said that Alexandros, having carried off [*harpasas*] Helen
from Sparta, was sailing away toward his own land. But when
he was in the Aegean, driving winds carried him into the
Egyptian Sea. And from there—for the winds did not let
up—he arrived in Egypt. In Egypt, he came to what is now
called the Canobic Mouth of the Nile and to the places where
fish is salted. [2] On the shore, there was a temple of Heracles
[= Hercules], and it is there now. If a house slave belonging to
any man whatsoever flees into this temple and puts on
himself sacred brand marks, giving himself over to the god, it
is not permitted to seize him. This custom [*nomos*] continues
from the beginning, and it remains in equal force up to my

time. [3] Therefore, having learned of this custom concerning the temple, Alexandros's servants deserted him. Sitting as suppliants of the god, they denounced Alexandros, wishing to harm him. They narrated at length the whole story of how things had gone concerning Helen and the injustice [*adikiēn*] that Alexandros had done to Menelaus. They made these accusations before both the priests and the guardian of the mouth of the Nile, whose name was Thonis.

[2.114] Having heard these men, Thonis sends the swiftest message to Proteus in Memphis, saying the following: [2] "A stranger has arrived, a man of the Teucrian [= Trojan] race, and he has committed an unholy act in Greece. For he seduced the very wife of a man who was hosting him in his house. He has arrived here, bringing her as well as a great deal of his host's property. He was carried away to your land by the winds. Are we to allow this man to sail away un-harmed, or are we to take for ourselves the things he has brought here?" [3] In response, Proteus sends back the following message: "This man—whoever he is—has commit-ted unholy actions toward his own host. Seize him and bring him to me so that I may see whatever it is that he will say."

[2.115] Hearing this, Proteus seizes Alexandros and constrains his ships right there. Proteus then takes Alexan-dros to Memphis along with Helen and the stolen property. In addition, he also takes the suppliants. [2] When they were all brought before Proteus, he asked Alexandros who he was and where he was sailing from. Alexandros told him his race and his country's name, and in particular he explained the voyage that he was making. [3] Afterward, Proteus asked Alexandros where he had gotten Helen from. When Alexandros gave a meandering reply and did not tell the truth, the suppliants who were present refuted him, relating the whole story of the wrongdoing. [4] Finally, Proteus rendered this account to them, declaring, "If I did not consider it of great importance to kill no guest-friend—since many people already have come to my land, driven off course by winds—I would have taken vengeance on you on behalf of the Greek. O, most wicked of men! You encountered hospitality and then committed a most unholy act. You seduced your host's wife. And even this was not enough for you. Having excited her passion, you stole her away and went off with her. [5] And even these actions alone were not enough for you. You have arrived here having also plundered other property belonging to your host. [6] Now, therefore, since I consider it very important not to kill a guest-friend, I will not release the woman and the property to you to take away. But I myself will guard them for my Greek guest-friend until he wishes to come and take them back himself. And I proclaim that you and your fellow travelers are to sail away from my land to some other place within three days' time. If not, you will be treated as enemies [*polemious*]."

[2.116] The priests claimed that this arrival of Helen to Proteus occurred. And it seems to me that Homer also learned this story. But since it was not equally as suitable for epic poetic composition as the other one which he did use, Homer let this version go. [2] And it is clear that he did [know this story]. In accordance with this version, Homer fashioned in the *Iliad* the wandering of Alexandros—how he was carried off course while bringing Helen and wandered to other places, and how he came to Sidon in Phoenicia. And nowhere else has Homer stepped back from this account. [3] Homer mentions this in his account of the exploits of Diomedes, and he says the verses in this way:

There were richly patterned robes, the work of Sidonian women,
which godlike [*theoeidēs*] Alexandros himself brought with him from
Sidon,

sailing upon the broad sea—the very route on which he brought back
Helen, descended from noble fathers.

[4] Homer also mentions [the story] in the *Odyssey* in these
verses:

> The daughter of Zeus also had such skillful and noble drugs,
> Which Polydamna, bedmate of Thon, had given to her
> (Polydamna), a woman of Egypt, where fruitful fields produce the
>   most
> drugs. Many of these, when mixed, are good, but many are ruinous.

[5] And Menelaus also says these other verses to Telemachus:

> Although I was still eager to return home here, the gods held me in
>   Egypt,
> because I did not accomplish for them perfect sacrifices of hundreds of
>   victims.

[6] In these verses it is clear that Homer knew of Alexandros's wandering to Egypt. For Syria borders Egypt, and the
Phoenicians who possess Sidon dwell in Syria.

[2.117] The fact that the verses of the *Cypria* [a lost
archaic epic poem] were composed not by Homer but by
someone else is most clear from the above verses and also
from this following passage. For in verses of the *Cypria* it is
said that on the third day after leaving Sparta, Alexandros
arrived in Troy bringing Helen, having experienced favorable
winds and a gentle sea. But in the *Iliad* Homer says that
Alexandros wandered off course while bringing Helen [i.e.,
before succeeding in bringing Helen to Troy]. Now, let's say
goodbye to the verses of Homer and the *Cypria*.

[2.118] When I asked the priests whether or not the
Greeks are telling an idle tale as to the events at Troy, they

declared the following on these matters: they said that they
knew it—by means of their investigations—from Menelaus
himself. [2] They say that after the abduction of Helen a huge
army of Greeks came to the Trojan land to help Menelaus.
Stepping onto the land from their ships and establishing their
encampment, the Greeks sent messengers to Troy. And
Menelaus himself went with them. [3] The priests say that
upon entering within the walls of Troy, these Greeks demanded back both Helen and the possessions that Alexandros had stolen and taken with him. The messengers also
demanded justice for these injuries. But, say the priests, the
Trojans told the same tale—both then and afterward, both
under oath and not—that they did not have either Helen or
the sought-after possessions. They said that all these things
were in Egypt. It would not be just, the Trojans said, for
themselves to have to pay the penalty for property held by
Proteus in Egypt. [4] The Greeks believed that they were
being laughed at by the Trojans. Thus, they besieged the city
until they seized it. But after they captured the city, Helen did
not appear. Instead, the Greeks learned the same story as the
previous one. Trusting therefore the first story, the Greeks
sent Menelaus himself to Proteus.

[2.119] Arriving in Egypt and sailing up to Memphis,
Menelaus told the truth of these matters. He met with great
hospitality, and he recovered Helen. She was completely
unharmed. In addition, Menelaus took back all his own
property. [2] Although Menelaus had this experience,
however, he was an unjust man toward the Egyptians. For,
they say, when Menelaus was eager to sail away, unfavorable
winds prevented this. Since this situation continued for such
a long time, Menelaus contrived a deed that was not holy.
[3] He took two children belonging to local men, and he
made them sacrificial victims. Afterward—when it was

discovered that he had done this—Menelaus fled with his
ship, hated and pursued, straight to Libya. Where he went
from there, the Egyptians are not able to say. The priests
declared that they knew some of these things from their
inquiries. But they said that the events occurring in their
own land they knew with accuracy.

[2.120] These are the things that the Egyptian priests
said. And I myself agree with their account concerning
Helen, as I consider the following: if Helen had been in Troy
[as Greek stories maintain], she would have been returned to
the Greeks whether Alexandros was willing or not. [2] For
surely neither Priam nor the other people related to him were
so damaged in their understanding as to wish to endanger
their own bodies and their children and city so that Alexandros could sleep with Helen. [3] If indeed they knew these
things in the beginning, then surely [they understood them]
after many Trojans had perished when they engaged in battle
with the Greeks—and every time battle occurred, two or
three or more of Priam's own sons were dying, if one must
speak drawing something from epic poetry. Well, with these
kinds of events happening, I myself expect that even if Priam
himself had been sleeping with Helen, he would have given
her back to the Greeks—especially intending to be freed from
the present troubles. [4] For the kingship was not even going
to go to Alexandros so that now that Priam was old, matters
would be in Alexandros's hands. Rather, Hector as the older
son (and more of a real man than Alexandros) was going to
take over the kingship when Priam died. It did not suit
Hector to entrust matters to a brother who committed
injustice and who was responsible for the terrible troubles
that were occurring, both privately for Hector himself and for
all the other Trojans. [5] But I say this because the Trojans did
not have Helen to give back. [I.e., Since the Trojans did not

return Helen, despite all of the motives they had for doing so, she must not have been in Troy.] The Greeks did not trust the Trojans when they were telling them the truth. This is how it appears to me in my opinion [*gnomēn*]: some divinity [*daimoniou*] was making preparations so that the Trojans, perishing in utter ruin, might make this [following] fact manifest to other men—namely that for great crimes the punishments from the gods are also great. And these things have been stated as they seem to me.

Midway through his account of Egypt, Herodotus explicitly transitions from detailing his own eyewitness experiences to narrating Egyptian *logoi*, "stories," explaining, "Up to this point, my vision, judgment, and inquiry [*opsis, gnōmē, historiē*] are saying these things. But from this point on, I am going to relate the Egyptian stories [*logous*] that I heard."[3] Herodotus will continue to include his own critique, explaining, "In addition, I will add something of my own vision [*opsios*]" (2. 99.1; cf. 2.104–105 and 2.106.1).

In the Egyptian tale of the Spartan queen Helen, Egyptians appear to share the Greeks' disgust at a violation of *xenia*, "guest-friendship." Ancient Greek epics and tragedies affirm the value of reciprocal obligations governing behavior between guests and hosts and condemn violations.[4] Greek tales maintain that by stealing his host's wife, Alexandros prompts a massive war destructive to himself, his family, his city, and to participants, noncombatants, and survivors on both sides of the conflict. Egyptian priests agree that Alexandros *harpasas*, "carried off" or "plundered," Helen from Sparta. And though the priests deny that Alexandros actually brought Helen to Troy, they deem the theft *adikiē*, "an injustice," to Helen's husband Menelaus (2.113). The priests are appalled at Alexandros's *anosion*, "unholy act," (2.114.2). King Proteus agrees that Alexandros "has committed unholy actions [*anosia*] toward his own host" (2.114.3).

For the second time in the *Histories*, Helen's story serves as a litmus test revealing cultural priorities. Egyptians, like Greeks, condemn violations of guest-friendship obligations. Egyptian and Greek moral outrage contrasts markedly with the Persians' manifest disinterest in denouncing Alexandros for an egregious moral transgression. As Herodotus previously relates, the Persian storytellers list Alexandros's theft of Helen as merely one in a series of reciprocal rapes. Their account does not affirm *xenia* as an important cultural value; they criticize not Alexandros for committing the rape or for violating *xenia* but the Greeks for making such a fuss about it (1.1–5).

Sharing Greek revulsion at a violation of the rules of hospitality, Proteus, the Egyptian king, finds himself in an awkward position: he would kill Alexandros, he says, to avenge his crime against Helen's Greek husband, if he himself did not consider it wrong to kill *xenoi*, "strangers/foreigners/guest-friends," who are constrained and protected (like their hosts) by the rules of *xenia*. Proteus calls Alexandros *kakiste*, "worst/most evil/most base," of men, but he recognizes that he himself cannot avenge a violation of *xenia* by violating *xenia*. Proteus accuses Alexandros of committing a "most unholy" deed in seducing and stealing his host's wife (2.115.4) and "having also plundered [*keraïsas*] other property" belonging to Menelaus (2.115.5). But Proteus refuses to violate the rules of guest-friendship by harming a guest, explaining, "If I did not consider it of great importance to kill no guest-friend, . . . I would have taken vengeance on you on behalf of the Greek" (2.115.4; similarly, 115.6). Proteus tries to stay within the bounds of *xenia*, opting to keep the stolen property, including Helen, and requiring Alexandros to depart within three days or forfeit his status as *xenos*, "guest," for the status of *polemios*, "enemy" (2.115.6).

Like Greek tales, the Egyptian version of Helen's story denounces violations of *xenia* and corroborates the fact that the Trojan War occurred, but it contradicts Homer's insistence on Helen's presence in Troy and on Menelaus's irreproachable efforts to retrieve her. The Egyptian priests agree that the Greeks sent a huge army against Troy to recover Helen and other stolen property. But they maintain that the Greeks besieged and sacked the city because they refused to believe the Trojans' claim that Helen and the stolen goods were not there (2.118).[5] According to the priests, only after conquering Troy and failing to find Helen do the Greeks remember the story about Proteus and send Menelaus to Egypt to retrieve Helen. The Egyptian priests add a terrible coda absent from Greek stories: prevented from sailing by adverse winds, Menelaus sacrificed two local children to the gods and then sailed for Libya with Egyptians in furious pursuit (2.119).

Although the Egyptian version contradicts Greek accounts of Helen's presence in Troy, Herodotus accepts it as essentially true. Herodotus never doubts the factual truth of the Trojan War and the ancient tales associated with it.[6] But he deduces that Helen must not have been in Troy when the Greek fleet arrived because if she had been, the Trojans would have returned her and the stolen property even if Alexandros refused. Surely the Trojan king and his people would not have risked their own lives, their children's lives, and their city, Herodotus reasons, just so that one prince could keep his stolen woman. The war lasted ten years, and Trojans were dying all the time, even the king's sons. The Trojans had plenty of opportunities to return Helen. Alexandros was not even heir to the throne. He could not possibly have had so much influence over the decision of his father or older brother Hector, who *was* heir to the throne. No, Homer's version only makes sense, Herodotus thinks, if Helen was never in Troy, but the

Greeks failed to believe the Trojans when they told them the truth (2.120).

Herodotus uses logic and empirical reasoning to evaluate and reconcile two contradictory versions of this ancient story, but his final takeaway lacks evidentiary proof. Herodotus concludes that Troy's destruction resulted from the gods' desire to demonstrate the inevitability of divine retribution for injustice. Herodotus connects criminal action with divine punishment, insisting that in his *gnomē*, "opinion," some *daimonios*, "divinity," sought to make manifest the fact that "for great crimes the punishments from the gods are also great [*megalōn adikēmatōn megalai eisi kai hai timōriae para tōn theōn*]. And these things have been stated as they seem to me" (2.120.5–6). Herodotus offers his interpretation, but he provides no evidence whatsoever to support his attribution of Troy's fall to supernatural causes.

By this point in Herodotus's analysis, the attribution of divine agency to this story seems superfluous. Herodotus has given a compelling, purely rational explanation for Troy's destruction with no need for unverified and unverifiable supernatural intentions or interventions. Drawing on his understanding of human nature, Herodotus assumes that the Trojans would have returned Helen if she had actually been in Troy. From the Trojans' failure to return Helen, he deduces that Helen never arrived in Troy. Troy fell because Alexandros chose to abduct Helen and because the Greek besiegers, refusing to think logically, failed to credit (or try to verify) the Trojans' claims that Helen was not there.

Human choices and actions in both the Greek and Egyptian versions of this story provide sufficient explanation for Troy's fall independent of any supernatural agency. The Egyptian tale corroborates the ancient Greek certainty that human wrongdoing produces predictably adverse consequences.

Archaic Greek epic tales repeatedly contrast divine with mortal acts of adultery: gods can commit rape with impunity; mortal men cannot. Citing epic verses to support the Egyptian account, Herodotus indirectly highlights the archaic Greek conception of moral transgressions as suitable for gods but self-destructive for human beings. Arguing that Homer knew the Egyptian version of Helen's story (2.116–117), Herodotus supplies a passage calling Alexandros *theoeidēs,* "godlike" (2.116.3). The adjective seems to describe not Alexandros's appearance or character but his *conduct.* Since only gods can steal women with impunity, Alexandros manifests "godlike" behavior in stealing Helen and anticipating no adverse repercussions.

Cautioning against reckless ("godlike") disregard for human moral precepts, both the Greek and Egyptian versions of Helen's story corroborate the traditional Greek understanding that stories offer moral instruction. Both versions encourage respect for the obligations of *xenia.* Herodotus's Greek contemporaries, like their parents and grandparents before them, accepted the many Greek tales of Helen and the Trojan War as their history. Troy did fall, and Menelaus did recover Helen. And one lesson of Homer's *Iliad* is that people do sometimes fight wars and cause horrific bloodshed and suffering for stupid, trivial reasons. Even the victorious Greeks and their loved ones suffer terribly, as the *Odyssey* shows. Herodotus's identification of divine vengeance as the cause of this extensive calamity lacks evidentiary support. But like ancient Greek epic poetry, his conception of divine vengeance identifies the catastrophic, inevitable, and predictable costs of glaring human failures of self-restraint, imagination, and logic. Herodotus claims that Homer knew that Helen never made it to Troy, but he rejected this version because it "was not equally as suitable for epic poetic composition" (2.116.1). Whether Helen was or was not ever in Troy, however, both the Egyptian and Greek versions of Helen's story illustrate the destructiveness of gratuitously harming someone and violating cultural ideals of decent and humane behavior.

Focused on human agency and the educational benefits of encountering foreign tales, Herodotus immediately provides a second opportunity for cross-cultural comparison. Ancient Greeks admired cleverness as a survival skill, but a colorful Egyptian tale of a powerful king and a wondrously clever thief celebrates cleverness regardless of its costs and consequences. Homer's *Odyssey* depicts cleverness enabling the famous trickster Odysseus to conquer Troy, survive ten years of wandering and hardship, return home, defeat rapacious suitors, rejoin his family, and recover his legitimate, benevolent autocratic authority. Although Odysseus's cleverness frequently causes suffering, it nevertheless ultimately benefits not only Odysseus himself but also his family and community. Not merely admirable in and of itself, cleverness in the *Odyssey* achieves admirable ends. By contrast, Egyptian priests tell Herodotus a gruesome tale of cleverness resulting in no beneficial social or political consequences:

[2.121] The priests said that Rhampsinitus took over the kingship of Egypt after Proteus. Rhampsinitus left as a memorial the west-facing gates of the Temple of Hephaestus. . . .

[α] The priests said that King Rhampsinitus had great wealth of silver, and that none of the kings who were later entrusted with royal power could surpass him—or even come close. They say that Rhampsinitus, wishing to store his wealth safely had a stone chamber constructed. One of its walls lay against the outer part of his house. But the man who built the treasure house plotted against the king, contriving the following: he made it so that one of the stones could be entirely removed from the wall with ease by two men or even one. [2] When the chamber was finished, the king stored his wealth in it. As time passed, the builder, nearing the end of his life, summoned his sons, for he had two. He explained to them how—taking forethought for them, so that they might have a life free from want—he had artfully devised the treasure house of the king when he built it. He explained to his sons clearly all the facts concerning the removal of the stone, and he gave them its measurements. He told them that by preserving this information they would be the treasurers of the king's money. [3] His life came to an end, and his sons did not long refrain from taking action. Going to the royal palace at night, they easily found the stone on the building. They grabbed the money and carried off a lot of it.

[β] When the king happened to open the chamber, he was amazed to see containers empty of money. But he was unable to blame anyone, since the seals were secure and the chamber locked. Since he opened the chamber two and three times and there always seemed to be less money (for the thieves did not cease plundering it), the king did the following: he commanded that traps be made and that these be set around the vessels containing the money. [2] The thieves came, as they had before, and one of them went into the chamber. Approaching a storage jar, he was immediately caught in a trap. As he understood how much trouble he was in, he immediately called his brother. He showed what the situation was, and he bid his brother enter as quickly as possible and cut off his head so that he would not be seen and recognized and thereby destroy his brother as well. It seemed to this other brother that the one caught in the trap spoke sensibly. Persuaded, he did as his brother asked, replaced the stone, and went away to his home, carrying the head of his brother.

[γ] When it was day, the king entered the chamber and was astounded to see the thief's body in the trap and without

its head—but the chamber was undamaged and had no point
of escape. Being completely at a loss, the king did the following: he hung the thief's headless corpse from a wall, and he
stationed guards around it. He commanded the guards to
seize and bring to him anyone they saw grieving or pitying
the dead man. [2] As the corpse hung there, the thieves'
mother was very distressed. She spoke to her surviving son
and commanded him to contrive—however he could—to
release his brother's body and bring it home. If he disregarded her commands, she threatened to go to the king
herself and reveal that her son had the money.

[δ] So bitterly did the mother seize upon her surviving
son. And though he told her many things, he did not persuade her. He therefore contrived the following: he got some
donkeys, and he filled some wineskins with wine and put
them on the donkeys. Then he drove the donkeys, and when
he was among the men guarding the hanging corpse, he drew
out two or three of the ends fastening the wineskins to
release the wine. [2] As the wine flowed out, the thief struck
his head and gave a great shout—as if he did not know which
of the donkeys to turn to first. When the guards saw so much
wine flowing, they ran into the road holding pails. They
collected the wine for themselves as it poured out, considering it their gain. [3] Pretending to be angry, the thief railed at
all of them. The guards consoled him, and in time he pre-
tended to calm down and to stop being angry. Finally, he
drove the donkeys out of the road and readied them again.
[4] As there was more talk, and one of the guards mocked
him and persuaded him to laugh, he gave the guards one of
the wineskins. And they, sitting down right where they were,
put their minds to drinking. They invited and urged the thief
to stay and drink with them. And, of course, he was persuaded, and he remained. [5] The guards welcomed him

cheerfully to the drinking, and he gave them another of the wineskins. Drinking copiously, the guards became excessively drunk. Overpowered by sleep, they lay down right there where they were drinking. [6] When it was far into nighttime, the thief took down his brother's body. To insult the guards, he shaved the right cheek of each of them. Placing the corpse upon the donkeys, he drove home. He had accomplished the thing that his mother had commanded.

[ε] When, however, the king received the report that the thief's corpse had been stolen, he considered this terrible/clever [*deina*]. He wholeheartedly wanted to discover who had contrived the scheme. The Egyptian priests say that the king did the following—though to me it does not seem credible: [2] he placed his own daughter in a chamber and commanded her to receive favorably all men equally. But before she lay with them, he said, she must compel each man to relate to her the cleverest and most unholy thing he had done in his life [*sophōtaton kai anosiōtaton*]. If anyone related the events that had occurred concerning the thief, she was to seize him and not let him escape. [3] While the daughter did as her father commanded, the thief, having learned the reason that this was being done, wished to prevail over the king by craft [*polutropiēi*]. He did the following: [4] He cut off the arm of a newly slain corpse at the shoulder. Holding this under his cloak, he went to the daughter of the king. Entering, he was asked the very same question as the others. He related that he had done the most unholy thing [*anosiōtaton*] when he had cut off the head of his brother who got caught in a trap in the king's treasure house. He said the cleverest thing [*sophōtaton*] he had done was to get the guards drunk and take down his brother's hanging corpse. [5] When the king's daughter heard this, she grabbed him. But in the darkness, the thief extended the arm of the corpse

to her. Taking hold of this, she held on, believing she was
holding onto the arm of the man himself. But the thief let it
go to her, and he left, fleeing through the doors.
[ζ] When these events also were reported to the king,
he was astonished at the man's great wisdom [*poluphrosunēi*]
and daring. Finally, he sent messengers to all the cities to
announce that he was giving immunity and promising great
rewards if the man came into his sight. [2] And the thief,
trusting this, came to him. Greatly esteeming the man,
Rhampsinitus gave him his daughter in marriage on the
grounds that he of all men knew and understood [*epistamenōi*] the most things. Rhampsinitus judged the Egyptians
superior to other men and this thief superior among
Egyptians.

This tale of Rhampsinitus and the Clever Thief contains
oral folktale elements also found in Europe and Asia.[7] And like
the Egyptian version of Helen's story, it too offers the educational benefits of cross-cultural comparison. The Egyptian and
Greek accounts of Helen's story emphasize a shared cultural
value, the necessity of respecting cultural norms and obligations. Egyptians, like Greeks, consider violations of the obligations of guest-friendship deplorable. The tale of Rhampsinitus
and the Clever Thief seems to suggest that Egyptians share
Greek admiration for extreme cleverness, as the thief displays
Odysseus-like attributes and may even prefigure Herodotus's
portrait of the Athenian general Themistocles.[8] But this story
actually exposes a completely antithetical ideal of admirable
achievement. The *Odyssey*—emerging long before democracy
was even a concept—commends cleverness as vital to survival
and to the restoration of wise, benevolent, autocratic authority. The tale of Rhampsinitus commends cleverness as a source
of callous brutality and self-enrichment. The story seems fan-

ciful. It is unlikely, if not impossible, that Rhampsinitus built a treasure house out of stone, though Herodotus cites surviving material evidence (2.121).[9] And some might choose to dismiss the tale as merely Egyptian humor and exaggeration.[10] But regardless of its veracity, this bizarre story celebrates an unaccountable autocrat's power to endorse and reward at whim. Though perhaps merely a lighthearted folktale, this story validates autocratic authority as a source not of communal wellbeing but of irresponsible, inhumane ideals of conduct.

Unlike the *Odyssey*, this Egyptian tale reduces cleverness to a capacity to harm others with impunity. In the *Odyssey*, cleverness helps Odysseus survive and recover his legitimate and beneficial hereditary authority. Undeniably, Odysseus's success also has dark, disturbing, antisocial implications as he fails to save his companions and brutally slaughters unarmed adversaries, and only divine intervention prevents the vengeance cycle from destroying his entire community.[11] Nevertheless, in the Greek epic, cleverness defeats unrestrained greed and irresponsible, self-serving leadership as it empowers Odysseus to punish the rapacious and abusive suitors despite their great numerical superiority. By contrast, the Egyptian tale of Rhampsinitus *affirms* rapacious greed and irresponsible leadership. This tale commends rather than condemns theft, insatiable self-enrichment, and callous disregard for human life. Cleverness enables the thief to steal without limit, decapitate his own brother, have sex with a prostitute who is somehow also a princess, marry the princess, and presumably thereby eventually inherit her father's throne and wealth. Will the clever thief become a good king? Impossible to tell. And no one seems to care.

Unlike the *Odyssey*, this Egyptian tale exposes a power structure and value system prioritizing material gain over human lives and relationships. Nothing *within* the tale deems this problematic. Unscrupulous cleverness ultimately brings the thief a king's admiration and great material rewards. The king admires cleverness consisting exclusively in taking advantage of others, deeming this *sophōtaton*, "cleverest" (2.121.ε.2)—as does the thief (2.121.ε.4)—apparently ignoring the word's broader sense of "most prudent," "most wise." And while Greeks and Egyptians condemn Alexandros's *aniosiōtaton*, "most unholy," deed of stealing his host's wife (115.4), Rhampsinitus rewards the thief for his self-proclaimed *anosiōtaton*, "most unholy" deed (2.121.ε.2 and 4). Emphasis on the thief's "craft" (*polutropiē*, 2.121.ε.3) and wisdom (*poluphrosunē*, 2.121.ζ.1) evokes the cunning and craft of the *Odyssey*'s *polutropos* Odysseus and *polumētis* Odysseus.[12] But Rhampsinitus equates cleverness alone with knowledge and understanding, rewarding the thief "on the grounds that he of all men knew and understood [*epistamenōi*] the most things. Rhampsinitus judged the Egyptians superior [*prokekristhai*] to other men and this thief superior among Egyptians" (2.121.ζ.2). The macabre features of this Egyptian tale—fratricide, a severed head, a mother threatening to denounce her child, a father prostituting his daughter, a severed arm—all underscore the atrocities resulting from reducing the concept of admirable intellectual achievement to a capacity for unscrupulous deception. Neither the thief nor the king finds the thief's actions immoral. Both esteem a use of cleverness that brings material rewards but disregards the value of human lives (the brother's, the daughter's). Both the king and the thief mistake material acquisition for success. In this story, cleverness trumps humanity.

Whereas the Egyptian tale of Helen affirms a long-held Greek moral value, this story validates by counterexample the Greeks' gradual trajectory away from autocratic government toward broader political decision-making (eighth to fifth centuries BCE). Mistaking deception for supreme intellectual achievement, King Rhampsinitus admires and condones atrocities.

Despite this story's folktale feel and even lighthearted tone, its grisly details exemplify the dangers of outsourcing moral decision-making to any single powerful, unaccountable individual (or group). The tale might have direct implications for Herodotus's Athenian contemporaries.[13] But its message also seems universal: an unfettered ability to reward and punish makes everyone vulnerable to the poor judgment and worst impulses of the powerful.

Emphasizing the capacity of unlimited, unaccountable, autocratic power to pervert moral judgment, the tale of Rhampsinitus and the Clever Thief exposes the need for political accountability and communal decision-making. By the 440s and 430s, when Herodotus was writing, a third generation of Athenians was continuing the Athenian democratic experiment, begun in 508 BCE. Recording the ancient Egyptian tale of Rhampsinitus, Herodotus illustrates the need for individual power holders to be accountable to the people subject to their power. No single individual can or should determine for everyone the elements of desirable, commendable conduct. Members of communities must debate such questions among themselves. Since opinions will differ, cultural norms and institutional mechanisms must function to protect minority interests and to balance individual needs and preferences against the requirements of humanity and justice. In the twenty-first century, a narrow definition of admirable achievement—the acquisition of wealth by any means and the ingenuity to take advantage of others—makes us easy prey for unscrupulous opportunists. Though a valuable skill, cleverness as an *exclusive* measure of value can, as the Egyptian story demonstrates, pervert human relationships, denigrate human life, and promote cruelty, violence, and murder. Our own culture's narratives shape our attitudes and aspirations. If modern entertainment and pop culture glamorize, like the Egyptian tale, unscrupu-

lous cunning, theft, violence, and murder, they threaten to undermine our capacity for humane moral judgment.

In narrating Egyptian tales, as in narrating Egyptian ways,
Herodotus occupies a vast area between the modern extremes
of insensitivity to—or rejection of—cultural differences ("moral
absolutism") and a complete absence of critical judgment ("cultural relativism"). The moral absolutist, confident in her own
moral certainty, rejects the possibility of learning anything from
others. The moral relativist, certain that all cultural practices
and beliefs are equally valid and valuable, refuses to judge the
ways of others. Both extremes prevent the possibility of learning from others, and both extremes remain stubbornly, proudly
ignorant of their own inadequacy. Moral absolutists fail to
perceive the intellectual prison of their own time and place.
Moral relativists reject the possibility of ever escaping it. Both
remain trapped. Neither has anywhere else to stand.

Archimedes famously claimed, "Give me a lever and a
place to stand, and I will move the world." Herodotus gives us
a place to stand. Neither insensitive to nor mindlessly accepting of all cultural differences, Herodotus examines them meticulously. His wide travels and careful recording of others' ways
and tales offered his contemporaries the opportunity to judge
and evaluate differences on their merits. It turns out that Babylonians and Egyptians, foreigners though they are for the
Greek Herodotus, do or understand some things better than
Greeks do. Greeks can learn from them. Sometimes Greek
practices, narratives, and ideals seem best. That is valuable to
discover, too. If after recognizing that alternatives exist and examining them critically you still prefer your own, then you
can be confident in your choice. You are not merely clinging
to the familiar out of fear or ignorance or lack of imagination.

Showing his audience the vast space between unthinking
rejection of the ways of others and uncritical acceptance of all

ways, Herodotus offers a vital invitation to evaluate foreign ways and stories and the ideals they commend. Both the Egyptian and Greek versions of Helen's story caution against violating cultural ideals of decent and humane behavior. Both versions emphasize the adverse consequences of gratuitously harming others or failing to respect reciprocal obligations. Both versions demonstrate by counterexample the value of abiding by cultural norms and responsibilities. The story of Rhampsinitus and the Clever Thief—in its perverse celebration of fraternal decapitation, warped familial relationships, and sexual exploitation—cautions against the moral distortions and depredations of authoritarianism. Exposing the need for alternatives to autocratic power, this tale validates the ancient Greeks' unprecedented rejection of autocratic government and their novel experiment in democratic decision-making.

Democratic politics, in theory at least, requires every voter to evaluate all ideas and narratives carefully so as to choose the best leaders and policies. Engaging with foreign ways and foreign narratives can be uncomfortable, but modern studies suggest that intellectual discomfort is vital to learning and growth.[14] Herodotus demonstrated this twenty-five hundred years ago. Like the world traveler Herodotus, every member of a pluralistic society has the opportunity and the responsibility to compare and assess evidence and draw rational, humane conclusions. Herodotus's account of Helen's story shows how to do it. His tale of Rhampsinitus and the Clever Thief suggests why we might want to.

10

On Tyranny

Herodotus proceeds from his exploration of Egypt to an account of the Persian king Cambyses, an impulsive autocrat of doubtful sanity. In portraying Cambyses, Herodotus highlights the destructiveness of one-man rule, whether as a consequence of absolute power itself or the character of this particular king. Unencumbered by empathy or altruism, unaccountable to his subjects, and motivated solely by rapacious self-interest, Cambyses epitomizes the dangers of tyranny. In his narcissism, irrationality, lust, and madness, Herodotus's Cambyses exemplifies the catastrophic extreme of irresponsible autocratic power.

Son of Cyrus, Cambyses ruled Persia for less than a decade (529–522 BCE). Herodotus's account of Persia and its history cannot be read as factual.[1] And his portraits of prominent Persians and Persian ways may be Greek-biased and fictionalized or derived from good, if tendentious, Persian source material.[2] But whether historically accurate or not, Herodotus's description of Cambyses' crimes exposes the logical consequences of ceding absolute authority to any individual not subject to the rule of law and not bound by custom or humanity:

[3.34] The following mad deeds were done by Cambyses against the other Persians: for it is said that he spoke to Prexaspes, whom he honored most. This man was entrusted to bring important messages to him, and his son was Cambyses' cupbearer, and this is no small honor. It is said that Cambyses said the following: [2] "Prexaspes, what sort of man do the Persians believe me to be, and what stories are fabricated about me?" And it is said that Prexaspes replied, "Oh, Master, you are praised greatly in regard to all other things—but they say that you are too devoted to the love of wine." [3] They say that Prexaspes said these things about the Persians, but that Cambyses became enraged and responded with the following: "Now, therefore, the Persians say that I, being devoted to wine, am out of my mind and not sensible. Their former words, therefore, were not true." [4] For previously, when Cambyses had asked Persians who were sitting with him—and Croesus—what sort of man he seemed to be in comparison to his father Cyrus, they answered that he was better than his father. For, they said, he held all that his father possessed, and he had acquired in addition both Egypt and the sea. [5] The Persians said these things. But Croesus being present and not pleased with this assessment said the following to Cambyses: "To me now, O child of Cyrus, you do not seem to be like your father. For you do not yet have a son such as yourself as your father left after him." Hearing these things, Cambyses was gladdened and he praised the judgment of Croesus.

[3.35] They say, therefore, that recalling these things, Cambyses spoke in anger to Prexaspes: "Ascertain now—you yourself—whether the Persians are speaking the truth or whether they themselves are out of their minds when they say these things. [2] For if—with your own son standing in the antechamber—I happen to shoot him in the middle of the heart, then the Persians appear to be speaking nonsense. But if I miss the mark, declare that the Persians are speaking the truth and that I am not of sound mind." [3] Having said these things and drawing the bow, Cambyses struck the boy with an arrow. The boy fell down, and they say that Cambyses commanded that his attendants split open the body and examine the wound. And when the arrow was found to be in the heart, they say that Cambyses—laughing and being very joyful—said to the boy's father: [4] "Prexaspes, it has become clear to you that I am not mad and that the Persians are out of their minds. But now, tell me: have you seen now anyone of all men who shoots a bow with such good aim?" And they say that Prexaspes, seeing that the man was not sound of mind and being fearful for himself, said, "Master, I do not think that a god himself would shoot so well." [5] These things were done at that time. But at another time, seizing twelve of the Persians—men equal in rank to the foremost ones— Cambyses buried them alive, head down, on no charge worth considering.

[3.36] Croesus the Lydian condemned Cambyses for doing these things, and he warned him with the following words: "O King, do not give everything over to your youth and passion but stop and get hold of yourself. Forethought, you know, is a good thing, and foresight is prudent. But you yourself are killing men who are your own citizens, seizing them on no charge worth considering. And you are killing children. [2] If you do many things of this sort, watch out that the Persians do not revolt from you. Your father Cyrus commanded me many times, ordering me to warn and advise you as to anything that I find to be good." Croesus, making his goodwill manifest, gave Cambyses this advice. [3] But Cambyses answered with the following words: "You yourself dare to advise me! You who were such a good governor of your own country?! And you advised my father well, do you think, bidding him cross the river Araxes and go against the Massagetae when they wished to cross into our land?! You destroyed yourself by leading your own country badly, and you destroyed Cyrus who was persuaded by you—but you did not do this with impunity! For you know, for a long time I have been in need of a pretext to seize hold of you." [4] Saying these things, Cambyses took his bow for the purpose of shooting Croesus down. But Croesus, jumping up, ran outside. And since Cambyses was not able to shoot Croesus, he commanded his attendants to seize and kill him. [5] But Cambyses' attendants, understanding his character, hid Croesus on this account: so that if Cambyses repented and sought after Croesus, they themselves, by revealing Croesus, would receive gifts as a reward for Croesus. But if Cambyses did not repent or long for Croesus, they would then do away with him. [6] And, surely, Cambyses did long for Croesus not much time afterward. And his attendants, learning this, reported to Cambyses that Croesus remained alive. Cambyses said that he was grateful that Croesus remained alive, but that those men, however, who had preserved him were not to escape with impunity but were to be put to death. And this he did.

[3.37] Cambyses did many mad things of this kind against the Persians and his allies. Remaining in Memphis, he even opened ancient burial vaults and examined the corpses. [2] Going further, he even entered the temple of Hephaestus and laughed scornfully at the cult statues many times. For there is a statue of Hephaestus that is most similar to the Phoenician Pataici [small statues], which the Phoenicians carry around on the prows of their warships. If anyone has not seen these, I will mark them out as a representation of a very small male person (*pugmaios*). [3] Cambyses also entered the temple of the Cabiri, which it is unlawful for

anyone to enter other than the priest. Having jeered a great
deal at these statues, he set them on fire. These statues are like
the ones of Hephaestus. And people say that they are the sons
of Hephaestus.

[3.38] In all respects, therefore, it is clear to me that
Cambyses was utterly mad. For otherwise he would not have
attempted to mock things that are sacred, lawful, and customary [*hiroisi te kai nomaioisi*]. For if someone should
propose to all men, urging them to choose out from all
customs the ones that are the best, after examining carefully,
all would choose their own. For all believe their own customs
to be the best by far. [2] It is not therefore fitting for any
man—other than one who is raving mad—to make such
things a subject of laughter. That all men have believed this
the case about customs can be concluded from many positive
proofs—but especially by the following: [3] Darius [a successor of Cambyses], in the course of his reign, called some
Greeks who were present and asked them how much money
it would take to persuade them to eat their dead fathers.
And they declared that on no condition would they do this.
[4] After this, Darius summoned some Indians—ones called
Kallatians—who do eat their dead parents. And with the
Greeks present and understanding through interpreters what
was said, Darius asked how much money the Indians would
accept to burn their dead fathers with fire [as Greeks did].
And the Indians shouted out very loudly and ordered him to
abstain from speaking ill-omened words. Thus, these things
have now been recognized by convention. And Pindar [Greek
poet, ca. 518–ca. 448/7 BCE] seems to me to have composed
his poem rightly in asserting that "Custom is King of all."

Throughout the *Histories,* numerous powerful monarchs
generate not communal well-being but death and destruction.

Herodotus portrays the lustful ambitions of kings driving historical events and promoting violence. Free to indulge their passions, autocrats in Herodotus's stories often transgress limits of justice and humanity, harming their own people as well as foreign enemies. The tale of Rhampsinitus and the Clever Thief (2.121) exposes the potential of royal authority to promote toxic ideals of conduct: the king blithely commends and rewards monstrous perversions of normal human relationships. Herodotus's account of Cambyses further emphasizes the destructiveness of autocratic rule, both for those subject to it and for the autocrat himself.

The Greek noun *turannis*, "tyranny," originally meant the regime of a nonhereditary autocrat, usually acquired by force, as distinct from a hereditary monarchy. Since such autocrats tended to behave badly, the Greek word gradually gained the negative connotations of the English "tyranny." Herodotus does not depict tyranny as an Eastern phenomenon. In fact, most tyrants in the *Histories* are Greek.[3] And the *Histories* suggests some positive as well as negative possibilities for *turannis*, "tyranny," in its original sense.[4] But *turannis* constituted an existential threat to the classical Athenian conception of *dēmokratia*.[5] Throughout this chapter I use "tyranny" in its exclusively pejorative modern English sense. Twenty-five hundred years ago, Herodotus unequivocally condemned tyrannical abuses of power, meticulously detailing numerous atrocities committed by unrestrained, unaccountable autocrats.

Herodotus's tale of Cambyses and Prexaspes exemplifies not only a tyrant's narcissistic craving for sycophantic affirmation but also his propensity for unwarranted anger and a depraved inclination to commit atrocities. Having asked Prexaspes, one of his most favorite and respected attendants, to declare the Persians' opinion of him, Cambyses erupts in anger at hearing the response. Prexaspes gives a cautious answer,

saying essentially, well, sir, they praise you for everything—
except they think that maybe you like wine too much. But this
effort at mild, tactful criticism convinces Cambyses that the
Persians consider him demented and crazed by wine. He now
doubts the Persians' truthfulness altogether, distrusting their
previous lavish praise (3.34). Enraged, Cambyses devises a di-
abolical and irrational "test": if he can shoot an arrow straight
through the heart of Prexaspes' son, who unfortunately happens to be nearby, that will prove the Persians untruthful and
the Persians themselves out of their minds. If Cambyses misses,
then the Persians are speaking the truth and he himself is not
of sane mind. This, of course, is the pseudo-logic of a lunatic.
If you had any doubt, Cambyses' gleeful laughter at seeing that
he does shoot the boy straight through the heart confirms that
like a madman Cambyses lacks a normal human capacity for
empathy and remorse, and he cannot value the innocent life of
a child. Cambyses himself draws the opposite conclusion,
claiming that this demonstrates that he is not mad and the
Persians are. In this poisonous political environment, with no
possibility of holding the tyrant to account, even mild criticism
has lethal consequences. Tyrannical authority also disallows expression of natural human emotions, as the bereaved father of
the murdered boy feels compelled to praise his deranged king's
marksmanship (3.35.3–4).

   As portrayed by Herodotus, Cambyses embodies the tyrannical extreme: he makes no effort to restrain his murderous impulses, rejects good advice, and values obedience alone.
Herodotus says that "on no charge worth considering" (though
it is difficult to imagine what could constitute a valid reason)
Cambyses buries alive twelve elite Persian men (3.35.5). Herodotus includes among Cambyses' tyrannical atrocities his attempt to murder Croesus, the former Lydian king who became
advisor to Cambyses' father Cyrus following the Persian

conquest of Lydia (1.84–89). When Croesus tries to caution the tyrant against murdering his own people, Cambyses orders Croesus killed (3.36.1–4). Understanding their king's mercurial nature as he himself does not—though not nearly as fully as they assume—the servants decide to save Croesus in case Cambyses changes his mind. Although Cambyses does change his mind, as the servants anticipated, he prioritizes obedience above all. Happy that Croesus survives, Cambyses rewards the servants for their disobedience not with gratitude, as they expect, but with death (3.36.5–6).

Though claims of Cambyses' numerous transgressions against both the living and the dead may well be distortions drawn from Herodotus's sources, Herodotus depicts the king's sacrilegious actions as manifestations of insanity.[6] Cambyses violates tombs and ancestral customs (3.37). His scorn for sacred rites and practices constitutes for Herodotus the clearest evidence of his madness (3.38.1).[7] Herodotus recognizes that people of every culture have strong attachment to their own laws and traditions, claiming that "all men have believed this the case about customs" or, more literally, "all people have recognized by convention [*nenomikasi*] matters concerning customs/traditions/laws [*nomous*]" (3.38.2). For Greeks, *nomoi* constitute general principles governing conduct, as distinct from commands issued by individuals.[8] Herodotus suggests that anyone violating ancestral customs must be mad.

Herodotus includes a powerful anecdote to corroborate his insistence on the intensity of human attachment to cultural traditions, describing the odd experiment attempted by Darius, a successor to Cambyses (3.38.3–4). Asked by Darius what it would cost to induce them to eat their dead fathers, some Greeks reply that they would not do it for any sum of money (3.38.3). Then Darius asks some Indians what it would cost to get them to burn their dead fathers, as the Greeks do. "And the

Indians shouted out very loudly," Herodotus says, "and ordered him to abstain from speaking ill-omened words" (3.38.4). In this anecdote, Greeks and Indians each adamantly reject each other's funeral practices. Herodotus's Greek contemporaries might have seen a contrast between admirable, emotionally restrained Greeks and intemperate, passionate barbarians, since Herodotus juxtaposes the calm Greek response with the Indians' violent outcry at the suggestion of violating ancestral customs. Modern readers, however, might mistake this anecdote for evidence of Herodotus's validation of cultural relativism.[9] But Herodotus never suggests that all customs are equally valid. Instead, the anecdote emphasizes the *power* of custom.[10] We are all deeply attached to our own.

Connecting his character portrait of the deranged tyrant Cambyses to his account of Persian imperialist expansion, Herodotus depicts tyranny as a source not only of wanton murder and glaring violations of cultural traditions but also of massive military conflicts. Following the lengthy description of Egypt in book 2, Herodotus resumes in book 3 his main narrative trajectory addressing Persian expansion and culminating in the conflict between Persia and Greece. He frames his extensive description of Egypt as a digression, for book 2 begins with Cambyses inheriting the rule of Persia from his father Cyrus and leading his Greek subjects (whom he considers his *douloi*, "slaves") in an attack against Egypt (2.1). Book 2 concludes with a description of the reign of King Amasis of Egypt (2.172–182), and book 3 opens with the claim that "against this Amasis, surely, Cambyses, son of Cyrus, was going to war" (3.1.1).

Uninterested in political or economic motives for military aggression, Herodotus once again finds causal agency in human impulse or desire. He attributes Cambyses' decision to invade Egypt to petty autocratic grievance. Unrestrained and unaccountable, the tyrant yields to his passions, and a personal quarrel becomes a motive for imperial conquest. Cambyses had previously asked the Egyptian king Amasis for his daughter in marriage, and Amasis had tricked him, sending a substitute instead. Cambyses invades Egypt to avenge the deception (3.1). Another man's personal grievance precipitates this quarrel between the Persian and Egyptian kings, for an Egyptian doctor, angry at Amasis for having sent him to Cambyses, previously advised Cambyses to request the Egyptian king's daughter. Desire for vengeance motivates the doctor, as he hopes to make Amasis either suffer the loss of his daughter or become Cambyses' enemy if he refuses (3.1.1–2). Even alternative stories concerning Cambyses' origins and intentions, though discounted by Herodotus, similarly include the vengeance motive (3.2–3). From the outset, Herodotus seeks the causes of human events (*aitiē, Hist.* 1, first sentence), and he now offers this cause (*aitiē,* 3.1) for Cambyses' invasion of Egypt: Cambyses launches a great war against Egypt to avenge a personal insult.

Willing to initiate war to avenge a personal affront, the tyrant lacks the ability to learn either from his own experience or from that of other people. Cambyses' desire for vengeance against Amasis persists, even after he succeeds in conquering Egypt. He has his men mutilate the dead king's corpse. When the embalmed corpse withstands their efforts, Cambyses violates not only Egyptian but also Persian customs by ordering it burned (3.16). Unlike Herodotus's Greek contemporaries, Cambyses evidently remains ignorant of Homer's crucial insight that vengeance is insatiable and reciprocal. Cambyses' violation of the corpse of Amasis echoes Achilles' desecration of his enemy's corpse in Homer's *Iliad.* But the archaic Greek epic exposes vengeance as unsatisfying and self-destructive: by violence, Achilles fails to appease his own thirst for revenge. He gains no solace or relief by slaughtering his dearest friend's killer and violating the dead man's corpse. And Achilles' own death—foretold though not depicted in the *Iliad*—will result, as he knows, from his vengeance killing of his beloved friend's killer. Achilles' rage, grief, and desire for vengeance subside not through violence but as a consequence of his profound (and in retrospect obvious) realization that vulnerability to suffering and death unites all human beings. This realization enables Achilles to share a moment of grief with his dead enemy's father. By discovering a capacity for empathy, Achilles recovers his humanity.[11]

Evidently ignorant of Homer's wisdom—or unable to appreciate it—Herodotus's Cambyses remains subject to his own foolish, tyrannical passions. Narcissistic, irrational, lustful, and crazed, Cambyses continues to exemplify the extreme evil of absolute autocratic authority. His rage and insanity destroy not only Egyptians but also many of his own warriors: launching a campaign against Ethiopia, Cambyses fails to prepare supplies for his troops, and he presses onward even after food runs out, heedless of his warriors' welfare. The troops resort to eating grasses and, finally, to cannibalism. Cambyses eventually turns the expedition back, but not until he has lost the majority of his army (3.25.5–7). Returning to Egyptian Memphis, Cambyses mistakes the Egyptians' celebration of an important religious festival for a celebration of his own failure in Ethiopia. Cambyses has his men kill the Egyptians who attempt to tell him the truth about the festival. Disrupting the festival, he orders the celebrants slaughtered and the officiating priests whipped (3.26–29).

Violating not only foreign but also Persian customs, Cambyses extends his crimes to incest and fratricide. Since he understands that Persian custom does not countenance his sexual desire for his own sister (Herodotus uses the same verb as for Candaules irrationally lusting for his own wife; cf. *ērasthē* at

1.8.1 and 3.31.2), Cambyses asks the royal judges whether any law or custom (*nomos*) sanctions such a union. Fearing Cambyses, the judges diplomatically reply that there is no law or custom (*nomos*) against it, and there is one that says the king can do whatever he wants (3.31.2–5). After marrying this sister and another sister soon after, Cambyses subsequently murders the latter (3.31.6). He previously has his brother assassinated in response to a dream (3.30). The Greek and Persian versions of the sister's murder differ in details, but both attribute the murder to Cambyses' response to his sister's implicit criticism of his previous murder of their brother (3.32).

Herodotus's portrait of the evils of tyranny not only includes murder, incest, fratricide, and violations of custom but also reaffirms Solon's warning that human fortunes inevitably fluctuate. Herodotus interrupts his account of Cambyses to tell of another tyrant, the wealthy Polycrates of Samos warned by his friend King Amasis of Egypt to beware of his extreme good fortune. Echoing Solon, Amasis insists that the gods are jealous, explaining, "I know of no one—I never heard any account of anyone—who was experiencing good fortune in all things and did not end his life badly, ripped up by the roots" (3.40.3). Since Amasis believes that the best life possible consists in alternating good and bad fortune, then for the continuously wealthy and successful Polycrates the future can only bring utter disaster. Amasis advises Polycrates, as a precaution, to throw away his most valued possession. Amasis's logic seems questionable; he assumes that the gods will not jealously punish a supremely fortunate man who deliberately discards his dearest possession. Polycrates opts to jettison an emerald signet ring, and *his* logic seems questionable. Is he trying to appease the gods' jealousy with a trivial choice, or is this truly (and pathetically) the thing he values most? Either way, the stunt fails. Polycrates tosses his ring into the sea (3.40–41), but a few days later, a fisherman catches an unusually large fish and presents it as a gift to the king. Lo and behold! Inside the fish lies the signet ring (3.43). Amasis interprets this as evidence that no person can protect another from what is coming to him and that Polycrates will not end well (3.43.1).

Affirming Solon's warning that human fortunes vary, the tale of Polycrates' ring also offers further evidence that autocratic power does not guarantee good judgment or admirable behavior. Both Amasis and Polycrates rely on their conception of divine causality, convinced, like Solon, that gods envy and seek to destroy human prosperity. Both share Croesus's misconception that wealth alone defines a man as fortunate. Amasis and Polycrates accept a trivial or symbolic sacrifice (the loss of a favorite ring) as valid appeasement of divine jealousy. The serendipitous return of the ring proves to both the failure of the strategy, but it does not prompt either to reflect on the role of human agency in human experience. Far from it. Seeing trouble approaching, Amasis callously and selfishly abandons Polycrates, breaking off the friendship to protect himself from suffering at his friend's misfortune (3.43.2). In fact, not Amasis but Polycrates opted to end the alliance on realizing that Cambyses intended to attack Egypt next.[12] But Herodotus's tale focuses on autocratic foolishness. His Polycrates never reassesses or revises his aggressive behavior. "Taking no heed of all advice [*pasēs sumbouliēs alogēsas*]," as Herodotus explains, Polycrates does indeed come to a disastrous end, attacked, deceived, and cruelly killed by a man he has perhaps deliberately or inadvertently offended (3.125.1–3). Though Herodotus himself deems Polycrates' fall from great good fortune confirmation of Amasis's prediction of divine action (3.125.4), his narrative illustrates autocratic narcissism and poor choices.

Like Cambyses, the autocrats Amasis and Polycrates provide no models to emulate. Amasis and Polycrates seem laughable in their effort to control the future. Herodotus's Greek contemporaries also knew that human fortunes were variable, but Greek stories recognize this variability as an inescapable fact of human existence that does not absolve human beings from taking responsibility for their own actions. In the *Iliad*, Achilles explains that Zeus distributes fates to human beings from two jars, one containing bad fates, the other good. Some people get only bad fates and suffer all their days. Other people get a mixture of good and bad fates. No one gets all good fates.[13] And everyone dies. Far from rejecting human agency, this understanding of human existence—sometimes called "the Greek tragic worldview"—emphasizes human responsibility for the quality of human life. In the *Odyssey*, Zeus does not deny divine responsibility for human suffering, but he points out that human beings blame gods for *all* of their troubles (*kaka*), whereas in fact they themselves—by their own foolishness—increase their own sufferings.[14] Ancient Greeks accepted that fate (or divine will, or luck, or chance) defines the contours of human existence. But they recognized, unlike the feckless Cambyses, Amasis, and Polycrates, that our own choices determine the quality of our lives. The realization that human fortunes alternate should make us all cautious and restrained when things are going well and hopeful (and enterprising) when they are not. It should make us delight in our friends' successes and ready to lend support when friends are in distress. The inability of the tyrant to do these things is a marker of his inhumanity.

Although tyrants in the *Histories* routinely come to bad ends, confirming the varying pattern of human fortunes, Herodotus's portrait of tyranny highlights the power of individual human decision-making. Choice, not chance, defines the life and death of Cambyses. Cambyses opts to murder his brother on the basis of a dream (3.30). (Polycrates, too, participates in the fratricidal pattern, becoming tyrant of Samos by killing one brother and exiling another, 3.39). Cambyses decides to avenge a personal insult and invade Egypt. This choice permits the Magi, a caste of Persian priests, to usurp the Persian throne. By opting to murder his own brother, Cambyses enables one of the Magi, who conveniently resembles the dead brother and possesses the same name, to claim that he, not Cambyses, is Cyrus's real heir (3.61–63). Cambyses now regrets killing his brother, realizing that the dream predicting his overthrow by his brother actually meant this usurper by the same name (3.64). (Modern historians disagree as to whether or not the usurper and Cambyses' brother were one and the same.)[15] Cambyses rushes off impetuously to attack the Magi, inadvertently stabbing himself with his own sword (3.63.3) and dying of the wound some days later (3.66.2). The Magi's choice to usurp Cambyses' autocratic power similarly ensures their violent end, as they are overthrown, after ruling just seven months, by a group of seven Persian noblemen using a combination of deception and violence (3.70–79).

Expanding the critique of unilateral political authority begun in book 1, Herodotus's portrait of tyranny in book 3 remains instructive today. Narcissistic, consumed by rage, relentlessly ambitious, and callously cruel, authoritarian leaders pursue their own interests at others' expense. Lacking self-restraint, forethought, and compassion, and accountable to no one, autocrats destroy other people and themselves. Cambyses' death by a self-inflicted wound aptly symbolizes the self-destructiveness of tyrannical rule. The twentieth and twenty-first centuries offer numerous more recent examples illustrating the inevitable, deadly consequences of unrestrained, unreflective autocratic rule. In exposing the enduring toxicity of tyranny,

Herodotus undermines any modern enthusiasm for a "powerful leader," or "strong man," or for any political officeholder permitted to violate the rule of law with impunity. Helping us to recognize twenty-first-century versions of this age-old venom, Herodotus defines tyranny as not merely a dangerous potential of authoritarianism but its essence.

11

On Types of Political Regimes

In telling the story of Cambyses, Herodotus exposes the dangers of autocratic narcissism; irrational and impulsive, the mad king transgresses law and custom. He epitomizes the catastrophic, self-destructive extreme of unrestrained, unaccountable political authority. After describing Cambyses' death, Herodotus posits some alternatives to autocracy. Seven Persian noblemen conspire together and violently overthrow the Magi, who had briefly usurped the Persian throne (3.70–79). The Seven then proceed to hold a calm debate regarding the best form of political regime (3.80–83) [522 BCE].

Narrating an implausible and almost certainly fictitious story, Herodotus depicts an unproductive political debate followed by a counterproductive political competition. The tale constitutes the first extant substantive example of political theory in Western literature.[1] In this story, each of three Persian noblemen speaks in favor of a different form of government, identified as "rule by the many," "rule by the few," or "rule by the one." The story may have had a Persian narrative at its base, but Herodotus anachronistically places in the mouths of Persians a century before his time the kinds of arguments current in the Greece of his own day.[2] The scene might signify—to

Herodotus's contemporary Greek audience—a surprising, un-Persian-like effort of Persians to have a productive conversation.[3] And yet, Herodotus can have obtained no eyewitness report for this conversation and its outcome. Moreover, elements, both included and omitted, distinguish Persian attitudes from contemporary Greek views.[4] And Herodotus's account does not flatter the Persians.

Though presented as a debate, the scene seems more like a series of rhetorical displays, for these Persians do not converse. Each speaker asserts his own opinion. They express agreement on some points, but none of the three addresses any criticism leveled by another speaker at the type of regime that he is commending. In the absence of real discussion, which would require addressing counterarguments, an ill-considered decision results. Merely a pretense of a productive exchange of arguments, this conversation illustrates by counterexample the value of actual discussion and debate. The Persians' subsequent process of selecting a monarch illustrates—also by counterexample—the necessity for rational determination of constructive leadership criteria:

[3.80] When the uproar calmed down and over five days had passed, the ones who had revolted against the Magi [i.e., the seven noblemen, leaders of the coup against the Magi] took counsel together about all matters. And speeches were spoken that are not credible to some of the Greeks—but they surely were spoken. [2] Otanes bid them place decision-making for the Persians in the public realm, saying the following: "It no longer seems best to me for there to be one monarch over us. For that is neither pleasant nor good. For you have seen the extent of the reckless, self-destructive violence [hubrin] of Cambyses, and you have enjoyed also the reckless self-destructive violence [hubrios] of the Magi.

[3] How could monarchy be a well-ordered thing, a system in which it is possible for a man who cannot be held to account to do whatever he wants? And this is because even the best man of all, placed in this office, would stand outside his accustomed thoughts [i.e., would not think as he otherwise normally would]. For reckless, self-destructive violence [*hubris*] is produced in him because of the good things present. And envy is rooted in a human being from the beginning. [4] And having these two things, he has all evilness. Filled with reckless, self-destructive violence [*hubri*], he does many outrageous things, and he does them out of envy also. Moreover, a man who is a tyrant [*turannon*] should be lacking in envy—since he has every good thing. But he is the opposite of this toward his citizens. He is jealous of the best citizens who are surviving and thriving, and he delights in the worst of the citizens. And he is best at taking on slanders [i.e., easily feels slighted or offended]. [5] And this is what is most incongruous of all: if you admire him with moderation, he is angered that he is not really and truly being worshipped. And if anyone really and truly worships him, he is angry at the flatterer. But now I come to saying the greatest evils: the tyrant disrupts ancestral customs, sexually assaults women, and kills men without trial. [6] First of all, the multitude holding sovereignty has the noblest name of all: political equality [*isonomiē*]. And, second, majority rule does none of the things that a monarch does. It assigns offices by lottery selection, and at the end of every term of office, the magistrate is held to account for his conduct in office. All resolutions are brought up on public authority. Therefore, I propose the opinion that we give up the monarchy and elevate the multitude to power. For in the majority is everything." Otanes, surely, put forward this opinion.

[3.81] But Megabyzus exhorted them to commit the government to an oligarchy, saying the following: "As to the things that Otanes said in proposing making an end of tyranny [*turannida*], understand that I declare these things also. But with respect to his advice that we give power to the multitude, Otanes failed to reach the best opinion. For there is nothing more devoid of understanding and fuller of reckless, self-destructive violence [*hubristoteron*] than a useless mob. [2] It is in no way tolerable for men escaping the reckless, self-destructive violence [*hubrin*] of a tyrant [*turannou*] to fall into the reckless, self-destructive violence [*hubrin*] of an unbridled, undisciplined, uneducated populace. For if the tyrant does anything, he does it knowingly. But it is not possible for the populace to know what they are doing. For how would anyone know who neither has been taught nor has seen anything noble and beautiful or proper? Such a person pushes on, falling into matters without thought, like a mountain stream swollen by rain and melted snow. [3] Now, let those who intend evil for the Persians make use of government by the people [*dēmōi*]. But let us—after selecting an assembly of the best men—confer power on them." Megabyzus brought forward this opinion.

[3.82] But, third, Darius made his opinion known, saying, "It seems to me that Megabyzus spoke rightly in what he said about the multitude, but not rightly as to the things that he said about oligarchy. For if all three regimes were set before us in theory, all being the best of their type—that is, the best form of majority rule, oligarchy, and monarchy, I say that monarchy is superior to the other two by far. [2] And I say this because nothing would seem better than one man who is best. For, employing the best judgment, he would guard the multitude blamelessly. In the same way, he would best keep silent as to his plans against enemies. [3] But in an oligarchy, many men cultivate excellence for the common good, and their private enmities usually become extremely severe. For each man wants to be in charge and wants to be victorious by means of his own opinions—with the result that they arrive at great enmities with each other. And out of these enmities, factions emerge. And from these factions, slaughter. And from slaughter, it ends in monarchy. And this sequence showed clearly by how much monarchy is the best regime. [4] In turn, when the people rule, it is impossible for wickedness not to arise. And with this wickedness occurring, common enmities do not arise among bad men. Instead, their friendships become strong. Joining up in their evildoing, these men conduct public affairs. And the situation is such until the time when one man, putting himself at the head of the populace, puts a stop to such men. From these actions, this man is admired by the populace. And, being admired, thereupon he thus becomes manifest as a monarch. And from this also it is clear that monarchy is the best regime. [5] To speak summing everything up in one statement: from where did we get our freedom and who gave it to us? Was it from the people, an oligarchy, or a monarch? Therefore, I hold this opinion: since we were freed by the agency of one man, I advise that we maintain that sort of regime. And besides this, my opinion is that we not dissolve ancestral customs that have been working well. For that would not be better."

[3.83] These three opinions were set forth, and four of the seven men preferred this last one. Since Otanes was defeated as to his opinion—being eager to establish equality under law [isonomiēn]—he spoke before all the conspirators, saying the following: [2] "Fellow conspirators, since indeed it is clear that it is necessary for one of us to become king— either chosen by lot, or whomever is chosen by the greater part of the Persians entrusting him with the position, or by some other contrivance—I myself will not contend with you now. For I wish neither to rule nor be ruled. I withdraw my claim to ruling on this condition, namely that I will be ruled by none of you—neither I myself nor my descendants, in perpetuity." [3] Having said these things, as the other six agreed to these conditions, Otanes did not compete for the monarchy but remained neutral. Even now, his family alone of the Persians continues to be free, and it is subject only to the extent that it wishes, while not violating Persian laws and traditions.

[3.84] The remainder of the Seven were planning how they would establish the kingship most justly. And it seemed best to them [*sphi edokse*] for Otanes and his descendants—if the kingship went to someone else of the Seven—to be given each year select Median clothing and the whole gift allotment that is most honored among the Persians. And they determined these special privileges for this reason: because Otanes was the first to plan the conspiracy and because he brought them all together. [2] These things, surely, were selected for Otanes, but they determined the following in common: that every one of the Seven who wished have the right to enter the palace without any official prior announcement—unless he chanced to find the king sleeping with a woman. And they agreed that the king not be permitted to marry anyone other than a descendant of the Seven who had joined in the rebellion. [3] Concerning the kingship, they resolved the following: when the sun rose and they had all arrived outside the city, whoever's horse was the first to neigh, this man would hold the kingship.

[3.85] But Darius had a clever groom whose name was Oibares. When the meeting ended, Darius said the following to this man: "Oibares, concerning the kingship, it seemed

best to us [hēmin dedoktai] to act according to the following
plan: when we are mounted on horseback, whoever's horse is
the first to neigh at sunrise, this man will hold the kingship.
Now, therefore, if you have any cleverness [sophiēn], devise
a scheme so that we hold this power and not anyone else."
[2] Oibares answered with the following: "O master, if indeed
by this method the kingship is to be yours or not, take
courage because of this and be heartened, since no one else
will be king before you. I have just the right sort of means of
accomplishing this." Darius said: "If, then, you have some
such cunning contrivance, it is the fitting time to prepare it
and not to put it off, since our contest will be at daybreak."
[3] Hearing this, Oibares did the following: when it was
nighttime, leading out one of Darius's mares—the one that
Darius loved most—Oibares tied her up at the limits of the
city. Then he led out Darius's stallion, and he led him around
the mare many times, bumping him against the mare. Finally,
he let the stallion mount the mare.

[3.86] With day beginning to dawn, the Six, as agreed,
were present on their horses. And riding out through the
edge of the city, when they were at this spot where the mare
had been tied the preceding night, right there, Darius's stallion,
running forward, whinnied. [2] And just at the moment that
the horse did this, lightning appeared in the cloudless sky, and
there was thunder. These occurrences finalized the decision
for Darius—just as if they happened from some coincidence.
And the other men, leaping down from their horses, prostrated
themselves before Darius.

[3.87] They say that Oibares contrived these things, but
there is also the following account (and both stories are told
by Persians): that Oibares, having rubbed the mare's genitals
with his hand, kept his hand concealed in his trousers. And at
the same time as the sun was rising, when the Six were about

to release their horses, Oibares pulled his hand out and brought it near the nostrils of Darius's stallion. And the stallion perceiving it—they say—neighed and whinnied.

[3.88] And surely Darius, son of Hystaspes, was accepted as king. And all the peoples in Asia were his subjects—the peoples who had been conquered by Cyrus and then later again by Cambyses—except for the Arabians.

In this passage, Herodotus depicts a debate that is not a debate and a competition that is not a competition. Our modern conception of political debate and political competition has become so degraded that we may miss the ironies, humor, and biting political critique of these scenes. Modern televised political "debates" consist of mudslinging and sound bites. News outlets report political contests as if they were sporting events, detailing not policy proposals but polling numbers. By comparison, these Persian noblemen offer logical-seeming arguments. They eloquently defend their preferred regime type, and they express agreement on some points. They seem to be talking to one another. But they are not. Laughably, none of the three counters or even acknowledges arguments made against his preferred regime type. The Seven make their choice without the benefit of reasoned discussion. Ironically, they use a majority vote to choose monarchy. Like the political debate, the tale of Darius's ascension to the kingship also seems unlikely to be true. But Herodotus depicts the Seven opting to permit luck or the gods to select the next monarch. He seems to have elided here evidence of Darius having some legitimate hereditary claim to sovereignty (cf. 7.11.2).[5] In Herodotus's telling, the Seven foolishly opt for an autocrat excelling not in constructive leadership abilities but in unscrupulous self-interest.

The first speaker, Otanes, in proposing majority rule for Persia, criticizes monarchy for making the ruler violent, unrestrained, and unaccountable. Otanes reminds his co-conspirators of the *hubris* of Cambyses and of the Magi (3.80.2). I translate *hubris*—admittedly awkwardly and repetitively—as "reckless, self-destructive violence" because although the English hybris (sometimes spelled "hubris") derives from the Greek *hubris,* the words do not have an identical range of meaning. In English, hybris has come to mean "arrogance" or "insolence," with "humility" or "modesty" its opposite. But *hubris* in Greek meant excessive, unrestrained desire, ambition, and overconfidence.[6] It frequently involved impulsive, short-sighted violence, specifically violence redounding to the harm of the perpetrator. The legal term *graphē hubreōs* meant a public indictment or prosecution for aggravated personal assault. In Greek, the opposite of *hubris* is not "humility" or "modesty" but *sōphrosunē,* meaning "wisdom," "prudence," "self-restraint," "moderation," even "chastity."[7] As the antithesis of *hubris, sōphrosunē* encompasses all the abilities required for maximizing the chances of achieving a successful life, whereas *hubris* destroys one's chances for a successful life. Herodotus has detailed Cambyses' many acts of reckless, self-destructive violence. Undoubtedly with the recent example of Cambyses in mind, Otanes criticizes monarchy not for its propensity to produce arrogance but because it liberates the ruler's most violent impulses and frees him to wreak havoc (3.80.3).

Otanes observes that monarchy not only liberates but actively cultivates the autocrat's worst instincts. Autocratic power produces *hubris* even in the best man (3.80.3). And again, by *hubris,* Otanes means not "arrogance" but "reckless, self-destructive violence," that is, the opposite of wisdom, prudence, self-restraint, the qualities necessary for success. Freedom from any external checks on his appetites also produces envy in the autocrat. The combination of reckless violence and envy results in *pasan kakotēta,* "complete evil." Filled with *hubris,* and acting also out of envy, the autocrat does numerous *atasthala,* "reckless, foolish things" (3.80.4). Logically, an autocrat should be completely free from jealousy since he has all good things. But, in fact, the autocrat envies the best men, associates with the worst, assumes (or imagines) slanders against him, and rejects both mild and excessive flattery (3.80.4–5). Otanes concludes by listing the tyrant's defining abuses: "He disrupts ancestral customs [*nomaia . . . patria*], sexually assaults women, and kills men without trial" (3.80.5).

Recognizing the evils of monarchy, Otanes argues that the "multitude" (*plēthos*) should rule. He calls this "political equality" (*isonomiē,* a noun combining *isos* "equal" and *nomos,* "law/custom/tradition"). The term was closely connected to *demokratia* and to *isēgoriē,* "equality of speech," the term Herodotus himself uses in describing democratic Athens (5.78).[8] The concept of "equality before the law" could be understood as the antithesis of monarchy or tyranny, and it lacked negative connotations that the term *dēmokratia* might have had for Herodotus's contemporaries.[9] Praising *isonomiē* as *pantōn kalliston,* "most noble (or beautiful) of all," Otanes extols its method of assigning political offices by lottery, holding magistrates accountable, and publicly presenting planning and policy. Otanes urges, therefore, "that we give up the monarchy and elevate the multitude [*plēthos*] to power. For in the majority is everything" (3.80.6).

In advocating majority rule, Otanes, this sixth-century BCE Persian nobleman, anachronistically describes the democratic procedures existing in the Athens of Herodotus's times a century later. Unlike the *representative* democratic republic of the modern United States, the radical Athenian democracy of the mid-fifth century BCE gave every male citizen, regardless of birth or wealth, a direct vote on policies (as in modern referenda). The Athenians selected nearly all political officehold-

ers not by election but by lottery, with candidates drawn from
the ten political "tribes" (artificial geographical groupings instituted by Cleisthenes in 508 BCE). Terms of office were limited
to one year, and men could not hold office more than once
every ten years. The system rested on the assumption that every
male citizen had an equal capacity to govern in the best interests of the community. To uncover any corruption or ineptitude, the Athenians also instituted a required, post-term public
euthunē, "audit," for officeholders. Deciding that military leadership alone required specific experience and expertise, the
Athenians chose ten generals annually (and without term limits) not by lottery but by election. They elected the great Athenian statesman and general Pericles, for example, twenty-nine
times.

Otanes' critique of monarchy and his anachronistic description of majority rule inadvertently expose logical incon-
sistencies in his argument. Otanes criticizes autocrats for
violating law, custom, and tradition (3.80.5). And his preferred
system of *isonomiē*, "political equality," may best promote individual freedoms and sustain rule by institutions and laws
rather than by unreliable human beings.[10] But Otanes fails to
acknowledge that rule by the multitude or "political equality"
itself constitutes a break with tradition (*nomoi*) by introducing
new norms and practices—including accountability, never a
feature of the traditional power structures of monarchy or ar-
istocracy. In attempting to constrain abuses of democratic authority by regularly investigating magistrates after their year of
service, the Athenians show a novel appreciation for the value
of public accountability. (Our own representative democratic
republic, by contrast, despite efforts to increase regulation or
"transparency," often fails to deter corruption or incompetence
or to hold public officials to account.) But Herodotus's contemporaries were only just beginning to recognize the tyrannical

potential of majoritarian voting itself. Athenian tragedies began to expose the dangers of mob rule (ochlocracy).[11] We can be even less naïve today. History demonstrates repeatedly that a majority vote, whether by referendum or by elected or appointed officials, is no guarantee of a just decision. We know that majorities often succumb to irrational passions and violate minority rights. A majority vote can validate and perpetuate traditional racist or misogynist customs. A majority vote can commend and even commit atrocities. Otanes ignores the fact that a direct democratic vote by all citizens offers scant protection against injustice. He fails to notice the glaring paradox in his own argument: majority rule rests on the assumption that an autocrat cannot restrain his own passions but that everyone else can.

Unlike Otanes, the next speaker, Megabyzus, recognizes the tyrannical potential of rule by the many, but he fails to perceive the same potential in oligarchy, or rule by the few, his preferred regime type. Accepting Otanes' critique of autocracy, Megabyzus criticizes majority rule for its ignorance and lack of restraint (issues never addressed by Otanes in commending *isonomiē*). Megabyzus attributes to the mob the same *hubris* that Otanes identifies in the tyrant, insisting that "there is nothing more devoid of understanding and fuller of reckless, self-destructive violence [*hubristoteron*] than a useless mob" (3.81.1). It is utterly intolerable, Megabyzus argues, to substitute the *hubris* of the *akolastou dēmou,* the "unrestrained" or "undisciplined" common people, for the *hubris* of the tyrant. The tyrant at least acts knowingly; the people do not. How could they? They have no education. They have never seen anything *kalon*, "noble," or *oikeion*, "proper." They shove and fall upon matters without any understanding, like a rain-swollen river torrent (3.81.2) Ignoring the tyrannical potential of an exclusive few, Megabyzus advocates oligarchy. Let our enemies be ruled by the *demos,* "the people," not us, he insists. We ourselves should select an assembly of the best men and bestow power on these, including ourselves, of course (3.81.3).

Darius, speaking third, suffers from similar selective vision, seeing the tyrannical potential of both majority rule and oligarchy but not monarchy, his preferred regime type. Darius completely ignores the recent example of Cambyses.[12] And he never addresses Otanes' criticisms of autocracy. Instead, Darius accepts Megabyzus's critique of majority rule but not his praise for oligarchy. Positing the theoretically best example of each of these three systems, Darius argues that monarchy far exceeds rule by the few or rule by the people (3.82.1), for the "best" man would, by definition, rule best. Darius criticizes oligarchy for failings never addressed by Megabyzus, claiming that oligarchs' competition for power produces private quarrels, political factions, and bloody civil strife, with monarchy the result (3.82.2–3). If the people rule, Darius claims, the result is the same: monarchy. The people conspire together and rule badly, until someone steps forward, stops the evildoers, earns admiration, and becomes monarch. Since both oligarchy and majority rule result in monarchy, Darius deems monarchy best (3.82.4). Under a monarch, the Persians gained freedom, Darius maintains, referring to Cyrus's liberation of Persia from subjugation to the Medes, and they should not abandon their traditional customs (3.82.5). (Persians believed that prior to Cyrus they had been subject to the Medes, though the claim is doubtful and lacks corroborating archaeological evidence.)[13] Freedom, for Darius, means liberation not from an autocrat but from foreign control.[14]

Darius's association of monarchy with freedom from foreign domination would have had deeply ironic and nontheoretical associations for Herodotus's Greek contemporaries in the 440s and 430s BCE. Democratic freedoms within Athens did not deter Athenian tyranny over subject states, still euphemistically termed "allies." But avoiding using the terms *turannis,* "tyranny," and *basileia,* "kingship," Herodotus's Darius invites critical Greek (as well as our own) self-reflection on autocratic power.[15] Having succeeded in repelling Persian imperial conquest a generation earlier (479 BCE), newly democratic Athens had in many respects come to replace Persia as a bullying, tyrannical imperial power now battling a Spartan-led Peloponnesian League. The Peloponnesians claimed to be fighting to liberate Greece from tyrannical domination by Athens, but this too seemed laughable. The Spartans' own tyrannical behavior following the Persian Wars had in fact spurred many Greek states to reject Spartan leadership and ally instead behind Athens.[16]

Anachronistically attributing these political arguments for "rule by the many," "rule by the few," and "rule by the one" to Persian speakers of a century before his own time, Herodotus crafts a caricature of democratic discussion and deliberation. It is not a debate, since it includes no exchange of ideas. No speaker ever addresses criticisms leveled at his own argument. And after each speaker states his opinion, four of the seven conspirators declare for Darius's recommendation of monarchy. Herodotus emphasizes the ironic outcome, as this majority vote results in autocracy (3.83.1). (Exemplifying identical absurdity, modern democratic elections sometimes elect "presidents for life.")[17] Herodotus further mocks the Persian conspirators by using democratic language to detail their undemocratic decisions. Stating that *sphi edokse,* "it seemed best to them," to exempt Otanes and his family from the monarchy (3.84.1), the Seven deploy official democratic terminology used by the Athenians a century later to announce political resolutions. Used as a legal term, *dokeō* announced decrees enacted by the *Boulē,* "Council," or *dēmos,* "Assembly/People" (as in *edokse tēi boulēi*, "it seemed best to the Council," or *edokse tēi dēmōi*, "it seemed best to the People"). Herodotus has Darius use the same official democratic language in relating the terms of the contest to his groom, as Darius explains *hēmin dedoktai*, "it seemed best to us" (3.85.1).

Laughable for their debate-that-is-not-a-debate and their democratically determined choice of monarchy, the Persians also ignore history and logic. The recent example of the crazed King Cambyses should promote skepticism regarding the theoretical construct of a "perfect" monarch. Actual autocrats—ancient and modern—tend to be mad and murderous (think Hitler, Stalin, Mao, Kim Jong Un, Putin). Even a perfect monarch would infantilize citizens, depriving them of adult autonomy and the responsibilities and freedoms of self-governance. And even a perfect monarch cannot guarantee an equally perfect successor or a peaceful transfer of power.

Ignoring recent experience and uncritically accepting Darius's arguments for rule by the one "best" man, the Persians should at least ask: Which qualities should this "best" man possess? How can we select for the person who is best in these qualities? Unlike the other six conspirators, Otanes, proponent of majority rule, realizes that they will have to choose lots, entrust the decision to the multitude, or use some other contrivance. But he opts himself out of the contest and his entire family out of the system since he wishes "neither to rule nor be ruled" (3.83.2–3). The other six conspirators, after establishing special privileges for themselves, adopt an inane selection procedure, deciding to ride out of the city at dawn and see whose horse neighs first. That man will be king (3.84.2–3).[18]

Thinking perhaps to leave the decision to divine will or chance, the Persians in fact select not for intelligence, wisdom, restraint, or benevolence but for unscrupulous cleverness. Persians seem to have used horses for divination.[19] But Herodotus's readers see that instead of identifying the "best" man for autocratic rule, the chosen selection procedure exposes the group to deception by its most dishonest, unprincipled member. Darius does not even devise his cheating method himself. His groom cleverly leads Darius's favorite mare and his stallion outside the city and lets them have sex (3.85). The next day, approaching that same place and recalling the fun of the day before, Darius's stallion whinnies (3.86.1). Herodotus also records a second version of this trick similarly involving the craftiness not of Darius but of his groom (3.87).

This counterproductive selection process elevates to the kingship a man lacking any qualms about cheating and perhaps least temperamentally suited to wise leadership. Previously, describing the conspiracy against the Magi, Herodotus contrasts the prudence of Otanes, the subsequent advocate of *isonomiē*, "political equality," with the rashness and ruthlessness of Darius. In planning the attack on the Magi, Otanes advises caution, restraint, and careful preparation (3.71.3), whereas Darius urges speed and prompt action (3.71.2). Darius threatens to expose the plot if the conspirators do not act immediately (3.71.5). He identifies lying and telling the truth as both aiming at the same goal (3.72.4), insisting that if gain were not the issue "equally the truthful man would be false and the lying man truthful" (3.72.5). Darius's certainty that everyone lies or tells the truth only for personal benefit undermines his subsequent praise for monarchy, as he has thus already blithely admitted that self-interest, not fact, determines his statements. Denigrating truth as purely opportunism, Darius prefigures the modern autocrat or would-be autocrat who dupes gullible devotees by insisting illogically, "Everyone lies. Believe me: trust no one."

Choosing Darius, the Persians gain a king who, as Herodotus's contemporaries well knew, will subsequently launch a vengeful, opportunistic, and spectacularly unsuccessful attack on Greece. In book 6, Herodotus will describe Darius's defeat by the Greeks at Marathon (490 BCE). Darius retreats afterward to Persia, determined to rebuild his forces and make another attempt, but he dies before he can attack Greece again. Darius's son Xerxes will replicate his father's vengeance-fueled quest, launching a second invasion of Greece (480–479 BCE) with similarly disastrous results—for Persia (described in books 7 through 9). Prostrating themselves before their new soon-to-prove-incompetent king (3.86.2), an act Greeks considered appropriate only toward gods,[20] these Persian noblemen appear both simple-minded and self-destructive.

We may laugh at the Persians' counterproductive selection process, but we should not feel too smug about modern democratic methods for choosing political officeholders. Modern political campaigns and elections frequently elevate people who are good at campaigning but not necessarily good at governing. Campaigning for election requires an aptitude (and enthusiasm) for pandering to constituents and financial backers and the charisma, impulsiveness, and even outrageousness that attract media attention. Governing requires self-restraint, forethought, wisdom, and compassion. Tragically, modern democratic selection processes tend to repel those who are most capable of ruling wisely and well.

Using a parody of debate and choosing monarchy by majority vote, the Persian noblemen ask the wrong question, and they get the wrong answer. They ask, what is the best form of government? The framers of the United States Constitution had the wisdom to ask instead, *what is the least bad form of government?* In consequence, the framers devised a system combining elements of monarchy (the executive or presidency), oligarchy (the Congress), and rule by the many (one vote per citizen). Perceiving the fundamental paradox of democratic theory, that the tyrant cannot restrain his passions but everyone else can, the framers instituted many checks and balances in the system. Winston Churchill accurately observed, "No one pretends that democracy is perfect or all-wise. Indeed, it has been said that democracy is the worst form of Government except for all those other forms that have been tried from time to time."[21]

This "least bad" system of equality for all under law (*isonomiē*) places serious demands on every citizen. Herodotus's tale of the Persians' non-debate and its consequences cautions against asking the wrong questions and failing to address counterarguments. The Persians' counterproductive method of selecting their monarch challenges modern democracies to devise election processes ensuring selection of the "best" leaders, that is, leaders able to respect the rule of law and the humanity of political opponents, leaders capable of promoting the public interest, not merely their own. In helping to craft the U.S. Constitution, John Adams famously sought to create a government not of men but of laws. The rule of law serves to rein in democracy's worst tendencies, constraining the tyrannical impulses of individuals and groups large and small. But preservation of the rule of law depends on the ability of human beings to recognize the necessity for law and their determination to maintain it. Since laws and judicial decisions will produce outcomes pleasing to some but not others, preservation of the rule of law requires everyone's commitment to seeking change exclusively by legal, peaceful means. The survival of the rule of law requires universal adherence to democratic norms of self-restraint, accountability, tolerance, compromise, and mutual cooperation.

Because it requires egalitarian ideals, institutions, and norms, democracy is novel, not normal. Consequently, democracy alarms and infuriates traditionalists—and rightly so, for it disrupts ancient hierarchical traditions. The rule of law has

the potential, for example, to overturn traditional misogynistic and racist norms often perpetuated by not only minority
but also majority rule. Disruption of traditional hierarchical
norms engenders anger and fear in people previously benefit-
ing from established political and social inequality. Even self-
proclaimed proponents of equality often strive not to eradicate
but to reverse traditional power relationships—a result achieved
by many so-called revolutionary movements. Regardless of
political party affiliation, today's extremists—radicals and conservatives alike—seek to impose hierarchies of power and opportunity. Targeting democratic institutions and norms,
extremists suppress dissent, introduce violence into the political
process, and erode civil liberties and human rights. Acceptance
of—or embrace of—political violence degrades the rule of
law regardless of the specific motivating moral conviction. Violations of democratic laws and norms produce reciprocal
violations, serving authoritarian ends in an ever-escalating,
destructive cycle. Extremists of diverse, even antithetical, ideological certainties ironically collaborate in undermining the
rule of law and promoting traditional authoritarian methods
and goals. Discrimination is historically normal. Equality for
all under law is not.

Herodotus demonstrates the need to reject traditional
hierarchical norms in favor of a historically anomalous form
of government, equality for all under the law (*isonomie*). In
depicting a failed Persian effort to compare and evaluate types
of political regimes, Herodotus highlights by counterexample
the valuable potential of democratic discussion and group
decision-making. Showing the foolishness of the Persians'
choice of monarchy and their selection of an unwise, unscrupulous, greedy monarch, Herodotus exposes the need for
actual, productive debate, farsighted reasoning, and merit-based
leadership. In this pseudo-debate and its aftermath, Herodotus

indirectly identifies the qualities of the "best" political authority: not unscrupulous cleverness but wisdom, forethought,
self-restraint, and concern for the welfare of others. Of the
three options proposed—rule by the many, rule by the few, rule
by the one—only the first offers the possibility of merit-based
leadership, oversight, and accountability. The story highlights
by counterexample the constructive potential of rule by the
many—but only if guided and constrained by law, accountability, and a wise appreciation for the value of both.

12

On Empiricism

Returning to his interests in geography and ethnography in book 4, Herodotus describes Scythia and its inhabitants, offering the earliest surviving geographic and ethnographic account of the Black Sea region (modern-day Bulgaria, Romania, Ukraine, south Russia, and Georgia), an area not entirely unknown to Herodotus's Greek contemporaries.[1] In contrast to his record of his travels in Egypt, it is not certain that Herodotus actually visited Scythia.[2] But here, too, Herodotus delivers a combination of both factual and fictional information, challenging some traditional Greek ideas but accepting others.[3] Meditating on the relationships among geography, culture, and power, Herodotus presents the Scythians as a surprising hybrid, possessing characteristics of both "others" and Greeks.[4]

Though Herodotus views Scythia through a Greek lens, his description promotes rational assessment of empirical evidence. Herodotus has even been called "the father of empiricism."[5] He models recognizably empirical methods, comparing and contrasting the foreign with the familiar. The process facilitates learning from the experiences of others. As in his account of Egypt, Herodotus includes as factual evidence not only claims of his own direct observation but also tales heard from local people. He subjects both types of evidence to logical critique. He integrates his geographic and ethnographic investigation into his main theme, the conflict between East and West. His empirical study of Scythia depicts the Scythians, in their unexpectedly successful resistance to Persian invasion, as a constructive model for any populace confronting existential threats. Herodotus begins with the evidence of three competing tales of the Scythians' origin:

[4.5] The Scythians say their own people is the youngest of all peoples and that it came to be in the following way: the first man to come into existence in this land—when it was not yet inhabited—had the name Targitaos. The Scythians say that the parents of this Targitaos were Zeus and the daughter of the river Borysthenes. This does not seem credible to me, but they do say it. [2] They say that Targitaos came into existence from some such origin, and he had three sons: Lipoxaïs, Arpoxaïs, and the youngest, Kolaxaïs. [3] During the reign of these sons, some pieces made of gold flew from the sky and fell into Scythia: a plow, a yoke, a single-edged axe, and a drinking bowl. They say that the eldest son, seeing the things first, went nearer, wishing to take hold of them. But as he approached, the gold caught fire. [4] When the eldest withdrew, the second son approached—and the gold did the same thing. They say that the gold surely drove these two away. But at the approach of the third and youngest son the fire went out, and he carried the gold things away to his home. In response to these events, the Scythians say, the older brothers agreed to give the whole kingdom to the youngest brother.

[4.6] From Lipoxaïs were born these Scythians who are called the race of the Auchatai. From the middle brother, Arpoxaïs, were born the Scythians who are called the Katiaroi and the Traspies. And from the youngest of them were born the royal ones who are called Paralatai. [2] The name for all of them together is Skolotoi, named after their king. But the Greeks named them Scythians. And this is how the Scythians say that they themselves came to be.

[4.7] And the Scythians say that all the years that occurred from the first king Targitaos to the crossing over of Darius against themselves were not more than a thousand— but just so many. The kings guard this sacred gold with greatest care. Every year, they approach it with prayers, propitiating it with great sacrifices. [2] It is said by the Scythians that whoever falls asleep in the open air while holding the sacred gold in the festival does not live out the year. Because of this, they say, the man is given as much land as he can ride around on his horse in one day. Since the country is large, Kolaxaïs established three kingdoms for his children, and he made one of these the largest—the one in which the gold is guarded. [3] The Scythians say that the area above—toward the North Wind [understood as a divinity by Herodotus's contemporaries] and belonging to the people dwelling above this region—is impossible to see or to traverse further because of the feathers pouring down. For they say that both the land and the air are full of feathers and these prevent viewing. [Herodotus later explains that he thinks by "feathers" the Scythians mean snowflakes (4.31).]

[4.8] The Scythians speak thus about themselves and the region above them. But the Greeks who inhabit the Pontus [region on the southern coast of the Black Sea] say the following: they claim that Heracles [= Hercules], driving the cattle of Geryon [a mythical monster with three heads and three bodies, three heads and one body, or three bodies and one head], reached this land which was then uninhabited— the land that the Scythians now occupy. [2] The Greeks say that Geryon lived beyond the Pontus, inhabiting the island Erytheia [mythical home of Geryon] near Gēdeira beyond the Pillars of Heracles [promontories flanking entrance to the Strait of Gibraltar] on the edge of the divinity Ocean. In a story [logōi], they claim that Ocean begins from the rising sun and flows around the entire earth. But they do not prove this by fact [ergōi]. [3] Hence, the Greeks say that when Heracles arrived in the land now called Scythian, winter and icy cold took hold of him. Drawing his lionskin up over himself, he went to sleep. And his mares that were pasturing in this spot, yoked to the chariot, vanished—they say—by a divine chance.

[4.9] And the Greeks say that when Heracles awoke, he searched, traversing every part of the area. Finally, he came to the land called Hylaia [the only wooded region in Scythia]. And there, they say, he found in a cave some half-girl, double-formed viper. The parts of her above the buttocks were that of a woman, the parts below that of a snake. [2] Seeing her and marveling, Heracles asked her if she had seen his mares wandering anywhere. She declared that she herself had them and that she would not return them to Heracles until he had sex with her. And Heracles did have sex with her for this payment. [3] But she kept delaying the return of the mares, wishing to be with Heracles for as long as possible. She knew that once he had the mares, he would want to depart. Finally returning them, she said, "I saved these horses for you when they arrived here. And you provided a reward, for I have three sons from you. [4] When these are full grown, what is it necessary to do? Tell me. Am I to settle them here (for I myself hold power over this land), or am I to send them to you?" The Greeks say that she asked this and that Heracles responded, [5] "When you see that the boys have become men, you would not err in doing the following: the one whom you see stretching this bow to its fullest extent and girding himself with this belt in this way, make this one an inhabitant of this land. But whoever of them falls short of these deeds which I command, send him away from the land. And doing these things you yourself will be glad, and you will do what I have commanded."

[4.10] They say that having drawn one of his bows (for until then he carried two), and having shown her the belt, Heracles handed over both the bow and the belt. On the end of its clasp, the belt had a golden drinking bowl. Having given her these things, Heracles went away. And when the boys became men, she gave these names to them: Agathyrsus to one, Gelonos to the next, and Scythes to the youngest. And remembering the command, she did what Heracles had bidden. [2] And, surely, two of her sons, Agathyrsus and Gelonos, could not accomplish the test set before them, and they went out of the land, banished by the woman who bore them. But the Greeks say that the youngest of them, Scythes, completed the test and remained in the land. [3] And from Scythes, son of Heracles, say the Greeks, the kings of the Scythians are always descended. And from the drinking cup on Heracles' belt, the Scythians carry drinking bowls hanging from their belts to this day. This alone his mother contrived for Scythes. And these are the things that the Greeks who inhabit Pontus say.

[4.11] There is also another story that maintains the following (and I myself subscribe to this story most): It is said that the Scythians, dwelling as nomads in Asia, being hard-pressed in war by the Massagetai, went away, crossing the river Araxes to Cimmerian land. (For the land which the Scythians now occupy is said to have been long ago that of the Cimmerians.) [2] At the approach of the Scythians, the Cimmerians took counsel, since a great army was approaching. And, of course, their opinions were divided, and fervent on both sides. But the better opinion was that of the Royals, the nobles ruling Scythia. For, surely, the opinion of the people [*dēmou*] held that the right way would be to depart and that it was not necessary to venture into danger against many men. But the opinion of the Royals was to fight it out for the land against the invaders. [3] Neither, therefore, were the people willing to be persuaded by the Royals, nor the Royals by the people. The people, surely, planned to depart from the land without a fight and hand it over to the invaders. But it seemed best to the Royals to lie in their own land when they had died and not to flee with the people. They calculated how many good things they had experienced and how many evils were likely to overtake them in fleeing from their homeland. [4] Since this seemed best to them, the Royals divided themselves, and being equal in number they fought against each other. All dead by their own hands, the Royals were buried by the Cimmerian people beside the river Tyras. (And their grave is still visible.) Having buried the Royals in this way, the people made their exodus from the land. And the Scythians, entering, took possession of a desolate land.

[4.12] Even now in the Scythian country there are Cimmerian walls, and there are Cimmerian ferry crossings. There is also a section of land named Cimmerian. And there is a Bosporus called Cimmerian. [2] It appears that the Cimmerians, fleeing the Scythians into Asia, founded the peninsula on which the Greek city of Sinope is now situated. It is also clear that the Scythians, pursuing them, attacked the Median land, having mistaken the road. [3] For the Cimmerians always fled along the land beside the sea. But the Scythians, holding the Caucasus on the right, pursued the Cimmerians until where they made the incursion into the Median land, having been turned toward the inland part of the road. And this is another story told in common by both Greeks and barbarians.

[4.13] And Aristaeus, son of Kaustrobios, a man of Proconnesus [modern Marmara Island, Turkey] said, in poetic verse, that he reached the tribe of the Issedones. Inspired by Phoibos Apollo, Aristaeus describes one-eyed men, the Arimaspians, living above the Issedones, and above these, the gold-guarding griffins, and above these the Hyperboreans [mythical people living at the northernmost part of the world] extending as far as the sea. [2] According to Aristaeus, these peoples—except for the Hyperboreans and beginning with the Arimaspians—always attacked neighboring peoples. And the Issedones were driven out from the land by the Arimaspians, and the Scythians by the Issedones. And the Cimmerians, living beside the southern sea, being hard-pressed by the Scythians, left their land. Thus, not even this account of Aristaeus agrees with the Scythians concerning this land.

Reporting these three different accounts of the Scythians' origins one after the other, Herodotus demonstrates his method of empirical analysis: assemble the evidence and subject it to rational, comparative scrutiny. Both the Scythian and Greek accounts contain folktale motifs and supernatural elements, including the fairy-tale standard three sons, three attempts, and a successful youngest son. Both include an ancestor of divine origin: Targitaos, in the Scythian account, born from Zeus and the daughter of a river, and Heracles, in the Greek account (also a son of Zeus, as Herodotus's Greek audience knew). In the Scythian tale, four golden objects fall magically from the sky and suddenly burst into flames, but the fire mysteriously subsides at the approach of the youngest brother.[6] The Greek version includes vanishing horses and a woman who is half female, half snake. Herodotus finds the claim of Targitaos's supernatural birth not credible (4.5.1). His preferred version is undoubtedly inaccurate,[7] but it contains neither folktale elements nor supernatural features. Herodotus also provides corroborating material evidence, maintaining that monuments still visible in the region support the story that the Scythians as nomads moved west from Asia to the region beyond the Black Sea, inciting the natives to flee (4.11–12). Herodotus finds further corroboration in the poetry of Aristaeus (4.13). In offering three tales and sanctioning only the third, he mirrors the pattern in the first two stories (three contenders and the third the winner).

Herodotus disdains the supernatural origin stories, but comparison nevertheless proves illuminating. In categorizing the world as "Greek" and "other," Herodotus exemplifies a rational method for examining evidence and engaging with otherness: identify both contrasts and similarities. This approach is comparable to the approach of ancient medical science.[8] And the effort produces valuable knowledge. Folklore and magic aside, the first two tales contrast Scythian with Greek ideals of achievement, suggesting that the Scythians ascribe success to luck, chance, or destiny, whereas the Greeks attribute success to personal prowess. In the Scythian version, the youngest son succeeds where his older brothers have failed because—well, he just does. The flaming objects magically stop burning at his approach. Distinguished merely as the youngest, this son demonstrates no particular skill or ability. In the Greek account, however, the third son succeeds by performing physical actions beyond his brothers' capabilities, drawing the bow and girding himself with the belt.

Herodotus's empiricism exemplifies not only rational comparison of evidence but also this Greek ideal of personal effort and achievement. Touring Scythia, he emphasizes his laborious endeavor to gather and assess eyewitness evidence, his own and others.' He acknowledges the limits of empirical investigation: the lack of eyewitnesses for the most distant regions (e.g., 4.16.1–2 and 4.25), difficulties posed by diverse languages (4.24), contradictions in secondhand information (e.g., 4.81.1). Whenever possible, Herodotus references corroborating material evidence: for example, affirming his claim regarding the number of Scythians with a huge bronze bowl made from melted arrowheads, one provided by each Scythian (81.3–6).

In Scythia, as in Egypt, Herodotus reveals the guiding influence of cultural assumptions. Just as a preconception of Egyptians as entirely "opposite" to Greeks shapes his depiction of Egypt, the certainty that the Scythians are both very unlike Greeks and also very like Greeks shapes Herodotus's account of Scythia.[9] Arduously assembling all available evidence, Herodotus depicts the Scythians as distinctly foreign in their cultural practices. Historical continuities in the region and surviving material evidence corroborate some of Herodotus's claims.[10] Archaeological evidence largely supports Herodotus's account of Scythian burial customs, including the strangling of numerous servants and horses and posing them around the burial site (4.72–73), ritual cannibalism (1.216.2–3; 4.26.1), scalping slain enemies (4.64), the use of human skulls as drinking cups (4.65), fondness for collecting the heads of dead enemies as trophies (4.103.3), and a penchant for intoxicating substances (4.75.1–2).

Herodotus characterizes Scythians as lacking rational self-control. Their liking for undiluted wine (e.g., 6.84) distances them from "normal" human practice as the Greeks understood it.[11] Ancient Greeks greatly diluted their wine with water, and they associated undiluted wine with lack of self-restraint and with feminine weakness. In Greek myth, Odysseus gives undiluted wine to the monstrous Cyclops to make him drunk and outsmart him.[12] Ancient Greeks attributed the drinking of undiluted wine to satyrs, comic hybrid creatures composed of human and bestial features. Attendants of the wine god Dionysus, satyrs constitute a counter-model for human beings, for they lack the human capacity to restrain their passions, sexual or otherwise.[13] Ancient Greeks aligned self-control with human beings as distinct from beasts, but more specifically with men, defining lack of self-control as a female characteristic.[14]

In recording the Scythians' un-Greek customs and proclivities, Herodotus highlights the Scythians' perhaps most questionable trait of all: their narrow xenophobia and blanket rejection of foreign ways. In contrast to Herodotus, manifestly interested in learning about and from others, the Scythians fear foreign practices. Herodotus cites the examples of the Scythian Anarcharsis, murdered by his own brother for adopting Greek religious rites honoring Cybele, mother of the gods (4.76), and the Scythian king Skyles, who prompts a popular rebellion and gets murdered by *his* brother for adopting Greek rites in honor of Dionysus, god of wine, madness, and revelry (4.78–80). From these stories, Herodotus concludes, "Thus do the Scythians protect their own customs [*nomaia*], and so great are the penalties they inflict on those who acquire additional foreign ways [*nomous*]" (4.80.5). These anecdotes of individual Scythians open to foreign customs complicate Herodotus's portrait of the distinction between the foreign and the familiar.[15] Herodotus implies, too, that some Greeks share Scythian closed-mindedness.[16] In exposing Scythian resistance to foreign ways, Herodotus implicitly critiques similar opposition to foreign influences among his Greek contemporaries.[17]

Herodotus's empiricism precludes such xenophobia but not prejudice. He does not fear foreign customs, as he claims Scythians do, but he *does* share the racial prejudice of his

Greek contemporaries. Accepting the Greek conception of two categories of identity, Greek and *barbaros*, "other," Herodotus is recognizably racist: he identifies characteristics not just typical of different peoples but inevitable for members of that group. But this prejudice—it is worth repeating—does not precisely align with modern racism. Herodotus does not base his prejudices and preferences on skin color or physical features— just as slavery in ancient Greece had nothing to do with skin color or ethnicity. Herodotus shows prejudice in attributing to individuals the characteristics of their ethnic group. But unlike modern racists, Herodotus defines group identity not by physical appearance but by geography, culture, and language.

And, crucially, although Herodotus displays prejudice in emphasizing the strangeness of Scythian cultural practices and geography, he focuses on their strategic *advantages*. Herodotus depicts Scythians as nomads, lacking Greek-style *poleis*, "citizen-communities," and inhabiting a region without typical geographic boundaries. He disparages the peoples of the area as *amathestata*, "most lacking in knowledge" (4.46.1), but he views the Scythians as an exception, because "by the Scythian race has been discovered most cleverly [*sophōtata*] of all the peoples that we know [*idmen*] the one greatest thing of all human affairs—though I do not, however, admire them in other respects. This is the greatest thing that has been discovered by them: how to prevent the escape of anyone attacking them. And if they do not wish to be found, they make it impossible for anyone to catch them. For the Scythians have no established citadels or walls. Carrying their households with them, they are all archers mounted on horses. They live not by cultivating fields but from their herds. Having their dwellings on carts, how would these people not be unconquerable and impossible to engage with?" (4.46.2–3). Though these claims are not factually true of all Scythians, Herodotus draws the deduction from the region's geography: expansive, grass-covered plains well watered by numerous rivers (4.47.1). Herodotus considers these rivers the Scythians' "greatest resources" (4.59.1) and the most significant feature of their land, "greatest by far and most plentiful in number" (4.82.1).

Herodotus splices his lengthy description of the Scythians' strategically advantageous lifestyle and geography into his account of Persian military expansion. Book 4 opens with the Persian king Darius's decision to attack Scythia. Motivated by a passion for revenge, like Cambyses in attacking Egypt (3.1–3), Darius wants to punish the Scythians for their earlier invasion of Media (4.1.1–2). After describing Scythian customs and geography, Herodotus returns in chapter 83 to Darius's planned expedition. Darius's brother tries unsuccessfully to dissuade him from attacking, "detailing the difficulty of dealing with the Scythians. Though giving good advice, he did not persuade Darius, and he stopped. And when all was prepared for Darius, he led out his army from Susa" (4.83.1–2). Herodotus can have had no direct evidence for this conversation, but the anecdote makes for good dramatic foreshadowing.

Herodotus's portrait of Darius revisits, in passing, the horrors of autocratic power so prominent in the portrait of Darius's tyrannical predecessor Cambyses (book 3). Passionate for vengeance and impervious to his brother's good advice, Darius mirrors not only Cambyses' revenge-fueled decision to attack Egypt but his rejection of his sister's sensible warning (3.32; 4.83.1–2). Darius also shares Cambyses' callous cruelty; he diabolically murders all three sons of a Persian who has the temerity to request exemption from military service for one son. Darius maliciously pretends kindness, replying to the man that "since he was a friend and making a reasonable request, he was going to leave behind all of his sons" (4.84.1). Delighted, the man expects his sons to be exempt from the campaign. Instead,

Darius orders all three killed. They do remain behind, dead
(4.84.2). Vengeful and jealous, Darius also executes a governor,
previously stationed in Egypt by Cambyses, for daring to rival
him in minting valuable coins (4.166).

For all his vengeful cruelty, Darius fails to conquer Scythia
(513 BCE), and the Scythians' resistance to invasion prefigures
Greek resistance to Persian invasion decades later.[18] Scythian
geography and lifestyle may be unique.[19] But Darius's attack
against Scythia foreshadows his and his son's failed campaigns
against Greece: Darius crosses into Europe by bridging the Bosporus (4.87–89), just as—Herodotus's contemporaries knew
and Herodotus will later describe—Darius's son Xerxes bridges
the Hellespont to attack Greece (7.33–37). Although described
by Herodotus as primitive, nomadic tribesmen, at the approach
of Darius and his forces, the Scythians immediately recognize
the value of unity. They urge their neighbors to join together
in repelling Darius's invasion, precisely as—again, Herodotus's
contemporaries knew—the Greeks will do years later in defeating Darius and then Xerxes. Herodotus explains that "reflect-
ing among themselves that alone they were not going to be able
to repulse the army of Darius in a fair stand-up fight, the Scythians sent messengers to their neighbors. And the kings of these
neighbors, having already gathered, were planning together
since this great army was attacking them" (4.102.1). Messengers
inform the various *ethnoi*, "peoples," of Scythia that Darius is
advancing from Asia into Europe (4.118).

The Scythians understand, as the Greeks will demonstrate
years later, the principle "united we stand, divided we fall."
Scythian arguments for unity prefigure arguments that Herodotus attributes to Athenians decades later advocating unified
Greek resistance to Persian invasion (8.56–64). The Scythians
seek united opposition to Darius's attack, urging their neighbors not to remain neutral and idle while watching the Persians

destroy Scythians but instead to join in opposing Darius's invasion. The Scythians threaten that otherwise they will either abandon the region or make an agreement with Persia, explaining, "For what are we to suffer if you are unwilling to exact vengeance on the enemy? And after this it won't be any easier at all for you, for the Persian is attacking you as much as us. And it won't suffice him, having subjugated us, to desist from subjugating you" (4.118.3). Herodotus attributes identical arguments to the Greek general Themistocles years later, urging the Greek *poleis* to remain together and fight the Persians at Salamis (480 BCE). When the Peloponnesians threaten to abandon Athens and retreat to the Isthmus of Corinth to defend themselves from there, Themistocles reminds them that defense of Salamis equally protects the Peloponnese and avoids leading the Persians further south (8.60β–γ). Like the Scythians, Themistocles also threatens that otherwise Athens will abandon Greece altogether and sail to Italy (8.62).

Not only rational arguments for unity but also clever strategy, tailored to Scythian geography and lifestyle, enlist the support of even reluctant neighbors. Some neighboring tribes opt to remain neutral unless Darius attacks them directly, arguing that Darius currently targets Scythians alone as payback for injustices that they committed by invading and dominating Persians (4.119). Instead of confronting Darius's forces directly, therefore, the Scythians retreat, using a scorched-earth policy, destroying water sources and grasslands (4.120.1). They intend, Herodotus explains, to lure the Persians into attacking unallied peoples and forcing them to fight (4.120.4). Deceived into thinking that the Scythians are fleeing (4.124), Darius keeps chasing and the Scythians keep retreating into the areas of nonaligned peoples, forcing them to participate in the fight (4.124–128). Continuing to attack and harass the Persian forces, the Scythians compel Darius to accept failure and retreat. (4.134–135).

Although Greek-like in their cleverness and unprecedented success in thwarting Persian invasion, Scythians remain foreign in Herodotus's depiction. Scythians appear like Greeks in their capacity to unify and outsmart Persian invaders, but unlike Greeks in that they themselves fall victim to Greek deception: at the Ister bridge, Ionian Greeks deceive the Scythians by pretending to destroy the bridge—Darius's escape route—but actually leaving it sufficiently intact (4.136–141). Ever after, Herodotus claims, Scythians disparaged the Ionian Greeks as the most worthless cowards of all men and the most devoted slaves (4.142).

Both foreign and familiar, the Scythians constitute empirical evidence of successful resistance to autocratic domination. Throughout the *Histories*, Herodotus ponders why Persian expansion succeeded against so many adversaries and yet failed against Greece in the Persian Wars (490–479 BCE). The defeat of the mighty Persian empire by a loose, Athenian-led coalition of small Greek citizen-communities shocked everyone. Scythia offered an earlier David and Goliath example. Though distinct from Greeks in their foreign ways, the Scythians nevertheless parallel Greeks in their cleverness, determination, and unprecedented success against Persia. We cannot know what Herodotus intended or how his contemporaries experienced his work. But his Greek contemporaries had fathers, uncles, and grandfathers who fought and even died to repel Persian invaders and drive them from Greece. Herodotus's depiction of the Scythians' tactics and their successful prevention of foreign domination would align with his contemporaries' knowledge of Greek resistance during the Persian Wars. Herodotus's observation that "the kings of the Scythians, hearing the name of 'slavery,' were filled with rage" (4.128.1) would remind his contemporaries of their own fathers' and grandfathers' refusal to allow a Persian king to subjugate Greece.

Empiricism enables Herodotus to see beyond ethnic and cultural differences to the commonalities beneath. Not threatened but fascinated by comparing Greeks and "others," Herodotus suggests that the distinction between "self" and "other" is a matter of perspective. Just as he views Egyptians as entirely opposite to Greeks, so, too, he depicts Greeks as "other" from the barbarian perspective.[20] As Herodotus explains in book 3, "custom is king" (3.38). Our own customs may look as bizarre to other people as their customs do to us. In this reminder that every ethnic group constitutes other people's "other," Herodotus does not affirm cultural relativism, the belief that all cultural values are equally valid. Empiricism requires not simply seeing and accepting cultural differences but *evaluating* them on their merits.

As empirical evidence, the Scythians not only prefigure later Greek resistance to Persian invasion but also provide a timeless template. Though ancient Greeks divided the world into "self" versus "others," Greeks had no strong panhellenic identity until the beginning of the fifth century, when Persian invasion encouraged Greeks to unite *as Greeks* to repel a foreign attacker. Hereditary identity, such as Ionian or Dorian, might influence alliances between citizen-communities, but Greeks saw themselves primarily as Athenian or Spartan or Theban, taking their identity from their own *polis*, "citizen-community." And Greek *poleis* battled one another almost incessantly, often with extreme brutality. But half a century after the Persian Wars, Greek citizen-communities survive as independent *poleis* precisely *because* Greeks—like Scythians—united in a time of crisis and used clever stratagems to prevent foreign imperial domination in 490 and 480 BCE.

Like everything that Herodotus commends, rational evaluation of empirical evidence requires effort—and sometimes discomfort. It is much easier to accept without question authoritative narratives that affirm our preconceptions, however prejudicial, fanciful, implausible, or evidence-free those narratives may be. Beginning with differing stories of the origins of the Scythians, Herodotus demonstrates the value of attentive comparative analysis. Though the Scythian origin story and the Greek one conflict, both include folktale and supernatural elements. Comparison reveals a distinctively Greek emphasis on individual effort and achievement. Herodotus discloses his own rational, empiricist predilection in his preference for the third account of the Scythians' origins, a purely rational story lacking any supernatural elements and attributed to no partisan source. Cultural differences can be alarming, distasteful, even repugnant, but by presenting these three stories in succession, Herodotus shows that the arduous process of identifying both otherness and sameness develops understanding.

Modeling a constructive, empiricist examination of Scythia, Herodotus pursues his investigation of the causes, trajectory, and limits of Persia's imperial expansion. He discovers that, unlike Egyptians or Lydians, the Scythians prove unconquerable adversaries. Their resistance to Persian domination affirms the Greek conception of achievement manifest in the Greek tale of the Scythians' origins; Scythian success against Persian invaders derives *not* from luck or destiny but from human resourcefulness and ingenuity. In the bellicose 440s and 430s, with enmities between Greek *poleis* intensifying, Herodotus depicts the Scythians' ability to unite as crucial to their survival. Herodotus's contemporaries failed to heed his message, and the Peloponnesian War (431–404 BCE), a brutal Greek-against-Greek war between the Athenian empire and a Spartan-led Peloponnesian League, exacted a terrible toll on Greece.

Herodotus finds Scythians both like and unlike Greeks and therefore useful as models and counter-models—just as ancient peoples and their experiences can be for us. As our own identities in the United States increasingly fragment into narrow and exclusive familial, ethnic, religious, moral, and/or political groupings, the Scythians provide a constructive paradigm for confronting the existential challenges of today. Modern nation-states, and the communities within them, face not only foreign enemies and global environmental and economic crises but also internal adversaries of political polarization, disinformation, and racial, social, and economic inequities. Suggesting an alternative to fear, lack of resourcefulness, and civil strife, Herodotus offers the Scythians as empirical evidence that unity, courage, and ingenuity promote communal strength. Able to learn from others' experiences, Herodotus validates empiricism as a tool vital to human survival and essential to freedom from foreign domination.

13

On Subjugation

Following his description of the Scythian model of successful self-defense, Herodotus offers a dramatic tale illustrating the costs of subjugation. He begins by reiterating the value of unity, providing a brief counterexample of *unsuccessful* self-defense. Whereas unity empowers the Scythians against invaders, disunity makes the Thracians weak and vulnerable to Persian domination. Although Herodotus identifies the Thracians as "the largest group of people [*ethnos*] of all—after the Indians," divisions between the various tribes make them vulnerable. Failure to unify makes the Thracians susceptible to conquest by a foreign adversary, whereas "if they could be ruled by one man or could all be like-minded [*phroneoi kata tōuto*], they would be unconquerable and the most powerful of all peoples [*ethneōn*] by a lot, in my opinion. But this is impossible for them, and lacking the means, it may never occur. For this reason, surely, they are weak" (5.3.1; and cf. 4.97; 4.118).[1]

As Thrace and Macedon fall under Persian control, Herodotus depicts submission to the Persian empire as an existential threat to Greek independence and values, a complete forfeiture of personal autonomy and moral decision-making. A tale of Persians at the Macedonian court illustrates both the devastations of autocratic subjugation and the costs of gullibility. When the king of Macedon willingly gives to the Persian king "earth and water," the symbols of complete subjection to Persia, he quickly learns that Persian demands do not stop at political surrender:

[5.17] [Following the Persian conquest of Paionia in Macedon, Darius's general] Megabazos . . . sends seven Persian men as messengers to the Macedonian land. These men were the most esteemed [*dokimōtatoi*] in the encamped army after Megabazos himself. These men were sent to Amyntas [king of Macedon] for the purpose of asking [*aitēsontes*] for earth and water for King Darius. [2] From Lake Prasias there is a very short route to the Macedonian land. First, there is a mine next to the lake, from which at a later time a talent of silver came in every day for Alexandros [son of King Amyntas]. After the mine, having crossed the mountain called Dysoron, one is in Macedon.

[5.18] Therefore, when these Persians who had been sent to Amyntas arrived and came into his presence, they asked for [*aiteon*] earth and water for King Darius. Amyntas gave these things, and he also invited the envoys to dine with him as his guests [*epi xeinia kaleei*]. Providing a magnificent dinner, he welcomed the Persians in a friendly manner. [2] When dinner was over, while the Persians were challenging each other in drinking, they said the following: "Macedonian guest-friend [*xeine*], for us Persians it is the custom [*nomos*] that whenever we put forth a great feast, then is the time to bring in our concubines and wedded wives to sit beside us. You now, since you welcomed us readily and you are hosting us greatly [*xeinizeis*]—and gave earth and water to King Darius—follow our custom [*nomōi*]." [3] In response to this, Amyntas said,

"O Persians, this is definitely not our custom. Ours is to keep men separated from women. But since you, being our masters [*despotai*], require this in addition, this also will be done for you." Having said so much, Amyntas sent for the women. And when summoned, they came and seated themselves in order opposite the Persians. [4] Thereupon, the Persians, looking upon the beautiful women, spoke to Amyntas, declaring that the thing that he had done was not wise. It would be better from the start, they said, for the women not to come, than for them to come and sit opposite the men—paining the men's eyes—instead of sitting beside them. [5] Forced by necessity, Amyntas commanded the women to sit beside the Persians. And when the women obeyed, the Persians immediately groped their breasts—these men were so very drunk with wine—and some of the Persians even tried to kiss them.

[5.19] Seeing this, Amyntas remained calm—although he found it very grievous—because he feared the Persians very much. But Alexandros, the son of Amyntas, being present and seeing these things, and being young and inexperienced of evil, could in no way restrain himself any longer. And so, being disgusted, he said the following to Amyntas: "Father, yield to your old age and go away and rest. Do not persist in the drinking. But I, remaining here on the spot, will provide for our guest-friends [*xeinoisi*] all that they need. [2] Understanding that Alexandros was intending to do some rash [or radical/revolutionary] actions [*neotera prēgmata*], Amyntas said, "Son, I understand your words, for you are nearly burning up with anger. I know that you are sending me away because you wish to do something rash [*neoteron*]. I need you, therefore, to do nothing politically disruptive [*neochmōsai*] against these men lest you destroy us. Instead, restrain yourself as you look upon these things that are being done. But concerning my own departure, I will obey you."

[5.20] Having asked this, Amyntas went away. And
Alexandros said to the Persians, "My guest-friends [xeinoi], it
is possible for you to have complete, easy access to these
women, whether you wish to have sex with all of them or
with however many of them you wish. [2] Concerning this,
you yourselves will give the sign. But now—for already
bedtime is almost approaching, and I see that you are full of
strong drink—send these women away to bathe, if it pleases
you. And afterward, welcome them back once they have
bathed. [3] Having said this—for the Persians consented—
Alexandros sent the women away to the women's quarters.
But Alexandros himself made ready, in the women's clothing,
smooth-cheeked young men, equal in number to the women.
And he provided each with a hidden dagger. Bringing in
these men, he said to the Persians, [4] "Persians [Persai], it
seems that you are being entertained hospitably with a
complete banquet lacking nothing. For it includes all the
other things—as many as we had—and in addition we have
supplied to you everything that we could find. And surely
this thing is the greatest of all: we will give to you freely our
own mothers and sisters in order that you may learn how
absolutely honored you are by us for the very things that you
deserve, and also that you may report back to the king who
sent you that a Greek man, his viceroy over the Macedonians,
has entertained you well with a feast and bed." [5] Having
said this, Alexandros seated beside each Persian man a young
Macedonian man disguised as a woman. When the Persians
tried to grope them, the Macedonians destroyed them.

[5.21] These Persians were destroyed by this fate, both
they themselves and their entourage. For, surely, wagons,
servants, and a full, abundant supply of equipment accompa-
nied them. And all of these vanished with all of them. [2] Not
long afterward, the Persians made a great search for these

men. But Alexandros put a stop to it by his cleverness
[*sophiēi*], giving [*dous*] a lot of money and his own
sister—whose name was Gygaia. Alexandros stopped the
search by giving [*dous*] these things to Boubares, a Persian
man, the general commanding the ones who were seeking
the men who had perished. The death of these Persians,
having been checked in this way, was passed over in silence.

[5.22] That these descendants of Perdiccas [the Macedo-
nians] were Greeks, as they themselves claim, I myself
happen to know. And, surely, in later stories I will show that
they are Greeks [8.137–9]. In addition, those of the Greeks
who manage the athletic contest at Olympia know that this is
so. [2] For when Alexandros chose to compete and went
down to the arena for this purpose, those of the Greeks who
were going to run the race excluded him, declaring that the
competition was to be contested not by barbarians but by
Greeks. But when Alexandros proved that he was from the
Greek citizen-community of Argos, he was judged to be a
Greek. And competing in the footrace, Alexandros tied for
first place. Now, these events occurred in this way.

This anecdote of Persian envoys at the court of the Macedonian king, with details including direct dialogue, emerges
as another of Herodotus's instructive parables, an educational
tale rather than a verifiably historical event. The tale may orig-
inate in Macedonian propaganda, but its numerous ironies and
ambiguities make it anything but a straightforward commendation of Macedonians as Greeks.[2] Herodotus here dramatizes
the high stakes of foreign domination. The Scythians' experience suggests that unity empowers resistance to foreign aggression (book 4). By contrast, acceptance of subjugation to Persia
makes the Macedonians vulnerable to Persian lack of self-
control, lack of respect for foreign customs, and abuse of greater

military power. Identifying the Persian king's envoys as *dokimōtatoi*, "most esteemed," among the Persians (5.17.1), Herodotus implicitly disparages Persian value judgments, as these men, highly respected in Persia, behave most improperly toward their Macedonian hosts. The envoys arrive "for the purpose of asking [*aitēsontes*] for earth and water," that is, for voluntary acceptance of complete subjection to the Persian king's authority (5.17.1). But the verb *aiteō* (repeated at 5.18.1) means both "to ask" and "to demand." The verb's force depends on the relative status of the one making and the one receiving the request/demand. Given the Persians' greater military might, if they "ask" for voluntary subjection, they "demand" it.

And subjugation has escalating costs. Having accepted Persian domination without a fight, the obliging Macedonian king invites the Persian envoys to dinner, offering friendly and generous hospitality (5.18.1). After dinner, the Persians demand that concubines and wedded wives be sent in to sit beside the men as is customary in Persia, insisting, "You now, since you welcomed us readily and you are hosting us greatly [*xeinizeis*]— and gave earth and water to King Darius—follow our custom [*nomōi*]" (5.18.2). The statement is not polite but peremptory, a command from a superior to a subordinate. The Macedonian king understands it as the absolute command that it is, for he responds, "O Persians, this is definitely not our custom. Ours is to keep men separated from women. But since you, being our masters [*despotai*], require this in addition, this also will be done for you" (5.18.3). The word *despotēs*, "master" (pl. *despotai*), source of the English "despot," means literally, "master of the house, power in the house."[3] The Macedonian king perfectly comprehends that he and his people are now completely subject to the Persians. But the presence of women does not satisfy the Persians. They do not want to sit opposite the women. They now want to sit next to them. So, the Macedonian king must allow this as well. And, of course, the Persians do not simply want to sit beside the women. Now very drunk, the Persians grope and try to kiss them (5.18.4–5).

The tale emphasizes not only Persian disregard for the Macedonians' customary separation of men from women but also their complete disdain for and disruption of the vital ancient Greek tradition of *xenia* itself, the system governing reciprocal obligations between guests and hosts. In the Egyptian tale of Helen, the Egyptian king Proteus refuses to violate *xenia* by harming his own guest (2.115.5)—despite his disgust at his guest's previous violation of *xenia* in Sparta (where the Trojan prince stole his host's wife). Not the current host, the Egyptian king, but the wronged host, Helen's husband, may be entitled to exact vengeance on his erstwhile guest. Whereas the Egyptian king Proteus refuses to violate *xenia* by harming his current guest-friend, the Persian envoys in Macedon heedlessly violate *xenia,* imitating the Trojan prince Alexandros/ Paris in committing sexual violence against the women of their current hosts. Just as the Trojan prince, by his own violation, released his host, Helen's husband, from the obligations of *xenia,* so too by demonstrating that as guests they themselves are not bound by *xenia,* the Persian envoys equally release the Macedonians from their responsibilities as hosts.

The Macedonians fully recognize that the Persians' conduct has freed them from the obligations of guest-friendship. Not *xenia* but fear constrains Amyntas, the angered but cautious Macedonian king. Understanding that his son plans something "rash" or "radical" (*neōtera,* repeated in the singular *neōteron*), he urges him "to do nothing politically disruptive [*neochmōsai*] against these men lest you destroy us" (5.19.2). The verb *neochmōsai* came to mean "to make political innovations," but in this context surely the king means "Do not revolt against these men who have us in their power." But neither *xenia* nor fear nor lack of ingenuity constrains the Macedonian king's youthful son (confusingly also named, like the Trojan prince) Alexandros. (This story contains ironic reversals of epic tales of both the Trojan prince Alexandros and the master trickster Odysseus.)[4] Cleverly replacing the women with beardless young men disguised as women and armed with daggers (5.20.1–3), Alexandros deceives the unsuspecting Persians. He insists ironically that the Macedonians are entertaining the Persians abundantly, sparing nothing. This hospitality includes offering up their very own mothers and sisters, both to demonstrate how the Macedonians honor the Persians and also to send a message to the king (5.20.4).

Completely missing the irony, the Persians also fail to notice that they have forfeited their respected and protected status as guests. In offering hospitality initially, Alexandros's father King Amyntas assumes a host's obligations under *xenia* (*epi xeinia kaleei*, 5.18.1) before feeling compelled to recognize the Persian envoys as "masters" (*despotai*, 5.18.3). And whereas Amyntas's son Alexandros first addresses the Persian envoys as *xeinoi*, "guest-friends" (5.20.1), in speaking ironically, he addresses them instead as just *Persai*, "Persians" (5.20.4). As the Persians continue to violate their responsibilities as guests under *xenia*, attempting to molest the "women" seated beside them, each disguised Macedonian kills his would-be violator (5.20.4). Having forfeited the protections of *xenia*, the Persian envoys have also given Alexandros license to "disappear" their entire entourage and accompanying equipment (5.21.1). Unconstrained by *xenia*, Alexandros is also free to conceal the whole event afterward by bribing the Persian general searching for the missing Persians (5.22.2).

This story follows the pattern in ancient Greek epic tales of violators of *xenia* succumbing to disguise and deception. In their rapacious appropriation of their hosts' women, the Per-

sian envoys in Macedon replicate the conduct and experience
of the Trojan prince Alexandros/Paris. After Paris violates *xenia* by stealing his host's wife, he and his people fall for the
Greeks' trick of the Trojan Horse, a benign-seeming gift containing fierce Greek warriors.[5] The suitors in the *Odyssey*, occupying uninvited the home of the absent Odysseus and
appropriating his possessions, similarly violate their responsibilities under *xenia*. They, too, subsequently fall victim to trickery, deceived by the beggar's disguise of the returning king.
Mistaking outward appearance for internal identity, the suitors lose their lives, slain by the avenging Odysseus.[6] Repeating
the pattern, the Persian envoys violate *xenia* by assaulting their
hosts' women. Like the Trojan Horse and Odysseus-disguised-
as-a-beggar, the Macedonian men-disguised-as-women are not
what they appear. Deceived by outward appearances, the Persian envoys fall prey to Macedonian vengeance.

Following Greek tradition in connecting violation of custom with destruction by deception, Herodotus once again
contrasts a barbarian (i.e., non-Greek) lack of sexual restraint
and gullibility with Greek self-control and superior cunning.
As in his tale of the Lydian king Candaules (1.6–14), opportunistic sexual predation and transgression of custom prove self-
defeating. King Candaules violates the customs of his own
people (1.8.3). The Persians in Macedon violate Greek customs.
Both fall victim to their own lack of impulse control. By contrast, the son of the Macedonian king retaliates not impulsively
but with careful, ingenious planning, and Herodotus takes
pains to identify the clever Macedonians as Greeks (5.22).[7] In
the context of the tale, the Macedonian custom of separating
men from women appears prudent, decent, and restrained.
And the Macedonian king's son seems crafty and adept.

But although this tale contrasts barbarian with Greek values regarding both *xenia* and the treatment of women, it does

not contrast Persian misogyny with Greek respect for women. Just like the Persians, the Macedonians view women not as autonomous human beings but as possessions. The Macedonian king Amyntas offers up Macedonian women—as he offers the lavish banquet—in a futile effort to appease despotic overlords. Even his son's desire to protect Macedonian women from Persian violation does not derive from concern for the women's experience, as Alexandros subsequently uses his own sister as part of a bribe to conceal the murders (*dous* twice, at 5.21.2, the verb *didōmi* meaning "to give" or "to bribe," depending on the context).

The story of Persians at the court of Macedon centers not on female autonomy or bodily integrity but on masculine power and control. In the *Histories,* transgressions against women symbolize transgressions against *nomos* "law/custom/tradition."[8] In demonstrating their disdain for *xenia,* the Persians directly challenge the ability of Macedonian men to protect their own women. Preventing rape, Alexandros signifies his rejection of Persian domination.[9] The attempted assault on Macedonian women symbolizes the Persians' attack on the authority, independence, integrity, and honor—the very masculinity—of Macedonian men. This conception of masculine honor requires men to protect their women.[10] By groping and seeking to violate Macedonian women, the Persians symbolically emasculate and seek to rape Macedonian men. Perhaps the cross-dressing feminizes the Macedonians.[11] But Alexandros's trick turns the tables. The young men costumed as women symbolically emasculate the Persians, killing them by penetrating them with daggers.

Focused not on female autonomy but on male power, this tale of subjugation and failed subjugation also validates the narrative authority of the investigating reporter. Emphasizing the contrast between Greek cleverness and barbarian gullibility, the

narrator aids his audience in seeing beneath the surface of
things so as to understand the true nature of events. The Histories repeatedly challenges theatrical display of the sort deployed by the Macedonian Alexandros while affirming the
interpretive role of the Herodotean narrator.[12] This tale epitomizes dramatic irony: Herodotus's readers are in on the Macedonians' deception as the Persians are not. We can appreciate
the double entendres as Alexandros promises his Persian
"guests" the complete banquet that they deserve, lacking nothing. We understand one thing, the Persians another, when Alexandros offers up the Macedonians' "own mothers and sisters,
in order that you may learn how absolutely honored you are
by us for the very things that you deserve" (5.20.4). And we can
appreciate the irony in the Persian would-be penetrators getting penetrated themselves. Alexandros stages a little drama,
replete with actors and costumes. Drawing back the curtain for
readers, Herodotus's narrator reveals the reality beneath the
dramatic illusion.

Ensuring that readers understand the reality beneath the
charade, Herodotus depicts the deceived Persians as a powerful, cautionary example. Like enthralled, undiscerning specta-
tors at the theater, the Persians erroneously conflate appearances
with reality, mistaking for women male actors wearing women's
clothing. Incautious, unperceptive, duped by surface appearances, the Persians fail to interpret visual evidence correctly—
with lethal consequences.

As narrative authority, Herodotus emphasizes that the
failure to perceive reality beneath surface appearances invites
subjugation—for Greeks as for barbarians. Herodotus's tale of
Athenians deceived by the tyrant Peisistratus (1.60.3–5) prefigures this tale of Persians deceived by Macedonians. Pretending to be escorted back to power by the goddess Athena,
Peisistratus very likely reenacts a religious procession and the

Athenians are not in fact duped.[13] But Herodotus mocks the
Athenians for their gullibility and extreme foolishness. Exposing the truth beneath the pretense, he disparages the tyrant's
trick as most mindless and puerile—particularly egregious for
Athenians, famed among Greeks for greatest wisdom and prudence (1.60.3). Peisistratus costumes a tall woman as a goddess. The Macedonians costume young men as women. The
Athenians mistake a mortal woman for a goddess. In the palace of the Macedonian king, the Persians mistake young men
for women. The principle is the same: in each instance, things
are not as they appear. The Athenians' failure to recognize a
mortal woman under the costume of a goddess costs them their
political freedom. The Persians' inability to see through the
young men's disguise costs them their lives.

Depicted as a triumph of Greek guile over Persian aggression, immorality, and gullibility, Herodotus's tale illustrates
the price of subjugation for dominated and dominators alike.
The Macedonian king learns that subjugation to Persia entails
complete forfeiture of Macedonian autonomy and values, since
acceding to one despotic demand invites another and another.
As the world rediscovered to its cost in 1938—and, sadly, continues to rediscover—no appeasement satisfies a ruthless,
powerful bully. But Herodotus's tale also illustrates the harm
of subjugation to oppressors as well as those oppressed. In
trampling Macedonian customs, the Persians erroneously trust
to their superior strength. Empowered to indulge their greed
and lack of discernment, they pay the ultimate price for their
rapacity and credulity.

After describing the Persian conquest of Thrace and
Macedon, Herodotus returns to his main theme: the conflict
between Persia and Greece and the Greeks' stalwart resistance
to Persian aggression. He will proceed to recount the Ionian
Revolt (499–494 BCE), a rebellion of Ionian Greeks (on the

Asian coast) against Persian imperial control. Herodotus offers a very unsatisfactory record of these events and the motives of the participants, but his narrative remains the only extant full account. We have very little to check Herodotus's claims against.[14] The Persians' ceaseless, escalating, atrocious demands at the court of the king of Macedon epitomize, like the Persian empire's relentless expansion, the rapacity of tyranny itself.

This tale of cultural values in conflict—though likely legendary and lacking historical verification—illustrates symbolically the grave threat that subjugation poses to Greek culture and autonomy. Subjugation brings material appropriation, of course. ("You are being entertained hospitably with a complete banquet lacking nothing. For it includes all the other things—as many as we had—and in addition we have supplied to you everything that we could find.") But this story depicts not only material greed but also moral depravity as the essence of Persian imperial expansion and the fundamental consequence of subjugation.

The tale memorably portrays subjugation as the obliteration of moral obligations and humane conduct. Subjugation appears to valorize predatory violence of masters against slaves and slaves against masters. Lack of decency and restraint precludes the functioning of mutually beneficial reciprocal norms—like *xenia*—between people with power and those subject to their authority. Violations of reciprocal obligations make deception, murder, and bribery seem necessary and admirable. Lack of moral discernment catalyzes this conflict between Persians and Macedonians as neither culture respects female bodily autonomy and both choose to treat women as possessions. We may not find the Greek custom of segregating women from men much more laudable than the Persian custom of placing women on the menu, but the story demonstrates that subjugation promotes mutual moral depravity. Persian military strength compels Macedonian compliance in violation of Macedonian custom. Macedonians, in turn, resort to deception and violence. Lacking any more creative or humane option, the Macedonians choose murder.

Herodotus's tale may validate Greek guile over Persian greed and gullibility, but in the twenty-first century we can admire the Macedonians' ruthlessness only at the cost of our humanity. Countering one atrocity with another, the Macedonians offer no useful moral example. Deception and violence will later prove vital to the Greeks' success in repelling Persian invasion. But in our own heavily armed times, with not only assault rifles but also nuclear weapons available, deception and murderous violence offer no solution to international and domestic conflicts.

Resistance to any form of subjugation—whether to a foreign foe, domestic authoritarian leader, or unquestioned dogma—originates in recognition of the vital human capacity for moral discernment. Pluralistic democratic government has the potential to offer citizens the freedom and responsibility to make humane moral judgments. If we do not care to do the hard work of sifting good from bad, right from wrong, in all their moral complexity, plenty of self-assured, undiscerning people are happy to relieve us of the burden, eager to subject us to their dogmatic certainties. But subjugation, as this tale shows, has escalating costs. It perverts moral judgment and encourages violence. Turning kindness, generosity, and trust into fatal weaknesses, subjugation promotes deception and violence as survival skills. Lethal to egalitarian politics, deception and violence victimize the vulnerable and enrich the unscrupulous. Egalitarian democratic norms and institutions require honesty, trust, and compassion. Subjugation risks making us—like the Persians and Macedonians in Herodotus's tale—something less than human.

14

On Political Equality

The tale of the Persians at the court of Macedon concerns subjugation to a foreign adversary, exposing the corrosive effect of subjugation on human relationships and moral judgment, debasing both oppressors and oppressed. Subsequently Herodotus contrasts autocratic rule with political equality *within* Greek citizen-communities. In these tales political equality appears as double-edged, a source of both strength and weakness.

Herodotus first provides an example of the advantages of autocratic decision-making, commending the Spartan king Cleomenes for his sensible resistance to deception and bribery. When Aristagoras, current ruler of Miletus, the leading Greek city in Ionia, decides to initiate a rebellion of Ionian Greeks against Persia, he attempts unsuccessfully to enlist Sparta's aid, using a combination of moral persuasion and material temptation. Though the Spartan political system had not one but two kings—Herodotus later explains why (6.52–55)—at this point King Cleomenes is ruling alone (5.39–42) (ca. 520–491 BCE). Herodotus reports accusations that Cleomenes was crazy, claiming, "Cleomenes, it is said, was not of sound mind and he was raving mad" (5.42.1). And Cleomenes will subsequently die

by cutting himself to bits, his madness attributed to divine
punishment for transgressing *nomos*, "law/custom/tradition"
(6.75.3–84).[1] But when Aristagoras, ruler of Miletus, arrives in
Sparta and tries to con Cleomenes, the Spartan king appears
not crazy but shrewd and sensible:

[5.49] Therefore, Aristagoras, tyrant of Miletus, arrived in
Sparta while Cleomenes held the kingship. And he went for
the purpose of talking with Cleomenes, as the Spartans
claim. Aristagoras was carrying a bronze writing tablet on
which a map of the entire earth was engraved and every sea
and all the rivers. [2] Arriving to speak with Cleomenes,
Aristagoras said the following to him: "Cleomenes, do not
marvel at my eagerness to come here, for the circumstances
are such: it is a disgrace for the children of the Ionians to be
slaves instead of free. And it is the greatest distress for us
ourselves and for you still more than for the rest of men, in as
much as you have set yourselves to lead Greece. [3] Now,
therefore, by the gods of the Greeks, rescue the Ionians once
and for all from slavery. They are men of the same blood as
you. And these things are able to proceed easily for you, for
the barbarians are not valiant, whereas you Spartans, with
respect to matters in war, have attained the greatest achievements regarding excellence. The barbarians' way of fighting is
the following kind: bows and short spears. They go into
battles wearing trousers and having Persian peaked hats on
their heads. [4] Thus, they are easily subdued. And those who
possess that continent have so many good things—more than
all other men together—beginning with gold and silver and
bronze and elaborately decorated clothing, beasts that go
under the yoke, and slaves. Wishing for these things in your
heart, you yourselves could have them. [5] And they live close
to each other, as I will declare: these here near the Ionians are

the Lydians, who inhabit a good land and are richest in
silver." Aristagoras said these things pointing to the map of
the earth which he carried engraved on the writing tablet.
"And next to the Lydians," said Aristagoras, "these are the
Phrygians who live toward the East. They are the richest in
sheep and cattle of all people I know and also the wealthiest
in crops. [6] Next to the Phrygians are the Cappadocians,
whom we call Syrians. The Cilicians border these, extending
to this sea here, in which this island here, Cyprus, lies. The
Cilicians pay in full fifty talents to the king [of Persia] as their
yearly tribute. And next to the Cilicians, these here are the
Armenians. They are also very rich in sheep flocks and cattle
herds. And next to the Armenians, the Matieni hold this
region here. [7] Next to them, this land here is Kissian. And
in it, surely, beside this river, the Choaspes, is Susa, where the
Great King makes his dwelling and where the treasure houses
for his possessions are. Once having captured this city, you
confidently already rival Zeus in wealth. [8] But don't you
think that it is expedient for you to delay fighting—for land
that is not large, nor so useful, and has narrow boundaries—
against the Messenians, who are well matched with you, and
against the Arcadians and the Argives [all in the Pelopon-
nese], who have no gold or silver at all? Any man is eagerly
willing to fight and die for those things. But since it is possible to rule over all of Asia easily, will you prefer anything
else?" [9] Aristagoras said these things, but Cleomenes
answered with the following: "O Milesian guest-friend, I am
delaying my answer to you until the day after tomorrow."

[5.50] At that time, they proceeded just so far. But when
the appointed day for the answer occurred and they came to
the agreed upon spot, Cleomenes asked Aristagoras how
many days the journey was from the sea of the Ionians to
the king of Persia. [2] And though Aristagoras was clever

(*sophos*) with regard to the other matters and was misleading Cleomenes well, he tripped up in this instance. For it was necessary for him not to say what was really true, since he wanted to tempt the Spartans into Asia. But Aristagoras did speak the truth then, declaring that the route up took three months. [3] And Cleomenes interrupted the remainder of the account that Aristagoras was rushing on to tell concerning the journey. Cleomenes said, "O Milesian guest-friend, remove yourself from Sparta before the sun goes down. For you are making no eloquent argument to the Spartans in wishing to lead them on a journey of three months from the sea."

[5.51] Having said these things, Cleomenes went home. But Aristagoras, taking in his hand the olive branch of a suppliant, went to the house of Cleomenes. Entering within, Aristagoras urgently begged Cleomenes to listen to him as a suppliant—and first to send away his small child. For indeed the daughter of Cleomenes was standing beside him. Her name was Gorgo. She also happened to be Cleomenes' only child, and she was about eight or nine years old. Cleomenes ordered Aristagoras to say to him what he wished and not to hold back because of the child. [2] Thereupon, surely, Aristagoras began by promising ten talents if Cleomenes would accomplish for him the things that he asked. When Cleomenes refused, Aristagoras proceeded to offer more and more money—to the point where he promised fifty talents. And the little child cried out, "Father, your guest-friend will corrupt you unless you depart and keep away from him!" [3] And Cleomenes, surely pleased by his daughter's advice, went into another chamber. And Aristagoras took himself completely away from Sparta. And it was not permitted to him to point out any further the details concerning the route up from the sea to the seat of the Persian king.

In seeking Spartan aid for the Ionian rebellion against Persia, Aristagoras uses flattery, moral arguments, and material enticements. He begins by reminding the Spartan king of Sparta's claims to leadership of Greece, insisting that enslavement by Persia therefore brings shame not only to Ionians but especially to Spartans (5.49.2). Asking Sparta to "rescue the Ionians once and for all from slavery," Aristagoras appeals to Spartan blood kinship with Ionian Greeks (5.49.3). The Spartans are Dorians, but Greek myths depicted ancient genealogical connections between ethnic groups.[2] Euripides' *Ion* (ca. 414–412 BCE)—though later than Herodotus's *Histories*— even identifies Dorus and Ion, the eponymous ancestors of the Dorians and Ionians, as half-brothers, making the two races technically "of the same blood."[3] In addition to evoking the Spartans' kinship obligations, Aristagoras describes the Persians as easy adversaries, identifying them as ill-equipped, cowardly, and no match for Spartan martial excellence (5.49.3– 4). Aristagoras details the Persians' abundance of material goods, easily acquired if Sparta only desires them (5.49.4). Listing the peoples of Asia and emphasizing their rich lands and plentiful possessions (5.49.5–7), Aristagoras asks the Spartan king, essentially, "Why fight against other Greeks in the Peloponnese, who have little? When you could easily acquire all this?" (5.49.8).

The encounter illustrates not only the seductions of aggression and avarice but also the temptation to rival divinities.[4] Urging Cleomenes to attack wealthy Persia instead of expanding Spartan power in the Peloponnese, Aristagoras overtly offers this mortal king an invitation to *hubris*. He confidently maintains that success will enable Cleomenes to rival (*erizete*, from *erizō*) Zeus in wealth (5.49.7). Herodotus's Greek contemporaries, familiar with Homeric epic tales, knew that no mortal can ever rival Zeus. In the *Odyssey*, the Spartan king

Menelaus corrects younger men's mistaken suggestion that his own shining, gilded mortal palace must be like Zeus's court, insisting, "Dear children, surely no one of mortals could rival Zeus [*erizoi*, from *erizō*], for his halls and possessions are immortal."[5] Believing oneself like a god, or more than mortal, epitomizes the Greek conception of *hubris*. *Hubris* defines the illusory expectation that one can harm others with impunity. Only divinities can do that.

The Spartan king Cleomenes, however, here proves resistant to *hubris*. Impervious to flattery, moral arguments, and material temptations, he does not act impulsively. Prudently, he requests a couple of days to consider Aristagoras's invitation (5.49.9). But at this next meeting, Aristagoras makes a huge mistake in telling the truth when asked the length of the journey from the Ionian coast to the Persian king. Herodotus observes that although Aristagoras has been making progress in his effort to mislead Cleomenes, here he errs fatally in admitting that the journey takes three months (5.50.2). This ends the discussion, as far as Cleomenes is concerned. He ejects Aristagoras, rejecting the very idea of marching three months inland from the sea (5.50.3).

Clearsighted and prudent, Cleomenes also appears resistant to bribery. He has resisted bribery before: years earlier, Maiandrios, ruler of Samos, similarly seeking Spartan help in fighting Persia, attempts to bribe Cleomenes with huge amounts of silver and gold cups [?515 BCE]. Herodotus characterizes Cleomenes then as *dikaiotatos andrōn*, "most just of men," in refusing to accept the bribe and having Maiandrios driven out of Sparta lest he corrupt some other Spartan (3.148). Resisting bribery once again, Cleomenes determinedly refuses Aristagoras's desperate, escalating offers of money (5.51.1). Eventually, however, Cleomenes' eight- or nine-year-old daughter Gorgo observes that her father risks being corrupted unless he removes himself from contact with Aristagoras (5.51.2). In nearly succumbing—rather than directly asserting a traditional Spartan disdain for material wealth—Cleomenes may foreshadow later Spartan acquisitiveness.[6] But once again Cleomenes drives away a would-be corrupter (5.51.3).

In describing Aristagoras's failed attempt at seduction, deception, and bribery, Herodotus crafts a story emphasizing the beneficial potential of autocratic authority. Herodotus ignores social and political considerations likely dissuading Cleomenes from assisting the Ionian Revolt, and he focuses instead on individual personalities and ambitions.[7] The tale seems to be another illustrative parable, since it is unlikely that the Spartan king made this decision unilaterally. He must have consulted the ephors, five annually elected Spartans who shared power with the two kings.[8] Nevertheless, Herodotus presents King Cleomenes' refusal to aid the Ionian rebellion as astute and commendable. The autocrat proves capable of discerning a statement of fact among a mass of disinformation. Aristagoras's self-defeating admission of the three-month journey along the Royal Road inland from the coast to the Persian capital, Susa (5.52–54), validates Cleomenes' sensible refusal to listen further. Herodotus rounds off the story by giving the culminating observation to the king's little daughter, who happens to be present at the meeting. By placing the final verdict in the mouth of a small child, Herodotus adds eloquent emphasis; even a little girl can see that Aristagoras is trying to corrupt the Spartan king. In this tale, the autocrat admirably resists temptation.

Herodotus will proceed to contrast this example of Spartan autocratic prudence with Athenian democratic imprudence, but first he backtracks to explain how the Athenians transitioned from tyranny to democracy. The Ionian Revolt begins (499 BCE) soon after the end of the Peisistratid tyranny (510 BCE) and the inception of direct democracy at Athens

(508/7 BCE). Aristagoras of Miletus, instigator of the Ionian rebellion, having been driven from Sparta after failing to gain the support of the Spartan king, goes straight to Athens, described by Herodotus as "having become free of tyrants in the following way" (*es tas Athēnas genomenas turannōn hōde eleutheras*, 5.55.1). Herodotus previously described how the tyrant Peisistratus initially took power in Athens (1.59–64). He now dispels the traditional story of the removal of the tyranny (5.55–65), insisting that the two men famed in Athenian lore as the tyrannicides, "tyrant killers," actually killed not the reigning tyrant, Peisistratus's eldest son and successor Hippias, but his younger brother (5.55.1) [514 BCE]. Herodotus later elaborates that in killing the tyrant's brother, these two men did not rid Athens of tyranny but only made the tyranny harsher (6.123.2). The tyrant killers became cult figures in the fifth century, symbols of Athenian political equality and emblematic of an archaic ideal of aristocratic achievement now extended to every male citizen of the democracy.[9] Here, however, after a detour describing a prior dream of the murdered man, the origins of the assassins, and the Phoenician origin of the Greek alphabet, among other things (!), Herodotus returns to "how the Athenians were freed from tyrants" (*hōs turannōn eleutherōthēsan Athēnaioi*, 5.62).

Herodotus conspicuously does not say that the Athenians "freed themselves" from tyranny, because Athenian liberation results largely from outside intervention. While Peisistratus's elder son continues to rule Athens, an exiled clan of aristocrats ("the Alcmaeonids") bribes the Pythian oracle at Delphi to give the same response to every Spartan consulting the oracle on public or private business: free Athens (5.63.1) [511 BCE]. Though Peisistratus's descendants and supporters ("the Peisistratids") defeat the Spartans' first attempt to overthrow their regime (5.63.3–4), they come under siege from a second Spartan attack led by King Cleomenes and supported by those among the Athenians who, Herodotus says, "wished to be free" (5.64) [510 BCE]. The Spartans' siege would not have succeeded, had the besiegers not managed to capture the children of the Peisistratids when their families attempt to sneak them out of Athens to safety (5.65.1). Forced to capitulate, the Peisistratids must give up their tyranny and leave the city, having held power in Athens for thirty-six years (5.65.2–3). "Thus," Herodotus concludes, "the Athenians were freed from tyrants" (5.65.5).[10]

Removal of a tyrant does not ensure a beneficial alternative or a livable society (as numerous more recent historical examples attest), but Athenian innovation quickly and constructively remedies the resulting power vacuum. Scholars continue to debate questions concerning Herodotus's account of the Athenian transition from tyranny to democracy, including the nature of his sources and the roles and motives of the elites and the *dēmos,* "people."[11] But following the removal of the tyranny, the Athenians implement an unprecedented political solution, and Herodotus praises the result, explaining, "Athens, being great even before, then freed from tyrants became greater" (5.66.1). Ousting the tyrants constitutes merely step one; a major reorganization of political ideals and allegiances follows. As two ambitious aristocrats now compete for power, one enlists popular backing. Cleisthenes, ancestor of the famous Athenian general Pericles, "attaches the people [*dēmos*] to himself as political supporters" (5.66.2). Cleisthenes ingeniously reorganizes the tribal structure of Athens (5.66.2), weakening the divisive power of the traditional aristocratic clans and also ameliorating competition between geographical regions within Attica.[12] Herodotus depicts Cleisthenes as no selfless democratic reformer, however, maintaining that Cleisthenes incorporates into his own party [*moira*] the *dēmos,* the non-aristocrats previously excluded from politics. "Having added the people [*dēmos*] as his ally," Herodotus claims, "he was stronger by far than his political adversaries" (5.69.2) [508/7 BCE]. When a Spartan invasion forces Cleisthenes out of Athens, the Athenians demonstrate their determination to retain the new system by revolting, recalling Cleisthenes, and even requesting Persian aid (5.70–3) [507 BCE].[13] The new political structure combined *isonomiē*, "equality under law," with *isēgoriē*, "equal right of assembly and free speech."[14]

Herodotus identifies the Athenians' novel political system as their source of military power. After the Athenians defeat yet another Spartan-led invasion (5.74–77) [506 BCE], Herodotus concludes, "Now the Athenians had grown greater, and it is clear that *isēgoriē* is an excellent thing not only in one way but in every way—if indeed the Athenians, when ruled by tyrants, were not better in war than any of their neighbors, but once freed from tyrants they became first by far. These facts make it clear, therefore, that when they were subjugated, they were willfully cowardly and neglectful of their duties, since they were being set to work by their master [*despotēs*]. Once freed, however, each man desired eagerly to attain achievements for himself" (5.78). Praising *isēgoriē*, Herodotus here unequivocally commends the political equality advocated unsuccessfully by Otanes during the Persian debate (3.80), termed there *isonomiē* (3.80.6). The Spartans, too, realize the advantage of liberty for the Athenians, since, Herodotus says, "Seeing the Athenians growing in power and in no way prepared to be prevailed on by them, the Spartans recognized that, free, the Attic race would be equally matched with their own, but that subjugated by tyranny the Attic race would be weak and ready to be obedient to authority" (5.91.1).

Although certain that Athenian political equality fuels military power, Herodotus also suggests that egalitarian decision-making makes the Athenians vulnerable to deception and temptation.[15] Having failed to deceive and bribe the Spartan king Cleomenes into supporting the Ionian rebellion (5.49–51), Aristagoras next tries his luck with newly democratic Athens. He arrives at an opportune time: seeking restoration to power, Peisistratus's son, the tyrant Hippias, has been unable to gain the support of Sparta's allies (5.91–3) and has enlisted Persian help (5.96.1) [?504 BCE]. The Persians' efforts on Hippias's behalf make manifest to the Athenians that the Persians are their enemies (5.96.2). "And, surely, in this crucial moment," says Herodotus, "Aristagoras of Miletus, having been driven out from Sparta by Cleomenes, arrived in Athens. For, of the remaining cities, this city was the most powerful by far" (5.97.1).

Herodotus previously praised democratic freedoms as a source of military might, but he now condemns democratic decision-making as impulsive, thoughtless, greedy, and irresponsible. In contrast to Cleomenes' example of autocratic prudence and self-restraint, political equality makes democratic Athens susceptible to false promises of easily acquired wealth and power. The Spartan king rejects Aristagoras's invitation to *hubris* (5.49.7), but the Athenians appear eager to succumb. In Athens, Aristagoras repeats temptations and promises recently offered to the Spartan king: the material possessions to be acquired, the ease of defeating the Persians (5.97.1). Aristagoras replaces the Spartan-tailored moral argument of blood kinship obligations between Dorians and Ionians with an Athenian-focused moral argument of political obligations, adding that "the Milesians are colonists from Athens, and it would be right for the Athenians, being greatly powerful, to protect them" (5.97.2). Though he failed to persuade the Spartan king, Aristagoras prevails with the Athenians, for "because he was very much in need, there was nothing that he did not promise them—to the point that he succeeded in seducing them. For it seems to be easier to mislead[16] many

men than one—if Aristagoras was not able to seduce one Spartan, Cleomenes, but he did this to thirty thousand Athenians"
(5.97.2).

Herodotus characterizes the Athenians' susceptibility to
seduction and greed as utterly foolish. Of the twenty ships that
the Athenians vote to send to aid the Ionians, Herodotus claims,
"These ships became the beginning of the evils [archē kakōn]
for both Greeks and barbarians" (5.97.3). His phrase echoes Homer's description of the ships that brought Alexandros/Paris
to Sparta. Homer calls those ships "the beginning of the evil
[archekakous]" for Paris himself and for the Trojans (Il. 5.62–4).[17]
Paris's ships enable him to steal the wife of his Greek host and
thereby catalyze the conflict between Greece and Troy, a catastrophe for both sides but particularly for Troy. In Herodotus's view, the twenty Athenian ships sent in 499 BCE to aid
the Ionian Revolt catalyze the Persian Wars between Greece
and Persia (490–479 BCE). By helping the Ionian Greeks capture and burn the Persian city of Sardis (5.100–101), including
a temple to the goddess Cybele, the Athenians motivate the Persian king Darius to attack Greece in revenge, for Herodotus
maintains that "alleging this as an excuse, the Persians later
burned the temples of the Greeks" (5.102.1).

Herodotus even suggests that if the Athenians had not
helped the Ionians to rebel and to burn Sardis, the Persian king
Darius might not have known that Athens existed. Darius's
ignorance of Greece echoes and exceeds the Spartan king
Cleomenes' ignorance of Persia. Cleomenes seems to have no
idea of the distance from the Ionian coast to the Persian king's
palace at Susa (5.50). Prior to the burning of Sardis, Darius does
not even know who the Athenians are. Infuriated at the attack
on Sardis, Darius knows that he will be able to punish the Ionian Greeks, but he has to ask his attendants, "Whoever are the
Athenians?" (5.105.1). After being informed, he shoots an ar-

row into the sky and prays, "O Zeus, let it be granted to me to take vengeance on the Athenians." Darius instructs a servant to remind him three times each time he is about to eat dinner, "Master [Despota], remember the Athenians" (5.105.2, repeated at 6.94).

In presenting Athenian support for the Ionian Revolt as the prime cause of the Persian Wars, Herodotus does not offer an impartial account of these events or the motives of participants.[18] Despite his Ionian origins (born in Halicarnassus on the coast of Asia Minor), Herodotus considers the Ionian rebellion a lost cause, praises the Spartan king's unwillingness to be lured into it (5.49–51), and criticizes the Athenians for allowing themselves to be seduced by an opportunist into fighting on the Ionians' behalf (5.97.2). After the Persians recapture some of the Ionian cities, Herodotus dismisses Aristagoras, instigator of the rebellion, as unprincipled and self-interested. He maintains that now "Aristagoras made it manifest that he was not of strong mind/spirit/understanding [psuxēn ouk akros]. He had thrown Ionia into disorder and mixed himself up in great matters. And seeing these things, he was planning an escape" (5.124.1). Shortly afterward, Aristagoras dies besieging a city in Thrace (5.126) [?497/6 BCE].

Herodotus's negative characterization notwithstanding, Aristagoras may well have had a legitimate desire to free the Ionian Greeks from Persian tyranny, and the Athenians likely had economic and strategic as well as moral motives in deciding to assist.[19] Herodotus criticizes Aristagoras for duping the Athenians, and he disparages the Athenians for foolishly bringing disaster on Greece, but many modern historians view Aristagoras more favorably and the Athenians as more reasonable. Though Herodotus emphasizes the Ionians' refusal of outside domination as their most compelling motive—Aristagoras's complaint that "it is a disgrace for the children of the Ionians to be slaves instead of free" (5.49.2)—economic hardships very likely prompted the rebellion. Athenian opinion was probably divided, but Athens, unlike Sparta, did have close ties with and knowledge of Ionia, and Persia's continued expansion enables Aristagoras to argue plausibly that mainland Greece will be Persia's next objective. Many Athenians will have worried about the Persian king's support for the exiled tyrant Hippias, now in Persia, although some might have welcomed the possibility of the tyrant's return. Persia did pose a threat to Athenian trade routes, and in voting to send twenty warships (5.97) the Athenians make a substantial commitment, for they had then only about fifty. Although the odds were against the rebellious Ionians, mainland Greek support might possibly have brought success. But Greeks have as yet no real sense of national unity, and Athenian support does not last. After the Athenians' withdrawal, perhaps a consequence of internal divisions of opinion, the Persians recapture many Ionian cities. The fact that Herodotus's home town, the Ionian city of Halicarnassus, never joined the rebellion may also have colored his view.

Though not unbiased in his account of events, Herodotus recognizes the ambivalent force of political equality. He presents the initial stage of Athenian democracy as both an inspiration and a cautionary warning—for his contemporaries in the 440s and 430s BCE and now for us. Uninterested in political, social, and economic causal factors, Herodotus continues to focus on human choices.[20] Although he portrays the Persian autocracy as relentlessly expansionist, he insists that Athenian support for the Ionian Revolt makes Athens the prime target of the subsequent vengeance of Persia's king.[21] Herodotus identifies political equality as a source of military might, repeatedly attributing Athenian power to the Athenians' transition from tyranny to democracy (5.66.1; 5.78; 5.91.1).[22] But political equality also proves a source of vulnerability.[23] While capable of making wise decisions, the Athenian people, acting collectively, also make foolish ones.[24] A potent source of communal cohesion, determination, and military strength, political equality includes the danger of collective impulsiveness and folly. Productive of both military strength and intellectual vulnerability, political equality emerges in the *Histories* as not the best but merely the least bad type of political regime. In book 3, before describing Darius's accession to the Persian throne, Herodotus portrays three Persian noblemen asserting the theoretical merits of "rule by the many" (*isonomiē*, equality before the law), "rule by the few," and "rule by the one" (3.80–83). In book 5, Herodotus provides a practical demonstration. The Persians' choice of "rule by the one" will prove a fatal error. Knowing already the events and outcome of the Persian Wars, Herodotus insists that democratic freedoms and political unity will empower the Athenians to defeat successive invasions launched by Persian autocrats. And yet, "rule by the many" also has its shortcomings. Collectively seduced by false promises of an easy victory and abundant plunder, Herodotus's Athenians launch an expedition heedless of potential risk.

Contrasting restrained autocratic prudence with impulsive democratic folly, Herodotus cautions against ceding moral and practical judgment to an injudicious crowd. Though biased—and probably historically inexact—Herodotus nevertheless recognizes that people may be more vulnerable to greed and gullibility in a crowd than individually. Swayed more by passion than reasoned argument, crowds regularly overestimate benefits and underestimate costs of proposed policies. Suggesting that political equality in 499 BCE exposes newly democratic Athens to the ill-considered opportunism of the multitude, Herodotus demonstrates the necessity for institutional protections against rash, imprudent majoritarian voting. The Athenians' susceptibility to a persuasive speaker's temptations and deceptions warns against removing or weakening protections against mob rule.

Herodotus's ambivalent portrait of political equality helps to undermine moral absolutism and to promote readers' aptitude for the creative negotiation and humane compromise required for democratic self-governance. The certainty that good and evil are fixed, mutually exclusive categories helps to sustain authoritarian political ideals and structures. Moral absolutism itself can promote pure evil, since monstrous atrocities require absolute moral certainty (e.g., Nazi genocide and Stalinist and Maoist purges and famines of the twentieth century). Herodotus undermines such absolutist certainty by pairing an example of sensible, prudent autocratic decision-making with an example of self-destructive democratic decision-making. Political equality may offer the best chance of individual and communal survival and success, but it remains no unalloyed good. Ill-informed and ill-advised majoritarian voting makes citizens in a democracy vulnerable to corrupt demagogues, panderers, and unscrupulous opportunists. Now as then, the preservation of democratic norms, laws, and institutions requires a clear-sighted ability—and desire—to appreciate the benefits and mitigate the harms of political equality. Democratic political equality remains constructive only if guided and constrained by critical moral discernment, expertise, caution, and foresight.

15

On Freedom

The Athenians' unprecedented democratic experiment, begun in 508/7 BCE, soon faces an existential threat. A decisive Persian victory in the naval battle of Lade, on the coast of Asia Minor (494 BCE), ends the Ionian Revolt. The Persian king Darius next targets islands in the Aegean, intending to cross to Greece afterward to punish Eretria and Athens for aiding the Ionians. Herodotus attributes to Darius the further intention of subjugating all of mainland Greece. Having conquered Eretria, burned its temples, and enslaved its populace, Darius intends the same fate for Athens (6.101–103), and in 490 he attacks Marathon at the northern edge of Attica (the Athenian acropolis and its surrounding communities).[1]

Herodotus remains our only extended source for the period, severely limiting our ability to assess his version of events. Writing more than a half century later, he commends Greek resistance to foreign invasion. Emphasizing once again the value of historical memory for constructively shaping present aspirations and decisions, Herodotus extols the Athenians' stalwart commitment to freedom from autocratic domination. As the vastly outnumbered Athenians prepare to defend their liberty at Marathon, however, smart money is on a Persian victory:

[6.105] First, when the generals were still in the Athenian citadel [the Acropolis], they sent the messenger Philippides to Sparta. Philippides was an Athenian day runner and especially practiced at this. This Philippides claimed—and reported to the Athenians—that the god Pan encountered him in the region of Mount Parthenion above Tegea. [2] Philippides said Pan shouted out his name, "Philippides!" and commanded him to ask the Athenians why they paid no attention to him, though he was well-minded toward them, had already been useful to them everywhere, and would yet be useful to them in future. [3] Believing these claims to be true—and once they had settled their own affairs well—the Athenians established a temple for Pan beneath the Acropolis. And because of this message, they propitiate Pan with yearly sacrifices and a torch race.

[6.106] This Philippides, having been sent then by the generals—on the very occasion when he said Pan appeared to him—was in Sparta on the second day after leaving the Athenian citadel [a distance of some 150 miles]. Arriving, Philippides said to the rulers, [2] "O Spartans, the Athenians need you to come to their aid and not to look on idly while the most ancient city among the Greeks falls into slavery at the hands of barbarians. For even now, Eretria has been reduced to slavery, and Greece has become weaker by one notable citizen-community." [3] Philippides reported to them the things he had been commanded to say. And it pleased the Spartans to help the Athenians. But it was not possible for them to do this immediately, since they were not willing to violate their custom. For it was the ninth day of the rising moon, and on the ninth, they said, they would not march out until the moon was full.

[6.107] The Spartans waited for the full moon. But Hippias, son of Peisistratus [former tyrant of Athens], was

leading the barbarians [the Persians] down to Marathon.
During the previous night, Hippias saw the following vision
in his sleep: he seemed to be sleeping with his own mother.
[2] He concluded, therefore, from the dream, that having
returned to Athens and having restored his rule, he would
end his life as an old man in his own land. For from this
vision he now concluded these things. And then, bringing
down the slaves from Eretria, Hippias made them disembark
on the island of the Styrians called Aegiliae. Having done so,
Hippias anchored the ships in Marathon. When the barbarians had disembarked onto the land, Hippias set them in
battle order. [3] And as he was arranging these things, a
sneezing and coughing came upon him more severe than he
was accustomed to. And since he was rather old, many of his
teeth were wobbly. One of his teeth therefore fell out because
of the force of his coughing. It fell out into the sand, and he
made a great effort to find it. [4] But since the tooth did not
appear, Hippias groaned, and he said to the men standing by,
"This land here is not ours, and we will not be able to make it
subject to us. For as much of it as was my share, the tooth
now has as its share."

[6.108] Hippias now concluded that the vision had been
accomplished in this way. When the Athenians had set
themselves in battle order in the precinct of the sanctuary of
Heracles, the Plataeans came to aid them in full force. For the
Plataeans had given themselves to the Athenians, and on
their behalf the Athenians had already undertaken numerous
labors. [2] The Plataeans had given themselves to the Athenians in the following way: hard-pressed by the Thebans, the
Plataeans first gave themselves to [the Spartan king]
Cleomenes, son of Anaxandrides, and the Spartans who
happened to be present. But the Spartans, not accepting, said
the following: "We live rather far away, and aid of such a sort

would be cold for you. For you could be enslaved often before
we learned anything of it. [3] We counsel you to give yourselves to the Athenians. They live near you. And they are men
who are not bad at aiding." The Spartans advised this not out
of goodwill toward the Plataeans but because they wished the
Athenians to have troubles by engaging in hostilities with the
Boeotians. [4] The Spartans now gave this advice to the
Plataeans, and the Plataeans did not distrust it. But when the
Athenians were performing their sacred rites to the twelve
gods, the Plataeans sat down as suppliants at the altar and
gave themselves over to them. Upon learning this, the
Thebans marched against the Plataeans, and the Athenians
went to help the Plataeans. [5] As these forces were about to
join in battle, the Corinthians did not look idly on. They
happened to be present, and with the arbitration entrusted to
them, they reconciled both sides. They marked out the land
with boundaries on the following terms: the Thebans were to
let alone any Boeotians unwilling to be classed as Boeotians
[i.e., joined to the Theban-controlled Boeotian League].
Having decided these things, the Corinthians then departed.
But as the Athenians were going away, the Boeotians attacked
them. But in the battle, the attacking Boeotians were defeated. [6] And the Athenians extended the boundaries that
the Corinthians had established for the Plataeans. They made
the river Asopus itself the boundary for the Thebans toward
the Plataeans—and also the settlement of Hysiae. The Plataeans, then, gave themselves to the Athenians in the way that
I have said. And they arrived then at Marathon to help the
Athenians.

[6.109] The opinion of the ten generals of the Athenians
were divided. Some did not want to engage in battle, for they
thought they were too few to fight the army of the Persians.
But some—and Miltiades among them—were urging an

attack. [2] And as they were evenly divided, and the worse opinion was winning, at that point Miltiades approached Callimachus. For there was an eleventh man entitled to vote, a man chosen by lot to be polemarch of the Athenians. And at that time the polemarch was Callimachus of Aphidna. Going up to Callimachus, Miltiades said the following: [3] "It is in your hands now, Callimachus, whether to enslave Athens or, having made Athens free, to leave for yourself a memorial for the entire life of humankind such as not even Harmodius and Aristogeiton [the famed "tyrannicides"] left. For right now the Athenians have arrived at their greatest danger, the greatest they have ever faced since first becoming Athenians. And indeed, if they bow down before the Persians, the sufferings that they will experience when they have been handed over to Hippias have been well understood. But if this city prevails, it can come to be first of Greek cities. [4] How, therefore, circumstances have become such as they now are, and how it has come to the point that you have authority over these matters, I will now explain. The opinions of us ten generals are evenly divided, with some urging to engage in battle, others not. [5] If we do not engage in battle now, I expect that some great factional conflict, bursting in upon the Athenians' minds and spirits, will shake them so violently that they medize [submit to the Persians]. But if we engage in battle before something rotten arises in some Athenians, we can prevail in the encounter—if the gods remain impartial. [6] All these things, therefore, pertain to and depend upon you now. For if you declare for my opinion, you have a homeland that is free and a city that is first of Greek cities. But if you choose for the ones eager to prevent a battle, the opposite of the good things I have detailed for you will come to be."

[6.110] Saying these things, Miltiades won Callimachus over. And with the polemarch's opinion added, it was decided to engage in battle. After this, the generals whose opinion was to attack, as their day of command came in turn to each of them, handed it over to Miltiades. But he, accepting it, did not yet make an attack until it was actually his day of command.

[6.111] And when his day of command came around to Miltiades, thereupon the Athenians were drawn up in order for the purpose of attacking in the following way. The polemarch Callimachus commanded the right wing, for the Athenians' custom at that time held that the polemarch was to command the right wing. The tribes followed in succession, lining up beside each other, according to their established numerical order. Last, the Plataeans were drawn up in order holding the left wing. [2] Ever after this battle, when the Athenians conduct sacrifices in their great quadrennial festivals, the Athenian herald prays, saying, "May good things come to both the Athenians and the Plataeans." [3] And then, with the Athenians drawn up in order at Marathon, the following was the case: the Greek battle line was equal in length to the Persian, but its middle section was only a few ranks deep, and in this way it was the weaker of the two. But each wing was strongly defended by its numbers.

[6.112] Thus, their army was drawn up, and the sacrifices were auspicious. Thereupon, as the Athenians were released, they hurled themselves at a run against the barbarians. The space between the two armies was not fewer than eight stades [approximately nine-tenths of a mile]. [2] The Persians, seeing the Athenians approaching at a run, prepared to receive them. They attributed to the Athenians a madness that was utterly self-destructive, seeing that they were few, and speeding on at a run with neither cavalry nor archers ready at hand. [3] The barbarians now assumed this. But when the Athenians clashed together with them in combat, the Athenians fought in a manner worthy to relate. For they

are the first of all the Greeks of whom we know to use a
battle-run against their enemies. And they were the first to
endure seeing Median clothing and the men clothed in it. Up
until then, even to hear the name "Medes" [= Persians] was a
source of terror for the Greeks.

[6.113] They were fighting at Marathon for a long time.
And the barbarians were victorious in the middle of the
battle line, where the Persians themselves and the Sacae had
been stationed. Breaking the line, they pursued the Greeks
inland. But at each wing, the Athenians and the Plataeans
were victorious. [2] Winning there, they allowed the routed
part of the barbarians to flee. And bringing together both
wings, they fought against the barbarians who had broken
the middle of their line. And the Athenians were victorious.
They pursued the Persians, cutting them down as they were
fleeing, until on reaching the sea, the Greeks demanded fire
and attacked the ships.

[6.114] And at this point in the struggle, the polemarch
Callimachus was killed, a man who had proved himself noble
and brave. Of the generals, Stesilaus, son of Thrasylaus, also
died. Kynegeirus [brother of the playwright Aeschylus], son
of Euphorion, died there too. As he seized the stern of a ship,
his hand was cut off by an axe, and he fell dead. Many other
famous Athenians also died there.

[6.115] In this way, the Athenians seized seven of the ships.
With the rest, the barbarians retreated by backing water.
Having retrieved the slaves from Eretria from the island where
they had left them, they sailed around Sounion. They wanted
to reach the Athenian citadel before the Athenians arrived. An
accusation later held among the Athenians that the barbarians
formed this plan because of a contrivance of the Alcmaeonidae [a noble family descended from Alcmaeon]. For the
accusation was that the Alcmaeonidae contrived to lift up and

show a shield as a sign to the Persians when they were already
on their ships.

[6.116] Now the Persians were sailing around Sounion.
But the Athenians ran to rescue the citadel as fast as their feet
could go. And they arrived before the barbarians did. Arriving from their encampment at the sanctuary of Heracles in
Marathon, they encamped at another sanctuary of Heracles,
the one in Kynosarges. The barbarians anchored their ships
off Phaleron. For at this time this was the Athenians' seaport.
After holding their ships there for a time, the barbarians
afterwards sailed back to Asia.

[6.117] In this battle at Marathon, about 6,400 of the
barbarians died and 192 Athenians. That is how many men
on both sides fell. [2] And it happened that the following sort
of marvel occurred there: an Athenian named Epizelus, son
of Cuphagoras, while fighting in the conflict and proving
himself to be noble and brave, was deprived of his vision. He
had not been struck or hit anywhere on his body. And from
this time on, he continued to be blind for the rest of his life.
[3] I heard the following account that they say Epizelus told
about his experience: he said that a huge hoplite warrior
seemed to stand opposite him. The man's beard covered his
entire shield. The apparition passed Epizelus by, he said, but
killed the man standing beside him. These are the things that
I learned that Epizelus said.

Recounting the battle of Marathon, Herodotus encourages his contemporaries to recall their own vision of their best
selves. Although he fails to offer a fully reliable account of this
first land battle in Greece between Greeks and Persians, Herodotus emphasizes Greek, and especially Athenian, achievements. Herodotus's numbers regarding military forces are
generally suspect, but we have little else to go on.[2] We can be

sure only that there were far fewer Greeks at Marathon than Persians, necessitating a shorter and thinner battle line (6.111.3).[3] Greatly outnumbered, the Greeks demonstrate superior skill and courage. Herodotus insists that the Athenians united to face the crisis (though in fact some Athenians may have favored the return to power of the now Persian-backed tyrant Hippias). Previous Athenian aid has also earned grateful Plataean assistance (6.108).[4]

The astonishing Greek victory over the Persians at Marathon became, for Athenians, a defining moment. The Greeks' success seemed miraculous. No one expected a small force of Greeks to rout vastly larger Persian forces. Except for the stalemate in Scythia, Persia had been conquering everything in its path. Success at Marathon gave the Greeks confidence, showing them that they actually had better training and strategy in infantry battles. Suddenly the Persians no longer seemed invincible. The victory at Marathon may also have contributed to the willingness of other Greek citizen-communities to unite to repel the second Persian invasion in 480 BCE.[5]

Herodotus's account of Marathon also disparages the Spartans for their antagonism and inactivity. Writing in the 440s–430s BCE, as tensions between Athens and Sparta escalate, Herodotus pointedly records the Spartans' failure to aid the Athenians and Plataeans at Marathon (6.106.3). He attributes the Spartans' earlier advice to the Plataeans to seek Athenian protection to a Spartan desire for Athenians "to have troubles by engaging in hostilities with the Boeotians" (6.108.3). The Greeks initially await a Persian attack, hoping for Spartan reinforcements, but the Spartans fail to arrive until two days after the battle. According to Herodotus, they merely tour the battlefield, praise Athens, and head home (6.120).

Herodotus presents not the Spartans but the Athenians and Plataeans as inspiring models of wisdom, endurance,

courage, and skill. Urging the battle in defense of Athenian
liberty, the Athenian general Miltiades aligns individual self-
interest with group survival, appealing to the polemarch Callimachus's desire to augment both his own personal glory and
the glory of the community (109.3). Herodotus details great feats
of physical endurance: the distance runner Philippides (Pheidippides in some sources) runs from Athens to Sparta to seek
Spartan help (6.105–6), and the Greeks at Marathon boldly attack *dromōi*, "at the run" (6.112). (The story that Pheidippides—
not Philippides, as Herodotus calls him—ran from Marathon to
Athens to announce the Greek victory and then dropped dead is
a later invention.)[6] The Greeks probably run only the last part of
the intervening mile, and probably not very fast, but it is very
difficult to run wearing heavy hoplite armor. Running into combat also demands great courage and discipline, since maintaining the hoplite phalanx even at the usual marching pace requires
organization, training, and skill. And the faster than usual advance would surely have intimidated the enemy.[7] With fewer
warriors, Miltiades strategically makes the Greek battle line long
to match the Persians' line but necessarily weak at its center.
When the center gives way, the Greek wings rout the Ionians
manning the Persians' wings and attack elite Persian forces manning the center (6.111.3; 113). Exhausted though they must have
been, the victorious Athenians race back to Athens in time to
prevent the Persians from landing at Phaleron, a bay of the Sa-
ronic Gulf only about three miles from Athens.[8] The Athenians'
swift arrival compels the Persians to accept failure and return to
Asia (6.116). Greek bravery and skill result in far fewer Greek
than Persian casualties (6.117.1). And contrary to normal Athenian custom, the fallen Greeks earn the most honorable burial
on the spot where they fell.[9]

　　Greek fortitude, bravery, and skill succeed against enor-
mous odds and amid the chaotic horror of ancient warfare.

Herodotus's description of the fighting recalls gory descriptions of hand-to-hand combat in Homer's *Iliad*, and his contemporaries also had firsthand experience of battle. The brother of the Athenian tragic playwright Aeschylus dies nobly at Marathon, his hand chopped off by an axe as he grabs the stern of a fleeing Persian ship (6.114). One survivor describes sudden, spontaneous—and permanent—blindness mid-battle, with his last sight that of an immense Persian warrior killing the man next to him (6.117). The story seems implausible, but so-called hysterical blindness has been attested in modern soldiers witnessing so much horror that the mind seeks to block it out.[10]

Herodotus's account of the violence memorializes Greek success derived from purely human energy and achievement. Though he begins and ends his description of the battle with supernatural tales, Herodotus gives these no authorial endorsement. He states only that Philippides *claimed* that he encountered the god Pan and that the Athenians believed him (6.105). In recording Epizelus's tale of a phantom apparition, Herodotus observes only that he heard that Epizelus said this (6.117.3). Similarly, Herodotus includes Hippias's dream and his interpretation of it without affirming its veracity (6.107). Herodotus concludes each supernatural tale by reiterating that he is reporting the claims and convictions of others (6.106.1, 108.1, 117.3). He never vouches for these stories' factual validity.

Agnostic on supernatural tales, Herodotus energetically corrects a false human narrative. He takes pains to exonerate from slander the Alcmaeonids, the family of Pericles, the great Athenian general of Herodotus's day.[11] Herodotus mentions the accusation that the Alcmaeonids somehow signaled to the Persians as they sailed toward Athens while the Athenians raced overland to arrive first (6.115). Perhaps the *Histories'* portrait of the Alcmaeonids in regard to tyranny undermines a rigid binary between support for freedom and opposition to tyranny.[12]

But here Herodotus unequivocally dismisses as false the accusation that the family sought to assist the Persians, deeming it absurd to suggest that the Alcmaeonids wanted Athens subjugated to the tyrant Hippias and to Persia, since the family were great tyrant haters (6.121.1). Praising the family at length for their staunch opposition to tyranny, Herodotus refuses to believe the slander, since the Alcmaeonids were exiled during the tyranny, and subsequently they forced the Peisistratids out (6.123.1). Herodotus instead attributes Athenian liberty to the Alcmaeonids, deeming them more responsible for ending the Peisistratid tyranny than the famed tyrannicides who, by killing the tyrant's brother merely "made the remaining Peisistratids more savage." Herodotus credits the Alcmaeonids for freeing Athens, "if they were truly the ones who seduced the Pythia to announce to the Spartans to free Athens, as I have shown before [5.63]" (6.123.2). Herodotus insists that the Alcmaeonids could have had no motive to betray Athens, since "there were no other men among the Athenians more esteemed [dokimōteroi] nor more honored" than they. Herodotus affirms that a shield was in fact displayed, but he can add nothing further (6.124).

In describing the battle of Marathon, Herodotus reminds his Greek contemporaries of the centrality of freedom to their own history and identity. But Herodotus's conception of freedom versus oppression does not align precisely with democratic versus autocratic political authority. For Herodotus, "freedom" means freedom from foreign domination. Herodotus frequently associates freedom with the rejection of tyranny.[13] But he does not depict rejection of autocracy as the clear motivation for the Ionian Revolt. He suggests that Persia backed local tyrants within the Ionian Greek citizen-communities (e.g., 4.137), but the rebellion included removal of just some tyrants (e.g., 5.37 and 5.38 vs. 5.103). Perhaps inspired by the Athenians' example, Aristagoras, ruler of Miletus and instigator of the Ionian Revolt, abandons his tyranny and proclaims *isonomiē*, "equality before the law" at Miletus. But after suppressing the Ionian rebellion, the Persians also establish democratic governments in some Ionian Greek cities (6.43).[14] Herodotus portrays the battle of Marathon not as an ideological conflict between democracy and tyranny but as an existential fight for Greek freedom from Persian domination.

Herodotus's commendation of Athenian valor and resolve at Marathon and his exoneration of the Alcmaeonids places the preservation of freedom at the center of Athenian identity. Throughout the fifth century, the Athenians crafted the tale of their unexpected victory at Marathon into "their finest hour" and used it to validate their claim to authority over Greece.[15] The surprise victory became a popular subject for artists, and there is some truth to the Athenians' self-aggrandizement. Though brutal subjugation of other citizen-communities later fueled the political, economic, and artistic achievements of Athens, Herodotus depicts the Athenians as preserving Greek autonomy at Marathon. They were helped by only one thousand Plataeans (and possibly fewer), and the Persians outnumbered them perhaps two or three to one. Had the Athenians (and Plataeans) failed to defeat the Persian invaders, the Greek citizen-communities, one by one, would have fallen under Persian rule.

Before describing events at Marathon, Herodotus emphasizes the brutality of Persian autocratic rule. Even Darius's own generals fear their monarch's wrath; on the eve of the final conflict in the Ionian Revolt, the battle of Lade, the Persian naval commanders fear that failure will subject them to *kakon ti*, "some evil," from Darius (6.9.1). Attempting to reconquer rebellious Ionian cities, the Persians instruct exiled, Persian-backed, former Ionian tyrants to threaten their people with horrible punishments if they refuse to surrender (6.9.4). One Ionian Greek general defines the stakes as a stark choice between freedom and slavery, and he urges his warriors to work hard now and avoid weakness and disorder if they wish to avoid punishment from the Persian king (6.11.2). After their victory at Lade, the Persians sack Miletus, enslave the survivors, and terrorize many Ionian cities. Two years later, Darius sends his son-in-law Mardonius to subjugate Thrace and solidify Persian control of the Aegean (492 BCE).[16] In victory, the Persian generals follow through on their threats: they castrate the most good-looking boys, send the most beautiful virgins to the king, and set the cities and their temples on fire. "Thus," Herodotus concludes, "the Ionians were enslaved for the third time, first by the Lydians, and twice in succession by the Persians" (6.32). Herodotus insists that the Persians intend to subjugate as many Greek cities as possible (6.44.1). Mardonius proceeds to enslave the Thracians, refusing to leave their territory "until he had brought them under his hand [*epixeirous*]" (6.45.1).

The brutal Persian onslaught seemed unstoppable. The capture of Miletus (494 BCE) offered terrifying evidence of Persian might and expansionist intentions. The following year, Herodotus says, the playwright Phrynichus dramatized the fall of Miletus in a tragedy that so upset the Athenians that they fined Phrynichus and ordered the play never performed again (6.21). Darius next sets his sights on Athens, for while the Athenians are engaged in a local conflict against Aegina, Herodotus relates, Darius stays focused on vengeance, "as his servant is constantly reminding him to remember the Athenians. And the Peisistratids [exiled family of the former Athenian tyrant] were beside him slandering the Athenians. At the same time, using this as a pretext, Darius wanted to subjugate all of the Greeks who had not given him earth and water" (6.94.1). Darius dispatches new generals, commanding them to enslave Athens and Eretria and bring the captives back to him (6.94.2).

Eretria's defeat and destruction both demonstrate the weakness of a divided community and illustrate Herodotus's contention that Darius intends pitiless enslavement for all Greece. The Greek *poleis* "citizen-communities" seem insufficiently aware of mutual interests, and the Athenians fail to aid the Eretrians, very likely wanting to save their own warriors for the defense of Athens.[17] Factional divisions within Eretria facilitate the Persians' victory, with some Eretrians thinking about fleeing and others, seeking personal advantages, planning to betray the city to the Persians (6.100.1–2). In conquest, the Persians show no mercy or restraint: they plunder and burn temples in revenge for the temples burned in Sardis, and they enslave the populace on Darius's instructions (5.101; 6.101.3). Eretria's fall makes Athens's predicament appear most dire. A few days later, the Persians sail for Attica, confident "that they would do to Athens the things they had done to the Eretrians" (6.102). The presence at Marathon of the elderly Hippias, former tyrant of Athens, accompanying the Persian fleet as an advisor suggests that the Persians intend to reinstall a tyranny with Athens subject to Persia. Having Athens as a support base, the Persians might later be able to subjugate all of Greece.[18]

If Herodotus's lead-up to the battle of Marathon suggests that the odds were against the survival of an independent Athens, the city's trajectory after the battle reveals extensive consequences of that survival. In 490, the Athenian democratic experiment was barely eighteen years old. The full flowering of Athenian direct participatory democracy did not develop until some thirty years later. (The system survived, with just a couple of interruptions, until 322 BCE.) The advent and survival of democratic government in Athens coincided with extraordinary innovations in drama, art, architecture, political thought, natural science, moral philosophy, and, of course, historiography.[19]

It is hard to imagine Athens's great artistic, political, and philosophical achievements throughout the fifth and into the fourth century BCE occurring under Persian autocratic rule.[20] As a poor subject-city of the Persian empire, Athens would have been unlikely to attract pioneering architects, artists, dramatists, natural scientists, and philosophers. Tribute payments to Persia would have made unaffordable the magnificent, innovative public building project on the Athenian acropolis, including the Parthenon (constructed 447–432 BCE). An Athens ruled by a Persian king could never have fostered productions of ancient Greek tragedies and comedies, genres of dramatic performance highly critical of both tyranny and the democratic status quo. No absolute autocrat could have tolerated the disruptions to traditional beliefs and hierarchies introduced by scientific and philosophical investigations and by historiography. A closed-minded autocratic society could never have permitted Socrates to wander freely around Athens for decades, challenging self-proclaimed experts to philosophical inquiry. (Socrates' eventual execution—under a fragile democracy recently restored after a brief oligarchic reign of terror—shows that even democratic tolerance remains a delicate flower.) And without Socrates, Plato might never have launched moral philosophy.

Despite fostering extraordinary artistic and intellectual accomplishments, the ancient Athenian democracy remained brutal, misogynistic, and imperialist, but Athenian democratic freedoms—imperfect as they were—initiated a movement, as yet unachieved today, toward equality and justice. The Athenian-led Greek coalition that defeated the Persian invasion subsequently evolved into Athenian dominance over formerly willing allies.[21] And modern attitudes toward Athenian imperialism continue to evolve.[22] Ironically, imperialism sustained Athenian achievements. But at the same time intellectual ferment *within* democratic Athens encouraged discussion, debate, dissent, criticism and self-criticism. State-sponsored Athenian drama exposed not only the toxicity of tyranny, the reciprocal costs of brutality, and the self-destructiveness of violent revenge but also the benefits—and nobility—of free speech, honesty, and compassion. Herodotus's own innovation, *historiē*, explicitly condemned authoritarianism and autocratic contempt for human life. Emphasizing the vulnerability of all human beings to suffering and death and condemning abuses of power, Athenian art and literature fostered the open-minded inquiry and empathy underlying universal principles of equality, justice, and humanity today.

Hindsight enables us to imagine the costs to humanity had the Persians succeeded at Marathon, but in memorializing Athenian achievement and attributing the continued freedom of Athens to extraordinary human effort, Herodotus does not directly valorize modern egalitarian ideals of freedom. The philosopher Isaiah Berlin identifies a negative and a positive type of freedom. Termed "freedom from" and "freedom to," the former is not incompatible with autocracy, nor does it require democracy.[23] Focused on "freedom from," Herodotus defines Greek liberty as freedom from foreign tyranny. And he portrays Athens as embodying the positive value of democratic freedom.[24] But the ancient Greek conception of "freedom from" was not incompatible with "freedom to," since freedom from foreign control permits and may even promote rule over other people.[25] Whether imposed by a foreign or domestic government, by one person, a few, or a majority of citizens, all forms of tyranny deny the "freedom to" of those subjugated, including freedoms of speech, association, and opportunity. Because "freedom to" can morph into tyranny over others, modern liberal democracy offers institutional mechanisms for balancing "freedom from" and "freedom to." The U.S. Constitution and Bill of Rights embody the effort to preserve individual rights and freedoms without endangering other citizens' health and well-being. The rule of law serves to protect "freedom from" and constrain the tyrannical potential of "freedom to."

Distinct from the modern democratic ideal of freedom, Herodotus's conception of freedom did not immediately transform into it. Victory at Marathon did not initiate the concept of universal equality and human rights—either in Athens or elsewhere. Even as Athenians throughout the fifth century prided themselves on their democratic government and political freedoms, they continued to keep people in slavery, subjugate women, enslave conquered peoples, and force allied cities to pay tribute. Similar hypocrisy enabled the framers of the U.S. Constitution in the eighteenth century to deem human enslavement compatible with freedom and justice for all. Prioritizing economic power and property rights over the lives of human beings, the founders doomed generations of human beings to enslavement and the nation to centuries of oppression, injustice, and violent civil discord. Even when slavery became illegal in the United States in 1863, it did not precisely disappear, morphing instead into insidious forms of noxious systemic oppression, despite the passage of anti-discriminatory constitutional amendments.[26] Following World War II and the defeat of fascist dictatorships, the United States positioned itself as the leader of the free world and the champion of human rights. Civil rights legislation followed two decades later, but racial and gender inequities nevertheless persist within the United States. The ancient Greek conception of freedom opposed foreign domination. But worldwide, individual freedom and universal human rights remained—and remain—necessary but elusive goals.

Without (anachronistically) validating modern liberal democratic values of equality and universal human rights, Herodotus's narrative of an idealized past nevertheless offered his contemporaries an inspiring model against which to measure themselves. His portrait of the Athenians as defenders of freedom and opponents of tyrannical oppression provided an easy-to-perceive alternative to the complicated reality of his contemporary Athens preceding and during the Peloponnesian War. By 431 BCE democratic Athens seems to have already become a self-proclaimed tyrant city.[27] Athens will proceed to ruthless suppression of rebellious so-called allies and violent subjugation of even formerly neutral citizen-communities.[28] Imperial aggression will cost Athens dearly in lives and wealth during and after the Peloponnesian War. Defeat will usher in a brief but horrific period of oligarchic bloodlust and terror in Athens (the Spartan-imposed Tyranny of the Thirty 404/403). In describing the victory achieved at Marathon by the generation before his own, Herodotus makes a prescient but apparently futile effort to encourage his contemporaries to reimagine their own goals and priorities.

In his effort to redirect Greek ambitions, Herodotus exploits the ambivalent force of historical memory. Ancient Greek connects memory with truth, since *alētheia*, "truth," means "not forgetting." But human memory powers both the primitive desire for vengeance and the noble passion for liberty. Memory of the Athenians' participation in burning Sardis reinforces and perpetuates Darius's desire for revenge, as he commands his servant to remind him three times a day, "Master [*despota*], remember the Athenians!" (5.105.2; 6.94). Turning the injunction on its head, Herodotus makes the phrase "Remember the Athenians!" a source of pride and inspiration. For Darius, historical memory means recalling an injury and affirming the desire for revenge. Herodotus repurposes historical memory to recall the extraordinary Athenian valor and determination that preserved Greek freedom.

By repurposing the role of memory in his account of the momentous battle of Marathon, Herodotus commemorates the value of history itself, the value of inquiring into the past so as to make an assessment. We can suspect—even identify—Herodotus's tendentious distortions without invalidating his project. George Orwell suggested that whoever controls the narrative of the past controls the future.[29] Narratives of our own past have tremendous power. They tell us who we are, how we want to see ourselves, and who we want to become. Herodotus offers a stirring tale of a Persian autocrat attempting to enslave Greeks and Greeks, though vastly outnumbered—and conspicuously unaided by Spartans—staunchly defending freedom. As dictators and would-be dictators gain power and momentum in our own times, Herodotus offers a shining historical example of the tenacity of the desire for freedom.

Herodotus's account of Marathon also provides a potent warning to powerful modern states contemplating unprovoked, opportunistic conquest of smaller sovereign countries. Nation-states are a modern construct, but the desire for political sovereignty and independence from foreign domination is not new. Herodotus's account of Marathon offered contemporary Athenians a cautionary example of aggressive imperial expansion improbably and decisively checked—a warning to set against successful Athenian imperial expansion from the 470s to the 430s BCE. As powerful nations attack or contemplate attacking smaller sovereign states today, Herodotus's tale of the Greek victory at Marathon illustrates the potent force of the human desire for freedom and the tremendous value of a unified response to an existential threat.

Given the worldwide rise today of violent totalitarian and fascist movements, Herodotus's reminder to his contemporaries of the centrality of freedom to their own identity equally serves as a vital reminder to modern liberal democracies confronting authoritarian forces both foreign and domestic. The ancient Greeks failed to include equality and universal human rights in their conception of freedom—as do many modern communities and states still. Despite Herodotus's idealized portrait of the Athenian commitment to freedom, the ancient Greeks never lived up to their own ideal of themselves and their virtues. But idealism always forges ahead of reality, and the gap between the actual and the ideal will never close if we give up on the ideals. To ignore or deny crucial distinctions between modern liberal democracies and brutal dictatorships (and terrorist organizations) is to serve the agenda of dictators, racists, misogynists, kleptocrats, and terrorists. The differences may be smaller than optimal and sometimes diminishing. But Herodotus's portrait of Athenian tenacity in the face of overwhelming odds should inspire us not to abandon the ideal of universal human freedom.

16

On Autocratic Leadership

Defeated at Marathon, the Persian king Darius determines to rebuild his forces for a second invasion of Greece (7.1). But he dies attempting to suppress an Egyptian revolt (486 BCE), and his son Xerxes inherits the throne and with it his father's passion for revenge. In describing Xerxes' decision-making process, accession to the kingship, and ill-advised assault on Greece (480 BCE), Herodotus advances his critique of autocratic leadership. Focused on the continued threat to Greek independence, Herodotus portrays the Persian king's greed and vengeful ambition as foolish, monstrous, and self-defeating.

Xerxes inherits autocratic power having demonstrated no aptitude for it, and he proves paradoxically both weak-willed and willful. Initially reluctant to attack Greece, Xerxes succumbs to the persuasion of self-interested advisors. Once he has set his course, Xerxes demonstrates the ability of autocratic leadership to insulate a ruler against receiving good advice. Surrounded by fearful flatterers reluctant to oppose his wishes, the headstrong autocrat remains unable to obtain wise counsel or know it when he hears it:

[7.7] Thus, Xerxes was persuaded to march against Greece. Thereupon, in the second year after Darius's death, Xerxes first made an expedition against the Egyptians who had revolted. Having subjugated them and having made Egypt much more enslaved than it was during Darius's time, Xerxes turned it over to his brother, Achaemenes, a son of Darius. . . .

[7.8] After the conquest of Egypt, as Xerxes was about to undertake the expedition against Athens, he convened a specially summoned gathering of the best Persians so that he could learn their opinions and so that he himself could declare to them the things he desired.

[7.8α] And when they were gathered, Xerxes said the following: "I myself will not be the first to institute this custom among you. Instead, having inherited it, I will use it. For, as I learn from our elders, we have never yet kept still since we took possession of sovereignty from the Medes, when Cyrus deposed Astyages. But in this way the god leads. And as we pursue many objectives, things turn out for the better for us. As for the people that Cyrus, Cambyses, and my father Darius conquered—I would not speak well in telling you about these, since you already know. [2] But when I myself took over this throne, I gave thought as to how I might not fall short of those who came before me in this honored office nor acquire less power for the Persians. And in taking thought, I find that glory [kudos] accrues to us as we acquire land that is not smaller nor poorer but more productive of all things. And at the same time, we get revenge and retribution. Therefore, I brought you together so that I may express what I have in mind to do.

[7.8β] "I intend, by bridging the Hellespont, to march my army through Europe to Greece so that I may take vengeance on the Athenians for all they did to the Persians

and to my father. [2] You have already seen that Darius was
eager to march against these men. But he died and was not
permitted to take vengeance. But on his behalf and that of the
other Persians, I will not stop until I capture Athens and set it
ablaze. For they were the ones who began doing injustice
against me and my father. [3] First of all, entering Sardis with
Aristagoras—our slave!—they set the sacred groves and
temples on fire. Second, you all doubtless know the things
that they did to us when we landed on their territory, when
Datis and Artaphrenes were generals [at Marathon].

[7.8γ] "For these reasons, I am prepared to march
against them. And as I make my calculations, I discover so
many good things in these plans. If we subdue them and
their neighbors dwelling in the land of Pelops, we will create
a Persian land that has the same borders as Zeus's sky. [2] For
then the sun will look down upon no territory bordering on
ours. Rather, in going with you through all of Europe, I will
make all the lands one territory. [3] For I ascertain that the
situation is thus: no city of men nor race of human beings
remains that will be able to go against us in battle—once the
ones I have listed have been done away with. Both those who
are guilty in our view and those who are blameless will bear
the yoke of slavery.

[7.8δ] "And in doing the following things, you would
please me: when I signal to you the time that it is necessary
for you to come, every one of you will need to be present
eagerly. And whoever arrives with his army most beautifully
well-prepared—I will give to him the gifts that are considered
most honorable in our land. [2] These things must be done
now in this way. But in order that I not seem to you to be
following merely my own counsel, I set the matter before you
all. And I command anyone who wishes to show forth his
opinion." Having said this, Xerxes stopped.

[7.9] After Xerxes, Mardonius spoke: "O Master [*despota*], you are the best—not only of all Persians who previously existed but also of all those who will come to be—you who hit the mark exactly both in saying other things that are best and truest and in saying that you will not allow the Ionians dwelling in Europe to laugh at us, since they are unworthy to do so. [2] And this is because it would be a terrible matter if, in wishing to acquire power, we have subjugated as slaves the Sacae, Ionians, Aethiopians, and Assyrians, and many other great peoples who have done the Persians no injustice, but we do not take vengeance on the Greeks who began doing wrong against us.

[7.9α] "What do we fear? A crowd of what magnitude? The power of what amount of money? We know their fighting. We know that their power is weak. We hold in subjection the sons of these men who inhabit our land, the ones called Ionians, Aeolians, and Dorians. [2] I myself have already made trial of these men, attacking them at the command of your father. And as I marched as far as Macedon and nearly to Athens itself, no one came to meet me in battle.

[7.9β] "Moreover, the Greeks are accustomed, I learn, to make their stand against enemies in a most ill-advised manner—both from thoughtlessness and from stupidity. For when they declare war against each other, they find the most beautiful and smoothest spot. And going down to this they do battle—with the result that the victors depart only after suffering great losses. Concerning the ones who are beaten, I won't even begin to say, for they are then utterly destroyed. [2] These men speak the same language. They use heralds and messengers. They ought to put an end to their disagreements by any method rather than battles. But if it is entirely necessary for them to make war, against one another, they ought to find somewhere where each side is most difficult to subdue and attempt to fight there. Therefore, the Greeks employ a method that is not useful. And when I marched as far as the land of Macedon, they did not come near the thought of doing battle.

[7.9γ] "O King, since you lead a multitude out of Asia and all its ships, who will oppose you by declaring war? As it seems to me, the affairs of the Greeks have not reached this degree of boldness. But if, then, I should be mistaken in my opinion, and the Greeks, raised up by thoughtlessness, should come against you in battle, they would learn that we are the best of men at the business of warfare. But let nothing, therefore, be untried. For nothing happens without cause. Rather, everything usually occurs for human beings from their making an attempt."

[7.10] Having said so much to smooth-coat Xerxes' opinions, Mardonius stopped. Since all the other Persians kept silent, not daring to offer an opinion opposite to the one already proposed, Artabanes, son of Hystaspes, trusting in his status as Xerxes' paternal uncle, said the following:

[7.10α] "O King, with no opposing opinions expressed, it is not possible to choose the better one. Instead, one must use the one stated. But if contrasting opinions are expressed, it is possible for us to distinguish the better one—just as we do not distinguish pure gold when it is by itself but only when we rub it against another gold piece. [2] And I myself counseled your father Darius, my own brother, not to take an army against the Scythians, men who inhabit no citadel anywhere on earth. But he, expecting these nomads to be subdued, was not persuaded by me. And in attacking, he lost many good men from his army [4.83–143]. [3] But you, O King, are about to attack men who are far better still than the Scythians, men who are said to be best both at sea and on land. There is danger in these circumstances, and it is right and just for me to declare this to you.

[7.10β] "You say that by bridging the Hellespont you are going to march your army through Europe into Greece. But suppose it turns out that you are defeated either on land or on sea—or even on both. For their men are said to be valiant. And this can be measured—if indeed the Athenians alone destroyed as great an army as the one that came with Datis and Artaphrenes into Attic territory. [2] And supposing it did not go well for them on both land and sea, but they engage with their ships and after winning a naval battle they sail to the Hellespont and then destroy the bridge? Surely this, my King, would be a dreadful thing.

[7.10γ] "But I myself do not contribute these possibilities by my own personal wisdom. Rather, it is the kind of suffering we once nearly brought on ourselves, when your father after bridging the Thracian Bosporus and the river Ister crossed against the Scythians. At that time, the Scythians were beseeching the Ionians by every means to destroy Darius's way of returning home. The guarding of the bridge over the Ister had been entrusted to the Ionians [4.136ff.]. [2] And then, if Histiaios, tyrant of Miletus, had followed rather than opposed the opinion of the other tyrants, Persian might would have been utterly ruined. Moreover, it is a dreadful thing even to hear that all the king's might came to be in the hands of one man.

[7.10δ] "Therefore, do not wish to enter into any such danger, since there is no necessity for it. Rather, be persuaded by me. Dissolve this special council. At another time, whenever it seems best to you, looking ahead by yourself alone, proclaim publicly what seems best to you. [2] For I find that planning well is the greatest advantage. For even if something you wish turns out the opposite, still the planning was done no less well, but the plan has been defeated by chance. But the man who planned shamefully has found a windfall, if

chance attends him. But nonetheless his planning was done
badly.

[7.10ε] "You see that the god strikes with a thunderbolt
living things that rise above others, and he does not allow
them to make a show of themselves. But small creatures do
not vex him at all. And you see that he always hurls his
thunderbolts against the greatest households and the tallest
trees. For the god loves to curtail all things that rise above
others. Thus, even a numerous army is destroyed by a small
one, in accordance with such a principle. Whenever the god,
begrudging their size, casts panic upon them or a thunderbolt, by themselves they are destroyed—unworthily. For the
god does not allow any other besides himself to have high
thoughts.

[7.10ζ] "So then, the hastening of everything produces
failures. And from failures, great penalties usually occur.
But good things reside in self-restraint. Even if they do not
immediately seem to be good, with time one would find
that they are.

[7.10η] "Now then, I advise this to you, O King. But you,
Mardonius, son of Gobryas, stop speaking foolish words
about the Greeks, who do not deserve to be ill-spoken of. For
by slandering the Greeks, you induce the king himself to
make war. And it seems to me that for this very purpose you
extend all your zeal. May this not now occur thus! [2] Slander
is a most dreadful thing. In it, two people do wrong and one
is wronged. For the slanderer accuses a man who is not
present. The one being misled does wrong before having
accurate knowledge. And the one absent from the conversation is wronged by being slandered by the one and by being
believed to be a bad man by the other.

[7.10θ] "But if then it is entirely necessary to march
against these men, come now, let the king himself remain in

the customary abodes of the Persians. And while we both
expose our children to danger, you, Mardonius, lead out the
army, having chosen the men you want and as large an army
as you wish. [2] And if matters proceed for the king in the
way in which you say, let my sons be killed, and me myself
along with them. But if matters proceed in the way I foretell,
let *your* children suffer these things, and you yourself with
them—if you make it home. [3] But if you do not wish to put
yourself under these conditions, and you will at any rate lead
out an army against Greece, I say that those of the Persians
left behind here will hear that you, Mardonius, having done
great harm to the Persians, have been torn to pieces by dogs
and birds somewhere in the land of the Athenians, unless of
course this happens earlier on the journey there—but after
you have come to know what sort of men you are persuading
the king to attack."

[7.11] Artabanus said these things. But Xerxes, enraged,
answered with the following words: "Artabanus, you are my
father's brother, and this will save you from receiving the
recompense you deserve for your foolish words. But since you
are a bad and fainthearted man, I will inflict upon you this
dishonor: you will not lead out the army against Greece with
me. Instead, you will remain here with the women. And
without you I will accomplish all the things I said I would.
[2] For may I not have been born the son of Darius, son of
Hystaspes, son of Arsames, son of Ariaramnes, son of Teïspes,
son of Achaemenes, if I do not take vengeance upon the
Athenians! Because I understand well that if we keep the
peace, they will not. Rather, they will certainly attack our
land—if it is necessary to make a calculation from the things
they have already done. These are the men who burned Sardis
and marched against Asia. [3] It is not possible, therefore, for
either side to retreat. But the contest lies before us, either to

act or to suffer, so that either all things here come to be under
Greek control, or all things there come to be under Persian
control. For there is no middle space at all for our enmity.
[4] It is a fine thing, therefore, that we who have suffered first
take vengeance—so that I may learn 'this terrible thing' which
I will suffer by attacking against these very men whom Pelops,
the Phrygian slave of my ancestors, so subjugated that even to
this day both the people themselves and their land are named
for the one who conquered them."

Herodotus once again crafts an illustrative (rather than
verifiably historical) narrative, this time a cautionary tale of an
autocrat thwarting productive debate. Herodotus very likely
lacked eyewitness reports for this farcical, specially summoned
advisory council. And any eyewitness account would necessarily have undergone five decades of distortion.[1] Perhaps the
convening of a council implies that the decision is not yet final.[2] But King Xerxes only pretends to seek good advice. Xerxes claims to assemble the noblemen to hear their views and
declare his desires (7.8.1). But, in fact, Xerxes does the reverse,
first stating his intentions and only afterward asking the noblemen's opinions. Recognizing that he need not list well-known
conquests of his autocratic predecessors, Xerxes asserts his determination to achieve not less than they. He insists that glory
(*kudos,* the glory conferred not, like *kleos,* by human beings but
by gods) derives from conquering vast tracts of productive
lands while simultaneously getting revenge.[3] Rather than seeking advice, Xerxes says he convened the noblemen to tell them
his plans (7.8α.1–2). By crossing the Hellespont and conquering and burning Athens, Xerxes intends to take vengeance on
the Athenians on his father's behalf (7.8β). Envisioning a Persia coterminous with the realm of Zeus (i.e., constituting the
entire world), Xerxes evokes not the wisdom but the greed and

ambition of the men he has convened to advise him (7.8γ). Xerxes proudly presents his imperialist objectives as morally indiscriminate, promising to enslave both the guilty and the innocent (7.8γ3) while offering prizes to whoever provides the best-prepared army (7.8δ.1).

Once Xerxes declares his motives and intentions, his subsequent request for other opinions is a sham, and everyone knows it.[4] Openly admitting to insincerity, Xerxes invites no discussion by concluding: "These things must be done now in this way. But in order that I not seem to you to be following merely my own counsel, I set the matter before you all. And I command anyone who wishes to show forth his opinion" (7.8δ.2). Xerxes does not seek advice; he only wants to *seem* to seek advice. Xerxes has absolute authority and has stated his intentions. Who would dare to disagree?

Predictably, therefore, the first speaker offers not reasoned critique but fawning flattery and admiration, commending Xerxes' judgment, motives, and plan (7.9–9γ). Xerxes' cousin Mardonius begins servilely by addressing Xerxes as *despota*, "master" (7.9.1), calling him *basileu*, "king," only when referencing his military leadership role (7.9γ1). (By contrast Artabanus, the only speaker to risk dissenting, consistently addresses Xerxes as *basileu*, "king" [7.10α1; 7.10α3; 7.10β2; 7.10η].) Mardonius declares Xerxes *aristos*, "best," of all Persians, and his vengeful intentions *arista kai alēthestata*, "best and truest" (7.9.1). Identifying Greeks as easy prey because they are busy battling one another, Mardonius disparages Greek fighting ability and proclaims Persian military might invincible (7.9α-γ).

Herodotus has previously portrayed Xerxes as susceptible to the enticements and pressures of Mardonius and other self-interested advisors, including the Peisistratids, family of the exiled former Athenian tyrant (7.6.2–5). Mardonius has been urging Xerxes to punish the Athenians for the sake of his reputation and as a warning to others against attacking Persia, adding tempting descriptions of Europe's beauty, fertility, and desirability as a new possession for the king (7.5.2–3). Preying on Xerxes' ambition and greed, Mardonius serves not Persia's interests but his own, motivated, according to Herodotus, "because he was a lover of new opportunities and because he wished to become viceroy of Greece" (7.6.1).

Vulnerable to self-serving advisors, Xerxes exemplifies the tendency of autocratic leadership to invite sycophancy and inhibit productive discussion. The king's specially summoned council superficially evokes a democratic debate.[5] But Mardonius tells Xerxes just what he wants to hear, and others remain silent, fearing to voice contrary opinions (7.10). Only one speaker dares to offer cautionary advice. Relying for safety on his status as Xerxes' paternal uncle, Artabanus begins— ironically—by commending to this willful autocrat the *democratic* principle of debate, insisting on the necessity of comparing contrasting opinions in order to choose the best one (7.10α.1). Artabanus reminds his nephew that Darius ignored his warning against attacking Scythia—with terrible results. And now Xerxes is preparing to attack even better warriors than the Scythians (7.10α.2–3). Artabanus recalls the Persians' unsuccessful invasion of Attica and the near disaster of Darius's invasion of Scythia, when the Ionians nearly destroyed the bridges needed for his retreat. Bridging the Hellespont would pose the same risk (7.10β–γ). Artabanus advises risk avoidance, careful planning, and restraint (7.10δ–ζ). Arguing that "the god loves to curtail all things that rise above others" (7.10ε), Artabanus echoes Solon's warning that human fortunes vary (1.32).[6] Artabanus condemns unfounded slander, criticizing Mardonius for trying to manipulate Xerxes and for inaccurately belittling Greek martial abilities (7.10η). Anticipating disaster, he urges that at the very least Xerxes himself should remain in Persia and not accompany the invasion (7.10θ).

But absolute power enables the autocrat to discount valid objections. Xerxes remains closed-minded, unable to assimilate or address reasonable counterarguments. He cannot benefit from others' previous experience or use factual information to reassess his plans. Artabanus's sound advice and dire prediction (soon to prove accurate) only enrage Xerxes and strengthen his vengeful resolve. Artabanus's prescient warning appears as ineffective as those of other "warner" figures in the *Histories*.[7] Xerxes forbids Artabanus from joining the invasion. He refrains from further punishment only because Artabanus is his father's brother—clearly implying that he *would* punish anyone else for voicing opposition (7.11).

This parody of an advisory council illustrates the impossibility of free and open discussion under a strong-willed, vengeful autocrat. As the scene demonstrates, an authoritarian leader can best ensure poor advice from subordinates by stating his own opinion first. Once the autocrat has declared his intentions, only a very brave person will venture counterarguments— usually to no avail. The greater the power of an authority figure, and the more arbitrarily he wields it, the more likely subordinates will offer merely flattery and approval. Like Xerxes, authoritarian leaders surround themselves with servile sycophants and cowardly enablers. As Artabanus observes, productive decision-making requires a free exchange of opinions in order to identify the best ones. The self-willed autocrat succumbs to his own impulses and appetites, unable to hear or assimilate dissenting views.

Following this non-advisory council, an even more questionable approach to decision-making further emphasizes the irrationality of autocratic leadership. In a memorable

anecdote—perhaps invented, perhaps embellished by Herodotus or his source—Herodotus describes nighttime dreams
strengthening Xerxes' determination to pursue his vengeful,
acquisitive, and doomed plan. After reconsidering his uncle's
advice and deciding not to invade Greece, Xerxes experiences
a recurrent dream commanding him to attack (7.12–14). Ter-
rified, believing the dream divinely sent, Xerxes asks his
uncle to wear his clothes, sit on his throne, and sleep in his
bed to see if he experiences the same dream (7.15). Artabanus
criticizes Xerxes' inability to benefit from the prior council,
reminding him that he previously chose the more dangerous
option (7.16α.2). Artabanus does not believe that dreams
come from the gods or that a dream would mistake him for
Xerxes, even lying in Xerxes' bed and wearing his pajamas.
But he obeys his king's command (7.16β–γ). Threatened by a
dream for trying to dissuade Xerxes from attacking Greece,
Artabanus reverses his opinion (7.17–18). When another dream
convinces Xerxes that he will succeed in enslaving the entire
world (7.19), he begins four years of preparation (7.20). Herodotus's account may appear to confirm the role of divinity in
Xerxes' decision.[8] The assumption that divine will could manifest via dreams may have aligned with Persian (and Greek)
attitudes.[9] Perhaps Xerxes even cleverly uses dreams to gain
unanimous support.[10] But Herodotus presents Xerxes as not
crafty but credulous. Herodotus's readers have already seen
that dreams offer no control over the future (e.g., 1.34–45;
1.107–130). And Herodotus's contemporaries know that the
decision apparently validated by these dreams will not serve
Xerxes well.

Herodotus depicts the Persian king's irrational, counterproductive decision-making as a consequence of inherited autocratic authority. To the assembled noblemen, Xerxes invokes
his hereditary status as motivation and justification for his

vengeful imperialist intentions ("May I not have been born son of . . . son of etc. . . . if I do not etc.," 7.11.2).[11] And yet, hereditary kingship seems suboptimal because it derives not from ability but from the legitimacy and timing of birth, attributes sometimes difficult to ascertain and easy to challenge. Herodotus previously underscores the senselessness of Xerxes' accession to the Persian throne: Xerxes' leadership skills never factor into his father's choice of a successor from sons born to two different mothers (7.2–3). Herodotus attributes the decision to Xerxes' mother Queen Atossa, suggesting that "Atossa held all the power" (7.3.4). Earlier Herodotus similarly demeans Darius's masculine authority, claiming that Atossa persuaded him to attack Greece in order to display and expand his power and prevent other Persians from conspiring against him (3.134). The principle of hereditary kingship also fosters self-interested leadership and political conflict to the detriment of communal welfare, as Herodotus demonstrates in a detailed account of the contentious origins of the Spartans' dual kingship (6.52–55, 61–70).

In the absence of aptitude, expertise, or wisdom, autocratic authority—whether inherited or appropriated—cannot guarantee good leadership. In the Persian debate regarding regime types, Darius advocates monarchy (3.82), but he acquires the throne by a non-meritorious selection process, his groom's ingenuity, and his own unscrupulousness (3.84–87). Darius wields his power imprudently, invading Marathon to the Persians' great cost. His son's hereditary accession appears equally unmerited, resulting from the accident of his birth and a woman's preference for her own son. Inheriting his father's kingship, vengeance motive, and self-defeating leadership style, Xerxes fails to evaluate facts and choose wisely. Like his father, he, too, will lead his people into disaster—as Herodotus's contemporaries well knew.

Describing Xerxes' ill-conceived assault on Greece, Herodotus depicts the Persian king as a cautionary example to any military commander—ancient or modern—contemplating a large-scale, long-range invasion. Trusting to the great size of his army, Xerxes proceeds to fulfill his uncle's prior warning against taking unnecessary risks (7.10γ–δ), for the expedition makes the Persian forces repeatedly vulnerable to violent storms (7.33–34, 42, 188–191). Artabanus foresees the difficulty of maintaining a large fleet and army for months far from home, since few harbors will be large enough and land resources will be insufficient. Xerxes remains confident that the army can carry enough supplies and local farmers will provide the rest (7.49–50). In fact, rivers and lakes dry up (7.20–21, 108–109, 127, 187, 196) and local food supplies fall short (7.118–120). Today's long-range military expeditions face comparable challenges supplying troops with food and materiel.

Misplaced confidence in numerical superiority deafens Xerxes to prescient counsel and prevents him from perceiving intangible realities beneath surface appearances. Xerxes cannot comprehend the warning of another advisor, the exiled Spartan king Demaratus, that the Greeks will nevertheless resist. Herodotus portrays Demaratus as both a traitor to Sparta and an exemplar of Greek values.[12] Demaratus describes Greeks as poor but virtuous, their *aretē*, "excellence," a product of *sophiē*, "wisdom/cleverness," their strength a product of *nomos*, "law, custom, tradition." Even if all other Greeks submit to Persia, the Spartans never will, Demaratus insists, regardless of the Persians' numerical advantage (7.102). Lacking any conception of internal valor, Xerxes laughs incredulously. If Spartans are ordinary men like Demaratus in size and appearance, Xerxes maintains, they cannot possibly resist a vastly greater army (7.103.1–2). When Xerxes admits that the courage Demaratus attributes to Greeks and especially to Spartans is unusual among

Persians, though "some will be willing to battle three Greeks at once" (7.103.5), Demaratus realizes that Xerxes' obsession with numbers is preventing him from getting the point. No, Demaratus is not claiming that each Spartan can take on ten enemy fighters or even two. Spartan determination and valor derive instead from their ability to work together and their respect for *nomos* (7.104). Spoken by a Spartan about Spartans, the statement nevertheless articulates the Athenian association of democracy with civic strength.[13] Demaratus's claims are so completely incomprehensible to Xerxes that he treats them as a joke (7.105).

But the joke is on Xerxes. At Thermopylae, a small force of Spartans, fighting courageously until death, succeeds in holding off the Persians' much greater forces (7.196–233).[14] Herodotus's account of Thermopylae affirms the power not of numbers but of courage, determination, and skill. The Spartans display not only a commitment to honor and glory but also greater military training and expertise, and the Persians' numerical superiority provides no advantage (7.210–212). The Persians ultimately prevail only because a traitor reveals a hidden mountain path (7.213–218).[15] Learning that the Greeks are surrounded, the Spartan general Leonidas dismisses the allies, but he chooses honor and glory over life itself, refusing to withdraw his small Spartan force (7.220–222). Many Greeks but also many Persians fall, including two of Xerxes' brothers (7.224–225). Commending Leonidas and the three hundred Spartans killed defending the pass, Herodotus records the inscription later set up at Thermopylae memorializing their sacrifice and dedication: "Stranger, report to the Spartans that we lie dead here / Obedient to their words" (7.228.2).

Unable to benefit from wise advice or appreciate the intangible goods of valor and skill, the autocrat retains misplaced confidence in his army's numerical superiority and outward appearance. Modern estimates of the forces vary, but all agree that Herodotus exaggerates the numbers.[16] And Herodotus emphasizes Xerxes' obsession with viewing his troops—from a marble throne on a hilltop (7.44), from a chariot, and from a ship (7.100).[17] Xerxes even exhibits his army to spies, certain that the Greeks will abandon their fight for freedom on learning the magnitude of the opposition (7.146–147). But Herodotus demonstrates that appearances can be deceiving. Fifteen Persian ships mistake Greek ships for their own and get captured (7.194). A Persian scout fails to see all the Spartans at Thermopylae and misinterprets what he does see, mistakenly believing that men exercising and combing their hair cannot be preparing for battle (7.208).[18] Watching the battle of Thermopylae from his throne, as if he were at the theater (7.212), Xerxes mistakes Spartan valor for *anaideiēi*, "shamelessness," and *aboulíēi*, "thoughtlessness" (7. 210.1). Before the battle, Xerxes cannot imagine that so few men will choose to fight against so many (7.209). But as Herodotus has already suggested, great numbers can be a liability rather than an advantage: the immense Persian fleet suffers massive losses in a storm (7.188, 190), and a draw in the naval battle at Artemisium and defeat at Salamis (described in book 8) lie ahead for the still more numerous Persians, as Herodotus's contemporaries understood.[19] Herodotus's lengthy catalogue of Persian forces (7.61–100) elevates the Greeks' achievement and emphasizes Xerxes' misjudgment.

Just as the numerical superiority of the Persian army masks its deficiencies in courage and skill, Xerxes' outward good looks and stature cloak the absence of wisdom and discernment within. Detailing Xerxes' forces, Herodotus offers a scathing, sardonic observation implying that successful leadership demands more than a pretty face and commanding physique: "Of so many tens of thousands of men, no one was

more worthy than Xerxes—because of his beauty and size
[*kalleos te heineka kai megatheos*]—to hold this power" (7.187.2).
Herodotus's distinction between outward appearance and
inner reality highlights the costs of prizing numerical superiority and impressive looks over valor, military skill, and intellectual ability. Plato (fourth century BCE) later draws an explicit
distinction between outer body and inner soul, but centuries
earlier Homeric epic had already begun to differentiate outward
beauty from inner prudence, presenting Odysseus, for example, as notable for his "appearance and size" and also for "knowing thoughts within" (*eidos te megethos* and *phrenas endon
eisas*) and "noble thoughts" (*phrenes esthlai*).[20] Homer's Odysseus remains his stalwart, clever self beneath various outward
transformations (warrior, shipwrecked sailor, decrepit old
beggar, splendid handsome king). Unable to perceive any dis-
connect between outward appearance and inner excellence,
Herodotus's Xerxes erroneously trusts that autocratic rule itself confers great advantage. Xerxes overestimates his own authority, commanding the Persian noblemen to fight bravely
(7.53), as if bravery could be summoned on command. Herodotus disparagingly deems the leaders of Xerxes' non-Persian
allies as not *stratēgoi*, "generals," but *douloi*, "slaves" (7.96.2). But
Xerxes cannot believe that free men, in an army of any size, will
fight as effectively as Persians driven by fear of their ruler and
by the whip (7.103). In fact, at Thermopylae autocratic leadership proves a liability; the advancing Persians, impelled not by
courage but by whips, trample each other (7.223).[21]

Exposing the fallacy of autocratic self-confidence, Herodotus also suggests that autocratic leadership impoverishes in-
tellectually even the lucky few whom it enriches materially. In
a subtle but potent anecdote, Herodotus depicts the Persian
preference for autocracy as a product of ignorance; Herodotus
describes a wealthy Persian, much honored by Xerxes, trying

to impress two Spartans with the material benefits of his subjection. Asked why they refuse to submit to Persia, although
the king would grant them lands to rule if they did (7.135.2),
the Spartans point out that the Persian is in no position to commend the life of slavery over a life of freedom, since he has
never experienced freedom. "For if you could try freedom,"
they explain, "you would advise us to fight for it not only with
spears but also with axes [i.e., civilian implements]" (7.135.3).

Herodotus associates autocratic leadership with not only
military and intellectual inadequacy but also moral depravity.
In contrast to the Spartans at Thermopylae, nobly sacrificing
their lives in defense of honor and freedom, the autocrat devalues human life. Impulsive, cruel, devoid of empathy, Xerxes
epitomizes atrocious autocratic brutality and arbitrary slaughter.
Like Cambyses and Darius before him, Xerxes corroborates the
accusation made by the proponent of political equality in the
Persian political debate: an autocrat "kills men without trial"
(3.80.5). Cambyses callously murders a brother (3.30), a sister
(3.31), an innocent young boy (3.35). Incensed by a devoted
supporter's hint of less than complete fidelity, Darius executes
three sons of a loyal Persian when asked to exempt one of them
from military service—having first cynically promised to leave
all three behind (4.84). Xerxes echoes his father's cruelty in
response to an analogous request: asked by a previously most
generous supporter to exempt one of his five sons from military service, Xerxes cuts the son in half and marches his army
off between the two halves (7.27–29, 38–39).[22] Xerxes' barbarity
may have a ritual background.[23] But Herodotus does not mention the possibility.[24] Persians as a group exhibit monstrous
disdain for human life. On crossing the river Strymon the
army buries alive eighteen local children—a Persian custom,
as Herodotus observes, having heard that Xerxes' wife once
ordered children of fourteen prominent Persian noblemen

buried alive as an offering "to the god said to be under the earth" (7.114). Whereas Herodotus's contemporary Greeks did not sacrifice human beings, the Persians fail to distinguish a human being from an animal, executing a captured Greek sailor in an effort to acquire a good omen before the battle of Thermopylae (7.180). After Thermopylae, Xerxes desecrates the corpse of the Spartan general Leonidas, ordering his head impaled on a stake (7.238).

Unable to value human life, the ruthless autocrat remains incapable of philosophical reflection. Xerxes' barbarity accompanies a bleak fatalism directly antithetical to the ancient Greek understanding of mortality as a positive force—perhaps *the* positive force in human life. Xerxes weeps on viewing his vast army, overcome by the brevity of human lifetimes. But he derives nothing from this insight. He merely accepts his uncle's fatalistic assessment that "since life is toilsome, death is the most preferable refuge" (7.44–46). For centuries before Herodotus, however, Greek epic poetry depicted the brevity of human life as the essential criterion for wise decision-making, the source of human achievement, and the impetus for human morality. Emphasizing that, unlike gods, human beings do not live forever and cannot act with impunity, the *Iliad* and *Odyssey* expose the uniquely human power to make either life-enhancing or self-defeating choices.[25] The Greeks assembling at Thermopylae recognize that the Persians are fully mortal, that mortal life always includes a mixture of success and adversity, and that therefore Xerxes is bound to fail (7.203.1–2). Awareness of the brevity of human life does not prompt Xerxes to reconsider his own goals and conduct.

Failing to appreciate that the brevity of human life makes every decision consequential, the overconfident, self-willed autocrat cannot learn from experience. Thermopylae confirmed Demaratus's claims about Spartan defensive valor, and Xerxes again asks his advice—and proceeds to ignore it. Xerxes chooses instead to follow the advice of a brother, who preys on Xerxes' insecurity and paranoia by suggesting that the exiled Spartan king may intend to betray Xerxes' interests (7.236.1). In military strategy, as in chess, the key to success lies in trying to imagine the opponent's capabilities and intentions, but Xerxes' brother argues the reverse, urging Xerxes to focus on his own interests rather than his enemies' plans, intentions, or numbers (7.236.2). And Xerxes unquestioningly follows his brother's advice rather than that of a man whose words have already proven prescient.

A cautionary reminder of Spartan autocratic discernment and Athenian majoritarian foolishness concludes book 7 and recalls Herodotus's assertion of the cause of the Persian invasion. Previously warning the Spartans of Xerxes' planned attack, the exiled Spartan king Demaratus cleverly inscribes a message on a wax tablet's wood frame before replacing the layer of wax. Gorgo, wife of King Leonidas, deduces that a message is under the wax (7.239). This story illustrates the Greek ability to discern reality beneath surface appearances. But it also recalls Herodotus's criticism of the foolish Athenian majoritarian decision that catalyzed the Persian Wars. For this same Gorgo, as a small child, warned her father, the Spartan king Cleomenes, against the corrupting bribery deployed by Aristagoras as he sought Spartan help for the Ionian Revolt (5.51.3). The Spartan king recognizes good advice and resists Aristagoras's enticements. But the Athenian populace succumbs (5.97)—motivating Darius and Xerxes to seek revenge by invading Greece (e.g., 5.102; 6.94; 7.8α2; 7.8β).

Despite this reminder of Spartan autocratic ingenuity and Athenian democratic folly, Herodotus repeatedly emphasizes the practical and moral deficiencies of autocratic leadership. Victim of his own anger and vengeful violence, Xerxes launches an expedition that will fail spectacularly—as Herodotus's contemporaries knew. Weak and easily manipulated, Xerxes ignores wise warnings, mistakes numerical superiority for actual superiority, treats human beings like animals, and fails to learn from experience. Though the Persians ultimately prevail at Thermopylae, Herodotus commends the Greeks' courage and resolute desire for freedom, and he condemns the Persian king's irrational materialism and barbarity.

In his disparaging portrait of Xerxes, Herodotus echoes Homer in exposing the inadequacy of hereditary political succession. Derived not from talent or achievement but from the accident of birth, inherited political authority and nepotism remain common features of autocratic (and oligarchic) leadership now as then. But centuries before Herodotus, with democratic ideals and institutions still hundreds of years in the future, Homer's epics already began to undermine confidence in the aristocratic principle of automatically inherited political power. The *Iliad*'s King Agamemnon, leader of the Greek forces at Troy, wields his inherited royal authority with stunning ineptitude, to the grave detriment of the warriors subject to his rule. In the *Odyssey*, Odysseus's son's claim to legitimate authority depends not on his father's status as king but on his own conduct; he must demonstrate his father's capacity for wise, benevolent sovereignty. The odds are against him, as Athena, goddess of wisdom, explains, insisting, "Few sons, you know, are equal to their fathers. More are worse, and few are better than their fathers."[26] The epic's human characters persist in believing nobility a product of inheritance, not conduct.[27] Odysseus's son resembles his father physically, as others observe, and during his travels he does begin to display the cunning, eloquence, and thoughtfulness characteristic of his father.[28] But if few sons can equal their fathers' achievements, as Athena maintains—and as goddess of wisdom she would know—then a political structure based on inherited authority cannot be optimal.

Revealing, like Homer, the regressive force of inherited political authority, Herodotus implicitly highlights the timeless problem of political succession. Throughout the eighth through sixth centuries BCE, *basileis,* "hereditary kings," *tyrannoi,* "autocrats who forcibly seized power," or hereditary oligarchies ruled Greek *poleis,* "citizen-communities." Herodotus emphasizes the brutality required to maintain autocratic power, as one tyrant metaphorically advises another to murder potential rivals, demonstrating by wordlessly lopping off the tallest ears in a cornfield (5.92). But no one lives forever, and children may lack their parents' talents—for good or evil. Tyrannies rarely lasted beyond the third or even the second generation. Though the Persians ignore the issue of political succession in discussing political regime types (3.80–82), democracy alone offers the possibility of peaceful regime change and nonviolent conflict resolution. Violent regime change characterizes autocracies. Kings and tyrants rarely die peacefully in their beds.

Autocratic leadership not only fails to resolve the problem of political succession, it also unleashes tyrannical appetites and impulses. Characterized by closed-minded moral certainty and misguided judgment, unfettered power discourages dissent and cannot incorporate valid counterarguments. Unable to learn from experience, Xerxes leads his people into disaster, as subsequent events will show. Cambyses, Darius, and Xerxes all corroborate the accusation, leveled against autocracy in book 3, that "the tyrant disrupts ancestral customs, sexually assaults women, and kills men without trial" (3.80.5). And tyrants' absolute power ensures their destruction.[29] Plato's description of the tyrant accurately describes Herodotus's Xerxes.[30] Enslaved to his own passions, as Plato recognizes, the tyrant serves no one's interests, not even his own.

In his depiction of Xerxes, Herodotus cautions against entrusting absolute power to *any* individual or group, small or large. Like all forms of unrestrained authoritarian leadership, Xerxes remains obstinate, vindictive, and unable to acquire wise counsel. Flatterers fear to check his impulses or challenge his ideas. Facing no external constraints, any absolute authority develops, like Xerxes, no internal ones. In demonstrating that a pretense of debate is as good as no debate at all, Xerxes' non-advisory council exposes not only the deficiencies of autocratic leadership but also the dangers of ideological bullying. Like a resentful, rapacious autocrat or cult leader—ancient or modern—any powerful, undiscerning, self-righteous group gets bad advice and makes self-destructive decisions if it silences dissent (even, or especially, in the interests of ideological purity). Intimidation (face-to-face or on social media) stifles debate, prevents creativity, and makes us all, like Xerxes, vulnerable to our own most self-defeating passions.

Herodotus's condemnation of autocratic leadership fosters appreciation for the constructive potential of peaceful democratic politics. Hereditary authority derives from accidents of birth. Democratic elections permit the possibility of merit-based leadership. Under a true democracy, officials leave when voted out of office and newly elected officials take over. Democracy endures if citizens have confidence in the legitimacy of elections and respect for the humanity of political opponents. Democracy survives if citizens and public officials value the rule of law and commit to nonviolent conflict resolution and peaceful legislative revisions. Unlike an autocrat, all leaders and groups in a participatory democracy must recognize their own strengths and weakness, seek wise, humane advisors, welcome opposing opinions, and incorporate factual evidence in making decisions.

Promoting attitudes required for preserving democratic institutions and norms, Herodotus's critique of autocratic leadership offers a timeless warning against closed-minded, authoritarian politics. In ancient Greece, autocrats inherited power or seized it by force. In modern times, authoritarian rulers can be democratically elected. They may abolish term limits and future elections and call themselves "presidents for life." They may undermine citizens' confidence in the integrity of elections and refuse to accept legitimate election results. Demonizing political enemies, authoritarian leaders provoke violence. Xerxes opposes not domestic political adversaries but foreign enemies, but in his ineffectual advisory council, even a Persian nobleman recognizes the folly of treating fellow citizens as enemies. Eager to exploit Greek internal divisions and animosities, Xerxes' sycophantic general Mardonius notes the foolishness of Greeks fighting Greeks, maintaining, "These men speak the same language. They use heralds and messengers. They ought to put an end to their disagreements by any method rather than battles" (7.9β.2). Herodotus seems to address his Greek contemporaries directly here.[31] But the warning transcends time and circumstances. By violence, intimidation, and intolerance of opposing views, vengeful autocratic leaders (and authoritarian movements) prevent us from discovering creative solutions to complex problems. Autocratic leadership sometimes achieves dominance but never social justice.

17

On Excellence

An inspiring portrait of human excellence accompanies Herodotus's condemnation of autocratic leadership. Despite suggesting throughout his narrative of the Persian Wars that divinities impede the Persians and assist the Greeks, Herodotus remains focused on human choices and actions.[1] His account of the naval battle at Salamis (480 BCE)—undoubtedly as disappointing to modern military historians as his descriptions of the battles of Marathon and Thermopylae—concentrates on illustrative anecdotes.[2] And once again we have little alternative evidence for comparison.[3] Writing a half century after the battle, Herodotus likely drew on eyewitness claims—surely embellished over the intervening decades. Much of his account remains unverifiable, though the Greeks did win.[4] The tragedian Aeschylus depicts the battle in his *Persians* (472 BCE), produced just eight years after the event. Though of limited historical utility, Aeschylus's play largely parallels the ideological perspective conveyed by Herodotus.[5]

More moralism than journalism, Herodotus's description of the battle of Salamis and preceding events extols the value of Greek democratic decision-making and military skill over Persian autocratic decision-making and military incompetence.

Herodotus depicts Greek courage, discernment, and humanity prevailing at Salamis over Persian cowardice, materialism,
and barbarity. But Herodotus combines praise for Athens as the
liberator of Greece with concerns about impending Athenian
imperialism.[6] His portrait of human excellence also cautions
against mistaking military might for moral virtue. Before the
battle, with Peloponnesian support still uncertain, the Greeks
gather at Salamis, unaware that the Persians have surrounded
their fleet:

[8.78] There was much heated debate among the generals at
Salamis. They did not yet know that the barbarians had
encircled them with their ships; they thought they remained
in place, just as they had seen them arranged during the day.
    [8.79] While the generals were arguing, Aristides, son of
Lysimachus, crossed from Aegina. He was an Athenian, but he
had been ostracized by the people. Having learned of Aristides' character, I myself have recognized that he was the best
and most just man in Athens. [2] Standing at the doors of the
council, Aristides called forth Themistocles—who was no
friend to him but the greatest personal enemy. But because of
the present troubles, Aristides determined to forget their
animosity, and he called Themistocles forth, wishing to
converse with him. Aristides had heard beforehand that the
Peloponnesians were eager to withdraw their ships to the
Peloponnese. [3] And when Themistocles went out to him,
Aristides said the following: "In any critical moment—and
surely particularly in this one—it is necessary for us to
compete over which of us two will do more good for our
homeland. [4] And I declare to you that it is an equal matter
for the Peloponnesians to speak a lot or a little about sailing
away henceforth. For I myself, having been an eyewitness, tell
you that now the Corinthians and Eurybiades himself [Spar-

tan general leading the Greek fleet] will not be able to sail away, even if they wish. For we are encircled by the enemies. Going inside, point out these things to the generals."

[8.80] And Themistocles replied with the following: "You give very useful orders, and you have reported well. For you arrive having yourself been an eyewitness of events that I myself wanted to occur. Understand that the Persians are doing these things because of me. For when the Greeks were unwilling to take themselves into battle, it was necessary to bring them over to it against their will. But since you arrived bringing a useful report, give the generals the report yourself. [2] For if I myself declare the same things, I will seem to be speaking fabrications. And I will not be persuasive. They will persist in believing that the barbarians are not doing these things. But you yourself, going forward, point out to them how circumstances stand. And when you point this out, if they are persuaded, this now is best. But if these things are not credible to them, it will be the same for us. For they will no longer be able to run their ships through, if we are surrounded everywhere, as you say."

[8.81] Coming forward, Aristides said these things, declaring that he came from Aegina and escaped the attackers' notice, slipping through only with difficulty. For the entire Greek encampment was now surrounded by Xerxes' ships. Aristides advised the Greeks to prepare to defend themselves. Having said this, he withdrew. But among the generals once again there was an argument, for the majority disbelieved the things that had been reported.

[8.82] But while the generals were distrusting Aristides' report, there arrived a warship of Tenian deserters commanded by Panaitios, son of Sosimenes. This very ship now brought the whole truth. And because of this deed, the Tenians were inscribed on a tripod [dedicatory offering] in

Delphi as among those who destroyed the Barbarian. [2] With this ship, then, having deserted to Salamis, and the Lemnian ship that had previously joined the Greeks at Artemisium, the Greek fleet was filled out to 380 ships. For at that time it was lacking exactly two ships for that number.

[8.83] Since the words spoken by the Tenians were now credible to the Greeks, they prepared to fight a naval battle. The light of day was beginning to shine through, and they convened a meeting of the fighting men on the ships. Of all the generals, Themistocles publicly made constructive statements. All of his words contrasted the better with the worse, the stronger with the weaker—in the nature of human beings and in the current situation. [2] Advising them to choose the better of these, and winding up his speech, Themistocles ordered them to board the ships. And they now did so. Just then, the warship which had gone away to fetch the descendants of Aiacus arrived from Aegina. Thereupon, the Greeks put all their ships out to sea. And as they did so, the barbarians immediately set upon them.

[8.84] The other Greeks were putting their ships sternwards, backing water, and they were running their ships ashore. But an Athenian man, Ameinias of Pallene, having sailed out, rammed an enemy ship. But his own ship became entangled, and the two ships were not able to get free. And so the other Greeks, coming to aid Ameinias, joined the fight. [2] The Athenians say that the beginning of the battle occurred in this way. But the Aeginetans [claim] that the ship that had gone away to Aegina to fetch the descendants of Aiacus was the one that began the battle. The following is also said: that an apparition of a woman appeared to them. This spoke and exhorted so that the whole army of the Greeks heard, reproaching them first with this: "O you fine ones! How long will you continue to back water?"

[8.85] And now the Phoenicians were ranged opposite the Athenians. For the Peloponnesians held the western wing of the Persian line, toward Eleusis, and the Ionians were opposite the Spartans. The Ionians held the eastern wing, toward the Piraeus. A few of the Ionians, moreover, deliberately played cowards, following Themistocles' commands. But more did not. [2] I am able to relate the names of many of the trierarchs who seized Greek ships, but I will mention none—except Theomestor, son of Androdamas, and Phylacus, son of Histiaius, both Samians. [3] I mention these two only for this reason: because Theomestor, on account of this deed, was installed by the Persians as tyrant of Samos. And Phylacus was officially registered as a Benefactor of the King and awarded much land. In Persian, Benefactors of the King are called "Orosangai."

[8.86] Concerning these men, then, that is how it was. But the majority of the king's ships were disabled, some destroyed by the Athenians, some by the Aeginetans. For the Greeks fought in good order and held their battle positions. But since the barbarians did nothing, neither as they were commanded nor prudently, events turned out just as this would ensure. The Persians were, however, better by far on this day than they themselves had been off Euboea [at the battle of Artemisium], every man displaying zeal and fearing Xerxes. And each man believed that the king was watching him.

[8.87] Now, in regard to the others, I am not able to say exactly how each of the barbarians or Greeks fought. But as for Artemisia, the following happened—and from it, she gained still more esteem from the king: [2] for when the king's affairs had reached great confusion, in this critical moment, Artemisia's ship was being pursued by an Attic ship. And not being able to escape (for other friendly ships were in

front of her, and her ship happened to be nearest the enemies),
it seemed best to her to do the following—and it turned out
to her advantage when she did it: for being pursued by the
Attic ship, Artemisia ran at full speed against a friendly ship
of Calyndian men. And the king of the Calyndians himself,
Damasithymus, was sailing on it. [3] Whether some quarrel
had occurred with him when they were still at the Hellespont, I am not able to say, nor whether Artemisia did this
deliberately or the ship of the Calyndians happened to fall in
her way by chance. [4] But as she struck and disabled it, by
good fortune she accomplished for herself a double success.
For when the trierarch of the Attic ship saw her ramming a
ship of barbarian men, he believed that Artemisia's ship was
either Greek or was deserting from the barbarians and
defending the Greeks. Turning away, he changed course
toward other ships.

[8.88] This turned out to Artemisia's advantage—that
she escaped and was not destroyed. But this also turned out
well in that though Artemisia had harmed Xerxes, from these
actions she was most esteemed by Xerxes. [2] For it is said
that the King, watching, perceived her ship as it did the
ramming. And then one of his attendants said, "Master, do
you see how well Artemisia fights and has disabled an enemy
ship?" And Xerxes asked if the deed was truly Artemisia's.
And his attendants declared that they clearly recognized the
figurehead of her ship. And they believed that the destroyed
ship was an enemy ship. [3] For these other matters, as has
been said, turned out to Artemisia's advantage, occurring by
the good fortune also that no one of the Calyndian ship
survived to become her accuser. And Xerxes is said to have
stated in response to what had been said, "My men have
become women, and my women men." They say that Xerxes
said this.

[8.89] In this battle, the general Ariabignes died. He was a son of Darius and brother of Xerxes. Also many other famous men of the Persians and Medes and their allies perished. But few of the Greeks died. For since they knew how to swim, those of the Greeks whose ships were destroyed and were not killed in the hand-to-hand fighting swam to Salamis. [2] But many of the barbarians perished in the sea, not knowing how to swim. And when the first ships turned to flight, thereupon most of the ships were destroyed. For the ones stationed in the back were attempting to pass to the front with their ships so as to display some achievement to the king. And they were wrecked against their own fleeing ships.

Despite the unexpected Greek victory at Marathon, succeeding events lengthen the odds against the Greeks at Salamis a decade later. Herodotus characterizes the Spartans' destruction at Thermopylae (480 BCE) as not a futile effort but an emblem of Greek valor and a harbinger of future victory. But the Persians' subsequent devastation of Attica nearly precipitates a complete Greek defeat. The naval battle off Artemisium (contemporaneous with Thermopylae but described after) results in a stalemate, despite an initial Greek victory and heavy Persian losses due to storms (8.1–18).[7] Learning of the defeat at Thermopylae, the Greek forces hasten to Salamis (8.21). The Athenian general Themistocles cunningly leaves messages encouraging Persia's Ionian supporters to desert to the Greeks or remain neutral, calculating, Herodotus assumes, that the messages will either induce defections or at least undermine Xerxes' confidence in his allies' loyalty (8.19, 22). But the Peloponnesians, losing hope of protecting northern Greece, prepare to defend their own territory farther south at the Isthmus of Corinth (8.40). The Athenians evacuate their households to Troezen, Aegina, and Salamis (8.41), and the Greek fleet, drawn from various communities, gathers at Salamis (8.42–48). Learning that the Persians have burned Thespiae and Plataea and are plundering and burning Attica, the alarmed Peloponnesians intend to withdraw to the isthmus (8.49–50)—until Themistocles threatens that Athens will abandon Greece altogether if the Peloponnesians depart (8.56–64). As the Peloponnesians still wish to head south (8.74), Themistocles convinces the Persians, via a secret messenger, that he himself wants a Persian victory, and he advises the Persians to prevent the Greeks from escaping (8.75). Accepting Themistocles' message as *pista*, "credible," the Persians surreptitiously encircle the Greek fleet at Salamis (8.76).

Facing long odds, the Greek generals at Salamis engage in productive debate. Their verbal dispute before the battle contrasts with the Persian king's unilateral command. The Spartan general leading the Greek fleet encourages discussion, beginning by asking for others' opinions (8.49), whereas Xerxes, in his pseudo-advisory council prior to the invasion, discouraged opposing views by stating his own intentions first (7.7–8). Disagreement among the Greek generals results from ignorance of fact, and new evidence resolves it, once the Tenian ship confirms Aristides' claim that the Persians have indeed encircled the Greeks (8.79–83). By contrast, Xerxes chose to invade Greece independent of—even in opposition to—factual considerations (7.10–11). Admittedly, in addressing the Greeks' divergent self-interests, the treachery of the Athenian general Themistocles proves more effective than his efforts at persuasion.[8] But before battle begins, Themistocles persuasively exhorts his fellow Greeks; he does not command their obedience or threaten violence (8.83), whereas the Persian king issued commands (e.g., 7.8δ), punishments, and threats (e.g., 7.11.1).

While discussion enables the Greeks to absorb facts and recognize wise counsel, the Persians ignore factual evidence and fail to learn from previous experience. Despite underestimating the Spartans at Thermopylae and therefore suffering heavy losses, the Persians cannot comprehend the willingness of a small Greek fleet to challenge their larger one (8.10). But in the naval battle off Artemisium, as in the land battle at Thermopylae, a smaller Greek force defies expectations, doing well in the initial engagement (8.11). Subsequently, shame at performing so poorly against so few ships (and fear of Xerxes' reaction) motivates the Persian commanders (8.15.1). And, as at Thermopylae, the venue off Artemisium, in this case not a mountain pass but a narrow strait, impedes the larger force, "for" Herodotus explains, "Xerxes' force was overcome by its own magnitude and multitude, with its ships thrown into disorder and dashing against each other" (8.16.2). Nevertheless, the Persians persist in valorizing quantity over quality, motivated by the belief that it would be terrible to lose to a smaller force (8.16.2). They ignore their experiences not only at Thermopylae and Artemisium but also in their siege of the Athenian Acropolis, where a tiny force of Athenians bravely fights to the death (8.51–54).

The Persians' inability to learn from experience includes a failure to benefit even from supernatural signs. Focused throughout on human desires and decisions, Herodotus incorporates reports of oracles and portents and people's responses to them (e.g., 8.36–39; cf. 8.41.2–3, 64), with oracles proving "correct"—but only after the fact (e.g., 8.20). He suggests that Greeks can benefit from supernatural warnings as well as wise counsel but Persians cannot.[9] The Athenians prove wise in previously accepting Themistocles' shrewd interpretation that an oracle advising them to trust to "a wooden wall" meant they must rely on their fleet (7.141.3). By contrast, the Persian king lacks the opportunity to respond to a definitive portent as he never even learns of it. Xerxes' autocratic power and unwillingness to hear dissent makes his subjects fear to tell him potentially useful, if unpleasant, information. As the Persians destroy Athens, burn the Acropolis, and plunder its sanctuaries (8.51–53), the Spartan exile Demaratus witnesses a large dust cloud coming from Eleusis and hears a supernatural voice. An Athenian exile informs Demaratus that this divine utterance foretells disaster for Xerxes (8.65.2). Although both men recognize the omen's clear warning, fear of Xerxes' anger prevents them from informing the king (8.65.5).

Insulated from unfavorable supernatural warnings, Xerxes also remains impervious to factual evidence and prudent counsel. Herodotus introduces Artemisia, Xerxes' sole female naval commander, as leader of a contingent of five ships deemed second best in the king's fleet (7.99.2–3). A real, historical figure, Artemisia draws the interest of ancient and modern scholars for Herodotus's insistence on her masculine bravery, represented as a denigration of Persian masculinity. But Herodotus's portrait, dismissed as implausible by Plutarch, particularly emphasizes Artemisia's wisdom and strategic intelligence.[10] And although Herodotus considers Artemisia's counsel the best offered by Persia's allies (7.99.3), Xerxes fails to follow her sage advice against risking a battle at Salamis (8.67–69). Artemisia reminds Xerxes that he has already accomplished his purposes by conquering Athens (8.68α.2). She wisely advises him to remain in place or advance into the Peloponnese, since either way the Greeks will flee to their own cities. Their supplies are low, and they will not want to remain to fight a sea battle for the Athenians (8.68β). If Xerxes launches a sea battle now, Artemisia recognizes, he will lose and also imperil his land army. Artemisia praises Xerxes as "best of all men," but she claims that his allies include "the worst slaves" (8.68γ). To the surprise of

Xerxes' other commanders, Artemisia's sole dissenting opinion does not anger the king but instead increases his regard for her—even as he ignores it. Xerxes seems unable to fathom any considerations other than his own personal role and influence; he attributes his men's poor performance at Artemisium to his absence, and he remains confident that they will fight well at Salamis under his direct oversight (8.69).

Unlike the narcissistic autocrat, the Greek generals not only make fact-based decisions and recognize wise counsel but also prioritize communal welfare over personal animosities. Though recently recalled from ostracism, Themistocles' political rival Aristides (ostracized 483 BCE) sets aside his personal enmity in the interests of Greek survival. (Ostracism by majority vote, essentially an *un*popularity contest, provided a safety valve enabling removal of a would-be tyrant. Requiring a citizen to leave Athens for ten years without forfeiting his property rights, ostracism could be exploited by political opponents, but in the current crisis, ostracized citizens had been recalled before their ten years were up.)[11] Recognizing that the Persian ships have encircled the Greeks, Aristides commends constructive rivalry, insisting that in the current troubles he and Themistocles should compete to determine who can most benefit the community (8.79.2–3). Themistocles willingly agrees to prioritize the survival of Greece, praising Aristides' suggestion and his report. Themistocles even implicitly acknowledges Aristides' greater reputation for trustworthiness, as he recognizes that the generals will find the claim of Persian encirclement more credible coming from Aristides than from himself (8.80.2).

Able to value constructive rivalry in the interests of communal survival, the Greeks also show themselves capable of foresight and skepticism in contrast to Persian unthinking credulity. Accepting Themistocles' prudent interpretation that the oracle about trusting to a "wall of wood" means the fleet, the Athenians similarly follow his shrewd advice to build two hundred ships after Marathon (7.140–144). Though Herodotus tacitly criticizes the judgment of Athenian voters by terming the formerly ostracized Aristides "the best and most just man in Athens" (8.79.1), at Salamis the Greeks prove discerning and reliant on factual evidence: hearing of the Persians' encircling action (8.80), the Peloponnesian commanders remain skeptical until convinced by the corroborating eyewitness report of deserters from the Persian fleet (8.81–82). By contrast, the Persians unquestioningly trust Themistocles' deceptive secret message luring them into attacking swiftly—against their own strategic interests (8.75–76). (Unlike Themistocles, Xerxes appears utterly inept at deception; even Persians find his ruse *geloion*, "laughable," when he tries unsuccessfully to conceal by burial the number of Persians killed at Thermopylae [8.24–25].)

Herodotus portrays Greek cleverness and skill triumphing at Salamis over barbarian disorganization, ignorance, and the desire to seem (rather than be) valiant. Undeniably tendentious, Herodotus observes that under attack, the Greeks fight in an organized, disciplined way, whereas the Persian forces do not—with predictable results (8.86). Herodotus claims that more Greeks survive than Persians because they know how to swim and that the Persians' disorder results in collisions between their ships, as the ones in the lead opt to flee (8.89). Although he maintains that the Persians do fight more energetically than at Artemisium, each believing the king is watching him (8.86), Herodotus depicts the desire to perform for the king as self-defeating, a cause of collisions between the fleeing ships (8.89.2).

Inserted into this Greek-ennobling account, Herodotus's tale of Artemisia's "own goal" devalues military accomplishment independent of context and accurate assessment. Watching safely from afar, and subsequently rewarding or punishing commanders and sailors at his whim (8.90), Xerxes fails to draw correct deductions from misleading appearances.[12] Whether Artemisia rams a friendly ship deliberately or accidentally, Herodotus cannot say. But the Greek commander of the pursuing ship incorrectly assumes that Artemisia has deserted the Persians and stops chasing her (8.87). From his lofty position above the fray, Xerxes cannot even recognize an allied ship, wrongly believing that Artemisia has sunk an enemy vessel (8.88.2). His advisors may have feared to set him straight.[13] Misinformed, Xerxes asks the wrong question, not "Did Artemisia strike an enemy ship?" but "Was that Artemisia's ship?"

In erroneously commending Artemisia's military "achievement," Xerxes not only illustrates the necessity of accurately contextualizing any martial victory but also exposes the foolishness of enjoying violence as entertainment. Picturing Xerxes viewing the battle as if it were a theatrical performance, Herodotus's contemporaries might recall Homer's depiction of the great god Zeus eagerly viewing the Trojan War from Olympus, delightedly watching men kill and be killed.[14] Xerxes' subjects consider him a god, but Greeks know that no man is a god. Greek epics and tragedies might portray human beings as "god-like," or admired like gods.[15] But mortality remained the crucial distinction. Despite his god-like panoramic view, the mortal king completely misinterprets what he sees, and unlike Zeus he remains vulnerable to violence himself. Zeus's example in the *Iliad* cautions mortals against thinking that any human being can enjoy watching violence with impunity. Like gods, we may be invulnerable to violence viewed from afar (or on a screen), but unlike gods, we are not impervious to violence in our own lives. Like mortality itself, the vulnerability to violence distinguishes human beings from divinities. Behaving like a god, the mortal autocrat shows that he is a fool.

Though Herodotus's depiction of Xerxes reaffirms the crucial distinction between men and gods, his story of Artemisia does little to challenge the traditionally sexist distinction between men and women. Mistaking Artemisia's "achievement," Xerxes implicitly disparages women as weak-willed and timid, exclaiming, "My men have become women and my women men" (8.88.3). Herodotus's portrait of Artemisia may subtly critique or mock contemporary Athenians' misogyny (and/or xenophobia and/or imperialism).[16] But Herodotus seems to share Xerxes' assessment, for he previously introduced Artemisia as an exception proving the rule, deeming her extraordinary and worth mentioning for her resolve and bravery, explaining, "Now I am not mentioning other division commanders, since I am not constrained to, but I do consider Artemisia an especial marvel [thōma]—a woman who served in the army against Greece." Artemisia took over her husband's tyranny after his death, and "went to war because of her own courage and manliness, there being no necessity for her to do so" (7.99.1). Herodotus particularly emphasizes Artemisia's unforced choice to support Xerxes and her active deployment of gender stereotypes in offering advice.[17] Artemisia's presence among Xerxes' forces could itself be viewed as an insult to Greek masculinity.[18] With perhaps grudging admiration, Herodotus depicts Artemisia as so much like a man that even she disparages women, as she ironically belittles female achievement in urging Xerxes before the battle of Salamis, "Spare your ships and do not make a naval battle. For their men are better and braver [kressones] at sea than your men by as much as men are better and braver than women" (8.68α.1). Herodotus believes that if the Greek captain pursuing Artemisia's ship had known it was hers, he would not have abandoned pursuit

(8.93.1). Deeply troubled at the thought of being opposed by a female commander, the Athenians offer a large bounty for Artemisia's capture, "for they deemed it a terrible thing for a woman to make war against Athens" (8.93.2).

Without challenging traditional sexism, Herodotus's account of Salamis extols Greek achievement and Athenian excellence in particular. Herodotus previously interrupts his narrative in book 7 to attribute the defeat of Persia unequivocally to Athenian valor at Salamis.[19] Acknowledging tensions between Athens and Sparta in his own times, Herodotus claims: "Here, by necessity, I am forced to deliver an opinion that is hateful to many people. But nevertheless, since it appears to me to be true, I will not restrain myself. [2] If the Athenians, fearing the approaching danger, had left their own territory, or if not leaving but remaining had given themselves to Xerxes, no one would have attempted to oppose the king at sea" (7.139.1–2). Once the Persians controlled the sea, land opposition would have been ineffectual. Any attempt to wall off Xerxes' land army at the isthmus would have failed. Each community would have abandoned the Greek alliance as Xerxes' fleet subjugated them one by one. Some Greeks might have fought to the death while others might have medized (submitted to Persian control), but Greece would have fallen to the Persians (7.139.3–4). Perhaps the Greeks' ultimate military success derived in fact not from the Athenian victory at Salamis but from Spartan success at the battle of Platea the following year.[20] But Herodotus explicitly praises Athenian excellence, concluding that "anyone who says that the Athenians were the saviors of Greece would not err from the truth. For whichever of the two paths they turned to, that was going to tip the scales. They chose for Greece to remain free. And they were the ones who roused the remainder of Greece—all of it that had not medized—and drove out the king, with the gods' help." Undeterred even by terrifying oracles, the Athenians held their ground against the Persian invaders (7.139.5–6).

Herodotus depicts this extraordinary Athenian courage, skill, and determination as but one facet of a broader contrast between ruthless Persian materialism and a farsighted Greek ability to value people over possessions. Marching toward Delphi prior to the battle of Salamis, the Persians exhibit merciless rapacity, burning and plundering towns and temples and killing many women by multiple rapes (8.32–33, 35). Reporting the Persians' plan to plunder Apollo's temple at Delphi, Herodotus claims to have heard that Xerxes had detailed knowledge of the temple's dedicatory offerings, particularly those of Croesus (8.35.2; cf. 1.48–52). Evoking Croesus's conversation with Solon (1.30–33), this observation implicitly aligns Xerxes with Croesus. Neither can comprehend the distinction between material possessions and true prosperity and happiness. Both mistake wealth for good fortune. Greeks, however, prioritize human survival over material possessions, as—prefiguring the Athenian evacuation of Athens—the Delphians abandon their treasure and their city to save themselves (8.36). Though Herodotus suggests that the behavior of a snake in the sanctuary on the Acropolis influences the Athenians' decision to save people over possessions, the Athenians understand that Athens endures as long as Athenians do (8.41). When a Corinthian commander belittles Themistocles as a man without a country, since the Persians have destroyed Athens, Themistocles vigorously defends the principle that Athens survives as long as its ships and warriors survive (8.61.2). To show how little he values the specific territory of Attica, Themistocles threatens that the Athenians will all depart for Italy if the other Greeks abandon Greece and sail to the Peloponnese (8.62).

This conception of "Athens" as the people rather than their homeland seems especially surprising because the Athenian connection to the land of Attica ran deep. Athenians considered themselves *autochthonous* or "born from the earth itself."[21] According to tradition, the first Athenian king, Erichthonios (or Erichtheus), originated from the unrequited lust of the lame god Hephaestus, who ejaculated on the leg of Athena, patron goddess of Athens. Disgusted, Athena wiped off the sperm with a piece of wool and tossed it away. The sperm grew in the ground and the baby Erichthonios emerged, his name a combination of *eris*, "wool," and *chthonos*, "ground." At Salamis, the Athenians' self-conception as *autochthonous* combined paradoxically with their willingness to vacate Athens in order to preserve Greece.[22]

Herodotus contrasts this Athenian wisdom to value people over territory and property with a barbarian disdain for human life. Following the defeat at Salamis, the Persian general Mardonius callously endangers his land forces, choosing to remain and fight in fear of punishment from Xerxes for having urged the invasion in the first place. Doubling down, Mardonius evinces no concern for his men, preferring to conquer Greece or die nobly in the attempt, even if Xerxes himself returns to Persia (8.100). Commending Mardonius's proposal to Xerxes, Artemisia shows similar disregard not only for Mardonius's life but for the lives of his 300,000 warriors. She reasons that Xerxes will ensure his own safety by returning to Persia and gain glory if Mardonius prevails, but he will lose nothing if Mardonius loses, for Xerxes' power in Asia will survive (8.101–102). Xerxes shares Artemisia's indifference to the human costs of a defeat. Her advice pleases him by aligning with his own thoughts, and his terror was such, according to Herodotus, that no advice would induce him to remain (8.103).

In a memorable anecdote, Herodotus vividly illustrates the Persian king's disregard for the lives of others. Many men die from hunger and disease during Xerxes' panicked retreat to the Hellespont (8.115), and when Xerxes' ship, sailing toward the Hellespont, encounters a storm, the ship's pilot explains that it must lighten its load to survive. The selfish autocrat invites the many Persians aboard to show their loyalty to him by jumping overboard—and they promptly do. Arriving safely in Asia, Xerxes rewards the ship's pilot with a gold crown for saving the life of his king but then has him executed because he destroyed many Persians (8.118). Prioritizing obedience over humanity, Xerxes here apes his tyrannical predecessor Cambyses, whose delight at Croesus's survival does not prevent him from executing the servants who disobeyed their king's order to kill him (3.36.5–6). Certain that Xerxes returned to Susa not by ship but overland, Herodotus finds the tale of Xerxes and the ship's pilot implausible. But he hardly exonerates Xerxes from a charge of inhumanity by insisting that the king would have had Phoenician rowers hurled overboard rather than lose any Persians, especially noblemen (8.119–120).

Against Xerxes' selfish and self-defeating barbarity, Herodotus juxtaposes the Athenian resolve to preserve Greek freedom. At Salamis, the Athenians yield to their allies' preference for Spartan leadership of the fleet, despite Athens supplying almost half of the ships (8.1–3), the best ones, and more than any other city (8.42). After Salamis, with the war not over and Greek victory still uncertain, Athenians seek to signal continued resolve in the face of Spartan mistrust. Resisting Mardonius's persuasion to submit to Persia, the Athenians publicly reject Persian promises of land and independence (with continued war the alternative), conveyed by the king of Macedon acting as intermediary (8.136, 140). Knowing the Spartans' fear of Athens accepting the Persian offer, the Athenians delay their response until the Spartans can be present to hear it (8.141). With the Spartans present, anxiously urging Athens to reject the Persian proposal and promising to supply Athenian women and other noncombatants with food (8.142), the Athenians grandly refuse, telling the Macedonian king that they know the Persians greatly outnumber them, "but nevertheless being eager for freedom, we are defending it in whatever way we are able. And do not try to mislead us into making an agreement with the barbarian. We will not be persuaded" (8.143.1). Reiterating their determination, the Athenians threaten violence against the Macedonian king if he ever dares to bring such arguments to them again in the guise of being helpful while in fact advising them to do things that are *athemista*, "lawless and godless" (8.143.2–3). Elsewhere, Herodotus exposes a confluence of idealistic and self-interested motives driving Athenian actions, but here he identifies the Athenian commitment to freedom as central to Greek identity.[23] The Athenians denounce as shameful the Spartan fear that Athens might come to terms with Persia, since they know well that "there is not enough gold anywhere or territory excelling in beauty or excellence that we would accept and could make us wish to medize and enslave Greece" (8.144.1).

Although this display of Athenian resolve exposes distrust and discord between Athens and Sparta, Herodotus continues to distinguish a Persian conception of excellence (external, quantifiable, material) from a Greek conception (internal, intangible, qualitative). One anecdote before the battle of Salamis encapsulates the Persians' failure to understand value in other than material terms. Learning that the Greeks are celebrating the Olympic festival and watching athletic and equestrian competitions, "Xerxes asks what they are contending for," and he is told that "an olive wreath is the thing given" to the winner. On learning that the prize is not money or possessions, one of the noblemen accompanying Xerxes exclaims in surprise, "Ah! Mardonius, against what kind of men have you led us to fight, who make a competition not about money but about excellence [*aretē*]?" (8.26). The Persians fail to see the ambiguity in the question "What do the Greeks compete for?" The question combines "What is the prize for victory?" with "What is the reason or motive for the contest?" The prize, the olive wreath, symbolizes victory. A marker of honor and glory, a wreath has little material value but great intangible value. The goal, *aretē*, "excellence, virtue," distinguishes Greek character and substance from Persian superficiality and material greed.[24]

In his account of the Greek victory at Salamis, Herodotus depicts human excellence as a product of democratic freedoms and vital to their preservation. The Persian king makes unilateral decisions. He lacks discernment and access to dissenting opinions. He draws incorrect inferences from misleading external appearances. In contrast, Greeks benefit from constructive debate. They excel in nonmaterial intellectual goods equally available to anyone. The undiscerning autocrat fails to benefit from wise counsel or learn from experience. He misinterprets visual information, mistaking Artemisia's sinking of an allied ship as a military success (8.87–88). Greek success derives not only from courage, determination, and ingenuity but also from the democratic arts of verbal persuasion, fact-based decision-making, and the wisdom to value human lives over material objects. The Greek concept of inner excellence ultimately triumphs over barbarian superficiality and rapacity. Although Greek unity remains provisional and fragile, Xerxes fails to exploit internal Greek divisions.[25] Herodotus contrasts Greek unity of purpose and willingness to fight to the death, at Salamis as at Thermopylae, with Persians who compete against one another for Xerxes' rewards and are reluctant to sacrifice their lives.[26] In the battle of Salamis, as at Marathon, Thermopylae, and Artemisium, communal defensive valor confronts vengeful autocratic opportunism, and Greek democratic freedoms prevail.

Herodotus suggests that the Greek concept of excellence triumphs, but in the figure of the wily Athenian general Themistocles the distinction between Persian materialism and Greek inner virtue begins to fracture.[27] Arguably, Themistocles plays the most decisive role in defending Greece. Although he himself has placed the Greek fleet in a precarious predicament, his talents for deception and prompt action preserve Greek unity and compel the Persians to fight. Themistocles cleverly attempts to detach Ionians from the Persian forces (8.19, 22). He makes intelligent, rational arguments to persuade the Greeks to remain at Salamis instead of fleeing to the Corinthian isthmus. He shrewdly appeals to Greek self-interest by pointing out that abandoning Salamis would simply bring the enemy down to the Peloponnese and endanger all of Greece (8.60α). Spelling out the advantages for fewer ships fighting against many in the narrow strait off Salamis, Themistocles reminds the Peloponnesians that by defending Salamis they will equally defend the Peloponnese farther south (8.60β). His calculated threat that Athens will abandon Greece makes other Greek commanders realize that without the Athenian ships they have no hope of defeating the Persians (8.62–64). Themistocles also tricks the Persians into initiating the attack at Salamis before the Peloponnesians can withdraw (8.75–76).

In his ingenuity and determination, Themistocles exemplifies the mutually beneficial relationship between a gifted individual and a high-achieving community. Herodotus claims that the Aeginetans and the Athenians performed *arista*, "the best deeds," at Salamis, and he names individual Greek commanders (8.93), but major credit must go to Themistocles for engineering the battle. When the Greeks divide the spoils of victory and award prizes for valor, each commander votes himself first prize, but everyone votes Themistocles second (8.122–123). The Spartans in particular give Themistocles great honor

and prizes (8.124). When a jealous Athenian belittles Themistocles, claiming that his honors were Athens's achievement
not his own, Themistocles retorts that not even a glorious
community could elevate such an untalented man as his critic.
Disparagingly addressing the man as *anthrōpos,* "a human being" (as distinct from a god), rather than *anēr,* "a masculine
man" (as distinct from a woman), Themistocles maintains, "I
would not have been honored thus by the Spartans if I were
from Belbina [a tiny insignificant island], nor would you, Man
[*anthrōpe*], be honored thus by the Spartans, even being an
Athenian" (8.125.2).

But if we have been envisioning Themistocles as a determined freedom fighter, using his talents selflessly in the service
of his community, Herodotus gradually undermines that im-
pression. Had the Peloponnesians abandoned northern Greece,
the Greek force would have dissolved and Greek independence
with it. But self-dealing more than public-spirited virtue seems
to motivate Herodotus's Themistocles. Accepting a large bribe
from the Euboeans to keep the Greek fleet at Artemisium, Themistocles pretends it is his own money and bribes two other
generals to remain (8.4–5). While the other recipients mistakenly believe the funds come from Athens, Themistocles secretly
pockets the remaining money (8.5.3). After Salamis, as the ter-
rified Xerxes races toward Persia, Themistocles first advises the
Greeks to destroy the bridges at the Hellespont, then adopts as
his own opinion the prudent advice of the Spartan general Eurybiades to allow the Persians to leave Europe, recognizing that
trapping Xerxes and his army in Greece will only ensure continued conflict there (8.108–109). Mindful of later events, Herodotus identifies Themistocles as concerned not for Greece but
for himself, explaining, "Themistocles said this intending to lay
up a store of credit with the Persian, in order that if therefore
any calamity from the Athenians overtook him, he would have
a place of refuge—accordingly the very thing that occurred"

(8.109.5). Sending a message to Xerxes claiming that he person-
ally restrained the Greeks from pursuing the Persian ships and
destroying the bridges, Themistocles insists that he sought to
do Xerxes a favor (8.110). It is tempting to suspect that had the
Greeks lost at Salamis, Themistocles might have claimed to
have sought to aid Xerxes all along.[28] As the Greeks end their
pursuit of Xerxes and besiege Andros, Herodotus mentions that
Themistocles has previously extorted money from that island
(8.111). With threats, Themistocles demands money from other
islands, too, and he accepts bribes without telling the other
Greek commanders (8.112), for "Themistocles did not stop
claiming more than his share" (8.112.1).

In the ambivalent figure of Themistocles, Herodotus begins to suggest that there is more to excellence than military
prowess. Herodotus counts on his contemporary audience's understanding of Themistocles' career path.[29] Themistocles will
end his career serving Xerxes' successor Artaxerxes, as Herodotus's contemporaries knew: Themistocles fled from Athens
to Argos sometime after 471 and then to Persia, ca. 461.[30]

This talented Greek general violates the distinction, emphasized throughout the *Histories,* between Greek internal
moral excellence and Persian material greed. Themistocles has
great power, resourcefulness, and an Odysseus-like capacity for
deception and strategy.[31] But he lacks steadfast loyalty to and
concern for his community. Undeniably, Themistocles played
an outsized role in saving Greece from Persian domination, but
ultimately he pursues his own interests at his people's expense.
A winner with few scruples, Themistocles demonstrates that
exceptional talent alone cannot guarantee consistently beneficial political leadership.

Like the portrait of Themistocles as both great war hero
and self-dealing opportunist, Herodotus's depiction of the glorious Greek victory at Salamis contains a timeless warning. In
his account of Salamis, Herodotus extols intellectual qualities

vital to democracy and generally discouraged under autocracy: ingenuity; expertise; verbal argument and persuasive speech; fact-based reasoning; nonviolent decision-making; constructive competition; concern for communal welfare—qualities constructively deployed by self-motivated achievers able to align their own interests with the community's welfare. In Herodotus's account of the battle of Salamis, the Greeks' ability to appreciate wise counsel contrasts with Xerxes' imperviousness to good advice. Greek shrewdness outsmarts Persian gullibility. Greek cleverness and competence defeat Persian folly and ineptitude. But in commending democracy-sustaining intellectual qualities, Herodotus also illustrates—via the example of the female Persian-allied naval commander Artemisia—the importance of context for evaluating military achievement. And in his ambivalent portrait of Themistocles, Herodotus cautions against mistaking power for human excellence.

Herodotus's account of Salamis invites his increasingly ruthless, avaricious contemporaries to recognize themselves in the brutal imperialist—and ultimately defeated—Persians of their fathers' and grandfathers' day. Herodotus may have reworked his source material to depict Themistocles as a cautionary example for his own imperialist Athens.[32] Drawing on knowledge of the subsequent careers of Themistocles and Athens, Herodotus may offer revisionist history.[33] He presents the positive and negative aspects of Themistocles' career, past and future, as emblematic of Athens's past and future.[34] Relying on his audience's knowledge of radical reversals in the roles of Themistocles and Athens (480 BCE vs. 431 BCE), Herodotus illustrates the cyclical pattern of historical change.[35] In the Persian Wars, according to Herodotus, expertise, rational calculation, unity of purpose, and effective organization defeat short-sighted acquisitiveness and opportunistic aggression, enabling the Greeks to repel their would-be conquerors despite great numerical inferiority. But fifty years later, a narrow conception of moral virtue as military and economic might has enabled Athens to wield tyrannical authority over other citizen-communities euphemistically called "allies." Efforts at financial extortion begin immediately after Salamis (e.g., 8.111–112). Increasingly during the fifth century, even as Athenians proclaimed principles of democratic freedom and equality at home, they violently subjugated other communities, sold conquered women and children into slavery, and kept people in bondage in Athens.

For Herodotus, a conception of universal human equality and universal human rights lies centuries in the future, but his nuanced portrait of human excellence begins to expose the fallacy of glorifying material wealth and military power while objectifying and subjugating other human beings. Cautioning against mistaking power for human excellence, Herodotus commends democratic virtues over autocratic vices. At Salamis, Greek discernment, ingenuity, and military skill triumph over Persian materialism, gullibility, and ineptitude, and Persian imperialist brutality proves myopic and self-destructive. But human beings are complicated creatures, and the later careers of Themistocles and Athens suggest that simplistic dichotomies of good versus evil generally fail to account for most real live people and events. In today's digitally enhanced, nuclear-armed, and volatile times, the seductions of wealth and power not only imperil democratic freedoms from within and without but also threaten human survival itself. Addressing his contemporaries—and now us—Herodotus implies that true, sustainable human excellence requires not economic and military strength alone but nonmaterial goods of democratic debate, ingenuity, expertise, and the capacity to align self-interest with communal good.

18

On Self-Control

The conclusion of the *Histories* reaffirms the value of narratives of the past for understanding and guiding the present. By showing the consequences of past human decisions, *historiē* promotes wiser choices in the present. We cannot know how accurately Herodotus depicts the final events of the Persian Wars.[1] By the end of the *Histories* Herodotus seems concerned that Greeks of his own day, a half century after the Persian Wars, risk losing the rational self-discipline that enabled their fathers and grandfathers to defeat foolish, acquisitive foreign invaders. The conclusion of the *Histories* reemphasizes the necessity for self-control.

The tale of Masistes' wife (9.108–113), a sordid story of barbarian lust, vengeance, and violent retribution, vividly demonstrates the destructiveness of *lack* of self-control. Herodotus introduces Masistes with an anecdote illustrating the lack of self-restraint distinctive of barbarians in the *Histories*. As the surviving remnants of the Persian army limp back toward Sardis, Masistes, a son of Darius and full brother of Xerxes, rashly insults another Persian commander, "calling him worse than a woman for how he had commanded his forces and declaring that he deserved to suffer every evil for having harmed the king's household. But among the Persians," Herodotus continues, "to be called worse than a woman is the greatest disgrace" (9.107.1). In ascribing to Persians this emphatic disdain for female nature, Herodotus exposes a great irony: Greeks understood the inability to control passion as the defining female characteristic, and Herodotus repeatedly attributes this inability to barbarian men.[2] The insulted Persian responds not rationally but passionately, furiously attacking Masistes with his sword—as if to demonstrate his lack of self-control. Fortunately for Masistes, other men intervene (9.107.2–3), but a failure to refrain from grievously insulting a fellow commander nearly gets him killed. Lack of self-control appears to be a family trait:

[9.108] Being in Sardis at that time, Xerxes fell in love [*ēra*] with Masistes' wife, who was also there. But as she was not able to be prevailed upon by him sending her messages—and out of respect for his brother Masistes—the king did not apply force. (And the same thought held the woman. For she well understood that she would not be compelled by force.) Prohibited from other actions, Xerxes thereupon arranged a marriage for his own son Darius with the daughter of this woman and Masistes, thinking that by doing this he would more likely gain possession of Masistes' wife. [2] Having joined Masistes' daughter and his son in marriage, and having performed the customary observances, Xerxes went away to Susa. And when he arrived there and led Darius's wife into his own house, in this way indeed Xerxes was done with Masistes' wife. He happened to change his mind and he fell in love with [*ēra*] Darius's wife, Masistes' daughter. This woman's name was Artaÿnte.

[9.109] As time proceeded, this came to be known in the following way: Amestris, Xerxes' wife, wove a great, elaborately embroidered cloak, worthy to be seen. And she

gave it to Xerxes. Well pleased [*hēstheis*], he put it on and
went to Artaÿnte. [2] Well pleased [*hēstheis*] also with
Artaÿnte, he bid her ask for whatever she wished to have in
exchange for her forced intercourse with him. For he said
that everything would be brought about for her if she asked.
And because it was necessary that things turn out badly for
her and her entire household, she said this to Xerxes: "Will
you give me whatever I ask you to give?" And he, thinking
that she would ask for anything rather than what she did ask,
promised and swore an oath. And since he had sworn, she
fearlessly asked for the cloak. [3] And Xerxes tried everything
he could, not wishing to give the cloak—for no other reason
than that he feared that in this way Amestris might find out
for certain that he was doing what she already guessed was
occurring. He offered Artaÿnte a city, immense gold, and an
army which no one would command other than she. (And an
army is really and truly a Persian gift.) But because he did not
persuade her, he gave her the cloak. And she, being exceed-
ingly joyful, wore it and exulted.

[9.110] And Amestris learned that Artaÿnte had the
cloak. But understanding what had been done, she did not
bear a grudge against this woman [Artaÿnte]. But expecting
that Artaÿnte's mother was responsible and had brought this
about, Amestris resolved to destroy Masistes' wife. [2] Amestris waited for her husband Xerxes to set forth the royal feast.
This feast was provided once yearly on the date the king was
born. In Persian the feast's name is "*tukta*"—but in the Greek
language "perfect." At that time only, the king has his head
anointed, and he gives the Persians gifts. Waiting for this day,
Amestris asked Xerxes for Masistes' wife to be given to her.
But he considered this a terrible and monstrous thing to hand
over his brother's wife—who was besides not to blame for this

situation—for Xerxes understood why Amestris was asking
for her.

[9.111] Finally, however, as Amestris persisted, and since
he was compelled by the custom [*nomou*] that when the royal
feast was provided, it was impossible for anyone asking for
something to fail in their request, very unwillingly Xerxes
assented. And handing over the woman, he did the following:
he ordered his wife to do what she wished, but sending for
his brother, he said the following: [2] "Masistes, you are
Darius's son and my brother. And in addition to this, you are
a good man. Do not continue to dwell with the woman with
whom you live now. But instead of her, I myself give you my
own daughter. Dwell with her. Do not keep as your wife the
woman that you have now. For it does not seem best to me."
[3] Masistes, wondering much at what had been said, said the
following: "O Master [*despota*], what cruel word are you
speaking to me? You command me to give up my wife, from
whom I have youthful sons and also daughters—one of
whom you yourself even arranged to be the wife of your own
son. And my wife happens to be very suited to my mind. And
you command me to marry your daughter? [4] And although
I do esteem it a great thing, King, to be thought worthy of
your daughter, I will, however, do neither of these things.
And in no way force me, though you want this. But another
man will appear for your daughter, a man not at all worse than
me. And allow me to dwell with my own wife." [5] Masistes
answered directly with such words. And Xerxes, enraged,
said the following: "Thus, Masistes, this has been accomplished by you: for now, neither would I still give you my
daughter to marry, nor will you dwell any longer with your
wife, so that you may learn to accept what is being given."
And when Masistes heard this, he went away out of reach,

saying only so much: "Master [*despota*], you have not yet destroyed me."

[9.112] And during this time in which Xerxes was speaking with his brother, Amestris, having sent for Xerxes' bodyguards, viciously mutilated Masistes' wife. Cutting off her breasts, she threw them to the dogs. And cutting out her nose, ears, lips, and tongue, she sent her back to her home viciously mutilated.

[9.113] And Masistes, not yet having heard anything of this, but expecting to have some evil, rushed into his home at the run. And seeing his horribly ruined wife, Masistes immediately after this took counsel with his sons. He made his way into Bactria with his sons and then doubtless also with some others, for the purpose of getting the district to revolt and to create the greatest of troubles for the king. [2] And this would have occurred, as it seems to me, if indeed Masistes had gone up inland to the Bactrians and Sacae sooner. For they liked him, and he was viceroy of the Bactrians. But since Xerxes, learning that Masistes was doing these things, sent an army against him, Xerxes killed him on the way—both Masistes and his sons and his army. Thus it was concerning Xerxes' love [*erōta*] and Masistes' death.

Herodotus thus frames his work with two tales of irrational, uncontrolled, barbarian lust. Recalling Herodotus's opening story of King Candaules (1.8–13), the tale of Masistes' wife depicts the consequences of unbridled, predatory sexual lust. In this instance, unresisted lust results not in regicide and regime change but in the horrible mutilation of an innocent woman and in fratricide. Undoubtedly, the *Histories* offers a Greek-inflected, tendentious portrait of Xerxes throughout.[3] Though perhaps invented or exaggerated, the tale of Xerxes' passion for Masistes' wife directly evokes Herodotus's initial

story of Candaules' passion for his own wife.⁴ Herodotus never
names either woman.⁵ And both stories begin in the same
abrupt, unmotivated way, precipitated by spontaneous lust
needing no prior impetus or clarification.⁶ In each instance,
Herodotus twice uses the same verb (*eraō*) for a king's unexplained and inexplicable lust (*ērasthē, erastheis,* 1.8.1; *ēra,* 9.108.1
and 9.108.2).⁷ Ironically, given the ancient assessment of women
as lacking self-control, both stories feature male impulsiveness
and lack of restraint alongside patient, calculated, female-
implemented vengeance. Like Candaules' wife, Xerxes' wife
coolly bides her time before exacting revenge (9.110.2).

In both stories, men's lack of impulse control accompanies a callous disregard for women's experience. Candaules
never considers his wife's feelings as he insists—in violation of
Lydian law/custom/tradition (*anomōn,* 1.8.4)—that his bodyguard view his wife naked (1.8.2–4). Though Xerxes cravenly
fears his own wife's reaction (9.109.3), the wishes or feelings of
Masistes' wife, her daughter Artaÿnte, or his own daughter
never factor into his calculations. Xerxes treats the women in-
terchangeably, casually transferring his lust from one to the
other, for once the daughter-in-law is in his own house, Xerxes
"happened to change his mind and he fell in love [*ēra*]" with
his son's wife, Masistes' daughter (9.108.2). Xerxes takes the
same pleasure in a live woman as in an inanimate object; the
same participle, *hēstheis,* "(having been) well pleased," describes
his reaction to the embroidered cloak and to intercourse with
his daughter-in-law (9.109.1; 109.2). Offering Masistes his own
daughter in place of his wife, Xerxes treats both women as mere
bargaining chips (9.111.2).

And as in the tale of Candaules, not the gods or fate but
human choices produce adverse consequences. Herodotus uses
the same form of foreshadowing in both tales, anticipating
Candaules' destruction, explaining, "for it was necessary that

things turn out badly for Candaules" (*chrēn gar Candaulēi genesthai kakōs*, 1.8.2) as he anticipates Masistes' destruction by insisting, "for it was necessary that things turn out badly for her [Artaÿnte] and her entire household" (*tēi de kakōs gar edee panoikiēi genesthai*, 9.109.2). Herodotus attributes this necessity not to divine will but to human decision-making, precipitated by the failure of either king to make any effort to resist acting on his desire. These events may appear divinely determined.[8] But Candaules' destruction results directly from his decision to expose his wife naked to his bodyguard's gaze, in heedless violation of *nomos* "law/custom/tradition" (1.8–9). Unlike Candaules, neither Xerxes nor his daughter-in-law suffers direct retribution for their choices.[9] Since tradition maintained that Xerxes was murdered by Artabanus, captain of his guard, Herodotus may have expected readers to assume divine punishment here, as elsewhere.[10] But as in the story of Candaules, events in the tale of Masistes' wife appear less predestined than freely chosen. Xerxes blithely sleeps with his daughter-in-law and incautiously flaunts his cloak in front of her (9.109.1). Paradoxically, Xerxes possesses absolute power but voluntarily submits to the constraints of custom.[11] He rashly promises to grant Artaÿnte's wish, making himself unable to deny her the gift of the cloak. Artaÿnte's own imprudent but voluntary choice to reject other, more lavish gifts dooms her innocent mother (9.109.2–3). Though bound by Persian custom to grant his wife's request, Xerxes might have refused; his autocratic authority surely affords here the same license to flout convention as he assumes in sleeping with his son's wife.[12]

The fraternal conflict seems equally unforced. Xerxes pretends that his brother's refusal to give up his wife and marry Xerxes' daughter causes him to take revenge on Masistes. But Xerxes has already given Masistes' wife to Amestris, so Masistes' refusal only causes Xerxes to rescind the offer of his daughter (9.111.5). Amestris opts to take horrific vengeance on her innocent sister-in-law even as the brothers converse (9.112). Xerxes' choice to permit his wife to harm Masistes' wife provokes Masistes' decision to take up arms against his brother (9.113.1). Concluding the story with the terse observation "so it was concerning Xerxes' love [erōta] and Masistes' death" (9.113.2), Herodotus emphasizes a causal connection between Xerxes' unchecked, predatory lust (erōs) and the destruction of his brother and his family.

In locating the "necessity" for suffering in human decision-making and a lethal lack of self-control, the grim tale of Masistes' wife aligns with numerous atrocities attributed to barbarians previously in the *Histories*. Cambyses' coldhearted murder of his siblings (3.30; 3.31) and an innocent boy (3.35), Darius's brutal execution of three sons of a loyal Persian (4.84), Xerxes' cutting a supporter's son in half and marching his army between the two halves (7.38–39), the Persian custom of burying children alive (7.114), the Persians' sacrificing of a captured Greek sailor as if he were a sacrificial animal (7.180), Xerxes' desecration of the corpse of the Spartan general Leonidas after the battle of Thermopylae (7.238) all mark Persians as distinct from Greeks in their barbarous brutality. In another gruesome tale, a man castrated, sold as a eunuch, and given as a gift to the Persian king tricks his mutilator, who makes his living castrating and selling beautiful boys, into bringing him his wife and children. He then forces the man to castrate his own four sons and the sons to castrate their father (8.105–106). Herodotus distinguishes this grisly retributive act from Greek notions of ethical behavior, for although the perpetrator (a Greek) calls his barbarous actions *dikē*, "justice" (8.106.3), Herodotus labels them simply *tisis*, "vengeance" (8.105.1), tacitly acknowledging that new atrocities never recompence previous ones.

Herodotus ascribes to unrestrained passion not only brutal atrocities but also the intellectual inadequacy perpetuating the Persian invasion. After the Persians' defeat at Salamis, Mardonius, commander of the remaining Persian forces in Greece, foolishly ignores the Thebans' sensible advice to bribe individual Greek leaders in order to pick off the Greek cities one by one (9.2.3). Instead, Mardonius succumbs to *deinos himeros,* "a terrible desire," and *agnōmosunē,* "want of sense or judgment," eager to show the king that he holds Athens a second time (9.3.1). Herodotus even has Mardonius attribute to the Athenians precisely the same irrationality that Herodotus attributes to him, for Mardonius erroneously expects the Athenians finally to give up their *agnōmosunē,* "want of sense or judgment" and accept his reiterated offer of land, autonomy, and the opportunity to rebuild their temples in exchange for allying with Persia (9.4.2, cf. 8.140). Herodotus continues to contrast the Athenians' wisdom of prioritizing human survival with the Persians' foolish, insatiable materialism, for by evacuating Athens to preserve its citizens, the Athenians thwart the Persians' lust for territory and plunder: reoccupying Athens, Herodotus says, Mardonius seized *erēmon to astu,* "a deserted citadel" (9.3.2).[13]

But even as he exposes irrational barbarian acquisitiveness and intellectual inadequacy, Herodotus begins to suggest that Greeks are not immune to unrestrained passion and barbarous acts. The Athenians perhaps even corroborate Mardonius's accusation that they lack sense or judgment (*agnōmosunē*), for they signal their vehement rejection of Mardonius's second offer to ally with Persia by stoning to death an Athenian who advised accepting it. For good measure, Athenian women stone to death the man's family as well (9.5).

This ominous hint of a Greek capacity for unrestrained brutality accompanies a worrisome foreshadowing of the Greek versus Greek conflicts of Herodotus's own day. Failing to learn the lesson of Salamis that unity confers strength, Greek citizen-communities still seem to envision their own interests narrowly. When Mardonius reoccupies Athens, the Spartans do not rush to the Athenians' aid. Reproaching Sparta for the delay and recalling their own prior service to Greece and continued determination to defend it, the Athenians ask Sparta to send an army immediately. But the Spartans continue to delay while building a wall at the Isthmus of Corinth (9.6–7). Herodotus recognizes the inconsistency between the Spartans' previous efforts to prevent the Athenians from medizing (8.140–144) and their apparent lack of concern now. By now, he suspects, the Peloponnesians have fully fortified the isthmus and feel less in need of Athenian support (9.8.2). But the Athenians also seem inconsistent, now contradicting their earlier claims of determined resistance by threatening to submit to Persia—before learning that a Spartan army is already heading north to help (9.10–11).[14] The Argives betray fellow Greeks, warning Mardonius of the Spartans' approach (9.12). Local Greek informants willing to betray the Greek cause appear to offer Mardonius conflicting news, for his actions seem erratic and unplanned. Having razed and burned Athens, he retreats to a more strategic position in Boeotia near Thebes, hoping to entice the Greeks into battle (9.13–15). Many Greek communities in Boeotia have already agreed to submit to Persia, though some more freely than others (9.17). The Thebans' willingness to advise Mardonius on how to divide the Greek cities after Salamis directly presages impending Greek versus Greek conflict: having medized in 480 BCE (7.132), the Thebans are, by Herodotus's day, staunch members of the Spartan-led Peloponnesian League, committed adversaries of the Athenian-led Delian League (turned Athenian empire in 454 BCE).

Although short-sighted intra-Greek animosities imperil Greek resistance in 479 BCE and presage future conflicts, the Persians remain vulnerable to a sole leader's unmediated passion. As in Xerxes' counterproductive advisory council (7.7–11), truth again falls victim to power.[15] The Persians' unquestioning obedience prevents their general Mardonius from even hearing cautionary advice. In a conversation recounted by a Greek dining at Thebes with Mardonius and fifty Persian noblemen, one Persian grateful for the Thebans' hospitality offers his Greek dinner partner an advance warning so that the Greek may make provisions for his own interests (9.16.2). The Persian tearfully predicts that few of Mardonius's troops will survive (9.16.3). Advised to tell Mardonius and the other Persian commanders, the Persian responds fatalistically, insisting that no human being can prevent "whatever is necessary to occur from the god, for no one believes even people speaking credible things. Although many of us Persians understand these things, we are obedient, constrained by necessity. And for human beings, this is the most hated distress: to understand many things but have power over none" (9.16.4–5).

This improbable but memorable anecdote illustrates once again how unquestioning obedience in a hierarchical power structure forestalls prudent counsel and makes everyone vulnerable to uncontrolled, autocratic whim. Autocrats gain and maintain power by discouraging or actively suppressing dissent; each maintains, "I alone know what is best for you. Do not trust anyone else." Like Darius and Xerxes before him, Mardonius fails to receive or benefit from sensible advice. Though the Persian in this tale blames *theos*, "god," and *anagkaiē*, "necessity," Herodotus's readers see that nothing about Mardonius's choices seems inevitable. Uninformed by definition and design, autocratic leadership will prove disastrous for Mardonius and his army. At the battle of Plataea in summer 479 BCE, Mardonius will lose most of his army.[16] Dating this conversation just prior to the Persians' definitive defeat at Plataea (9.16.5), Herodotus highlights the dire consequences of failing to hear or heed informed guidance.

In contrast to the Persians, subject to their general's irrational impulses and deprived of dissenting opinion, the Greeks at Plataea begin to manifest a sensible, unified, democratically led opposition. With ten days of unfavorable omens deterring either side from attacking, the Athenians succeed only with the aid of other Greeks in routing the Persian cavalry harassing the Greeks (9.19–21; 9.23.2). The Greek forces grow stronger during this interlude, as more Greeks come to join (9.33, 36, 38, 40). Meanwhile, Greek democratic decision-making elevates experience and expertise: with the Spartans occupying the most honorable battle position, the right wing, verbal argument resolves a dispute between the Athenians and the Tegeans, both wanting the second most honorable position, the left wing. In a hoplite phalanx, each warrior's shield, held in his left hand, protects half his body, and his spear-carrying right arm and half of his chest gain protection from the shield of the man on his right. A battle line tends to move right, either gradually or rapidly, as each warrior naturally seeks the protective covering of his righthand neighbor's shield. The bravest warriors resist that rightward drift, making the right wing the place of honor. The left wing also confers considerable honor, for cowards on the left would squeeze everyone rightward. Asserting their claim to the left wing, the Athenians argue most persuasively, citing especially their victory at Marathon a decade earlier. The Spartan warriors act as jury, shouting their approval of the Athenians' claim (9.26–28). The Spartan general Pausanias concedes Athenian martial preeminence: on learning that the Persians will attack the next morning, he offers the Athenians the most prestigious right wing, acknowledging their prior success at

Marathon. Even the Persians recognize Athenian military superiority, for Mardonius then shifts his forces accordingly, eager to keep Persians opposite Spartans, though ultimately the Greeks revert to their original positions and the Persians to theirs (9.46–47).

While constructive democratic decision-making informs Greek strategy and elevates expertise, a counterproductive unilateral command structure continues to subject the Persians to their general's foolish, unmediated passion. Mardonius arranges his forces as he prefers with no discussion (9.31). He responds to events not rationally but emotionally, for by the eleventh day of the standoff at Plataea, Mardonius *periēmektee* "was greatly aggrieved" (9.41.1). Herodotus for a second time attributes intellectual inadequacy to Mardonius, as he again rejects prudent advice to withdraw his forces to safety and try to bribe individual Greek leaders. Though the advice comes this time not from the Thebans but from a Persian nobleman, Herodotus maintains that "Mardonius's judgment/opinion [*gnome*] was stronger [*ischuroterē*] and more senseless [*agnōmonesterē*] and in no way in agreement [*oudamōs suggignōskomenē*]" with this sage proposal (9.41.4).

Mardonius's lack of judgment extends to misinterpreting supernatural warnings, for—as always in the *Histories*—human desires and choices determine events afterward confirmed by supernatural signs. Motivated by passion, unable to recognize sound advice, Mardonius decides to ignore unfavorable omens and attack immediately (9.41). Autocratic authority permits no opposition, since "with Mardonius thinking this right, no one spoke out against him, so that his opinion [*gnōmē*] prevailed, for he held his power over the army from the king" (9.42.1). Certain of victory, Mardonius mistakenly cites an oracle predicting success for the Persians, as long as they do not plunder Apollo's temple at Delphi (9.42.3–4). Herodotus explains that this oracle did not, in fact, apply to the Persians (9.43), as of course it could not have. The Persians are about to lose this coming battle, as Herodotus's contemporaries well know. Oracles and supernatural explanations are, by definition, always correct—as is always clear after the fact. And indeed, after the Greeks rout the Persians completely at Plataea, Herodotus cites an oracle confirming Mardonius's death as "justice [*dikē*] for the murder of Leonidas," the Spartan commander at Thermopylae (9.64.1). Since none of the fleeing Persians sought refuge in a nearby precinct consecrated to Demeter, Herodotus offers an ex post facto explanation, speculating, "I suppose—if it is necessary to make any suppositions about divine matters—that the goddess herself did not accept them because they set fire to her temple in Eleusis" (9.65.2).

Herodotus describes the Greek victory at Plataea, the final land battle of the Persian Wars, not as a consequence of divine will belatedly confirmed by supernatural signs but as a collective effort by diverse citizen-communities determined to preserve Greek freedom. Alexandros of Macedon, now eager to hedge his bet, conveniently overlooks his prior willingness to serve as Persia's envoy when Mardonius tried to bribe the Athenians into submitting to Persia (at 8.140). Warning the Athenians now of imminent Persian attack, Alexandros insists—unashamedly—on his own identity as a Greek and a staunch defender of Greek freedom (9.45). Despite tensions between Athenians and Spartans, the Greek generals decide collectively to retreat to a more advantageous location (9.51). Though distrustful of Spartan statements, "understanding the purposes of the Spartans as intending some things but declaring others" (9.54.1), the Athenians nevertheless make a determined—though ineffective—effort to aid the Spartans. Calling for Athenian support, and claiming that their allies have betrayed them both, the Spartan commander Pausanias insists that now they "must defend and protect each other as best we can. If the cavalry had begun by attacking you, it would have been necessary for us, and those with us, the ones who are not betraying Greece—the Tegeans—to aid you" (9.60.1–2). The Athenians immediately try to help, suffering considerable casualties in the process, for "when the Athenians heard these things, they rushed to come to the rescue and to defend to the utmost," though an attack by Boeotian allies of the Persian king thwarts their efforts (9.61.1). The Spartans and Tegeans succeed together in killing Mardonius and routing the Persians (9.62–5).

In depicting the victory at Plataea as a collective effort by disparate Greek citizen-communities, Herodotus recalls a more cooperative, constructive time than his own. It may be anachronistic to attribute Panhellenic propagandist intentions to Herodotus.[17] But how strange Pausanias's appeal to mutual obligations—and the Athenians' energetic response—would have seemed to Herodotus's audiences in the 430s–420s, when tension, distrust, and even violence have characterized relations between Sparta and Athens for decades. As at Marathon and Salamis, Greek identity remains community specific, but Greeks succeed at Plataea *together*. Superior Greek weaponry and skills ultimately prevail over the Persians' lack of hoplite arms, inadequate training, and inferior tactical abilities (9.62.3). Although Thebans persist in fighting Athenians, even as the Persians flee in disorder toward the Hellespont after Mardonius's death (9.63, 66–68), Athenian help finally enables the Spartans to sack the Persians' walled camp, killing most of the Persians. Herodotus affirms this constructive teamwork, emphasizing specific contributions of different citizen-communities and enumerating the losses of Tegeans, Athenians, and Spartans (9.70). (As always, Herodotus's numbers are unreliable, but if we think in percentages, well—lots

of dead Persians. Also many dead Greeks.) Achieving victory
together, the Greeks retain the identity of their communities,
for Herodotus observes that "the Tegeans and Athenians were
brave [agathoi], but the Spartans outdid them in excellence/
virtue [aretē]" (9.71). Praising a number of individuals by name,
Herodotus scrupulously identifies each as Spartan or Athenian
(9.71–74).

Herodotus not only highlights successful Greek teamwork but also reasserts Greek decency and restraint as distinct
from Persian barbarity.[18] After Plataea, the Spartan general Pausanias rejects another man's advice to desecrate Mardonius's
corpse. A man from Aegina argues that by impaling Mardonius's head, as Xerxes did the head of Leonidas, the Spartan
general defeated at Thermopylae (7.238), Pausanias will increase
his glory and avenge the violation of his uncle's corpse. Disturbingly, this advice comes from a Greek.[19] And the man expects
his advice to please Pausanias (9.78). Instead, Pausanias reasserts Greek moral standards over Persian barbarism, replying,
"I admire your goodwill and foresight, but you have missed the
target of good judgment [gnōmēs mentoi hēmartēkas chrēstēs],
for having exalted me, my homeland, and my accomplishment,
you are hurling me down to nothing by advising me to defile a
corpse. And if I do this, you declare that I will enhance my reputation. These actions are more fitting for barbarians to do
than for Greeks. And even in barbarians we find them hateful"
(9.79.1). Pausanias angrily continues, "Would that I not glad-
den the Aeginetans by doing this nor those who find such actions pleasing. It is sufficient for me to please the Spartans by
doing and saying things that are sanctioned and approved by
the laws of nature [hosia]. I declare that Leonidas, whom you
urge me to avenge, has been greatly avenged. He has been
honored—both himself and the others who died at Thermopylae—by these countless souls here. As for you, however, never

again approach me with such an argument nor counsel me. Be grateful that you are departing unharmed" (9.79.2).

Herodotus continues to contrast humane Greek self-control with barbarian acquisitiveness and ruthless vengeance. Pausanias resists the lure of money, rejecting bribes offered by Theban leaders following their surrender (9.86–88). Herodotus juxtaposes Greek valor and austerity with Persian materialism, deeming the Athenians "the best and bravest" of the Greeks (9.105) while mentioning Persian "treasure chests of money" among the plunder discovered after the battle (9.106.1). Pausanias yet again rejects the passion-driven barbarity characteristic of non-Greeks (and women) in the *Histories*, refusing to punish sons of a Theban leader for their father's misdeeds, "declaring that the sons were not at all responsible for their father's association with Persia" (9.88.1). Pausanias's admirable restraint in this instance contrasts with Herodotus's earlier descriptions of vengeance inflicted on a man's sons for evil committed by their father (8.105–106) and Athenian women's stoning of the wife and children of a man deemed a traitor (9.5).

Commending rational self-restraint, Herodotus exposes materialism itself as a manifestation of an irrational and self-destructive lack of self-control. After Plataea, marveling at the material treasures discovered in the conquered Persian camp, the Greek victors perceive the irony of Persians possessed of so much yet coming to take more from comparatively impoverished Greeks (9.80–83). Herodotus contrasts the Persians' lavish furnishings and food with the simple, austere Spartan fare, for on seeing Xerxes' tent filled with gold and silver, Pausanias pointedly has his servants prepare a Spartan meal for comparison.[20] Pausanias invites the Greek commanders to view the disparity, explaining, "Men of Greece, I gathered you here for this reason: I wanted to show to you the foolishness [*aphrosunē*] of the leader of the Persians. Having this sort

of way of life, he came to us—we who have such an impoverished way of life—for the purpose of taking it away from us"
(9.82.3). Herodotus's contemporaries would appreciate the
irony: rich in material possessions, the Persians came to plunder simple, austere, nonmaterialistic Greeks—and instead
wound up plundered themselves.

Although Herodotus commends Greek decency over Persian barbarity and contrasts admirable Greek austerity with
decadent Persian materialism, the conclusion of the *Histories*
points ominously toward the alternating pattern of human fortunes.[21] Describing the final battle of the Persian Wars, a naval
battle at Mycale on the Ionian coast (479 BCE),[22] Herodotus
evokes the original impetus for the Persian invasion in 490. As
the remnants of the Persian land army flee to Asia (9.89), the
Greeks urge the Ionian Greeks to rebel from Persia (9.90–91).
Herodotus claims that the naval battle of Mycale occurred
simultaneously with the land battle at Plataea, finding divine
influence in the story that despite the great geographical distance, a report of the victory at Plataea increased Greek confidence and enthusiasm at Mycale prior to victory (9.100–101).
Herodotus identifies this battle—with intense fighting and high
casualties on both sides (9.102–103)—as a second Ionian Revolt
(9.104). He thereby connects Persia's final defeat at Mycale to
the origins of the Persian Wars, for in reasserting control over
Ionian Greeks in the first revolt (499–494), Darius conceives
the passionate desire for vengeance on the Athenians, a key motive for his 490 invasion (5.105.2; 6.94). Calling Mycale a second Ionian Revolt, Herodotus implies that Persian fortunes
have come full circle, with Persian victory in 494 precipitating
Persian defeat in 479.

In alluding to the cyclical pattern of historical change,
Herodotus suggests that Greek moral leadership and self-
restraint remain fragile, vulnerable to the ruthlessness and

temptations born of success.[23] The once-restrained Pausanias will later succumb to corruption, as Herodotus's contemporaries knew. Herodotus cannot have known how Thucydides would later portray Pausanias.[24] But he does reference Pausanias's later career (5.32; 8.3.2). And he could count on his contemporaries appreciating ironic contrasts between Pausanias's earlier and later exploits.[25]

Though the *Histories* almost seems to trail off at the end with a pair of perhaps random-seeming anecdotes, both tales contain dire warnings for Herodotus's contemporaries. In the first story, merciless Greek cruelty echoes that of barbarians throughout the *Histories* and foreshadows the increasing Greek-on-Greek atrocities of subsequent decades. Emphasizing egregious Athenian cruelty following the defeat of the Persians, Herodotus appears to condemn vengeance inflicted by mortals.[26] After subjugating Sestos at the Hellespont, the Athenians brutally execute the city's captured ruler, hanging him from a wooden plank. Xanthippus, the Athenian general authorizing this punishment also happens to be the father of Pericles, architect of later Athenian imperialism.[27] The Athenians have previously resisted material bribes.[28] But whereas Pausanias had earlier spared the sons of a Theban traitor, absolving them of responsibility for their father's actions (9.88), the Athenians stone to death the son of the about-to-be-executed ruler of Sestos before his eyes (9.116–120).[29]

A second tale explicitly advises self-control, as Herodotus concludes the *Histories* with an ominous prediction made years before by King Cyrus, father of Cambyses and predecessor of Darius and Xerxes.[30] Cyrus connects material luxury with physical and moral weakness, warning the Persians as they consider moving into richer lands "to prepare to be no longer rulers but ruled by others. Because from soft regions men usually become soft. For it is not possible for there to grow from the same land both excellent produce and men who are good and brave in the arts of war" (9.122.3).

Like the tale of Masistes' wife, these final two cautionary anecdotes seem to warn Herodotus's contemporaries against becoming lustful, inhumane, decadent, and soft, like Persians of their fathers' and grandfathers' times. Herodotus connects imperial expansion with self-destruction, and he repeatedly complicates the distinction between Greeks and Persians.[31] Athenian vengeance at Sestos appears barbaric, and Cyrus's warning against luxurious living prefigures the grasping Athenian imperialism of Herodotus's day. At Plataea and Mycale, the Persians' passion-driven, unilateral decision-making and the Greeks' lack of unified identity cause massive suffering and death. Rational restraint, coordinated action, and expertise enable the Greeks, finally, to repel the Persian invaders in 479 BCE. But Herodotus addresses contemporary Greeks of the 440s/430s, all heading disturbingly down the path well trodden by the Persians before them. Athenian success in liberating Ionia from Persian domination appears as a necessary precursor to Athenian domination of Ionia.[32] Over decades, the Athenians effectively transform the Delian League—formed after the victories in 480 and 479 as a defense against future Persian aggression—into the Athenian empire (moving the league's treasury from Delos to Athens in 454). Using violence and intimidation to turn former allies into tribute-paying subjects, Athens has amassed great wealth. The Athenian lifestyle, once restrained and austere, has become more luxurious. An expansionist Athenian empire and a Spartan-led league of Peloponnesian Greeks increasingly engage in violent conflict. Instead of austere, restrained Greeks resisting greedy barbarian invaders, rapacious Greeks now oppose rapacious Greeks.

Mirroring the cyclical pattern of history, the conclusion of the *Histories* recalls its opening tales and their theme: the

consequences of lack of self-control. Herodotus begins his inquiry by reporting the Persians' versions of familiar tales of
men's inability to refrain from stealing other men's women, the
series of reciprocal rapes precipitating the Trojan War, a conflict catastrophic for both Trojans and Greeks (1.1–5). In the first
tale narrated not as a report of tales told by others but offered
on Herodotus's own authority, a Lydian king's irrational insecurity and inability to control his lust cost him his throne and
his life (1.8–13). King Candaules subjects his wife to a virtual
rape, displaying her naked before his bodyguard. In turn,
Candaules suffers a virtual rape, penetrated by the knife of this
same bodyguard. (The Persian emissaries at the Macedonian
court, unable to refrain from assaulting the wives and daughters
of the Macedonian nobility, suffer equivalent symbolic rape,
knifed by young men cleverly disguised as women [5.19–21].)
Similarly unable to restrain his lust for Masistes' wife, Xerxes
gratuitously precipitates the innocent woman's mutilation and
the destruction of his own brother and his family (9.108–113).

In its depiction of barbarians as particularly unable to
control lustful impulses, the conclusion of the *Histories* affirms
the timeless value of self-control by both negative and positive
example. The unilateral authority exemplified by Xerxes and
Mardonius leaves powerful leaders uninformed and unencumbered by rational internal or external constraints. Disdain for
knowledge, truth, human lives, and experience makes leaders
and followers alike vulnerable to irrational passion. By contrast,
in spite of internal divisions, Greeks deploy not passion but reason, deliberating rationally and coordinating their efforts to
defeat the Persian invaders at Plataea and Mycale. Willing to
work together, Greeks value persuasive speech, and they acknowledge expertise. Attributing to autocratic barbarians a
self-defeating lack of self-control, Herodotus highlights the

Greeks' cooperative democratic decision-making and prudent self-discipline.

For Herodotus and his Greek contemporaries, lack of self-control constitutes shameful weakness and effeminacy. In this ancient conviction that women, unlike men, lack emotional self-control, we can see the noxious precursor of a sadly still-enduring feature of modern misogyny. But embedded in the ancient misogynistic and prejudicial view of male versus female capacities, there lies a universal warning against failures of impulse control. Herodotus distinguishes barbarians from Greeks by their predatory sexual lust and insatiable material acquisition, consumption, and display. Throughout the *Histories*, the inability to refrain from prioritizing things over people and treating people as if they were things appears foolish and self-destructive.

By Herodotus's day, however, Athens seems poised to replicate the alternating pattern of human fortunes. The *Histories* characterizes Athenians in the Persian Wars as staunch opponents of tyranny and brave defenders of freedom against barbarian conquest. But within decades, Greek versus Greek violence of the Peloponnesian Wars will cost Athens its empire and, for a time, its democratic government. The Athenians' long rise to power and prosperity lasted from the defeat of Persia in 479 down to the 430s–420s BCE. At the peak of their imperial success and unprecedented democratic experiment, the Athenians—once dedicated defenders of Greek autonomy against autocratic imperialistic Persian barbarity—gradually and then more rapidly succumb to materialism and inhumanity. Controlling a powerful empire, the Athenians treat subject citizen-communities (still euphemistically called "allies") with increasing brutality and rapacity. Herodotus's contemporaries might well perceive the irony of Athens's transformation from erstwhile defender of Greek freedom to current tyrannical oppressor of Greek citizen-communities.[33] Athenian lack of self-control will precipitate two violent, if relatively short-lived, oligarchic coups (411 and 404/3 BCE) and the defeat of Athens by Sparta aided by—irony of ironies—Persia (404 BCE).

In commending Greek self-control and humanity over Persian lack of self-restraint and barbarity, Herodotus identifies timeless tools for delaying disaster. Undermining any impulse to blame suffering on the gods or destiny, Herodotus identifies the power of human choices. The ancient Athenians failed to achieve their own ideals of democratic freedoms let alone modern liberal democratic ideals of universal human rights, equality, and individual autonomy. And, undeniably, the *Histories'* layered complexity and evolving perspective supports various deductive conclusions.[34] But Herodotus repeatedly reminds his contemporaries—and now us—that irrational passion, autocratic leadership, and internal divisions create vulnerability, while self-control, constructive democratic decision-making, and unity confer strength.

It is difficult not to view Athens's rise-and-fall trajectory in the fifth century BCE as a cautionary model for the United States in the twenty-first century CE. Athens once rallied Greek communities to a decisive defeat of foreign military aggression. Two generations later, Herodotus's impulsive, aggressive, grasping Athenian contemporaries in the 430s appear to be abandoning their claim to moral leadership—as the United States risks abandoning its moral leadership role today. By Herodotus's day, the sons and grandsons of the courageous, restrained Athenian victors in the Persian Wars seem to have forgotten the value of self-control. During the Persian Wars, violent internal divisions increased the vulnerability of diverse Greek citizen-communities to an invading army. Three-quarters of a century later, Greek versus Greek violence brought the Athenian empire to an end. In the decades following the Allied victory in World War II, the United States did much to guarantee a rules-based world order between sovereign states, while vastly increasing its political supremacy and material wealth. But three-quarters of a century later, U.S. power and moral authority are slipping, with civil discord inviting extremist violence from within and without (fueled by disinformation both domestic and foreign). As grasping Greek versus Greek violence doomed the Athenian empire, lack of self-control and the risk of domestic political violence imperil both the United States' constitutional democratic republic and a rules-based world order.

As the modern world faces its greatest crises since World War II—epidemics of violence within and between countries; environmental, humanitarian, and economic catastrophes; dire threats to public health—there is little evidence of the self-control that Herodotus depicts as key to survival. Though the ancient Greeks never achieved a just, humane, egalitarian society, Herodotus's *Histories* aligns with ancient Greek epics and tragedies in fostering justice, humanity, and equality as desirable goals.[35] Confronting a powerful adversary for whom no lives matter—Cambyses, Darius, and Xerxes care as little for Persian lives as for Greek ones—moral clarity remains vital. Self-control stands in opposition to the predatory sexual lust and vengeful bloodlust of modern terrorists and autocrats no less than that of ancient kings. Self-control allows us to hear and heed expert advice and to benefit from productive verbal argument. Self-control permits rational cooperation and constructive democratic decision-making. Prevailing over anger and fear, self-control enables us to respect the humanity of political opponents and even enemies. Self-control permits unequivocal condemnation of violent atrocities irrespective of the victims' identities or the perpetrators' motives. Self-control subordinates the self-destructive passions of greed, hatred, fear, vengeance, and sexual violence to the far-sighted wisdom of truth, justice, and humanity.

Conclusion
Preserving Humanity

Herodotus's extraordinary invention, *historiē*, aids the preservation of humanity in both senses of the word: the human species itself and our unique capacity for just, compassionate moral action. Herodotus's *Histories* cautions against unthinking allegiance to any person or dogma. Exposing the destructive and self-destructive essence of autocracy, the *Histories* reminds us of our obligations to ourselves and to others as conscious, self-aware human beings. *Historiē*, the effort to preserve, understand, *and evaluate* events and narratives, past and present, has unique potential to sustain current and future generations. Focused on human conduct and its consequences, the man who invented history models and cultivates evidence-based critical discernment, humanity's best defense against atrocities and extinction.

Crucially, the *Histories* attributes the responsibility for preserving humanity not to supernatural forces but to human beings. Like ancient Greek epics and tragedies, the *Histories* examines human choices and their results. But unlike ancient epic poets and tragic playwrights, Herodotus concentrates spe-

cifically on human agency, excluding supernatural protagonists and validating supernatural causal explanations only with
hindsight. Herodotus never doubts the potency of divine forces.
He recognizes, as we must, that divine will, destiny, fate, or
chance remain beyond human control. But the *Histories* suggests that by taking responsibility for our own conduct, we gain
control of that large piece of human experience precipitated by
our own words and actions. In the *Histories,* not gods or fate
determine human fortunes but human appetites, choices, analyses, and reasoning—or lack of reasoning. Many disasters, as
Herodotus shows, are in fact not inevitable but unnecessarily
self-inflicted. The *Histories* encourages us to focus on these.

Herodotus's invitation to concentrate on factors within
our control also sustains humanity in the alternate sense of the
word. The *Histories* warns repeatedly against abusing power
and objectifying other people—or admiring and assisting those
who do. Far from encouraging readers to emulate ruthless autocrats or to elevate would-be autocrats to leadership roles,
Herodotus exposes autocratic rulers as a danger to both themselves and the people subject to their power. Absolute power
makes the powerful victims of their own worst impulses and
impervious to wise counsel. Tales of sexual predation and other
self-destructive autocratic atrocities illustrate the disastrous
consequences of irrational passions, unfounded self-confidence,
insatiable material greed, contempt for human life, and lack
of impulse control. By contrast, *humane* human qualities—
evidence-based reasoning, cooperative decision-making, forethought, self-restraint, respect for human life—appear to
maximize the chances for survival and happiness.

Vital for humanity, *historiē* constitutes a supremely noble
human accomplishment. Like the singers of epic tales before
him, Herodotus aims to preserve great and marvelous deeds—
but now using prose, making his own achievement the public

record, display, and evaluation of human achievements. Constantly detailing his own investigative process and opinions, Herodotus models the role of the *histor*, a person capable of assessing facts so as to make a constructive judgment. He explicitly reserves the right to make his own analyses, claiming, for example, "I am under an obligation to say what has been said, but I am by no means under an obligation to trust it. And let this statement of mine hold for my entire account" (7.153.3). Free to make his own evaluative judgments, Herodotus liberates readers to make their own. *Historiē* entails not the constraints of uncritical belief but the freedom of rational investigation and evidence-based ethical judgment.

In its focus on human agency, the *Histories* illustrates the deep connection between fact-based critical thinking and democratic political ideals, institutions, and norms. Herodotus invented history when democracy was a novel, evolving political experiment. I write as the appetite for both history and democracy has begun to diminish and the connection between the two has begun to erode. Like no other political system, democracy has the potential to guarantee individual rights and freedoms and nonviolent regime change. But in giving citizens immense power and responsibility, democracy potentiates both the constructive and the destructive force of individual choices. The *Histories* identifies critical moral discernment as a fundamentally democratic survival skill empowering us to identify harmful and helpful options for ourselves as individuals and as members of communities large and small. Available to everyone, the capacity for evidence-based, logical evaluation enables us to acknowledge moral complexity, a basic prerequisite for mutually beneficial, humane decision-making and peaceful conflict resolution.

With the Athenian democratic experiment barely two generations old, Herodotus modeled for his contemporaries not merely a new genre of narrative but a way of engaging constructively with narrative, a method of distinguishing fact from fiction. Fusing storytelling with factual investigation and rational assessment, Herodotus challenged traditional certainties regarding unsubstantiated beliefs and events long distant in time. Despite incorporating his own critical assessments, Herodotus encourages readers to make their own evidence-based evaluative judgments. He thereby impedes senseless subservience to any unverified or unverifiable narrative or authoritative narrator.

Not as a set of facts but as a way of reading and thinking, *historiē* fortifies readers against mindless acceptance of any evidence-free, counterfactual narratives—including Herodotus's own stories. Although Herodotus introduced the principle of verification for distinguishing fact from fiction, he records numerous unverifiable stories of long-ago events, some of them manifestly fabricated or impossible. Drawing on multiple sources unavailable to us today, Herodotus also selected and shaped his material for his own purposes in ways we cannot know. Even to assess the historical accuracy of his account of the Persian Wars of the early fifth century—just a generation or two before his own times—we find ourselves much in the position of Herodotus himself in relation to traditional ancient Greek epic tales: these events happened too long ago for factual verification, and we possess limited alternative source material. But all of Herodotus's tales, plausible and implausible, foreign and familiar, demand the same intellectual scrutiny.

In subjecting a wide variety of human conduct, choices, and stories to rational scrutiny, the *Histories* undermines simplistic moral binaries of good versus evil, enabling us to perceive reality in all its morally confounding complexity. As a Greek writer, Herodotus distinguishes Greeks from non-Greeks, and he retains confidence in Greek cultural superiority, but his geographical and ethnographical investigations demonstrate the enriching value of ethnic and cultural diversity. His inquiries reveal that the concept of "us versus them" is situational. We ourselves are other people's Other, just as they are ours. Protagonists in the *Histories* are complicated guys (mostly guys) saying and doing a variety of things, some admirable, some decidedly not. Herodotus depicts Persians *and* Greeks, Spartans *and* Athenians, as cautionary examples. His examples of leadership—good and bad—as well as his nuanced depictions of freedom and excellence encourage us to reassess our own definitions and goals.

Moral complexity is effortful and uncomfortable, however, and self-criticism is painful. As two-eyed, two-handed, two-footed creatures, we often frame reality by antitheses: left/right, on one hand/on the other hand. We tend to prefer either/or to the complex reality of both/and. Authoritarian movements divide the world into "friend" and "foe," relieving us of the burden of moral choice. Seduced by simplistic definitions of right versus wrong (as in, us: right; them: wrong), we come to feel part of something greater than ourselves, even though many—even most—disagreements actually contain elements of right and wrong on both (or multiple) sides. A preference for intellectual ease, salacious entertainment, and moral certainty makes us dangerously receptive to corrupt authoritarian political extremists and their cynical enablers.

Tragically, modern digital technology enhances exponentially the difficulty of resisting divisive authoritative falsehoods. News outlets and social media, aiming not to inform but to capture attention and promote addiction, publicize and validate enticing, hateful, and fraudulent claims. Digital algorithms feed us our preferred narratives, exploit our most destructive weaknesses, and foment hatred and intolerance—all the while eroding our capacity for independent critical thought and moral evaluation. Generating groups impervious to reality, each group locked into its own silo of unverified and unverifiable certainties, our most inventive and lucrative technologies train us to seek not information but affirmation. Allowing digital tools to use us—to command and control our time, attention, and personal information—we risk forfeiting our autonomy and moral agency. Artificial Intelligence exacerbates the problem, since despite its astounding constructive potential AI cannot unerringly identify falsehoods—at least not yet. And not, it seems, soon enough. AI has the capacity to undermine human confidence in democratic norms, institutions, and the rule of law. It can feign but not replicate or substitute for human judgment, expertise, and compassion.

Disinformation, like all fiction, is seductive. Some people prefer it to reality. Fiction by definition does not have to be factual, reality-based, or even internally consistent. Autocrats use fictional narratives to ensnare followers and test their loyalty. Even well-meaning, intelligent people can succumb. The more evidence free, illogical, or outlandish the narrative, the more the autocrat demonstrates his power and followers demonstrate their abject fealty. Enthusiastic acceptance of patent falsehoods becomes the measure of political loyalty. Autocrats and aspiring autocrats strive to maintain the fiction that everyone is as corrupt as they; that everyone lies, cheats, steals, and commits sexual assault; that human beings are incapable of self-government. Not by persuading but by making us impervious to persuasion, the flood of falsehoods diminishes our desire and ability to engage in evidence-based analysis and good-faith argument.

Authoritarian leaders will always endanger humanity, but authoritarian followers pose the greater peril. Radicalized by unverified or unverifiable authoritative fictions, counterfactual historical narratives, or supernatural explanations for scientifically understood natural phenomena, we may choose feelings over facts, automatically rejecting claims with which we disagree. Groupthink exerts powerful pressure, and anger makes us feel righteous, important, and part of a like-minded community. Many of us prefer virtue signaling to problem solving. Whatever our moral and political convictions, virtue signaling is easy. Problem solving is difficult.

All past human experience attests that *historiē* is difficult. Though Herodotus's *Histories* fosters the intellectual discernment and emotional restraint required for democratic self-government, the Athenian experiment in direct democracy lasted less than two centuries. Athenian ideals of freedom and equality did not preclude slavery, the subjugation of women, or brutal imperialist conquest of other citizen-communities. Fearing the tyrannical capacity of the Athenian model of direct democracy and seeking to avert the dangers of both autocracy and mob rule, the framers of the U.S. Constitution crafted a constitutional democratic republic. Though colloquially termed a "democracy," the modern U.S. constitutional republic differs greatly from the ancient Athenian version in institutions and norms. But the framers, too, fell well short of ensuring equal rights for all human beings. Like the ancient Athenians, they failed to reject human enslavement, male-only suffrage, and imperial domination. Over decades, the United States has moved (too slowly, imperfectly) toward greater recognition of universal human equality. Having lasted nearly two and a half centuries, our constitutional democratic republic now seems particularly fragile.

Herodotus reminds us that human choices sustain historical memory and each generation must continually reinvigorate democratic ideals, institutions, and norms for itself. Exposing the dangers of insular autocratic decision-making and the hazards of falling for deceptions and disguises, the *Histories* emphasizes the value of historical memory for enlarging understanding and guiding present action. Herodotus unmasks not only the fraudulent promise of authoritarianism but also the constructive and destructive potential of political equality. Applied to every narrative, critical discernment protects against mistaken certainties and ill-conceived decisions.

Historical inquiry remains an ever-evolving but vital process. A multiplicity of modern scholarly interpretations of the *Histories* attests to the work's complexity and the value of unceasing investigative analysis. Accurate historical assessment requires a factual basis, but the facts of history are always multifaceted and morally complex. History constantly evolves, as historians inevitably investigate and interpret the past in light of the present. New evidence emerges, and contemporary attitudes and agendas change. Demonstrating that *historiē* requires and rewards open-minded, meticulous assessment *and reassessment* of all available evidence, the *Histories* promotes the evidence-based critical reasoning required to address modern efforts to erase or distort both the past and the present.

Herodotus's deliberate intentions remain unknowable, but his invention of history seems designed to encourage his contemporaries to govern themselves wisely. The *Histories* shows that the past offers illustrative examples and the opportunity to evaluate them critically. The morally complicated model of ancient Greece can help illuminate the truth of our own history. For us, too, past and present injustices, villainy, and cruelty accompany examples of admirable, noble achievements. Neither the wholly positive view of the United States as "land of the free and home of the brave" nor the wholly negative view of the United States as a brutal, racist, colonial power is the whole truth. The truth is that in the United States—and perhaps in other parts of the world as well—our memories are both too long and too short. We nourish ancient hatreds and

forget historical facts. Ignorance of the past ensures ignorance
of the ideals, goals, and consequences of both tyranny and democracy. Herodotus insists that truth means not forgetting.

Herodotus's *Histories* suggests that humanity—in both
senses of the word—cannot survive without a citizenry capable
of independent, nuanced, critical thought. Illiberal ideological
orthodoxies come in many guises: identity politics masquerading as patriotism or even universalism, tribalism masquerading
as opposition to tribalism, injustice masquerading as opposition to injustice. Assailing freedom of thought and freedom
of expression, extremist orthodoxies substitute convenient
fictions for facts, loyalty for expertise. Uncritical acceptance
of authoritative fictions precludes the rational argument, mutual understanding, humane decision-making, and creative
compromise required for self-governance. Dogmatic certainty
may be seductive to people of good faith deeply troubled by
injustice. But extremists seek vengeance and power, not justice
or equality. Extremist illiberal orthodoxies deny the reality of
the fundamental humanity of every human being.

The man who invented history encouraged his contemporaries to resist becoming enthralled. He invited them instead to think and choose for themselves. Like Homer and the
tragedians, Herodotus develops the radical idea that our identity derives not from inherited qualities or socioeconomic
status but from our own individual conduct. Exposing the
fraudulent promise of authoritarianism 2,500 years ago, the
Histories provides a warning not only to anyone thinking
of becoming an autocrat but also and especially to anyone
willing to cede power to one. Subsequent human history
demonstrates—repeatedly and without exception—that authoritarian movements, whatever they claim, aim at rule by
the few in the interests of the few, at terrible cost to everyone
else and, in the end, to the rulers themselves. Fortifying us

against mindless indoctrination, *historiē* frees us to acknowledge human achievements and human suffering—even when
they may be ideologically inconvenient.

Cultivating our intellectual discernment and our ability
to recognize ourselves in others, Herodotus introduced *historiē*
as humanity's best chance for survival. Good faith, evidence-
based logical argument fosters democratic ideals of equality,
justice, and humanity—and the institutions and norms that
sustain them. Creative cooperation and the ability to distinguish facts from fictions enable verbal conflict resolution to
replace physical violence. Citizens of newly democratic Athens
in the fifth century BCE confronted foreign enemies and internal adversaries, plague, and their own violent impulses—as
do we. Herodotus emphasizes that internal divisions make
communities weak and vulnerable to devastation whereas unity
promotes strength. He reminds us that reductive, polarized
thinking pits us against one another—at the precise moment
when our very survival depends on our ability to face facts, co-
operate, and innovate *together*. The false promise of authoritarianism appeals to people who have not really thought it
through. Herodotus helps us to think it through. The ancient
Athenians never realized the great egalitarian, humane potential of democratic government. Herodotus equips us to do
better.

Notes

Introduction

1. Herodotus, *Histories* 1.152–153.

2. Asheri, *Commentary*, 2–5; Thomas, "Intellectual Milieu of Herodotus," 61; Munson, *Telling Wonders*, 3, 267–268; Baragwanath, "Returning to Troy," 289 and n6.

3. Excellent discussions of Herodotus and his methods include Myres, *Herodotus: Father of History*; Momigliano, "Place of Herodotus in the History of Historiography," 31–45; Immerwahr, *Form and Thought in Herodotus*, 5–7; Evans, "Father of History or Father of Lies," 11–17; Meier, "Historical Answers to Historical Questions," 41–57; Gould, *Herodotus*; Lateiner, *Historical Method of Herodotus*; Moles, "Truth and Untruth in Herodotus and Thucydides," 88–120; Christ, "Herodotean Kings and Historical Inquiry," 167–202; Romm, *Herodotus*; Hartog, "Invention of History," 384–395; Bakker, "Making of History: Herodotus' *historiēs apodexis*," 3–32; Cartledge, *Thermopylae*, 213–219; Roberts, *Herodotus*; Popkin, *From Herodotus to H-Net*, 27–31; Pelling, *Herodotus and the Question Why*.

4. Fornara, *Herodotus*, 41–48, 57–58; Strasburger, "Herodotus and Periclean Athens," 296–299.

5. Momigliano, "Place of Herodotus in the History of Historiography," 34–35.

6. *ktēma eis aiei*, Thucydides, *History of the Peloponnesian War* 1.21–22.

7. Fornara, *Herodotus*, 59–62; Raaflaub, "Herodotus, Political Thought, and the Meaning of History," 221–248. See also Kingsley, *Herodotus and the Presocratics*.

8. Grethlein, "How Not to Do History," 195–218.

9. Pelling, *Herodotus and the Question Why*, 236.

10. Immerwahr, *Form and Thought*, 17.

11. Fowler, "Herodotus and His Prose Predecessors," 29.

12. Nagy, *Pindar's Homer*, 262, 315–320.

13. *Iliad* 18.497–508.

14. *Herodotum patrem historiae* (Cicero, *de Legibus* 1.5).

15. *Pseusmata kai plasmata* (Plutarch, *de Herodoti Malignitate* 854f).

16. Asheri, *Commentary*, 6; Roberts, *Herodotus*, 101–103.

17. See especially Baragwanath and de Bakker, "Intro: Myth, Truth, and Narrative in Herodotus's *Histories*," 1–56.

18. Fowler, "Herodotus and His Prose Predecessors," 32; Sheehan, *Guide to Reading Herodotus' Histories*, 17.

19. Arieti, *Discourses on the First Book of Herodotus*, 38–39.

20. On the development of Athenian political institutions 508/7–ca. 450 BCE, see, for example Fornara and Samons, *Athens from Cleisthenes to Pericles*, 37–75; Krentz, "Appendix A: The Athenian Government in Herodotus," 723–726. On Herodotus's relationship to democratic thought, see Forsdyke, "Athenian Democratic Ideology and Herodotus' *Histories*," 329–358, and "Herodotus, Political History, and Political Thought," 224–241.

21. On Herodotus's methodology and use of prose, see, e.g., Drews, *Greek Accounts of Ancient History*, 20–44; Fowler, "Herodotus and His Prose Predecessors," 29–45; Griffiths, "Stories and Storytelling in the *Histories*," 130–144; Scanlon, *Greek Historiography*, 11–14, 17–21; Pelling, *Herodotus and the Question Why*, 58–79. Most of the first generation of Greek prose writing survives only in fragments, if at all. But two book-length works, Herodotus's *Histories* (ca. 440s/430s BCE) and Thucydides' *History of the Peloponnesian War* (ca. 431–411 BCE) survive in their entirety.

22. Luraghi, "Importance of Being *Logios*," 439.

23. Griffiths, "Stories and Storytelling," 131.

24. E.g., Forsdyke, "Ancient and Modern Conceptions of the Rule of Law," 184–212.

25. See my own *Enraged*, 22–28, and *Embattled*, 32–34, 63–65.

26. For excellent discussions, see Stockton, *Classical Athenian Democracy*, 19–116, and Raaflaub, "Power in the Hands of the People," 31–66.

27. Canevaro, "Majority Rule vs. Consensus," 109–147.

28. Martin, *Ancient Greece*, 171–177. And see Katz's discussion of modern scholars' belated interest in this topic, in "Women and Democracy in Ancient Greece," 41–68.

29. See Kamen, *Greek Slavery*, 27–31 and passim.

30. Rose, "Theorizing Athenian Imperialism," 19–39.

31. Anderson, "Tyranny and Social Ontology in Classical Athens," 17–23.

32. For Herodotus's relationship to Tragedy, see Griffin, "Herodotus and Tragedy," 46–59.

33. Baragwanath, "Returning to Troy," 287–312.

34. Sheehan, *Guide to Reading Herodotus' Histories*, 27–31.

35. The division of the work into nine books was not done by Herodotus (Immerwahr, *Form and Thought*, 79; Priestley, *Herodotus and Hellenistic Culture*, 192).

36. Waterfield, "On 'Fussy Authorial Nudges' in Herodotus," 488–491.

37. Pelling, *Herodotus and the Question Why*, 129–145.

38. Scullion, "Herodotus and Greek Religion," 192.

39. Sheehan, *Guide to Reading Herodotus' Histories*, 25.

40. Dewald, "Myth and Legend in Herodotus' First Book," 75–76; Pelling, *Herodotus and the Question Why*, 146–149.

41. Lateiner, *Historical Method of Herodotus*, 205–207.

1

On Faith

1. E.g., Roberts, *Herodotus*, 2–5.

2. I translate *historiē* as "results of the inquiry," following How and Wells in their understanding of *historiē* as "properly 'inquiry' and so the 'result of inquiry,'" *Commentary*, 53. Modern translations differ: e.g., "researches" (de Sélincourt, *Herodotus: The Histories*, 41); "history" (Grene, *History: Herodotus*, 33); "research" (Purvis, in Strassler, *Landmark Herodotus*, 3); "exposition of the enquiries" (Asheri, *Commentary*, 8). See also Bakker, "Making of History," 13–19, and Press, *Development of the Idea of History in Antiquity*, 23–24. Pelling defines *historiē* as "a word that focuses on the gathering of material as well as on its exposition" (*Herodotus and the Question Why*, 23).

3. Bakker, "Making of History," 13–14.

4. Hartog, "Invention of History," 393. See also Marincola, "Herodotean Narrative and the Narrator's Presence," 121–137; Dewald, "Narrative Surface and Authorial Voice in Herodotus' *Histories*," 147–170; Luraghi, "Meta-*historiē*," 76–91.

5. *Iliad* 18.497–508.

6. Bakker, "Making of History," 6–8.

7. *Iliad* 1.1–2.

8. *Odyssey* 1.1–2.

9. Nagy, *Homeric Questions*, 20–22, and *Homer the Pre-classic*, 3–28.

10. Hesiod, *Theogony* 1.

11. Hesiod, *Works and Days* 1.

12. E.g., Griffiths, "Stories and Storytelling," 135–140.

13. On Herodotus's relation to his poetic predecessors, see especially Nagy, "Herodotus the *Logios*," 175–184, and Marincola, "Herodotus and the Poetry of the Past," 13–28.

14. De Jong identifies the Herodotean narrator as "omni-present," "omniscient," and "self-conscious," in "Narratological Aspects of the *Histories* of Herodotus," 259–260.

15. Baragwanath and de Bakker, *Myth, Truth, and Narrative*, 1–19. *Ta genomena*, includes "things done" and "things said" (Bakker, "Making of History," 19).

16. Marincola, "Herodotus and the Poetry of the Past," 17–19.

17. Nagy, "Herodotus the *Logios*," 180–184.

18. E.g., *Iliad* 9.189; *Odyssey* 1.338. On *kleos*, see especially Nagy, "Herodotus the *Logios*," 15–18.

19. Hesiod, *Works and Days* 1.

20. Marincola, "Herodotus and the Poetry of the Past," 16–17.

21. On Herodotus's interest in causality and its connection to moral evaluation, see especially Pelling, *Herodotus and the Question Why*, 5–11.

22. *Odyssey* 1.3.

23. Aeschylus, *Agamemnon* 176. *Pathos* derives from the verb *paskhō*, meaning to suffer or be affected by anything, good or bad. The noun *pathos* means anything that befalls someone, therefore a "suffering" or "misfortune," or sometimes merely an "incident" or "experience."

24. Both *apodexis*, the noun "display," and *apodekhthenta*, the aorist passive participle "(having been) displayed," derive from the verb *apodeiknumi* meaning "to show forth, bring forth, produce, make known." Nagy, "Herodotus the *Logios*," 177–179; Asheri, *Commentary*, 72–73. The combination *apodexis historiēs* indicates some distance in time between Herodotus and the events he will describe (Lateiner, *Historical Method of Herodotus*, 8–10).

25. Bakker, "Making of History," 25–28.

26. *Odyssey* 1.32–34.

27. E.g., Sophocles' *Ajax* and Euripides' *Hippolytus* and *Bacchae*.

28. Griffiths, "Stories and Storytelling," 140–142. See also Dewald, "Myth and Legend in Herodotus' First Book," 75–78.

29. Immerwahr, "Aspects of Historical Causation in Herodotus," 166.

30. Anhalt, *Embattled*, 104–108.

31. Immerwahr, *Form and Thought*, 19.

2

On Myth

1. Pelling calls these Persian storytellers (*logioi*) "experts in tales" (*Herodotus and the Question Why*, 25). Nagy identifies them as Asiatic Greeks, "who represented the world view of the Persian Empire," observing that

Herodotus of Halicarnassus was himself an Asiatic Greek and, implicitly, a *logios* as well ("Herodotus and the *Logioi* of the Persians," 188). See also Węcowski, "Hedgehog and the Fox," 149–150.

2. E.g., Dewald, "Myth and Legend in Herodotus' First Book," 59–85; Chiasson, "Myth and Truth in Herodotus' Cyrus *Logos*," 225–226.

3. E.g., Drews, *Greek Accounts of Ancient History*, 89; Lateiner, *Historical Method of Herodotus*, 41; Thomas, *Herodotus in Context*, 268; Węcowski, "Hedgehog and the Fox," 150–152; Dewald, "Humour and Danger in Herodotus," 147; Henderson, "Old Comedy and Popular History," 144–159.

4. E.g., Bromberg, *Global Classics*.

5. Węcowski, "Hedgehog and the Fox," 153; Blondell, *Helen of Troy*, 148. Stahl identifies Herodotus's "moral partisanship" throughout the *Histories* in "Blind Decisions Preceding Military Action," 132–133.

6. Munson, "Herodotus and the Heroic Age," 195. Herodotus links the historical with the mythical past by depicting the Trojan War as a metaphor for the Persian War (Munson, 199–200). See also Bowie, "Mythology and the Expedition of Xerxes," 269–286, and Baragwanath, "Returning to Troy," 287–312.

7. *Odyssey* 8.521–531.

8. E.g., Aeschylus's *Agamemnon* and Euripides' *Hecuba* and *Trojan Women*.

9. E.g., Aeschylus, *Suppliants* 15–18, 274–276, 291–324, 531–599.

10. E.g., *Iliad* 14.321–322.

11. E.g., Euripides' *Medea*.

12. Blondell, *Helen of Troy*, 36–37, 69–72, 93, 103,147, 151–153, 166–180, 187–193, 205–206, 241, 244–245.

13. Thompson, *Herodotus and the Origins of the Political Community*, 32.

14. Arieti, *Discourses on the First Book of Herodotus*, 9–10. For Herodotus's depiction of Persia, see Flower, "Herodotus and Persia," 274–289. Sheehan provides bibliography for the modern rejection of the Hellenocentric view of Greece vs. Persia (*Guide to Reading Herodotus' Histories*, 28).

15. E.g., Aeschylus's *Clytemnestra*, Sophocles' *Antigone*, Euripides' *Medea*. And see especially Roisman, *Tragic Heroines in Ancient Greek Drama*.

16. E.g., the sacrifice of Iphigenia in Aeschylus's *Agamemenon*; portrait of Tecmessa in Sophocles' *Ajax*; Antigone in Sophocles' *Antigone*; captive women in Euripides' *Trojan Women*; female sacrificial victims in Euripides' *Hecuba* and *Children of Heracles*.

17. E.g., Moritz v. Commissioner of Internal Revenue, 469 F. 2d 466 (1972); Weinberger vs. Wiesenfeld 420 U.S. 636 (1975); Califano vs. Goldfarb 430 U.S. 199 (1977).

18. Clay identifies a fundamental connection in Greek thought between seeing and knowing ("Homer's Trojan Theater," 236).

19. E.g., Griffin, "Herodotus and Tragedy," 53.

20. Anhalt, *Embattled*, 138–139, 146–155.

21. E.g., *Persians* (472 BCE), *Suppliants* (ca. 467 BCE), *Agamemnon* (458 BCE).

22. *Hecuba* (ca. 424 BCE) and *Trojan Women* (415 BCE). See Gregory, *Euripides and the Instruction of the Athenians* 85–120; Anhalt, *Enraged*, 165–177.

23. Pelling, *Herodotus and the Question Why*, 167–168.

24. Myres, *Herodotus*, 74–75.

25. E.g., McNamee, *Zucked*, especially 81–110. McNamee outlines "the typical path for disinformation or a conspiracy theory" on the internet (123–127).

26. E.g., Popkin, *From Herodotus to H-Net*, 15–19.

3
On Sexual Violence

1. Sansone, "Herodotus on Lust," 1–3.

2. Sansone, "Herodotus on Lust," 17–28.

3. Dewald, ""Narrative Surface and Authorial Voice," 151, 163.

4. Pelling, *Herodotus and the Question Why*, 108–109.

5. De Jong, "Narratological Aspects of the *Histories*," 255–256.

6. Arieti, *Discourses on the First Book of Herodotus*, 16n29.

7. Griffiths, "Stories and Storytelling," 140.

8. Plato, *Republic* 2.359a–360d. On variants of the Gyges tale, see Asheri, *Commentary*, 81–82. Danzig discusses Plato's version as a response to Herodotus's version, in "Rhetoric and the Ring," 169–192. See also Griffin, "Herodotus and Tragedy," 50–51.

9. Sansone, "Herodotus on Lust," 11–12.

10. E.g., Hamel calls Candaules "an ill-starred fellow" (*Reading Herodotus*, 8).

11. Grene, *History*, 36; Purvis, in Strassler, *Landmark Herodotus*, 8.

12. Long, *Repetition and Variation in the Short Stories of Herodotus*, 9–38; Arieti, *Discourses on the First Book of Herodotus*, 19–20.

13. E.g., Thucydides' Alcibiades argues that his own achievements enhance his ancestors' reputation (Thucydides, *History of the Peloponnesian War* 6.16.1).

14. Blondell, *Helen of Troy*, 148–149.

4
On Fact

1. Munson, "Celebratory Purpose of Herodotus," 96–97; Hooker, "Arion and the Dolphin," 146.

2. Ehrenberg, *From Solon to Socrates*, 24, 104.

3. Immerwahr, *Form and Thought in Herodotus*, 35, 41–42; Flory, "Arion's Leap," 411; Griffiths, "Stories and Storytelling," 131, 133; Munson, "Celebratory Purpose of Herodotus," 95. For various scholarly explanations, see Long, *Repetition and Variation in the Short Stories of Herodotus*, 51–60, and Hooker, "Arion and the Dolphin," 141. But cf. Gray, who finds connections to the broader narrative and validation of Herodotus's own investigative method ("Herodotus' Literary and Historical Method," 16–19; 22).

4. How and Wells, *Commentary*, 63–64; Pickard-Cambridge, *Dithyramb, Tragedy, and Comedy*, 10–13, 97–101; Campbell, *Greek Lyric*, vol. 3, 16–25; Asheri, *Commentary*, 91–93. Arion was not the first to use the name dithyramb (e.g., Archilochus, Fragment 120 in Gerber, *Greek Iambic Poetry*, 161). Arion may have influenced Stesichorus. No fragments of Arion's work survive.

5. Munson, "Celebratory Purpose of Herodotus," 96. See also Gould, *Herodotus*, 29–30, and Lateiner, *Historical Method of Herodotus*, 199.

6. Bowra, "Arion and the Dolphin," 121–122.

7. Asheri, *Commentary*, 92. Higham offers modern anecdotes of dolphin riders ("Nature Note," 82–86), but Flory identifies "a tension . . . between fact and fiction" in the tale ("Arion's Leap," 419). On possible traditional sources for the tale, see Gray, "Herodotus' Literary and Historical Method," 23–24.

8. Bowra, "Arion and the Dolphin," 133–134.

9. Gray, "Herodotus' Literary and Historical Method," 13–14. The Homeric *Hymn to Dionysus* associates the god with dolphins (*Hymn 7 to Dionysus* 50–53). In the *Hymn to Apollo*, the god takes dolphin form and arrives by ship in Taenarum (*Hymn 3 to Delian Apollo* 400–443). Arieti suggests a possible pun on Delphi-*delphinos* (*Discourses*, 36 and n56), but Herodotus neglects to mention the famous sanctuary to Poseidon at Tainaron. Arion's song constitutes an act of worship (How and Wells, *Commentary*, 64), but Herodotus has "edited out the god" (Griffiths, "Stories and Storytelling," 140). Herodotus substitutes a "fabulous" for a "supernatural rescue" (Sheehan, *Guide to Reading Herodotus' Histories*, 37–38). Herodotus also excludes the folktale motif of the protagonist magically summoning or bewitching the dolphin for aid (Flory, "Arion's Leap," 413 and n5; Sheehan, *Guide to Reading Herodotus' Histories*, 70).

10. Flory, "Arion's Leap," 421; Munson, "Celebratory Purpose of Herodotus," 100.

11. Griffiths, "Stories and Storytelling," 138–140. Sheehan terms the leap "a supremely theatrical moment" (*Guide to Reading Herodotus' Histories*, 69–70) and finds parallels with the leaps of Prexaspes (3.75) and Boges (7.107), arguing that for all three "integrity and honour is more important than self-preservation" (209).

12. Wood, *Histories of Herodotus*, 23–26; Arieti *Discourses*, 36. Noting Arion's willingness to give up his money and his dedication to his art, Arieti views the tale as corroboration of Solon's claims about the limited duration of happiness and a lesson in "how the gods help one who is good and pious" (38).

13. Munson, *Telling Wonders*, 253.

14. Fornara, *Herodotus*, 19.

15. Long, *Repetition and Variation*, 58–60. How and Wells note the use on coins of the image of a hero riding a dolphin (*Commentary*, 64).

16. Flory, "Arion's Leap," 412n4; Arieti, *Discourses*, 37.

17. Munson, "Celebratory Purpose of Herodotus," 98.

18. On "the story pattern of 'the enquiring king,'" see de Jong, "Helen *Logos* and Herodotus' Fingerprint," 127–142. But cf. Arieti's suggestion that Herodotus might "intend for us to see Periander and the sailors as cut from the same cloth, both untrustworthy and untrusting" (*Discourses*, 37). Arieti views Periander as "an archetype of the wicked tyrant" (37n58), rejecting David Konstan's argument that justice prevails under Periander's rule (Konstan, "Stories in Herodotus' *Histories*: Book 1," 14).

19. Flory, "Arion's Leap," 417.

20. Arieti, *Discourses*, 37–38.

21. Hooker, "Arion and the Dolphin," 142, 144; Griffiths, "Stories and Storytelling," 142.

22. Long, *Repetition and Variation*, 54.

23. Munson identifies: "overwhelming aggression against a numerically weaker victim . . . barbarism and civilization, physical force and moral excellence, divine punishment and rewards" ("Celebratory Purpose," 98–100).

24. Benardete, *Herodotean Inquiries*, 15; Friedman, "Location and Dislocation in Herodotus," 168–171. Friedman sees in Arion's choice "the despair of placelessness" and its connection to "the poet's performance of his craft" (171).

25. Gray, "Herodotus' Literary and Historical Method," 15–16; Fowler, "Herodotus and His Prose Predecessors," 81.

26. Thucydides, *History of the Peloponnesian War* 1.22.4.

27. Aristotle, *Poetics* 1451 b4–12.

5

On Happiness

1. On Solon's role in Athens, see especially Forrest, *Emergence of Greek Democracy*, 147–174; Ehrenberg, *From Solon to Socrates*, 50–77; Martin, *Ancient Greece*, 109–112; Krentz, "Appendix A: The Athenian Government in

Herodotus," 723–725. On the historicity of Croesus, see Ehrenberg, *From Solon to Socrates*, 105–106, and Martin, *Ancient Greece*, 124.

2. Ehrenberg, *From Solon to Socrates*, 407n1.

3. Wallace, "Redating Croesus," 168–181.

4. Arieti, *Discourses*, 45 and n69.

5. Chiasson, "Herodotean Solon," 249–262.

6. Raaflaub, "Herodotus, Political Thought, and the Meaning of History," 241–246. Good discussions of this story abound. Long, *Repetition and Variation*, 62–73 and 176–177; Shapiro, "Herodotus and Solon," 348–364; Chiasson, "Herodotus' Use of Tragedy in the Lydian *Logos*," 5–36; J. Kindt, "Delphic Oracle Stories and the Beginning of Historiography," 34–51; Pelling, "Educating Croesus: Talking and Learning in Herodotus' Lydian *Logos*," 141–177; Kingsley, *Herodotus and the Presocratics*, 1–8.

7. Arieti, *Discourses*, 41.

8. For a succinct description of Solon's institutional reforms, see Raaflaub, "Power in the Hands of the People," 38–39. More extensive accounts include Forrest, *Emergence of Greek Democracy*, 160–174; Ehrenberg, *From Solon to Socrates*, 62–76; Stockton, *Classical Athenian Democracy*, 19–22.

9. Arieti, *Discourses*, 45–56.

10. Roberts, *Herodotus*, 25.

11. Raaflaub, "Herodotus, Political Thought, and the Meaning of History," 234.

12. Thompson, *Herodotus and the Origins of the Political Community*, 14–16.

6
On Self-Deception

1. Thonemann, "Croesus and the Oracles," 152–167.

2. E.g., Roberts, *Herodotus*, 76–88.

3. Arieti, *Discourses*, 72–73.

4. Kurke, *Coins, Bodies, Games, and Gold*, 152.

5. Hamel, *Reading Herodotus*, 20.

6. Arieti notes Croesus's failure to learn from the Spartans' experience (*Discourses*, 82).

7. Arieti, *Discourses*, 104–106.

8. Arieti, *Discourses*, 55–56.

9. Arieti, *Discourses*, 128.

10. Pelling, "Urine and the Vine," 71–73.

11. Pelling, "Urine and the Vine," 74–75; Billows, *Marathon*, 113–115.

12. Arieti, *Discourses*, 195.

13. Eugene O'Neill, *A Moon for the Misbegotten: A Play in Four Acts* (New York: Vintage Books, 2009).

7
On Deception

1. Subsequently, Peisistratus must flee Athens again, but he regains power a third time (1.61–64).

2. Anhalt, *Embattled*, 9–11, 49–50, 151–152.

3. Noting that "certainty is impossible," How and Wells suggest the following dates: first tyranny, 560–559 BCE; first exile, 555 BCE; second tyranny, 550 BCE; second exile, 549 BCE; third tyranny, 539 BCE; death of Peisistratus, 527 BCE; expulsion of Hippias, 510 BCE (How and Wells, *Commentary*, 84). Schreiner argues for just one period of exile ("Exile and Return of Peisistratos," 13–17).

4. Baragwanath, *Motivation and Narrative in Herodotus*, 151.

5. Jennifer Finn, "Herodotus' *Poor Man of Nippur*," *Classical World* 112, no. 2 (2019): 13–16, 22–6.

6. Asheri, *Commentary*, 160; Hamel, *Reading Herodotus*, 38.

7. *Iliad* 6.269–311.

8. *Iliad* 24.25–30.

9. Aristotle's account essentially accords with Herodotus's (*Constitution of the Athenians* 14.4). And see Connor, "Tribes, Festivals, and Processions," 40–50; Sinos, "Epiphany and Politics in Archaic Greece," 73–91; Blok, "Phye's Procession," 18–19, 40, 44–48.

8
On Foreign Ways

1. E.g., Rood, "Herodotus and Foreign Lands," 290–305; Roberts, *Herodotus*, 49–64.

2. Lloyd, "Appendix C: The Account of Egypt," 742.

3. Fornara, *Herodotus*, 21 and passim.

4. Lloyd, "Appendix C: The Account of Egypt," 737–743.

5. Dewald, "Narrative Surface," 149–151; Marincola, "Herodotean Narrative," 121–122.

6. "Divine elements" (*theia apēgēmatōn*, 2.3.2) vs. "human deeds/matters" (*anthrōpēia prēgmata*, 2.4.1).

7. Gruen, *Ethnicity in the Ancient World*, 13–16.

8. Attributing the origins of the American caste system to colonial times, Isabel Wilkerson notes the existence of slavery throughout world history and the comparative newness of modern racial oppression, in *Caste*, 17–44.

9. Derbew, *Untangling Blackness in Greek Antiquity*, 98–101, 110.

10. Gruen, *Ethnicity in the Ancient World*, 42–55.

11. *Odyssey* 17.322–323.

12. Osborne, *Athens and Athenian Democracy*, 84–103.

13. For a compendium of ancient sources on Greek and Roman slavery, see Bathrellou and Vlassopoulos, *Greek and Roman Slaveries*.

14. Pelling, *Herodotus and the Question Why*, 41.

15. Pelling, "East Is East and West Is West," 51; Rood, "Herodotus and Foreign Lands," 296–298; Stahl, "Blind Decisions," 132–133.

16. Pelling, "East Is East and West Is West," 51–54.

17. Lloyd, "Egypt," 415–418.

18. Pelling, "East Is East and West Is West," 56.

19. Pelling, "East Is East and West Is West," 61.

20. Wenghofer, "Sexual Promiscuity of Non-Greeks," 515–534.

21. Wenghofer, "Sexual Promiscuity," 518–520.

22. Wenghofer, "Sexual Promiscuity," 521.

23. Wenghofer, "Sexual Promiscuity," 526–527. On women in the *Histories*, see Roberts, *Herodotus*, 65–75.

24. E.g., D. Fehling, *Herodotus and His "Sources,"* 243; Lloyd, "Egypt," 430–434.

25. Munson, discussing *Histories* 3.38 (*Telling Wonders*, 171–172).

9
On Foreign Tales

1. See especially de Jong, "Helen *Logos*," 127–142.

2. West, "Rhampsinitos and the Clever Thief," 323. West deems this tale not authentically Egyptian but "a scurrilous Greek fantasy" (325).

3. Luraghi, "Meta-*historiē*," 77–78.

4. E.g., *Odyssey* 7.155–181. See Vandiver's discussion of Herodotus's use of the traditional concept of *xenia* drawn from epic poetry, in "Strangers Are from Zeus," 143–166.

5. Euripides' tragedy, *Helen* (ca. 414–412 BCE), develops the idea that Helen remained in Egypt and never reached Troy.

6. Vandiver, "Strangers Are from Zeus," 151.

7. West, "Rhampsinitos and the Clever Thief," 324. On Herodotus's use of folklore elements here and elsewhere, see especially Luraghi, "Stories before the *Histories*," 87–112.

8. West, "Rhampsinitos and the Clever Thief," 325–326.

9. Asheri, *Commentary*, 327.

10. E.g., Dewald, "Humour and Danger," 149–150.

11. See, e.g., Loney, *Ethics of Revenge*, 173–192, 203–225, and Barker and Christensen, *Homer's Thebes*, 235–239.

12. E.g., *Odyssey* 1.1 and 9.1.

13. Identifying Rhampsinitus "rewarding where he should have punished," Arieti finds implicit criticism of Athenian imperialism (*Discourses*, 207–209).

14. E.g., Grant, *Hidden Potential*, 23–41.

10

On Tyranny

1. Flower, "Herodotus and Persia," 280. For a modern account of ancient Persia, see Llewellyn-Jones, *Persians*.

2. See Sancisi-Weerdenburg, "Personality of Xerxes," 579–590, vs. Munson, "Who Are Herodotus' Persians?" 457–470.

3. Pelling, "East Is East and West Is West," 53–54.

4. Strasburger, "Herodotus and Periclean Athens," 309–310, 313; Billows, *Marathon*, 140, 148–153; Lane, *Birth of Politics*, 74–80; Shepherd, *Persian War in Herodotus and Other Ancient Voices*, 67.

5. Anderson, "Tyranny and Social Ontology in Classical Athens," 30–31.

6. Egyptian propaganda was most hostile to Cambyses (Asheri, *Commentary*, 433–434).

7. Baragwanath, *Motivation and Narrative in Herodotus*, 108.

8. Redfield, "Commentary on Humphreys and Raaflaub," 252.

9. E.g., Asheri maintains that "the relativistic spirit of Ionian science permeates this chapter" (*Commentary*, 435–437), while Humphreys counters the relativist assumption in "Law, Custom, and Culture in Herodotus," 211–220. And, similarly, Thomas, "Intellectual Milieu of Herodotus," 69–70.

10. E.g., Rood, "Herodotus and Foreign Lands," 299; Cartledge, *Thermopylae*, 251–252; Sheehan, *Guide to Reading Herodotus' Histories*, 118–119, with additional bibliography. But cf. Kingsley, *Herodotus and the Presocratics*, 49–53, 56, 75, 200–201, 207–210.

11. Anhalt, *Enraged*, 93–94, 102–114.

12. Cartledge, *Thermopylae*, 220.

13. *Iliad* 24.525–533.

14. *Odyssey* 1.32–34.

15. E.g., Flower, "Herodotus and Persia," 279, vs. Pelling, "Speech and Action," 127–129.

11

On Types of Political Regimes

1. Hansen, *Athenian Democracy in the Age of Demosthenes*, 14; Cartledge, *Greeks*, 93–95.

2. Lateiner, "Herodotean Historiographical Patterning," 197–198. On the debate's historicity, see Asheri, *Commentary*, 471–473. Asheri notes the absence of technical terms for government by the one, the few, and the many, calling the debate as we have it from Herodotus "a Greek debate on Greek ideas composed by Herodotus, well-integrated into the main narrative and made emphatic at a time when the Greek public was interested in problems of this type" (472). Herodotus "implies that democracy had been proposed in Susa more than ten years before its institution in Athens" (473). See also Moles, "Truth and Untruth," 88–120, and Barker, *Entering the Agon*, 182–188.

3. Pelling, "Speech and Action," 124.

4. Pelling, "Speech and Action," 139–143, 146.

5. Pelling, "Speech and Action," 129–130.

6. Cairns, "Hybris, Dishonour, and Thinking Big," 1–32.

7. Plato makes this opposition explicit (Cairns, "Hybris," 25, 27, 31).

8. Lane, *Birth of Politics*, 71–72.

9. Pelling, "Speech and Action," 136–139; *Herodotus and the Question Why*, 193–195.

10. Lateiner, "Herodotean Historiographical Patterning," 209.

11. E.g., Sophocles' *Ajax* and Euripides' *Hecuba*.

12. Pelling, "Speech and Action," 145.

13. Flower, "Herodotus and Persia," 279.

14. Asheri, *Commentary*, 476.

15. Pelling, "Speech and Action," 148, 152–155.

16. Fornara and Samons, *Athens from Cleisthenes to Pericles*, 81–82.

17. Zakaria calls this phenomenon, "One man, one vote, one time," *The Future of Freedom*, 121.

18. Asheri notes the sacredness to the Persians of both the sun and horses (*Commentary*, 477).

19. Murray, "Herodotus and Oral History," 43–44.

20. Asheri, *Commentary*, 169.

21. Churchill, November 11, 1947.

12

On Empiricism

1. West, "Scythians," 446–447; Wheeler, "Appendix E: Herodotus and the Black Sea Region," 748.

2. West, "Scythians," 442.

3. Wheeler, "Appendix E: Herodotus and the Black Sea Region," 748–755, and "Appendix F: Rivers and Peoples of Scythia," 756–761.

4. Hartog, *Mirror of Herodotus*.

5. Thomas, "Intellectual Milieu of Herodotus," 71, citing Müller, "Herodot—Vater des Empirismus?" 299–318.

6. On folktale themes in the Scythians' origin story, see Asheri, *Commentary*, 575–576 (with bibliography).

7. Strassler, *Landmark Herodotus*, 287, note to 4.12.3. On the lack of archaeological evidence to confirm that the Scythians arrived from Asia, see Asheri, *Commentary*, 579–580, and Sheehan, *Guide to Reading Herodotus' Histories*, 135–136.

8. Pelling, *Herodotus and the Question Why*, 80–93, 120.

9. Munson, *Telling Wonders*, 76, 99, 107. Romm identifies Herodotus's reliance on "symmetries and polarities" in his understanding of geography ("Appendix D: Herodotean Geography," 245).

10. West, "Scythians," 448–454.

11. Wheeler, "Appendix E: Herodotus and the Black Sea Region," 752–755.

12. *Odyssey* 9.345–374.

13. Lissarrague, "Sexual Life of Satyrs," 55–57, 61–66.

14. Carson, "Putting Her in Her Place," 142–145, 147, 154–156; Wenghofer, "Sexual Promiscuity of Non-Greeks," 528–529.

15. Derbew, *Untangling Blackness in Greek Antiquity*, 113–116, 122–123.

16. Pelling, "East Is East and West Is West," 54–55.

17. Munson, *Telling Wonders*, 118–121.

18. Sheehan, *Guide to Reading Herodotus' Histories*, 208–211, with additional bibliography.

19. Pelling, *Herodotus and the Question Why*, 118.

20. Cartledge and Greenwood, "Herodotus as a Critic," 365–367.

13
On Subjugation

1. Van Wees, "Herodotus and the Past," 334–335.

2. Fearn, "Narrating Ambiguity," 98–127.

3. On Herodotus's use of *despotēs*, see Brock, *Greek Political Imagery from Homer to Aristotle*, 108–110.

4. Fearn, "Narrating Ambiguity," 106–108.

5. E.g., *Odyssey* 4.271–289 and 8.492–520.

6. *Odyssey* 22.

7. In opposing Philip of Macedon in the fourth century BCE, however, Demosthenes maintains that the Macedonians are *not* Greeks (*Philippics* 3.31).

8. Baragwanath, *Motivation and Narrative*, 153.

9. Fearn, "Narrating Ambiguity," 103–104.

10. Walcott, "Herodotus on Rape," 144.

11. Fearn, "Narrating Ambiguity," 113–114

12. Anhalt, "Seeing Is Believing," 269–280.

13. Krentz, "Appendix A: The Athenian Government in Herodotus," 724–725.

14. Momigliano, "Place of Herodotus in the History of Historiography," 3; Cawkwell, "Appendix H: The Ionian Revolt," 762. For a full account, see especially Murray, "Ionian Revolt," 461–490; Forsdyke, "Greek History," 533–545; Cawkwell, *Greek Wars*, 61–86; For modern correctives to the traditional Greek-centered view of Persia, see Briant, *From Cyrus to Alexander*, and Morgan, *Greek Perspectives on the Achaemenid Empire*.

14
On Political Equality

1. Stadter, "Herodotus and the Cities of Mainland Greece," 245.

2. Hall, *Ethnic Identity in Greek Antiquity*, 41–65, 182–185.

3. Euripides, *Ion* 1575–1593.

4. Forsdyke, "Greek History," 532.

5. *Odyssey* 4.78–79.

6. Pelling, "Aristagoras (5.49–55, 97)," 189–192.

7. Billows, *Marathon*, 181–184.

8. Ehrenberg, *From Solon to Socrates*, 125–126.

9. McGlew, "Tyrannicide Citizen in Fifth-Century BCE Athens," 37–38, 45–46. 50–52.

10. For other ancient accounts with further details, see Thucydides, *History of the Peloponnesian War* 6.53–59, and Aristotle, *Constitution of the Athenians*, 18–19. On causes of the exile of the Alcmaeonidae, see *Histories* 5.71 and Thucydides, *History of the Peloponnesian War* 1.126.

11. Forsdyke, "Greek History," 538–542. And see, e.g., Ober, "Athenian Revolution of 508/507 BCE," 215–232. See also Raaflaub, "Power in the Hands of the People," 31–66, vs. Ober, "Revolution Matters," 67–85.

12. Aristotle, *Constitution of the Athenians*, 20–22; Ober, *Democracy and Knowledge*, 139–143; Krentz, "Appendix A: The Athenian Government in Herodotus," 725–726; Billows, *Marathon*, 152–167.

13. Ober, "Revolution Matters," 71–74.

14. Billows, *Marathon*, 156; Shepherd, *Persian War in Herodotus and Other Ancient Voices*, 73–75.

15. Pelling, "Aristagoras," 186–187, 189.

16. For *diaballein* Pelling suggests "put one across" ("Aristagoras," 179).

17. *Iliad* 5.62–64. How and Wells, *Commentary*, vol. 2, 57–58; Immerwahr, "Aspects of Historical Causation in Herodotus," 181.

18. Cawkwell, "Appendix H: The Ionian Revolt," 762–766.

19. All claims in this paragraph are drawn from Ehrenberg, *From Solon to Socrates*, 125–129, and Cawkwell, "Appendix H: The Ionian Revolt," 762–768.

20. Forsdyke, "Greek History," 528–531; Cawkwell, *Greek Wars*, 62–68; Harrison, *Writing Ancient Persia*, 20–26, 30–33.

21. Van Wees, "Herodotus and the Past," 345–347; Harrison, "Persian Invasions," 555–558. For an account of the Ionian Revolt, see Shepherd, *Persian War in Herodotus and Other Ancient Voices*, 78–110.

22. Baragwanath, *Motivation and Narrative*, 196. On the association of tyranny with civic weakness and democracy with civic strength, see, e.g., Forsdyke, "Athenian Democratic Ideology," 332–333 and passim, and Moles, "Herodotus and Athens," 39.

23. Forsdyke discusses the strengths and weaknesses of *isēgoriē* as Herodotus depicts it ("Greek History," 533–534).

24. Munson, *Telling Wonders*, 208–211.

15
On Freedom

1. On the battle of Marathon, see How and Wells, *Commentary*, vol. 2, 110–114; Ehrenberg, *From Solon to Socrates*, 134–142; Hammond, "Expedition of Datis and Artaphrenes," 491–517; Billows, *Marathon*; Shepherd, *Persian War in Herodotus and Other Ancient Voices*, 111–153.

2. Tritle, "Warfare in Herodotus," 211–215.

3. For modern estimates, see Billows, *Marathon*, 198–199, 240–241.

4. Billows, *Marathon*, 203–227.

5. Ehrenberg, *From Solon to Socrates*, 142.

6. E.g., Plutarch, *Moralia* 347c, and Lucan, *Pro Lapsu* 3. On "Philippides" vs. "Pheidippides," see How and Wells, *Commentary*, vol. 2, 107. The modern Marathon run originated in 1896 (Billows, *Marathon*, 49–52).

7. Billows, *Marathon*, 73–82, 218–220.

8. Billows, *Marathon*, 228–33.

9. Ehrenberg, *From Solon to Socrates*, 139–141; Billows, *Marathon*, 33, 227.

10. Tritle, *From Melos to My Lai*, 215.

11. Moles, "Herodotus and Athens," 40–42.

12. Baragwanath, *Motivation and Narrative*, 149.

13. Brock, *Greek Political Imagery from Homer to Aristotle*, 110.

14. Ehrenberg, *From Solon to Socrates*, 130; Baragwanath, *Motivation and Narrative in Herodotus*, 179; Cawkwell, "Appendix H: The Ionian Revolt," 767.

15. Tritle, "Warfare in Herodotus," 214, citing Immerwahr, *Form and Thought in Herodotus*, 248; Billows, *Marathon*, 28–40.

16. Ehrenberg, *From Solon to Socrates*, 130–131.

17. Ehrenberg, *From Solon to Socrates*, 135.

18. Ehrenberg, *From Solon to Socrates*, 134–138.

19. Martin, *Ancient Greece*, 149–157; Billows, *Marathon*, 28–30.

20. Billows, *Marathon*, 249–261.

21. Martin, *Ancient Greece*, 137–141.

22. E.g., Harrison, "Through British Eyes," 25–37.

23. Berlin, "Two Concepts of Liberty," 174–178, 204, 208–209.

24. Forsdyke, "Greek History," 537.

25. Baragwanath, *Motivation and Narrative*, 192–197; Pelling, *Herodotus and the Question Why*, 186–189.

26. See Alexander, *New Jim Crow*, and Katznelson, *When Affirmative Action Was White*.

27. Thucydides, *History of the Peloponnesian War* 2.63.2. Brock, *Greek Political Imagery from Homer to Aristotle*, 124–125.

28. Thucydides, *History of the Peloponnesian War* 1.98–102, 3.25–51, and 5.84–116.

29. "Who controls the past controls the future. Who controls the present controls the past." George Orwell, *1984*, 60th anniversary ed. (New York: Plume, 2009), 34.

16
On Autocratic Leadership

1. Sancisi-Weerdenburg, "Personality of Xerxes," 584.

2. Immerwahr, "Aspects of Historical Causation in Herodotus," 187–189.

3. Kurke distinguishes *kudos* from *kleos*, "Economy of *Kudos*," 132.

4. Pelling, "Speech and Action," 123–124, and "Speech and Narrative in the *Histories*," 108–110.

5. Pelling, *Herodotus and the Question Why*, 122–123.

6. Shapiro, "Proverbial Wisdom in Herodotus," 102; Pelling, *Herodotus and the Question Why*, 12.

7. De Jong, "Narratological Aspects of the *Histories*, 280–281.

8. Pelling, *Herodotus and the Question Why*, 153–156.

9. Scullion, "Herodotus and Greek Religion," 197; Sheehan, *Guide to Reading Herodotus' Histories*, 200–201 (with additional bibliography).

10. Strauss, *Battle of Salamis*, 40.

11. Harrison, "Persian Invasions," 559.

12. Forsdyke, "Greek History," 546.

13. Forsdyke, "Athenian Democratic Ideology," 343–350.

14. Strauss, *Battle of Salamis*, 31–51; Shepherd, *Persian War in Herodotus and Other Ancient Voices*, 231–248, 251–256, 256–269, 274–284.

15. Tritle, "Herodotus and Warfare," 215–216; Cartledge, *Thermopylae*, 146–148.

16. Flower, "Appendix R: The Size of Xerxes' Expeditionary Force," 819–820.

17. Konstan, "Persians, Greeks, and Empire," 62–67.

18. Cartledge, *Thermopylae*, 135–138.

19. Cartledge, *Thermopylae* 9, 152. For accounts of the battles of Thermopylae and Artemisium, see Hammond, "Expedition of Xerxes," 546–563, and Shepherd, *Persian War in Herodotus and Other Ancient Voices*, 219–289.

20. *Odyssey* 11.337 and 11.367.

21. Forsdyke, "Athenian Democratic Ideology," 351–354. And see Cartledge's account of the battle (*Thermopylae*, 141–152).

22. Thomas sees evidence of "Herodotean exaggeration" in "the fateful favor" story pattern, while conceding that "a Greek coloring is not necessarily a sign of Greek invention" ("Herodotus and Eastern Myths and *Logoi*," 235–244).

23. Sheehan, *Guide to Reading Herodotus' Histories*, 205–206.

24. Shapiro, "Proverbial Wisdom," 107n70.

25. Anhalt, *Enraged*, 75, 99–102, 112; *Embattled*, 75–79, 89, 114.

26. *Odyssey* 2.276–277.

27. E.g., Menelaus at *Odyssey* 4.62–64.

28. E.g., *Odyssey* 3.124–125, 4.140–150, and 4.204–206.

29. Immerwahr, *Form and Thought*, 169–182.

30. Plato, *Republic* 9.574e–576a.

31. Munson, *Telling Wonders*, 145–146.

17

On Excellence

1. Harrison, "Persian Invasions," 561–563.

2. Immerwahr, *Form and Thought*, 238–239; Hammond, "Expedition of Xerxes," 569–590; Tritle, "Warfare in Herodotus," 210, 216–218.

3. See Shepherd, *Persian War in Herodotus and Other Ancient Voices*, 306–352.

4. Strauss provides an excellent account (*Battle of Salamis*, 141–208).

5. Harrison, "Persian Invasions," 571–572.

6. Immerwahr, *Form and Thought*, 215–223.

7. Strauss, *Battle of Salamis*, 11–30.

8. Pelling, "East Is East and West Is West," 57.

9. Harrison, "Persian Invasions," 570–571.

10. Lockwood, "Artemisia of Halicarnassus," 147–170.

11. Ehrenberg, *From Solon to Socrates*, 99–100; Stockton, *Classical Athenian Democracy*, 33–41. For a recent discussion, see Węcowski, *Athenian Ostracism and Its Original Purpose*.

12. Herodotus depicts Xerxes as "the supervisor who does not see" (Immerwahr, *Form and Thought*, 282).

13. Strauss, *Battle of Salamis*, 183.

14. *Iliad* 11.81–83; 20.22–23.

15. Brock, *Greek Political Imagery from Homer to Aristotle*, 10–13.

16. Sebillotte-Cuchet, "Warrior Queens of Caria," 241–242; Lockwood, "Artemisia," 154.

17. Lockwood, "Artemisia," 153–154.

18. Strauss, *Battle of Salamis*, 98.

19. Harrison, "Persian Invasions," 574–575.

20. Cartledge, *Thermopylae*, 164–166, and note to pp. 165–166.

21. E.g., *Iliad* 2.547–548 and 20.215–237; *Histories* 8.55.

22. Pelling, "Bringing Autochthony Up-to-Date," 482.

23. Baragwanath, *Motivation and Narrative*, 161–168.

24. Konstan, "Persians, Greeks, and Empire," 60–61, 67–69.

25. Harrison, "Persian Invasions," 566–569.

26. Strauss, *Battle of Salamis*, 193.

27. Konstan, "Persians, Greeks, and Empire," 70–74.

28. I am grateful to an astute anonymous reader for Yale University Press for this suggestion.

29. Fornara, *Herodotus*, 66–74.

30. Thucydides, *History of the Peloponnesian War* 1.134–388; Plutarch, *Life of Themistocles* 26–29; Diodorus Siculus, *Library of History* 11.56

31. E.g., Asheri, *Commentary*, 48.

32. Blösel, "Herodotean Picture of Themistocles," 194–197.

33. Baragwanath, *Motivation and Narrative*, 315–316.

34. Moles, "Herodotus and Athens," 43–48.

35. Fornara, *Herodotus*, 77–81.

18
On Self-Control

1. Barron, "Liberation of Greece," 592–622.
2. Wenghofer, "Sexual Promiscuity of Non-Greeks," 515–534.
3. Sancisi-Weerdenburg, "Personality of Xerxes," 579–590.
4. Lateiner, *Historical Method*, 141–148; Dewald, "Wanton Kings, Pickled Heroes," 66–69; Blok, "Women in Herodotus' *Histories*," 230–232; Pelling, *Herodotus and the Question Why*, 32; Blondell, *Helen of Troy*, 149.
5. Larsen, "Kandaules' Wife, Masistes' Wife," 225–244; Roberts, *Herodotus*, 69–71.
6. Sansone, "Herodotus on Lust," 12–13.
7. Welser, "Two Didactic Strategies," 361–362.
8. Pelling, *Herodotus and the Question Why*, 107–108.
9. Pelling, *Herodotus and the Question Why*, 32–33.
10. Welser, "Two Didactic Strategies," 363–366.
11. Sancisi-Weerdenburg, "Personality of Xerxes," 585–586.
12. Baragwanath, *Motivation and Narrative*, 279–280. But cf. Sansone, "Herodotus on Lust," 31–32.
13. On the sack of Athens, see Hammond, "Expedition of Xerxes," 563–569.
14. Fornara, *Herodotus*, 85.
15. Cartledge and Greenwood, "Herodotus as a Critic," 351.
16. See Shepherd's account of the battle of Plataea, in *Persian War in Herodotus and Other Ancient Voices*, 388–460.
17. Asheri, *Commentary*, 48.
18. Pelling, "Speech and Narrative," 114–116.
19. Harrison, "Persian Invasions," 567; Gruen, *Ethnicity in the Ancient World*, 14–15.
20. Harrison, "Persian Invasions," 553–554.
21. Van Wees, "Herodotus and the Past," 36. Good discussions include Boedeker, "Protesilaos and the End of Herodotus' *Histories*," 30–48; Herington, "Closure of Herodotus' *Histories*," 149–160; Dewald, "Wanton Kings, Pickled Heroes, and Gnomic Founding Fathers," 62–82.
22. See Shepherd's account of the battle of Mycale, in *Persian War in Herodotus and Other Ancient Voices*, 461–475.
23. Hamel, *Reading Herodotus*, 289–290.
24. E.g., Thucydides, *History of the Peloponnesian War* 1.95, 128–135.
25. Fornara, *Herodotus*, 62–66.
26. Welser, "Two Didactic Strategies," 367–371.
27. Harrison, "Persian Invasions," 567.

28. Van Wees, "Herodotus and the Past," 347–348.
29. Flower, "Herodotus and Persia," 286–287.
30. Arieti, *Discourses,* 202.
31. E.g., Pelling, "East Is East and West Is West," 59–64.
32. Stadter, "Herodotus and the Athenian *archē,*" 348–350, 355–356.
33. Pelling, "Speech and Narrative," 113 and n41.
34. Baragwanath, *Motivation and Narrative in Herodotus,* 318–322.
35. See Anhalt, *Enraged* and *Embattled,* passim.

Bibliography

Alexander, Michelle. *The New Jim Crow: Mass Incarceration in the Age of Colorblindness.* New York: New Press, 2020.

Anderson, Greg. "Tyranny and Social Ontology in Classical Athens." In *Tyranny: New Contexts. Dialogues d'histoire ancienne supplément,* 21, edited by Sian Lewis, 15–35. Besançon: Presses universitaires de Franche-Comté, 2021.

Anhalt, Emily Katz. "Seeing Is Believing: Four Women on Display in Herodotus' *Histories.*" *New England Classical Journal* 35, no. 4 (2008): 269–280.

———. *Enraged: Why Violent Times Need Ancient Greek Myths.* New Haven: Yale University Press, 2017.

———. *Embattled: How Ancient Greek Myths Empower Us to Resist Tyranny.* Stanford: Stanford University Press, 2021.

Arieti, James A. *Discourses on the First Book of Herodotus.* Lanham, MD: Rowman and Littlefield, 1995.

Asheri, David, Alan Lloyd, and Aldo Corcella. *A Commentary on Herodotus, Books I–IV.* Edited by Oswyn Murray and Alfonso Mureno, translated by Barbara Graziosi, Matteo Rossetti, Carlotta Dus, and Vanessa Cazzato. Oxford: Oxford University Press, 2007.

Bakker, Egbert, J. "The Making of History: Herodotus' *historiēs apodexis.*" In *Brill's Companion to Herodotus,* edited by Egbert J. Bakker, Irene J. F. de Jong, Hans van Wees, 3–32. Leiden: Brill Academic Publishers, 2002.

Baragwanath, Emily. *Motivation and Narrative in Herodotus.* 1st ed. Oxford Classical Monographs. Oxford: Oxford University Press, 2008.

———. "Returning to Troy: Herodotus and the Mythic Discourse of His Own Time." In *Myth, Truth, and Narrative in Herodotus,* edited by Emily Baragwanath and Mathieu de Bakker, 287–312. Oxford: Oxford University Press, 2012.

Baragwanath, Emily, and Mathieu de Bakker, "Intro: Myth, Truth, and Narrative in Herodotus's *Histories*." In *Myth, Truth, and Narrative in Herodotus*, edited by Emily Baragwanath and Mathieu de Bakker, 1–56. Oxford: Oxford University Press, 2012.

Barker, E. T. E. *Entering the Agon: Dissent and Authority in Homer, Historiography, and Tragedy.* Oxford: Oxford University Press, 2009.

Barker, E. T. E., and Joel Christensen. *Homer's Thebes: Epic Rivalries and the Appropriation of Mythical Pasts.* Washington, DC: Center for Hellenic Studies, 2020.

Barron, J. P. "The Liberation of Greece." In *The Cambridge Ancient History*, 2nd ed., vol. 4: *Persia, Greece, and the Western Mediterranean c. 525–479 BCE*, edited by John Boardman, N. G. L. Hammond, D. M. Lewis, R. O. A. M. Lyne, 592–622. Cambridge: Cambridge University Press, 1988.

Bathrellou, Eftychia, and Kostas Vlassopoulos. *Greek and Roman Slaveries.* Blackwell Sourcebooks in Ancient History. Hoboken, NJ: Wiley-Blackwell, 2022.

Benardete, Seth. *Herodotean Inquiries.* The Hague: Martinus Nijoff, 1969.

Berlin, Isaiah. "Two Concepts of Liberty." In *Isaiah Berlin: Liberty*, edited by Henry Hardy, 166–217. Oxford: Oxford University Press, 2002; orig. pub. 1958.

Billows, Richard A. *Marathon: How One Battle Changed Western Civilization.* New York: Overlook Duckworth, 2010.

Blok, J. S. "Phye's Procession: Culture, Politics and Peisistratid Rule." In *Peisistratos and the Tyranny: A Reappraisal of the Evidence*, edited by H. Sancisi-Weerdenberg, 17–48. Amsterdam: Brill Academic Publishers, 2000.

———. "Women in Herodotus' *Histories*." In *Brill's Companion to Herodotus*, edited by Egbert J. Bakker, Irene J. F. de Jong, Hans van Wees, 225–242. Leiden: Brill Academic Publishers, 2002.

Blondell, Ruby. *Helen of Troy: Beauty, Myth, Devastation.* Oxford: Oxford University Press, 2013.

Blösel, Wolfgang. "The Herodotean Picture of Themistocles: A Mirror of Fifth-Century Athens." In *The Historian's Craft in the Age of Herodotus*, edited by Nino Luraghi, 179–197. Oxford: Oxford University Press, 2001.

Boedeker, Deborah. "Protesilaos and the End of Herodotus' *Histories*." *Classical Antiquity* 7 (1988): 30–48.

Bowie, A. M. "Mythology and the Expedition of Xerxes." In *Myth, Truth, and Narrative in Herodotus*, edited by Emily Baragwanath and Mathieu de Bakker, 269–286. Oxford: Oxford University Press, 2012.

Bowra, C. M. "Arion and the Dolphin." *Museum Helveticum* 20 (1963): 121–134.

Braun, Thomas. "Hecateus' Knowledge, of the Western Mediterranean." In *Greek Identity in the Western Mediterranean: Papers in Honour of Brian*

Shefton, edited by Kathryn Lomas, 287–334. *Mnemosyne Supplements* 246. Leiden: Brill Academic Publishers, 2004.

Briant, Pierre. *From Cyrus to Alexander: A History of the Persian Empire.* University Park: Eisenbrauns, an imprint of The Pennsylvania State University Press, 2002; orig. pub. 1996.

Brock, Roger. *Greek Political Imagery from Homer to Aristotle.* New York: Bloomsbury, 2013.

Bromberg, Jacques A. *Global Classics.* Abingdon: Routledge, 2021.

Cairns, D. L. "Hybris, Dishonour, and Thinking Big." *Journal of Hellenic Studies* 116 (1996): 1–32.

Campbell, D. A., ed. *Greek Lyric,* vol. 3: *Stesichorus, Ibycus, Simonides, and Others.* Cambridge, MA: Harvard University Press, 1982–1983.

Canevaro, Mirko. "Majority Rule vs. Consensus." In *Ancient Greek History and Contemporary Social Science,* edited by Mirko Canevaro, Andrew Erskine, Benjamin Gray, and Josiah Ober, 101–156. Edinburgh: Edinburgh University Press, 2018.

Carson, Anne. "Putting Her in Her Place: Woman, Dirt, and Desire." In *Before Sexuality: The Construction of Erotic Experience in the Ancient Greek World,* edited by David M. Halperin, John, J. Winkler, and Froma I. Zeitlin, 135–169. Princeton: Princeton University Press, 1990.

Cartledge, Paul. *The Greeks: A Portrait of Self and Others.* Oxford: Oxford University Press, 1993.

———. *Thermopylae: The Battle That Changed the World.* Woodstock and New York: Overlook Press, 2006.

Cartledge, Paul, and Emily Greenwood. "Herodotus as a Critic: Truth, Fiction, Polarity." In *Brill's Companion to Herodotus,* edited by Egbert J. Bakker, Irene J. F. de Jong, Hans van Wees, 351–371. Leiden: Brill Academic Publishers, 2002.

Cawkwell, George, L. *The Greek Wars: The Failure of Persia.* Oxford: Oxford University Press, 2005.

———. "Appendix H: The Ionian Revolt." In *The Landmark Herodotus: The Histories,* edited by Robert Strassler, translated by Andrea Purvis, 762–768. New York: Pantheon Books, 2007.

Chiasson, C. C. "The Herodotean Solon." *Greece, Rome, and Byzantine Studies* 27 (1986): 249–262.

———. "Herodotus' Use of Tragedy in the Lydian *Logos.*" *Classical Antiquity* 22 (2003): 5–36.

———. "Myth and Truth in Herodotus' Cyrus *Logos.*" In *Myth, Truth, and Narrative in Herodotus,* edited by Emily Baragwanath and Mathieu de Bakker, 113–132. Oxford: Oxford University Press, 2012.

Christ, Matthew R. "Herodotean Kings and Historical Inquiry." *Classical Antiquity* 13 (1994): 167–202.

Clay, J. S. "Homer's Trojan Theater." *Transactions of the American Philological Association* 137 (2007): 233–252.

Connor, W. R. "Tribes, Festivals, and Processions: Civic Ceremonial and Political Manipulation in Archaic Greece." *Journal of Hellenic Studies* 107 (1987): 40–50.

Danzig, Gabriel. "Rhetoric and the Ring: Herodotus and Plato on the Story of Gyges as a Politically Expedient Tale." *Greece & Rome* 55, no. 2 (2008): 169–192.

Derbew, Sarah F. *Untangling Blackness in Greek Antiquity.* Cambridge: Cambridge University Press, 2022.

Dewald, Carolyn. "Narrative Surface and Authorial Voice in Herodotus' *Histories*." *Arethusa* 20, nos. 1 and 2 (1987): 147–170.

———. "Wanton Kings, Pickled Heroes, and Gnomic Founding Fathers: Strategies and Meaning at the End of Herodotus' *Histories*." In *Classical Closure: Reading the End in Greek and Latin Literature,* edited by D. H. Roberts, F. Dunn, and D. Fowler, 62–82. Princeton: Princeton University Press, 1997.

———. "Humour and Danger in Herodotus." In *The Cambridge Companion to Herodotus,* edited by Carolyn Dewald and John Marincola, 145–164. Cambridge: Cambridge University Press, 2006.

———. "Myth and Legend in Herodotus' First Book." In *Myth, Truth, and Narrative in Herodotus,* edited by Emily Baragwanath and Mathieu de Bakker, 59–85. Oxford: Oxford University Press, 2012.

Drews, Robert. *The Greek Accounts of Ancient History.* Cambridge, MA: Harvard University Press, 1973.

Ehrenberg, Victor. *From Solon to Socrates: Greek History and Civilization during the Sixth and Fifth Centuries BCE.* London: Routledge, 1991; reprint of 1968 edition.

Evans, J. A. S. "Father of History or Father of Lies: The Reputation of Herodotus." *Classical Journal* 64 (1968): 11–17.

Fearn, David. "Narrating Ambiguity: Murder and Macedonian Allegiance." In *Reading Herodotus: A Study of the Logoi in Book 5 of Herodotus' Histories,* edited by Elizabeth Irwin and Emily Greenwood, 98–127. Cambridge: Cambridge University Press, 2007.

Fehling, D. *Herodotus and His "Sources": Citation, Invention, and Narrative Art.* Translated from the German by J. G. Howie. Leeds: Francis Cairns, 1989.

Finn, Jennifer. "Herodotus' *Poor Man of Nippur*." *Classical World* 112, no. 2 (2019): 13–38.

Flory, Stewart. "Arion's Leap: Brave Gestures in Herodotus." *American Journal of Philology* 99, no. 4 (1978): 411–421.

Flower, Michael. "Herodotus and Persia." In *The Cambridge Companion to Herodotus,* edited by Carolyn Dewald and John Marincola, 274–289. Cambridge: Cambridge University Press, 2006.

———. "Appendix R: The Size of Xerxes' Expeditionary Force." In *The Landmark Herodotus: The Histories,* edited by Robert Strassler, translated by Andrea Purvis, 819–823. New York: Pantheon Books, 2007.

Fornara, Charles W. *Herodotus: An Interpretive Essay.* Oxford: Oxford University Press, 1971.

Fornara, Charles W., and Loren J. Samons II. *Athens from Cleisthenes to Pericles.* Berkeley: University of California Press, 1991.

Forrest, W. G. *The Emergence of Greek Democracy: 800–400 BC.* New York: McGraw-Hill, 1966; reprint 1976.

Forsdyke, Sara. "Athenian Democratic Ideology and Herodotus' *Histories.*" *American Journal of Philology* 122 (2001): 329–358.

———. "Greek History c. 525–480 BC." In *Brill's Companion to Herodotus,* edited by Egbert J. Bakker, Irene J. F. de Jong, and Hans van Wees, 521–549. Leiden: Brill Academic Publishers, 2002.

———. "Ancient and Modern Conceptions of the Rule of Law." In *Ancient Greek History and Contemporary Social Science,* edited by Mirko Canevaro, Andrew Erskine, Benjamin Gray, and Josiah Ober, 184–212. Edinburgh: Edinburgh University Press, 2018.

Fowler, Robert. "Herodotus and His Prose Predecessors." In *The Cambridge Companion to Herodotus,* edited by Carolyn Dewald and John Marincola, 29–45. Cambridge: Cambridge University Press, 2006.

Friedman, R. "Location and Dislocation in Herodotus." In *The Cambridge Companion to Herodotus,* edited by Carolyn Dewald and John Marincola, 165–177. Cambridge: Cambridge University Press, 2006.

Gerber, Douglas E. *Greek Iambic Poetry.* Loeb Classical Library, vol. 259. Cambridge, MA: Harvard University Press, 1999.

Gould, J. *Herodotus.* New York: St. Martin's Press, 1989.

Grant, Adam. *Hidden Potential: The Science of Achieving Greater Things.* New York: Viking Press, 2023.

Gray, V. J. "Herodotus' Literary and Historical Method: Arion's Story (1.23–24)." *American Journal of Philology* 122 (2001): 11–28.

Gregory, Justina. *Euripides and the Instruction of the Athenians.* Ann Arbor: University of Michigan Press, 1991.

Grene, David, trans. *The History: Herodotus.* Chicago: University of Chicago Press, 1987.

Grethlein, Jonas. "How Not to Do History: Xerxes in Herodotus' *Histories.*" *American Journal of Philology* 130, no. 2 (2009): 195–218.

Griffin, Jasper. "Herodotus and Tragedy." In *The Cambridge Companion to Herodotus*, edited by Carolyn Dewald and John Marincola, 46–59. Cambridge: Cambridge University Press, 2006.

Griffiths, Alan. "Stories and Storytelling in the *Histories*." In *The Cambridge Companion to Herodotus*, edited by Carolyn Dewald and John Marincola, 130–144. Cambridge: Cambridge University Press, 2006.

Gruen, Erich S. *Ethnicity in the Ancient World—Did It Matter?* Berlin: Walter de Gruyter, 2020.

Hall, Jonathan M. *Ethnic Identity in Greek Antiquity.* Cambridge: Cambridge University Press, 1997.

Hamel, Debra. *Reading Herodotus: A Guided Tour through the Wild Boars, Dancing Suitors, and Crazy Tyrants of the History.* Baltimore: Johns Hopkins University Press, 2012.

Hammond, N. G. L. "The Expedition of Datis and Artaphrenes." In *The Cambridge Ancient History*, 2nd ed., vol. 4: *Persia, Greece, and the Western Mediterranean c. 525–479 BCE*, edited by John Boardman, N. G. L. Hammond, D. M. Lewis, and R. O. A. M. Lyne, 491–517. Cambridge: Cambridge University Press, 1988.

———. "The Expedition of Xerxes." In *The Cambridge Ancient History*, 2nd ed., vol. 4: *Persia, Greece, and the Western Mediterranean c. 525–479 BCE*, edited by John Boardman, N. G. L. Hammond, D. M. Lewis, R. O. A. M. Lyne, 518–591. Cambridge: Cambridge University Press, 1988.

Hansen, M. *The Athenian Democracy in the Age of Demosthenes.* Oxford: Blackwell, 1991.

Harrison, Thomas. "The Persian Invasions." In *Brill's Companion to Herodotus*, edited by Egbert J. Bakker, Irene J. F. de Jong, Hans van Wees, 551–578. Leiden: Brill Academic Publishers, 2002.

———. "Through British Eyes: The Athenian Empire and Modern Historiography." In *Classics and Colonialism*, edited by Barbara Goff, 25–37. London: Duckworth, 2005.

———. *Writing Ancient Persia.* London: Bloomsbury, 2011.

Hartog, François. *The Mirror of Herodotus: The Representation of the Other in the Writing of History.* Translated by J. Lloyd. Oakland: University of California Press, 1988.

———. "The Invention of History: The Pre-History of a Concept from Homer to Herodotus." *History and Theory* 39 (2000): 384–395.

Henderson, J. "Old Comedy and Popular History." In *Greek Notions of the Past in the Archaic and Classical Eras: History without Historians*, edited by John Marincola, L. Llewellyn-Jones, et al., 144–159. Edinburgh: Edinburgh University Press, 2012.

Herington, John. "The Closure of Herodotus' *Histories." Illinois Classical Studies* 16 (1991): 149–160.

Higham, T. F. "Nature Note: Dolphin Riders. Ancient Stories Vindicated." *Greece & Rome* 7, no. 1 (1960): 82–86.

Hooker, J. T. "Arion and the Dolphin." *Greece & Rome* 36, no. 2 (1989): 141–146.

How, W. W., and J. Wells. *A Commentary on Herodotus.* Vols. 1 and 2. Oxford: Oxford University Press, 1912; reprint 1991.

Humphreys, Sally. "Law, Custom, and Culture in Herodotus." In *Herodotus and the Invention of History,* edited by Deborah Boedeker and John Peradotto. *Arethusa* 20, nos. 1 and 2 (1987): 211–220.

Immerwahr, Henry R. *Form and Thought in Herodotus.* American Philological Association Monograph Series, no. 23. Atlanta: Scholars Press, [1966], 1986.

———. "Aspects of Historical Causation in Herodotus." In *Herodotus,* vol. 1: *Herodotus and the Narrative of the Past,* edited by Rosaria Vignolo Munson, 157–193. Oxford: Oxford University Press, 2013. Reprint of *Transactions of the American Philological Association* 87 (1956): 241–280.

Jong, I. J. F. de. "The Helen *Logos* and Herodotus' Fingerprint." In *Myth, Truth, and Narrative in Herodotus,* edited by Emily Baragwanath and Mathieu de Bakker, 127–142. Oxford: Oxford University Press, 2012.

———. "Narratological Aspects of the *Histories* of Herodotus." In *Herodotus,* vol. 1: *Herodotus and the Narrative of the Past,* edited by Rosaria Vignolo Munson, translated by J. Kardan, 253–291. Oxford: Oxford University Press, 2013.

Kamen, Deborah. *Greek Slavery.* Berlin: Walter de Gruyter, 2023.

Katz, Marilyn A. "Women and Democracy in Ancient Greece." In *Contextualizing the Classics: Ideology, Performance, Dialogue, Essays in Honor of John J. Peradotto,* edited by Thomas M. Falkner, Nancy Felson, and David Konstan, 41–68. Lanham, MD: Rowman and Littlefield, 1999.

Katznelson, Ira. *When Affirmative Action Was White: An Untold History of Racial Inequality in Twentieth-Century America.* New York: W. W. Norton, 2005.

Kindt, J. "Delphic Oracle Stories and the Beginning of Historiography: Herodotus' Croesus *Logos." Classical Philology* 101 (2006): 34–51.

Kingsley, K. Scarlett. *Herodotus and the Presocratics: Inquiry and Intellectual Culture in the Fifth Century BCE.* Cambridge: Cambridge University Press, 2024.

Konstan, David. "The Stories in Herodotus' *Histories:* Book 1." *Helios* 10 (1983): 1–22.

————. "Persians, Greeks, and Empire." In *Herodotus and the Invention of History*, edited by Deborah Boedeker and John Peradotto. *Arethusa* 20, nos. 1 and 2 (1987): 59–73.

Krentz, Peter. "Appendix A: The Athenian Government in Herodotus." In *The Landmark Herodotus: The Histories*, edited by Robert Strassler, translated by Andrea Purvis, 723–726. New York: Pantheon Books, 2007.

Kurke, Leslie. "The Economy of *Kudos*." In *Cultural Poetics in Archaic Greece: Cult, Performance, Politics*, edited by Carol Dougherty and Leslie Kurke, 131–163. Cambridge: Cambridge University Press, 1993.

————. *Coins, Bodies, Games, and Gold: The Politics of Meaning in Archaic Greece*. Princeton: Princeton University Press, 1999.

Lane, Melissa. *The Birth of Politics: Eight Greek and Roman Political Ideas and Why They Matter*. Princeton: Princeton University Press, 2014.

Larsen, S. "Kandaules' Wife, Masistes' Wife: Herodotus' Narrative Strategy of Suppressing Names of Women (Herodotus 1.8–12 and 9.108–113)." *Classical Journal* 101 (2006): 225–244.

Lateiner, Donald. "Herodotean Historiographical Patterning: 'The Constitutional Debate.'" In *Herodotus*, vol. 1: *Herodotus and the Narrative of the Past*, edited by Rosaria Vignolo Munson, 194–211. Oxford: Oxford University Press, 2013. Reprint of *QS* 20 (1984): 257–284.

————. *The Historical Method of Herodotus*. Toronto: University of Toronto Press, 1989.

Lissarrague, François. "The Sexual Life of Satyrs." In *Before Sexuality: The Construction of Erotic Experience in the Ancient Greek World*, edited by David M. Halperin, John J. Winkler, and Froma I. Zeitlin, 53–81. Princeton: Princeton University Press, 1990.

Llewellyn-Jones, Lloyd. *Persians: The Age of the Great Kings*. New York: Basic Books, 2022.

Lloyd, Alan B. "Egypt." In *Brill's Companion to Herodotus*, edited by Egbert J. Bakker, Irene J. F. de Jong, Hans van Wees, 415–435. Leiden: Brill Academic Publishers, 2002.

————. "Appendix C: The Account of Egypt: Herodotus Right and Wrong." In *The Landmark Herodotus: The Histories*, edited by Robert Strassler, translated by Andrea Purvis, 737–743. New York: Pantheon Books, 2007.

Lockwood, Thornton C. "Artemisia of Halicarnassus: Herodotus' Excellent Counsel." *Classical World* 116, no. 2 (2023): 147–170.

Loney, Alexander C. *The Ethics of Revenge and the Meanings of the Odyssey*. New York: Oxford University Press, 2019.

Long, T. *Repetition and Variation in the Short Stories of Herodotus*. Frankfurt am Main: Athenäum, 1987.

Luraghi, Nino. "The Stories before the *Histories*: Folktale and Traditional Narrative in Herodotus." In *Herodotus*, vol. 1: *Herodotus and the Narrative of the Past*, edited by Rosaria Vignolo Munson, 87–112. Oxford: Oxford University Press (2005), 2013.

———. "Meta-*historië*: Method and Genre in the *Histories*." In *The Cambridge Companion to Herodotus*, edited by Carolyn Dewald and John Marincola, 76–91. Cambridge: Cambridge University Press, 2006.

———. "The Importance of Being *Logios*." *Classical World* 102, no. 4 (2009): 439–456.

Marincola, John. "Herodotean Narrative and the Narrator's Presence." In *Herodotus and the Invention of History*, edited by Deborah Boedeker and John Peradotto. *Arethusa* 20, nos. 1 and 2 (1987): 121–137.

———. "Herodotus and the Poetry of the Past." In *The Cambridge Companion to Herodotus*, edited by Carolyn Dewald and John Marincola, 13–28. Cambridge: Cambridge University Press, 2006.

Martin, Thomas R. *Ancient Greece: From Prehistoric to Hellenistic Times*, 2nd ed. New Haven: Yale University Press, 2013; orig. pub. 1996.

McGlew, James. "The Tyrannicide Citizen in Fifth-Century BCE Athens." In *Tyranny: New Contexts. Dialogues d'histoire ancienne supplément*, 21, edited by Sian Lewis, 37–56. Besançon: Presses universitaires de Franche-Comté, 2021.

McNamee, Roger. *Zucked: Waking Up to the Facebook Catastrophe*. New York: Penguin Press, 2019.

Meier, Christian, "Historical Answers to Historical Questions: The Origins of History in Ancient Greece." In *Herodotus and the Invention of History*, edited by Deborah Boedeker and John Peradotto. *Arethusa* 20, nos. 1 and 2 (1987): 41–57.

Moles, John. "Truth and Untruth in Herodotus and Thucydides." In *Truth and Fiction in the Ancient World*, edited by C. Gill and T. P. Wiseman, 88–120. Exeter: Exeter University Press, 1993.

———. "Herodotus and Athens." In *Brill's Companion to Herodotus*, edited by Egbert J. Bakker, Irene J. F. de Jong, Hans van Wees, 33–52. Leiden: Brill Academic Publishers, 2002.

Momigliano, A. "The Place of Herodotus in the History of Historiography." In *Herodotus*, vol. 1: *Herodotus and the Narrative of the Past*, edited by Rosaria Vignolo Munson, 31–45. Oxford: Oxford University Press, 2013. Reprint of *History* 43, no. 147 (1958): 1–13.

Morgan, J. *Greek Perspectives on the Achaemenid Empire*. Edinburgh: Edinburgh University Press, 2016.

Müller, D. "Herodot—Vater des Empirismus?" In *Gnomosyne: Menschliches Denken und Handeln in der frühgriechischen Literatur: Festschrift für Wal-*

ter Marg zum 70. Geburtstag, edited by G. Kurz, D. Müller, and W. Nico-
lai, 299–318. Munich: Beck, 1981.

Munson, Rosaria Vignolo. "The Celebratory Purpose of Herodotus: The Story
of Arion in *Histories* 1.23–24." *Ramus* 15 (1986): 93–104.

———. *Telling Wonders: Ethnographic and Political Discourse in the Work of
Herodotus.* Ann Arbor: University of Michigan Press, 2001.

———. "Who Are Herodotus' Persians?" *Classical World* 102, no. 4 (2009):
457–470.

———. "Herodotus and the Heroic Age: The Case of Minos." In *Myth, Truth,
and Narrative in Herodotus,* edited by Emily Baragwanath and Mathieu
de Bakker, 195–212. Oxford: Oxford University Press, 2012.

Murray, Oswyn. "The Ionian Revolt." In *The Cambridge Ancient History,*
2nd ed., vol. 4: *Persia, Greece, and the Western Mediterranean c. 525–479
BCE,* edited by John Boardman, N. G. L. Hammond, D. M. Lewis,
R. O. A. M. Lyne, 461–490. Cambridge: Cambridge University Press, 1988.

———. "Herodotus and Oral History." In *The Historian's Craft in the Age of
Herodotus,* edited by Nino Luraghi, 16–44. Oxford: Oxford University
Press, 2001.

Myres, John L. *Herodotus: Father of History.* Oxford: Clarendon Press, 1953.

Nagy, Gregory. *The Best of the Achaeans: Concepts of the Hero in Archaic Greek
Poetry.* Baltimore: Johns Hopkins University Press, 1979, revised 1999.

———. "Herodotus the *Logios.*" In *Herodotus and the Invention of History,*
edited by Deborah Boedeker and John Peradotto. *Arethusa* 20, nos. 1 and
2 (1987): 175–184.

———. *Pindar's Homer: The Lyric Possession of an Epic Past.* Baltimore: Johns
Hopkins University Press, 1990.

———. *Homeric Questions.* Austin: University of Texas Press, 1996.

———. *Homer the Pre-classic.* Berkeley: University of California Press, 2010.

———. "Herodotus and the *Logioi* of the Persians." In *No Tapping around
Philology: A Festschrift in Honor of Wheeler McIntosh Thackston Jr.'s
70th Birthday,* edited by A. Korangy and D. J. Sheffield, 185–191. Wies-
baden: Harrassowitz Verlag, 2014.

Ober, Josiah. "The Athenian Revolution of 508/507 BCE: Violence, Author-
ity, and the Origins of Democracy." In *Cultural Poetics in Archaic Greece:
Cult, Performance, Politics,* edited by C. Dougherty and L. Kurke, 215–232.
Oxford: Oxford University Press, 1993.

———. "Revolution Matters: Democracy as Demotic Action (A Response to
Kurt Raaflaub)." In *Democracy 2500? Questions and Challenges* (AIA Colloquia and Conference Papers 2), edited by I. Morris and Kurt Raaflaub,
67–85. Dubuque, Iowa: Kendall/Hunt, 1998.

———. *Democracy and Knowledge: Innovation and Learning in Classical Athens.* Princeton: Princeton University Press, 2008.

Osborne, Robin. *Athens and Athenian Democracy.* Cambridge: Cambridge University Press, 2010.

Pelling, Christopher. "The Urine and the Vine: Astyages' Dreams at Herodotus 1.107–108." *Classical Quarterly* 46 (1996): 68–77.

———. "East Is East and West Is West—or Are They? National Stereotypes in Herodotus." *Histos* 1 (1997): 50–66.

———. "Speech and Action: Herodotus' Debate on the Constitutions." *Proceedings of the Cambridge Philological Society,* 48 (2002): 123–158.

———. "Speech and Narrative in the *Histories.*" In *The Cambridge Companion to Herodotus,* edited by Carolyn Dewald and John Marincola, 103–121. Cambridge: Cambridge University Press, 2006.

———. "Educating Croesus: Talking and Learning in Herodotus' Lydian *Logos.*" *Classical Antiquity* 25 (2006): 141–177.

———. "Aristagoras (5.49–55, 97)." In *Reading Herodotus: A Study of the Logoi in Book 5 of Herodotus' Histories,* edited by Elizabeth Irwin and Emily Greenwood, 179–201. Cambridge: Cambridge University Press, 2007.

———. "Bringing Autochthony Up-to-Date." *Classical World* 102, no. 4 (2009): 471–483.

———. *Herodotus and the Question Why.* Austin, Texas: University of Texas Press, 2019.

Pickard-Cambridge, A. W. *Dithyramb, Tragedy, and Comedy.* Oxford: Clarendon Press, 1962.

Popkin, Jeremy D. *From Herodotus to H-Net: The Story of Historiography.* Oxford: Oxford University Press, 2016.

Press, Gerald A. *The Development of the Idea of History in Antiquity.* Montreal: McGill-Queen's University Press, 2003.

Priestley, J. *Herodotus and Hellenistic Culture: Literary Studies in the Reception of the Histories.* Oxford: Oxford University Press, 2014.

Raaflaub, Kurt A. "Herodotus, Political Thought, and the Meaning of History." In *Herodotus and the Invention of History,* edited by Deborah Boedeker and John Peradotto. *Arethusa* 20, nos. 1 and 2 (1987): 221–248.

———. "Power in the Hands of the People: Foundations of Athenian Democracy." In *Democracy 2500? Questions and Challenges* (AIA Colloquia and Conference Papers 2), edited by I. Morris and Kurt Raaflaub, 31–66. Dubuque, Iowa: Kendall/Hunt, 1998.

Redfield, James. "Commentary on Humphreys and Raaflaub." In *Herodotus and the Invention of History,* edited by Deborah Boedeker and John Peradotto. *Arethusa* 20, nos. 1 and 2 (1987): 249–253.

Roberts, Jennifer. *Herodotus: A Very Short History.* Oxford University Press, 2011.

Roisman, Hanna M. *Tragic Heroines in Ancient Greek Drama.* London; New York: Bloomsbury, 2021.

Romm, James. *Herodotus.* New Haven: Yale University Press, 1998.

———. "Appendix D: Herodotean Geography." In *The Landmark Herodotus: The Histories,* edited by Robert Strassler, translated by Andrea Purvis, 744–747. New York: Pantheon Books, 2007.

Rood, Tim. "Herodotus and Foreign Lands." In *The Cambridge Companion to Herodotus,* edited by Carolyn Dewald and John Marincola, 290–305. Cambridge: Cambridge University Press, 2006.

Sancisi-Weerdenburg, Heleen. "The Personality of Xerxes, King of Kings." In *Brill's Companion to Herodotus,* edited by Egbert J. Bakker, Irene J. F. de Jong, Hans van Wees, 579–590. Leiden: Brill Academic Publishers, 2002.

Sansone, David. "Herodotus on Lust." *Transactions of the American Philological Association* 146, no. 1 (2016): 1–36.

Scanlon, Thomas F. *Greek Historiography.* Hoboken, NJ: Wiley-Blackwell, 2015.

Schreiner, J. H. "The Exile and Return of Peisistratos." *Symbolae Osloenses* 56 (1981): 13–17.

Scullion, Scott. "Herodotus and Greek Religion." In *The Cambridge Companion to Herodotus,* edited by Carolyn Dewald and John Marincola, 192–208. Cambridge: Cambridge University Press, 2006.

Sebillotte-Cuchet, Violaine. "The Warrior Queens of Caria (Fifth to Fourth Centuries BCE)." In *Women and War in Antiquity,* edited by Jacqueline Serris-Fabre and Alison Keith, 228–246. Baltimore: Johns Hopkins University Press, 2015.

Sélincourt, Aubrey de. *Herodotus: The Histories.* Harmondsworth: Penguin Books, 1954; revised with an introduction and notes by A. R. Burn, 1972.

Shapiro, Susan O. "Herodotus and Solon." *Classical Antiquity* 15, no. 2 (1996): 348–364.

———. "Proverbial Wisdom in Herodotus." *Transactions of the American Philological Association* 130 (2000): 89–118.

Sheehan, Sean. *A Guide to Reading Herodotus' Histories.* London: Bloomsbury Academic, 2018.

Shepherd, William. *The Persian War in Herodotus and Other Ancient Voices.* Oxford: Osprey, 2019.

Sinos, R. H. "Epiphany and Politics in Archaic Greece." In *Cultural Poetics in Archaic Greece: Cult, Performance, Politics,* edited by C. Dougherty and L. Kurke, 73–91. Oxford: Oxford University Press, 1993.

Stadter, Philip A. "Herodotus and the Cities of Mainland Greece." In *The Cambridge Companion to Herodotus,* edited by Carolyn Dewald and John Marincola, 242–256. Cambridge: Cambridge University Press, 2006.

———. "Herodotus and the Athenian *archē.*" In *Herodotus,* vol. 1: *Herodotus and the Narrative of the Past,* edited by Rosaria Vignolo Munson, 334–356. Oxford: Oxford University Press, 2013. Reprint of *Annali Della*

Scuola Normale Superiore Di Pisa: Classe Di Lettere E Filosofia 22 (1992): 781–809.

Stahl, H.-P. "Blind Decisions Preceding Military Action." In *Thucydides and Herodotus,* edited by E. Foster and D. Lateiner, 125–53. Oxford: Oxford University Press, 2012.

Stesichorus, Ibycus, Simonides. *Greek Lyric,* vol. 3: *Stesichorus, Ibycus, Simonides, and Others,* edited and translated by David A. Campbell. Loeb Classical Library 476. Cambridge, MA: Harvard University Press, 1991.

Stockton, David L. *The Classical Athenian Democracy.* Oxford: Oxford University Press, 1990.

Strasburger, Hermann. "Herodotus and Periclean Athens." In *Herodotus,* vol. 1: *Herodotus and the Narrative of the Past,* edited by Rosaria Vignolo Munson, translated by J. Kardan and Edith Foster, 295–320. Oxford: Oxford University Press, 2013. Originally in *Historia* 4 (1955): 1–25.

Strassler, Robert, ed. *The Landmark Herodotus: The Histories,* translated by Andrea Purvis. New York: Pantheon Books, 2007.

Strauss, Barry. *The Battle of Salamis: The Naval Encounter That Saved Greece—and Western Civilization.* New York: Simon and Schuster, 2004.

Thomas, Rosalind. *Herodotus in Context: Ethnography, Science, and the Art of Persuasion.* Cambridge: Cambridge University Press, 2000.

———. "The Intellectual Milieu of Herodotus." In *The Cambridge Companion to Herodotus,* edited by Carolyn Dewald and John Marincola, 60–65. Cambridge: Cambridge University Press, 2006.

———. "Herodotus and Eastern Myths and *Logoi*: Deioces the Mede and Pythius the Lydian." In *Myth, Truth, and Narrative in Herodotus,* edited by Emily Baragwanath and Mathieu de Bakker, 233–253. Oxford: Oxford University Press, 2012.

Thompson, Norma. *Herodotus and the Origins of the Political Community: Arion's Leap.* New Haven: Yale University Press, 1996.

Thonemann, Peter. "Croesus and the Oracles." *Journal of Hellenic Studies,* 136 (2016): 152–167.

Tritle, Lawrence. *From Melos to My Lai: War and Survival.* London: Routledge, 2000.

———. "Warfare in Herodotus." In *The Cambridge Companion to Herodotus,* edited by Carolyn Dewald and John Marincola, 209–23. Cambridge: Cambridge University Press, 2006.

Vandiver, Elizabeth. "Strangers Are from Zeus: Homeric *Xenia* at the Courts of Proteus and Croesus." In *Myth, Truth, and Narrative in Herodotus,* edited by Emily Baragwanath and Mathieu de Bakker, 143–166. Oxford: Oxford University Press, 2012.

Walcott, Peter. "Herodotus on Rape." *Arethusa* 11 (1978): 137–147.

Wallace, Robert W. "Redating Croesus: Herodotean Chronologies, and the Dates of the Earliest Coinages." *Journal of Hellenic Studies* 136 (2016): 168–181.

Waterfield, Robin. "On 'Fussy Authorial Nudges' in Herodotus." *Classical World* 102, no. 4 (2009): 485–494.

Weçowski, Marek. "The Hedgehog and the Fox: Form and Meaning in the Prologue of Herodotus. *Journal of Hellenic Studies* 124 (2004): 143–164.

———. *Athenian Ostracism and Its Original Purpose: A Prisoner's Dilemma.* Oxford: Oxford University Press, 2022.

Wees, Hans van. "Herodotus and the Past." In *Brill's Companion to Herodotus,* edited by Egbert J. Bakker, Irene J. F. de Jong, Hans van Wees, 321–349. Leiden: Brill Academic Publishers, 2002.

Welser, Christopher. "Two Didactic Strategies at the End of Herodotus' *Histories* (9.108–122)." *Classical Antiquity* 28, no. 2 (2009): 359–385.

Wenghofer, Richard. "Sexual Promiscuity of Non-Greeks in Herodotus' *Histories.*" *Classical World* 107, no. 4 (2014): 515–534.

West, Stephanie. "Scythians." In *Brill's Companion to Herodotus,* edited by Egbert J. Bakker, Irene J. F. de Jong, and Hans van Wees, 437–456. Leiden: Brill Academic Publishers, 2002.

———. "Rhampsinitos and the Clever Thief (Herodotus 2.121)." In *A Companion to Greek and Roman Historiography,* vol. 2, edited by John Marincola, 322–327. Oxford: Wiley-Blackwell, 2008.

Wheeler, Everett L. "Appendix E: Herodotus and the Black Sea Region." In *The Landmark Herodotus: The Histories,* edited by Robert Strassler, translated by Andrea Purvis, 748–755. New York: Pantheon Books, 2007.

———. "Appendix F: Rivers and Peoples of Scythia." In *The Landmark Herodotus: The Histories,* edited by Robert Strassler, translated by Andrea Purvis, 756–761. New York: Pantheon Books, 2007.

Wilkerson, Isabel. *Caste: The Origins of Our Discontents.* New York: Random House, 2020.

Wood, H. *The Histories of Herodotus: An Analysis of Formal Structure.* The Hague: Mouton, 1972.

Zakaria, Fareed. *The Future of Freedom: Illiberal Democracy at Home and Abroad.* New York: W. W. Norton, 2007; orig. pub., 2003.

Index

absolutism, 8–9
abuses of power, 3
Achaemenes, 259
Achilles, 19–20, 22, 162–63, 166
Adams, John, 186
Aeschylus, 9, 13, 23, 41–42, 108, 247, 283
Agamemnon, 22, 34, 37
Agamemnon (Aeschylus), 108; *pathei mathos*, 23; wisdom, coming from experience and suffering, 23
Agathyrsus, 193
Ajax (Sophocles), 108
Alcmaeonidae, 243–44
Alcmaeonids, 247; Athenian liberty, attribution to, 248
aletheia (truth), 32–33, 66
Alexandros (Paris), 37, 108, 133, 135, 208–11, 214–15, 232; "godlike" behavior, 142; theft and rape of Helen, 32–33, 35–36, 132, 136–39, 141–42, 149
Alexandros of Macedon, 213–14, 216–17, 321
allegory, 59, 66, 68–69, 74; moral, 64

Amasis, 70, 161–62, 166; divine causality, 165; signet ring, loss of, 164–65
Ameinias of Pallene, 286
Amestris, 311–12; cloak of, 309–10, 314–15
Amyntas, 208–10, 213–14, 216
Anarcharsis, 198
Anaxandrides, 239
Andromache and Hecuba, 38
Andros, 305
Aphrodite, 126
apodexis, 18, 24, 346n24
Apollo, 62–63, 65, 92, 103, 109
Archilochus, 49, 54
Archimedes, 151
Argives, 317
Argos, 29, 34, 71, 78, 211, 305
Ariabignes, 289
Arieti, James A., 349n9, 350n12, 350n18, 354n13
Arion, 67, 80, 350n12, 350n24; dithyramb, 61, 349n4; dolphin ride, 59–63, 65–66, 68, 74; evidentiary proof, 66, 68; tale of, as moral allegory, 64
Arismaspians (one-eyed men), 195

379

guest-friendship, 134, 138, 147, 208,
213
gullibility, 2, 106, 110, 207–8, 215–18,
220, 235, 306–7; of popular
majorities, 12; tricksters, 107
Gygaia, 211
Gyges, 46–54, 57–58, 62–63, 68, 76,
93

hamartas, 92–93
happiness, 15, 31, 40, 68–69, 74,
77–80, 82, 298, 334, 350n12; as
elusive, 81; wealth, mistaken for,
15, 83
Harmodius, 241
Hecuba, 41
Helen (Euripides), 353n5
Helen of Troy, 56, 131–32, 134–35,
137–38, 140–41, 143, 147, 149, 152,
213, 353n5; rape of, 30, 33–35, 45,
56, 139; theft of, 30, 32–33, 36–37,
133, 136, 139, 142
Hephaestus, 19, 113, 143, 156–57,
299
Hera, 108
Heracles/Hercules, 34–35, 46, 49,
93, 121, 132, 191–93, 195, 239, 244
Herodotus, 1, 11–12, 20, 32, 34, 45,
52–53, 65, 68–69, 76, 90, 99,
147–48, 170, 178, 181, 185, 212,
219–20, 225–26, 228–29, 231, 233,
255, 266–67, 269–71, 308, 315–17,
346n24, 346–47n1, 349n9,
350n18, 355n2, 356n9, 360n22;
absolutism, undermining of, 8;
accountability, of powerful, 150;
ancestral customs, violating of
as mad, 160; ancient myth,
challenging of, 28–29; apodexis,
24; on Artemisia, portrait of,
292, 294–96, 306; assessing of,
7; Athenian commitment to

freedom, as central to Greek
identity, 301; Athenian political
system, 230; Athenian susceptibility to seduction and greed,
232; Athenian wisdom, 299;
Athenians, as gullible, 106–7;
Athenians, lack of discernment,
109, 111; attentive comparative
analysis, 205; author as investigator, 19; authorial responsibility,
61–62; authoritarianism, condemning of, 253, 340; authoritative narratives, analysis and
assessment, 14; authority of faith,
rejection of, 18; autocracy, as
opposite of liberty, 106; autocratic leadership, 258, 275–76,
278–79, 281–83, 318, 334; autocratic narcissism, 165, 169;
autocratic rule, 158, 221, 227;
barbarians vs. Greeks, 215,
329–30; barbaroi, 116–17, 124,
126; battle of Plataea, 319–21;
battle of Marathon, 238–49, 251,
256; battle of Salamis, 283,
284–89, 294, 297–99, 302–3,
305–6; battle of Thermopylae,
273–74, 289; "best" man rule,
183–84, 187–88; best selves, 244;
breaking with tradition, 42;
broadmindedness and rationality of, 122; causal agency in
human impulse, 161–62; causality,
56; cause and effect, patterns of,
81; causes and consequences of
human conflict, 22, 56; cautionary warnings, 15; commemorating
human events, 22; communities
and individuals, rising and
falling of, 78, 96; comparison
and analysis, 44; conflict, focus
on, 13; corroborating evidence,

as inventor of history, 6, 17, 341; lack of self-restraint, as driver of self-destruction, 15; leadership, 337; learning from past events, 56; majoritarian voting, 235; majority vote, as autocracy, 182; Masistes' wife, 309–13; materialism, as manifestation of lack of self-control, 324; as mendacious, 5; method of inquiry, 114–15, 118–20, 122, 124–25; misinterpretation, 126–27; modern historiography, anticipating of, 62; moral discernment, 10; moral evaluation, 10; myth, reconsidering of, 39–40; myth and history, distinction between, 7–8, 42–44, 50, 74; mythic material, 28; narrative authority, 110; narrative storytelling, 13; non-Greek peoples, fascination with, 115; objective comparative evaluation, 131; objective truth, 7; one-man rule, destructiveness of, 153; as open-minded, 130–31; oracles and dreams, 95, 118–19, 122; origins of the gods, 122–24; "otherness," openness to, 10, 16; pattern of historical change, 80; patterns of behavior, 55; on Persian disregard for lives of others, 299–300; Persian storytellers, 35–37, 40, 43–44; political debate, 176, 182; political equality, 236; political equality, ambivalent force of, 234; as political thinker, 4; as prejudiced, 10; productive debate, need for, 187–88; prose writing, employing of, 22; as purveyor of falsehoods, 5; racial prejudice of, 198–99; rational

conclusions, 119; rational thought and self-control, 4; reality-based rational judgment, 27; regime change, 54; rejection of others, and acceptance of all ways, 151–52; on Scythians, 196–206, 211; self-control, 326, 328–31; self-deception, 91, 93, 95–98; self-deception, vulnerability to, 89; self-reflection, 121; self-understanding, 27; sexual violence, self-destruction of, 50; skepticism, encouraging of, 111, 129; stories, 6–7; subjugation, 207, 217–18; on successful leadership, 274–75; supernatural forces, turning away from, 26–27, 125, 334; supernatural signs, 93–94, 97, 106, 109, 196, 247, 291, 320–21; susceptibility to deception, 107, 111; traditional hierarchical norms, rejection of, 187; Trojan War, as metaphor for Persian War, 347n6; truth, as not forgetting, 341; tyrannical abuses of power, condemning of, 158; tyranny, 161, 164, 167–68, 179–80; tyranny, dangers of, 153, 158; tyranny, and individual decision-making, 166; unity, value of, 207; unquestioning trust in one's judgment, 88; as unreliable narrator, 9–10; value of history, commemoration of, 256; vengeance, condemnation of, 326; verifiability, criterion of, 6, 44, 74, 89, 98, 336; verifiable narrative, introducing of, 2; on women, 126; Xerxes, as cautionary example, 272, 278, 281

Romania, 189
Romm, James, 356n9
rule: aristocratic, 105; autocratic,
 100, 102, 104, 158, 167–68, 183–84,
 221, 249, 252, 275; best man, 181,
 183–84; majority rule, 171–72,
 178–81, 183, 187–88; mob rule, 180,
 235–36; one-man rule, 153; by the
 people, 173, 181; rule by few, 169,
 180–82, 188, 235; rule by many,
 169, 180, 182, 185, 188, 235; rule by
 one, 169, 182–83, 188, 235; rule of
 law, 3, 8, 153, 167–68, 186–87, 254,
 281, 338; tyrannical, 167
Russia, 189

Sardis, 46, 69–70, 74–76, 84, 74–76,
 232, 251, 255, 260, 265, 308–9
Schreiner, J. H., 352n3
Scythia, 189, 211, 245, 262–63, 268;
 ability to unite, 205; as *amathestata*, 199; burial customs, 197;
 Darius's attack on, 200–203; as
 David and Goliath example, 203;
 geography of, 199–202; human
 fortune, as varying, 268; as lacking
 rational control, 197; as models
 and counter-models, 205–6; as
 nomads, 199, 201; origins of,
 190–95, 205; resistance to Persian invasion, 190, 201; strategic
 advantages of, 199–200; supernatural origin stories, 196; as
 unconquerable adversaries, 205;
 "united we stand, divided we
 fall," 201–2; xenophobia of, 198
self-control, 308, 331–32, 315, 324,
 326–27, 331–32; failures of
 impulse control, warning
 against, 329; lack of, 328–30;
 timeless value of, 328

self-deception, 83–84, 89, 92–96,
 110; democratic elections, 97–98
sexual inequality, 39
sexual predators, 37–40, 57;
 suffering for victims and
 themselves, 50–51, 58
Sheehan, Sean, 349n11
Skyles, 198
slavery, 57, 92, 117–18, 161, 199, 203,
 219, 222, 225, 233–34, 238–39, 243,
 254, 260–61, 275, 292, 307, 339,
 353n8; and freedom, 250, 276
social media, 3, 111, 129, 337
Socrates, 54, 252
Solon, 82, 84, 298; chance, 81;
 Croesus, meeting between,
 68–80, 83, 88, 90; divine power,
 as jealous and disruptive, 94;
 fortune, as impermanent, 92,
 164–65; good fortune, as more
 desirable than wealth, 79; happiness, 80; "look to the end of
 everything," 96; reforms of,
 104–6; supernatural forces, 81,
 94; surface appearances, caution
 against, 88; wealth, as impermanence of, 78–79
Sophocles, 9, 108
Sparta, 1, 99, 104, 135, 213, 221–22,
 225, 228, 231–32, 238, 246, 272,
 297, 317; Athens, antagonism and
 distrust between, 245, 301, 322;
 defeat of Athens, 330; Tyranny
 of the Thirty, 255
Spartans, 1, 86, 91, 224, 226–27, 238,
 239, 240, 245, 246, 248, 256, 272,
 273, 276, 278, 287, 289, 291, 299,
 303, 304, 317, 319, 321, 322, 323, 337;
 as Dorians, 225; kinship, 225; as
 slaves, 92; tyrannical behavior, 182
Stalin, Joseph, 183, 236